06

India
FROM MIDNIGHT
TO THE MILLENNIUM
AND BEYOND

India

FROM MIDNIGHT
TO THE MILLENNIUM
AND BEYOND

Shashi Tharoor

Arcade Publishing • New York

FIRST ARCADE PAPERBACK EDITION

Copyright acknowledgments appear on page 371.

Map of India designed by Jeffrey L. Ward

Though the author works for the United Nations, the views expressed in this book are entirely personal and are not to be construed in any way as representing the views of that organization or of the author in his official capacity.

Library of Congress Cataloging-in-Publication Data
    Tharoor, Shashi, 1956–
        India : from midnight to the millennium and beyond / by Shashi Tharoor.
                p.   cm.
      ISBN 1-55970-384-9 (hc)
      ISBN 1-55970-803-4 (pb)
      1. India — Civilization — 1947- 2. India — History — 1947-
    3. India — Politics and government — 1947- I. Title.
    DS428.2.T47   1997
    954.04 — dc21   97-8376

Published in the United States by Arcade Publishing, Inc.
Distributed by Time Warner Book Group

Visit our Web site at www.arcadepub.com
Visit the author's Web site at www.shashitharoor.com

10 9 8 7 6 5 4 3 2 1

Designed by API

PRINTED IN THE UNITED STATES OF AMERICA

In loving memory of my father
CHANDRAN THAROOR
(December 17, 1929–October 23, 1993)
who taught me to believe in
"an India for Indians,"
this book is dedicated
to my mother
LILY THAROOR

It would not matter what kind of mess they made — and they would make a mess, if they governed themselves, the people of India. They would probably make the greatest muddle possible.

—D. H. Lawrence, *Aaron's Rod*

My legacy to India? Hopefully, it is 400 million people capable of governing themselves.

—Jawaharlal Nehru

If there is one place on the face of the earth where all the dreams of living men have found a home from the earliest days when man began the dream of existence, it is India.

—Romain Rolland

Contents

Preface to the 2006 Edition

S ince this book was written, India's 650 million registered voters have lined up in the hot sun four times in seven years to determine anew who will govern them. The details of the results of these electoral exercises will not be found in this volume, but they do not undermine its thesis. Indeed, the last Indian general election of the millennium will be remembered for having brought up a vital question of national identity that is central to this book's spirit: Who is an Indian?

As Indian political parties geared up for the 2004 polls, this question arose again. Before the previous elections, in 1999, the leading opposition, the Congress Party, had split over the issue of the eligibility of its Italian-born president, Sonia Gandhi, to lead the country. The controversy dominated the election campaign, with the ruling National Democratic Alliance openly declaiming a choice between *videshi* (foreign) and *swadeshi* (indigenous) rule.

It is all the more ironic that when a group of Indian nationalists had convened the first-ever Indian National Congress in 1885 — giving birth to the party that won the country's freedom from British rule six decades later — they chose as their president Allan Octavian Hume, a liberal Scotsman. Well into the twentieth century, the party's most redoubtable leaders (and elected presidents) included the

English-born Annie Besant and the Muslim Maulana Abul Kalam Azad, who was born in Mecca.

A century later, the same Congress Party split over another foreign-born president. Three powerful Congress politicians, Sharad Pawar, Purno Sangma, and Tariq Anwar — with classic Congress secularism, a Hindu, a Christian, and a Muslim — averred that Mrs. Gandhi was unfit to be prime minister because she had been born in Italy. In the extraordinary letter they delivered to her and subsequently leaked to the newspapers, the three party leaders declared, "It is not possible that a country of 980 million, with a wealth of education, competence, and ability, can have anyone other than an Indian, born of Indian soil, to head its government." Mrs. Gandhi promptly resigned, precipitating a crisis that ended with the expulsion of the three nativists from the party and her triumphant return as party president. But the genie was out of the bottle; indeed, the trio went so far as to ask Mrs. Gandhi to propose a constitutional amendment requiring that the offices of president and prime minister be held only by natural-born Indian citizens. "Our soul, our honor, our pride, our dignity, is rooted in our soil," they explained. The ruling NDA coalition promptly declared that they would, if reelected, pass such a law themselves.

As it happened, they did not, though they spent the next five years in power at the head of a coalition government. But this territorial notion of Indian nationhood is a curious one for a party with the Congress's eclectic traditions. The republic's founding fathers had consciously refused to adopt the American requirement that its head of government be native-born. Even more curious is the implicit repudiation of the views of the Congress's greatest leader, Mahatma Gandhi, who tried to make the party a representative microcosm of an India he saw as pluralist, diverse, and all-inclusive — a "house with all the doors and windows open" through which the winds from around the world would blow, without sweeping Indians off their feet.

Under Gandhi and Nehru, Indian nationalism became a rare animal. It was not based on any of the conventional indices of national identity. Not language, since India's constitution recognizes eighteen official languages, and thirty-five other languages are spoken by more than a million people each. Not ethnicity, since the "Indian" accommodates a diversity of racial types in which many Indians have more in common with foreigners than with Poonawallahs and Bangaloreans. Punjabis and Bengalis, for instance, have more in common with Pakistanis and Bangladeshis, respectively, than with other Indians. Not religion, since India is a secular pluralist state that is home to every religion known to mankind, with the possible exception of Shintoism. Not geography, since the natural geography of the subcontinent — framed by the mountains and the sea — was hacked by the Partition of 1947. And not even territory, since by law anyone with one grandparent born in pre-Partition India — outside the territorial boundaries of today's state — is eligible for citizenship. Indian nationalism has therefore always been the nationalism of an idea. It is, as I have tried to demonstrate in this book, the idea of an "ever-ever land" — emerging from an ancient civilization, united by a shared history, sustained by pluralist democracy.

When India celebrated the forty-ninth anniversary of its independence from British rule in 1996, its then–prime minister, H. D. Deve Gowda, stood at the ramparts of Delhi's sixteenth-century Red Fort and delivered the traditional Independence Day address to the nation in Hindi, India's "national language." Eight other prime ministers had done exactly the same thing forty-eight times before him, but what was unusual this time was that Deve Gowda, a southerner from the state of Karnataka, spoke to the country in a language of which he did not know a word. Tradition and politics required a speech in Hindi, so he gave one — the words having been written out for him in his native Kannada script, in which, of course, they made no sense.

Such an episode is almost inconceivable elsewhere, but it represents the best of the oddities that help make India India. Only India could be ruled by a man who does not understand its "national language"; only in India, for that matter, is there a "national language" that half the population does not understand; and only in India could this particular solution have been found to enable the prime minister to address his people. One of Indian cinema's finest "playback singers," the Keralite K. J. Yesudas, sang his way to the top of the Hindi music charts with lyrics written in the Malayalam script, but to see the same practice elevated to the prime ministerial address on Independence Day was a startling affirmation of Indian pluralism.

For the simple fact is, we are all minorities in India. There has never been an archetypal Indian to stand alongside the archetypal Englishman or Frenchman. If America is a melting pot, then to me India is a *thali*, a selection of sumptuous dishes in different bowls. Each tastes different, and does not necessarily mix with the next, but they belong together on the same plate, and complement each other in making the meal a satisfying repast.

The rise of Hindu nationalism as a political phenomenon in recent years has articulated an alternative view of Indian identity, one that is explicitly narrow and definitional. Its pro-Hindu and pro-Hindi, sectarian and antisecular view of Indianness has so far not found sympathy with three-fourths of the electorate. But the ascent of Sonia Gandhi to the leadership of the Congress Party, and the very real prospect that she could win power broadened the debate. The usual chauvinists and xenophobes were joined by political opportunists of various stripes. The spokesperson of the socialist Samata Party, for instance, illiberally declared that it was "an insult to the self-respect of [India] to have a foreigner at the helm."

But is Sonia a "foreigner"? She is an Indian by marriage and naturalization, not birth, but traditional Indian culture has always absorbed the daughter-in-law completely into the family fold. Sonia Gandhi has lived in India for thirty-seven years — considerably longer than in her native Italy — and has made her home in India despite the assassination in 1991 of her husband, Rajiv. She has declared, "I am Indian and shall remain so till my last breath. India is my motherland, dearer to me than my own life." But Sonia Gandhi is not the issue. The real issue is whether Indians should let politicians decide who is qualified to be an authentic Indian.

India's national identity has long been built on the slogan "Unity in diversity." The "Indian" comes in such varieties that a woman who is fair-skinned, sari-wearing and Italian-speaking, as Sonia is, is not more foreign to my grandmother in Kerala than one who is "wheatish-complexioned," wears a *salwar-kameez,* and speaks Punjabi. Our nation absorbs both these types of people; both are equally "foreign" to some of us, equally Indian to us all.

India's founding fathers wrote a constitution for their dreams; we have given passports to their ideals. To start disqualifying Indian citizens from the privileges of Indianness is not just pernicious, it is an affront to the very premise of Indian nationalism. An India that denies itself to some Indians would no longer be the India Mahatma Gandhi fought to free.

How has India changed since this book was first written? Two phenomena have been the most striking: the country's dramatic economic progress, averaging 5.9 percent annually at the cusp of the millennium and rising, and the eruption of religious violence, most notably in 2002 in the state of Gujarat, when perhaps 2,000 people, mainly Muslims, lost their lives. The two seemingly incompatible statistics tell their own story, of an India torn between history and hope.

One Indian city, Bombay, seems to epitomize all of India's contradictions. It is India's commercial capital, the home of the country's main stock exchange, a city that pays 38 percent of India's taxes; it manufactures the grandiose dreams of "Bollywood" (making four times as many films annually as the United States); it houses the country's most opulent hotels and boasts of commercial rents higher than Manhattan or Tokyo; and it supports India's most innovative theaters and art galleries. But the contradictions in Bombay are appalling — a bottle of champagne at one of many five-star hotels sells for one and a half times the national average annual income but 40 percent of the city has no safe drinking water; the world's largest film industry thrives but plumbing, telephones, and law and order break down regularly; the city supports several hundred slimming clinics while

millions starve in filthy slums. And violence lurks not far from the surface in a city where Hindu-Muslim riots erupted in 1992 and where
the reach and power of the criminal underworld rivals that of Chicago
in the 1920s.

Ten years after the Bombay riots, it was Gujarat that exploded,
when the torching of fifty-nine Hindu pilgrims in a train compart-
ment led to a pogrom of Muslim civilians. "I'll tell you what your
problem is in India," an American businessman said. "You have too
much history. Far more than you can use peacefully. So you end up
wielding history like a battle-ax against each other."

All right, he didn't really say it. The American in question is a fictional character in *Riot*, my novel about a Hindu-Muslim riot that
erupts during a campaign to construct a Hindu temple on the site occupied for four and a half centuries by a Muslim mosque. While 2002
headlines, months after the novel's publication, spoke of a renewed
cycle of killings and mob violence over the same issue, I received
dozens of comments on the eerie similarity between art and life. Some
callers point to the afterword in my novel, where I alert readers to a
threat by Hindu extremists to commence construction of their temple
in defiance of court orders. I seek no credit for prescience. The tragedy
in India is that even those who know history seem condemned to
repeat it.

It is one of the ironies of India's muddled march into the twenty-
first century that it has a technologically inspired vision of the future
yet appears shackled to the dogma of the past. The temple town of
Ayodhya, in India's most populous state, Uttar Pradesh, has no computer software labs; it is devoted to religion and old-fashioned industry. In 1992, a howling mob of Hindu extremists tore down an unused
sixteenth-century mosque, the Babri Masjid, which occupied a prominent spot in a town otherwise overflowing with temples. The mosque
had been built in the 1520s by India's first Mughal emperor, Babur;
the Hindu zealots vowed to replace it with a temple to the Hindu god
Ram, which had stood on the spot for millennia before the Mughal

invader tore it down to make room for his mosque. In other words, they wanted to avenge history, to undo the shame of half a millennium ago with a reassertion of their glory today.

India is a land where history, myth, and legend often overlap; sometimes Indians cannot tell the difference. Some Hindus claim, with more zeal than evidence, that the Babri Masjid stood on the exact spot of Lord Ram's birth, and had been placed there by the Mughal emperor as a reminder to a conquered people of their own subjugation. Historians — most of them Hindus — reply that there is no proof that Lord Ram ever existed in human form, let alone that he was born where the believers say he was. More to the point, there is no proof that Babur actually demolished a Ram temple to build his mosque. Of course, proof is not a valid currency on issues of faith, but to destroy the mosque and replace it with a temple, these scholars argue, would not be righting an old wrong but perpetrating a new one.

To most Indian Muslims, the dispute is not about a specific mosque — which had been abandoned since most of Ayodhya's Muslim minority emigrated to Pakistan upon the Partition in 1947 — but about their place in Indian society. For decades after independence, successive Indian governments had guaranteed their security in a secular state, permitting the retention of Muslim Personal Law separate from the country's civil code and even financing the hajj to Mecca. Three of India's presidents were Muslims, as were innumerable cabinet ministers, ambassadors, generals, and supreme court justices. Since the 1970s, India's Muslim population has exceeded Pakistan's. The destruction of the mosque seemed an appalling betrayal of the compact that had sustained the Muslim community as a vital part of India's pluralist democracy.

The Hindu fanatics who attacked the mosque had little faith in the institutions of Indian democracy. They saw the state as soft, pandering to minorities out of a misplaced and westernized secularism. To them, an independent India, freed after nearly a thousand years of alien rule (first Muslim, then British), and rid of a sizable portion of its Muslim population by the Partition, had an obligation to assert its own identity, one that would be triumphantly and indigenously Hindu. They are not fundamentalists in any meaningful sense of the term, since Hinduism is uniquely a religion without fundamentals: there is no Hindu pope, no Hindu Sunday, no single Hindu holy book, and indeed no such thing as a Hindu heresy. They are, instead, chauvinists, who root their Hinduism not in any of its soaring philosophical or spiritual underpinnings — nor, unlike their Islamic counterparts, in the theology of their faith — but rather in its role as a source of identity. They seek revenge in the name of Hinduism-as-badge, rather than in Hinduism-as-doctrine.

In doing so they are profoundly disloyal to the religion they claim to espouse, which stands out not only as an eclectic embodiment of tolerance but as the only major religion in the world that does not claim to be the only true religion. All ways of worship, Hinduism asserts, are equally valid, and religion is an intensely personal matter related to the individual's self-realization in relation to God. Such a faith understands that belief is a matter of hearts and minds, not of bricks and stone. The true Hindu seeks no revenge upon history, for he understands that history is its own revenge.

The Hindu zealots who chanted insultingly triumphalist slogans may have helped incite the worst elements on the Muslim side, who set fire to a railway carriage carrying temple campaigners (though one inquiry suggests the train fire may have simply been accidental); in turn, Hindu mobs have torched Muslim homes and killed innocents. As the courts deliberate on a solution to the dispute, the cycle of violence goes on, spawning new hostages to history, ensuring that future generations will be taught new wrongs to set right. We live, Octavio Paz once wrote, between oblivion and memory. Memory and oblivion: how one leads to the other, and back again, has been the concern of much of my fiction. As I pointed out in the last words of *Riot*, history is not a web woven with innocent hands.

As the twenty-first century began, with India's computer scientists and software engineers bringing investment and employment to the "Silicon Plateau" around Bangalore, and with the likes of Bill Gates helping convert the medieval city of Hyderabad into a high-tech "Cyberabad," the question began to be asked in India, Can we become a world leader? What makes a country a world leader? Is it population, in which case India (with 1.1 billion people in 2005) is on course to top the charts, overtaking China as the world's most populous country (with 1.6 billion) by 2050? Is it military strength (with the world's fourth-largest army) or nuclear capacity? After a series of nuclear explosions in 1998 India's status is clear, if not universally recognized. Is it economic development? There, India has made extraordinary strides in recent years; it is already the world's fifth-largest economy in PPP (purchasing-power parity) terms and continues to climb, though too many of its people are destitute, living amid despair and disrepair. Or could it be a combination of all these, allied to something altogether more difficult to define — the power of example?

In answering this question, India must determine where its strengths lie as it seeks to make this new century its own. Much of the conventional analyses of India's stature in the world relies on the all-too-familiar indices of GDP, impressive economic growth rates (5.9 percent a year over the last five years, and talk of 7 to 8 percent in the next five), and its undoubted military power. But if there is one attribute of independent India to which observers have not perhaps paid enough attention, it is a quality India would do well to cherish and promote in today's world: its soft power.

"Soft power" consists of those attributes that attract and persuade others to adopt the country's agenda, rather than relying purely on the dissuasive or coercive "hard power" of military force. What does this mean for India? It means giving attention, encouragement, and active support to the aspects and products of a society that the world would find attractive — not in order to persuade others to support us, but rather to enhance the country's standing in their eyes. Bollywood is already doing this by bringing its brand of glitzy entertainment not just to the Indian diaspora in the United States and Britain but to the

Syrians and Senegalese — who may not understand the Hindi dialogue but catch the spirit of the films, and look at India with stars in
their eyes as a result. (An Indian diplomat friend in Damascus told me
a few years ago that the only publicly displayed portraits that were as
big as those of then-president Hafez al-Assad were those of the
Bollywood star Amitabh Bachchan.) Indian art, classical music, and
dance have the same effect. So does the work of Indian fashion designers, which recently dominated the show windows of New York's
chic Lord and Taylor department store. Indian cuisine, spreading
around the world, raises our culture higher in people's reckoning (the
way to foreigners' hearts is often through their palates). When India's
cricket team triumphs or its tennis players claim grand slams (so far
only in doubles); when a bhangra beat is infused into a Western pop
record or an Indian choreographer invents a fusion of kathak and ballet; when Indian women sweep the Miss World and Miss Universe
contests; or when a film like *Lagaan* claims an Oscar nomination —
when each of these things happens, India's soft power is enhanced.
And when some Americans speak of the IITs with the same reverence
they used to accord to MIT or Caltech, and the Indianness of engineers and software developers is taken as synonymous with mathematical and scientific excellence, it is India that gains in respect.

But it is not just these material accomplishments that enhance
India's soft power. Even more important are the values and principles
for which India stands — above all our precious pluralism, which used
to be widely admired till the barbarous mobs at the Babri Masjid and
the *goondas* of Gujarat devastated both their victims and the country's
image. India must reclaim its true heritage in the eyes of the world.
Its democracy, its thriving free media, its contentious NGOs, its
energetic human rights groups, and the repeated spectacle of its
remarkable general elections have all made of India a rare example of
the successful management of diversity in the developing world.

After the elections of 2004 Sonia Gandhi resolved the existential
dilemma by winning election as the prime minister-designate of the
ruling coalition and then renouncing the office in favor of another.

The sight in May 2004 — in a country 82 percent Hindu — of a Roman Catholic leader (Sonia Gandhi) making way for a Sikh (Manmohan Singh) to be sworn in as prime minister by a Muslim (President Abdul Kalam) caught the world's imagination and won its admiration. No strutting nationalist chauvinism could ever have accomplished for India's standing in the world what that one moment did — all the more so since it was not directed at the world.

It was an affirmation of an ancient civilizational ethos in a new political era — taking India from midnight to beyond the millennium.

— Shashi Tharoor
(January 2006)

Chronology of Major Events
Mentioned in India:
From Midnight to the Millennium and Beyond

1947 August 15, India becomes independent

1948 January 30, assassination of Mahatma Gandhi

1950 January 26, adoption of the Constitution of the Republic of India

1952 first General Elections; Congress government elected

1954 Prime Minister Jawaharlal Nehru adopts goal of "socialist pattern of society"

1956 States Reorganization Act creates ethno-linguistic states

1957 second General Elections; Congress under Nehru increases its majority; Communist government elected in Kerala state

1959 Indira Gandhi, as president of the Congress Party, leads successful campaign for dismissal of the elected Communist government in the state of Kerala

1962 war with China; third General Elections

1964 death of Prime Minister Jawaharlal Nehru; succeeded by Lal Bahadur Shastri

1965 war with Pakistan

1966   death of Prime Minister Shastri at Tashkent peace conference; succeeded by Indira Gandhi

1967   fourth General Elections; Congress majority slashed; several opposition governments formed in the states; formerly secessionist DMK party assumes power in Tamil Nadu

1969   nationalization of banks, followed by split of Indian National Congress Party; Prime Minister Indira Gandhi rules with support of left-wing parties

1971   fifth General Elections; Mrs. Gandhi wins overwhelmingly; Bangladesh crisis (largest refugee influx in human history); war with Pakistan; creation of Bangladesh (formerly East Pakistan)

1974   Jayaprakash Narayan leads movement for "Total Revolution"; Supreme Court decides in Keshavananda Bharati case that right to property is not part of the basic structure of the Constitution

1975   Prime Minister Indira Gandhi found guilty by court of electoral malpractice; June, State of Emergency declared, including arrests of opposition leaders, press censorship, and Sanjay Gandhi's "five-point program"

1976   passage of the Forty-second Amendment to the Indian Constitution to enact Emergency-era changes

1977   March, Emergency ends in sixth General Elections; Mrs. Gandhi and Congress (Indira) crushed; Janata Party government takes power under Prime Minister Morarji Desai

1979   Janata Party splits, with rival faction under Charan Singh seeking Mrs. Gandhi's support to form government; withdrawal of this support leads to seventh General Elections

1980   January, seventh General Elections; Mrs. Gandhi restored to power as prime minister; June, Sanjay Gandhi killed in air crash of stunt plane over Delhi; Mandal Commission report recommending additional reservations for "other backward classes" submitted, and quietly shelved

1981   Rajiv Gandhi wins by-election to his brother's seat in Parliament

1982   Asian Games held in New Delhi, prompting major infrastructure development in the capital

1983   Sir Richard Attenborough's film *Gandhi* wins eight Academy Awards

1984   July, Sikhs' Golden Temple assaulted by Indian Army in "Operation Bluestar"; October, Mrs. Gandhi assassinated; Rajiv Gandhi becomes prime minister, calls eighth General Elections, and wins biggest landslide in Indian electoral history; anti-defection law passed

1985   Rajiv Gandhi attacks corruption and inefficiency at Congress Party's centenary celebrations; "new economic policy" announced; Shah Banu alimony case ruling by Supreme Court

1986   passage of Muslim Women (Protection of Rights Upon Divorce) Act

1987   controversy arises over allegations of corruption in Bofors gun purchase

1988   first of an eight-year run of good monsoons; Babri Masjid/Ram Janmabhoomi controversy erupts over disputed mosque at Ayodhya

1989   ninth General Elections; National Front coalition defeats Rajiv Gandhi's Congress government; minority government led by Janata's V. P. Singh takes office

1990   Mandal controversy arises over Prime Minister Singh's decision to implement 1980 recommendation of further job reservations for "other backward classes"; twelve students die in protest immolations; Bharatiya Janata Party launches nationwide agitation over Ayodhya

1991   Prime Minister Singh's government falls, with rival faction under Chandra Shekhar seeking Rajiv Gandhi's support to form government; withdrawal of this support leads to tenth General Elections; gold reserves pawned to stave off default on international debt; Rajiv Gandhi assassinated by Sri Lankan Tamil suicide bomber; Congress government formed under Prime Minister Narasimha Rao; economic reforms launched

1992   Supreme Court upholds Mandal; Harshad Mehta stock-market scandal erupts; December, demolition of Babri Masjid at Ayodhya by Hindu mob; serious Hindu-Muslim riots in several cities

1993 Hindu-Muslim tensions continue; bomb explosions rock Bombay; Washington conference of Vishwa Hindu Parishad; Congress wins confidence vote in Parliament, allegedly after illegal payoffs to opposion members

1994 October, sugar scandal erupts; November, Andhra Pradesh state elections lost by Congress

1995 September, statues of Ganesh reported to be drinking milk; Kerala state declared 100 percent literate

1996 Congress suffers worst-ever electoral defeat; Hindutva-inclined BJP emerges as largest single party, supports coalition government from the outside

1997 former "Untouchable" K. R. Narayanan elected president

1998 Bharatiya Janata Party forms and leads new coalition government; carries out nuclear test explosions

1999 Prime Minister Vajpayee makes historic bus trip to Pakistan and signs peace declaration; Pakistani forces cross Kashmir cease-fire lines in Kargil sector, lose brief but bloody war

2000 May, India marks the birth of its one billionth citizen; U.S. president Bill Clinton makes historic visit

2001 massive earthquakes strike western state of Gujarat; Vajpayee meets new Pakistani president Musharraf in unsuccessful summit in Agra; suicide attack on Indian parliament in December raises tensions with Pakistan

2002 large-scale rioting and killing in Gujarat leaves over 1,000, mainly Muslim, dead; July, Dr. A. P. J. Abdul Kalam, a Muslim and architect of India's missile program, elected president

2003 tensions with Pakistan ease

2004 Congress Party returns to power in surprise election victory as head of new coalition government

India

FROM MIDNIGHT
TO THE MILLENNIUM
AND BEYOND

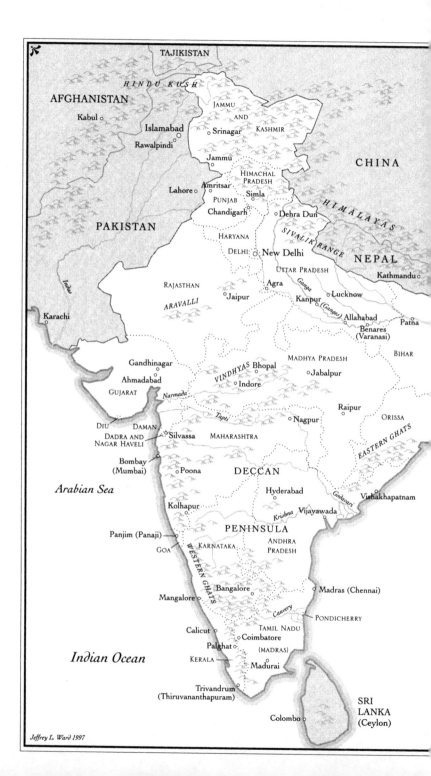

TAJIKISTAN

HINDU KUSH

AFGHANISTAN

Kabul ○

JAMMU
AND
KASHMIR

Srinagar ○

CHINA

Islamabad ○
Rawalpindi ○

Jammu ○

HIMACHAL
PRADESH

HIMALAYAS

Lahore ○

Amritsar ○
PUNJAB
Chandigarh ○

Simla ○

Dehra Dun ○

SIVALIK RANGE

PAKISTAN

HARYANA

DELHI ○ New Delhi

NEPAL

Kathmandu ○

UTTAR PRADESH

RAJASTHAN

ARAVALLI

Agra ○
Jaipur ○

Ganga

Lucknow ○

Kanpur ○

Ganges

Allahabad ○

Karachi ○

Indus

Benares
(Varanasi)

Patna ○

BIHAR

Gandhinagar ○

Ahmadabad ○

GUJARAT

Narmada

VINDHYAS Bhopal ○

Indore ○

MADHYA PRADESH

Jabalpur ○

Raipur ○

ORISSA

DIU ○
DADRA AND
NAGAR HAVELI

DAMAN

Tapti

Silvassa

MAHARASHTRA

Nagpur ○

EASTERN GHATS

Bombay
(Mumbai) ○

Poona ○

DECCAN

Arabian Sea

Kolhapur ○

Hyderabad ○

Godavari

Vishakhapatnam ○

Krishna

Vijayawada ○

Panjim (Panaji) ○

GOA

PENINSULA

KARNATAKA

ANDHRA
PRADESH

WESTERN GHATS

Bangalore ○

Madras (Chennai) ○

Mangalore ○

Cauvery

PONDICHERRY

Calicut ○

Palghat ○

TAMIL NADU

Coimbatore ○

(MADRAS)

Indian Ocean

KERALA

Madurai ○

Trivandrum
(Thiruvananthapuram) ○

SRI
LANKA
(Ceylon)

Colombo ○

Jeffrey L. Ward 1997

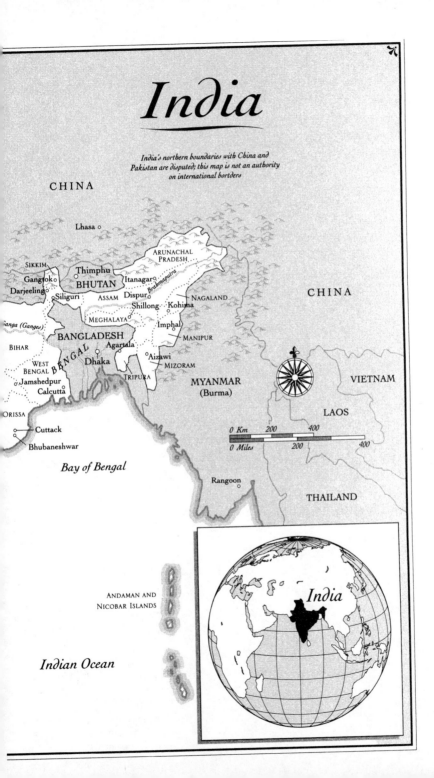

India

India's northern boundaries with China and Pakistan are disputed; this map is not an authority on international borders

CHINA

Lhasa

ARUNACHAL PRADESH

SIKKIM

Gangtok
Thimphu   Itanagar
Darjeeling BHUTAN
Siliguri   ASSAM   Dispur   *Brahmaputra*

CHINA

Shillong Kohima   NAGALAND

Ganga (Ganges)   MEGHALAYA   Imphal

BIHAR   BANGLADESH   Agartala   MANIPUR

WEST BENGAL   Dhaka   Aizawl

Jamshedpur   TRIPURA   MIZORAM

Calcutta   MYANMAR   VIETNAM
(Burma)

ORISSA   LAOS

Cuttack   0 Km   200   400

Bhubaneshwar   0 Miles   200   400

Bay of Bengal   Rangoon

THAILAND

ANDAMAN AND
NICOBAR ISLANDS   India

Indian Ocean

Introduction

On August 15, 1997, independent India turns fifty years old. What has been the story of those first fifty years? What does the twenty-first century hold for India? And why should either of these questions matter?

Twenty-one years ago, when I was fresh out of college and about to go to the United States for postgraduate studies, a leading Indian national newspaper asked me to do an article for their Independence Day supplement. The Emergency had just been declared; politicians had been locked up, the press censored; even one of my short stories, a police-detective effort called "The Political Murder," had been banned by censors who thought the very notion of a political murder dangerous and antinational. Around me, newspapermen and journalists were cowed and resentful. The freedoms for which our independence struggle had been waged seemed in peril; and yet weren't we, the literate minority, disqualified by our privileged status from objecting to measures designed, as the government claimed, to benefit "the common man?" I was angry, cynical, and confused — a combination of emotions appropriate both to my age and to the times. This is how I began my article:

Independent India is twenty-eight years old today. I was nineteen a few months ago. In school they told me I was the citizen of tomorrow. Around me I saw the citizens of today, and wondered what purpose I was going to serve. They seemed worn and jaded and cynical. To my fellow-citizens-of-the-future, Independence Day merely meant early mornings in starched uniforms on parade grounds, relieved only by the comforting thought of no more classes. In college they were more sensible. They just gave us a holiday, and the chowkidar unfurled the flag.

I look at a fading photocopy of the piece today, and marvel that they published it at all. By August, of course, censorship by unimaginative government babus had given way to self-censorship by imaginative subeditors, and mine were evidently more daring than most. "Independence," I went on in adolescent passion,

> conjures up visions of mammoth patriotic rallies outside Red Fort; a reminder of freedom and self-reliance and the hope of unexploited progress. But when the drums have been beaten and the cavalcade has passed, the cheering invariably seems to subside into a desultory grumble. Our capacity for unproductive complaint is seemingly limitless; but then we appear to have developed the art of destructive criticism to the proportions of a national characteristic. Perhaps it is because, as a former colony, we are used to bemoaning our lot without being able to do anything about it. . . .
>
> The divisions [that matter] are less between Indian and Indian — whether Hindu-Muslim, Brahmin-untouchable, landlord-peasant or bureaucrat-revolutionary — than between Indian and India. And what is far more fearsome than economic stagnation or political apathy is that atrophy of the line of association that binds the one's fortunes indissolubly to the other's. For otherwise we have the strange spectacle of a nation without nationals, of Indians who are not involved in India.

"Atrophy." "Indissolubly." I was nineteen, I liked big words. But beneath the overdeveloped vocabulary I had a message from my generation. After a couple of paragraphs savaging "cocktail-toting polemicists" at "boxwallah gatherings" for their lack of a "sense of belonging" to India, I argued: "That one is an all-too-dispensable part [of the Indian reality] is surely all the more reason why one should take one's role all the more seriously, instead of affecting the dislocated detachment that has become the untaxed perquisite of citizenship." That was my point: we had to belong, we had to care, we had to be involved in what became of our independence. This "sense of belonging"(the phrase with which I titled the article) would be vital "to me and those of my generation who now stand on the threshold of that which has, over the last twenty-eight years, been made to mean so little."

It was easy enough to say this, I suppose, when I was holding a ticket to the United States and escaping from my responsibility to do anything about it. But as I read these words now, I wonder how much they might resonate in the mind and spirit of a nineteen-year-old collegian in today's India. A year and a half after I wrote this article, boys and girls very much like me, children of executives in Hindustanized multinationals, accustomed to ease and privilege, came out in the streets of Calcutta and Delhi, threw off the apolitical detachment I had described, and campaigned door-to-door to unseat an authoritarian government. They asserted the "sense of belonging" I was afraid we had all lost.

Today the issues that confront India are, in a strikingly different way, as important as those that faced my contemporaries two decades ago. There is no immediate threat of a suspension of our basic freedoms, as there was then. But in this book I propose to argue that India is, in a phrase first used (though in a different context) by the British historian E. P. Thompson, "the most important country for the future of the world." For Indians stand at the intersection of four of the most important debates facing the world at the end of the twentieth century:

· *The bread-versus-freedom debate.* Can democracy "deliver the goods" to alleviate desperate poverty, or do its inbuilt inefficiencies only impede rapid growth? Is the instability of political contention (and of makeshift coalitions) a luxury that a developing country cannot afford? As today's young concentrate on making their bread, should they consider political freedom a dispensable distraction?

· *The centralization-versus-federalism debate.* Does tomorrow's India need to be run by a strong central government able to transcend the fissiparous tendencies of language, caste, and region, or is that government best which centralizes least?

• *The pluralism-versus-fundamentalism debate.* Is the secularism established in India's Constitution, and now increasingly attacked as a westernized affectation, essential in a pluralist society, or should India, like many other Third World countries, find refuge in the assertion of its own religious identity?

• *The "Coca-colonization" debate, or globalization versus self-reliance.* Should India, where economic self-sufficiency has been a mantra for more than four decades, open itself further to the world economy, or does the entry of Western consumer goods bring in alien influences that threaten to disrupt Indian society in ways too vital to be allowed? Should we raise the barriers to shield our youth from the pernicious seductions of MTV and McDonald's?

These are not merely academic debates; they are now being enacted on the national and world stage, and the choices we make will determine the kind of India our children will inherit in the twenty-first century. And since the century will begin with Indians accounting for a sixth of the world's population, their choices will resonate throughout the globe.

In the pages that follow I embark upon a sweeping and highly personalized examination of contemporary India, with these debates in mind. This book is not a survey of modern Indian history, though it touches upon many of the principal events of the last five decades. It is not "reportage," though I do draw anecdotally upon my own travels and conversations in India. It is instead a subjective account, I hope both informed and impassioned, of the forces that have made (and nearly unmade) today's India, and about the India that I hope my sons will inherit in the second half-century after independence.

Not all agree with my vision of India. There are those who wish it to become a Hindu Rashtra, a land of and for the Hindu majority; those who wish to raise higher the protectionist barriers against foreign investment that are slowly beginning to come down; those who believe that a firm hand at the national helm would be preferable to the failures of democracy (one prominent nationalist even called recently for the army to take over the government). As far back as 1949, during the debates on the draft Constitution of India, its principal draftsman, Dr. B. R. Ambedkar, had pointed out that Indian democracy was as old as its ancient village republics. India had political assemblies with elaborate parliamentary rules of procedure at a time when most of the rest of the world suffered under despotism or anarchy. "This democratic system," Ambedkar said movingly, "India lost. Will she lose it a second time?"

I will argue that the only possible idea of India is that of a nation greater than the sum of its parts. An India that denies itself to *some* Indians could end up being denied to *all* Indians.

In asserting this, a few words of explanation are in order. This book is a paean to India, yet it emanates from the pen of a United Nations official who has lived outside India for most of his adult life. I am, indeed, often asked how I can reconcile my passionate faith in India with my internationalist work for the United Nations. I see no contradiction; indeed, both emerge from the same pluralist convictions. The Indian adventure is that of human beings of different ethnicities and religions, customs and costumes, cuisines and colors, languages and accents, working together under the same roof, sharing the same dreams. That is also what the United Nations, at its best, seeks to achieve. It is arguably easier for Indians than for most others to work with people who are unlike them, since that is what we are brought up to do at home.

The second explanation, however, deals with that collective "we." Who are the Indians of whom I speak so proprietarily? In his magisterial essay on life and thought in Mexico, *The Labyrinth of Solitude*, Octavio Paz observed that his thoughts were not concerned with the entire Mexican population, but rather with those among them "who are conscious of themselves, for one reason or another, as Mexicans." The same applies, for comparable reasons, to this book, which speaks of an India that exists in the imagination of most, but not all, of my countrymen and countrywomen. Paz went on to serve as Mexico's ambassador to India in the 1960s, and I imagine he saw that, as in the Mexico he was writing about in 1950, several historical epochs and states of development coexist simultaneously in India. This is still the case, and it would be foolish as well as presumptuous to seek to speak for them all in a general notion of Indianness. In the last fifty years not all Indians have learned to think of themselves as Indians, and to speak of an Indian identity is really to subsume a number of identities that vary depending upon class, caste, region, and language. But this variety is in itself integral to my idea of Indianness; the singular thing about India is that you can only speak of it in the plural. India is fundamentally a pluralist state; its pluralism emerges from its geography, is reflected in its history, and is confirmed by its ethnography. It is this that I hark to in my writing, which — when it succumbs to generalization — will generalize for the many rather than for the mass.

This is hardly a new predicament. The narrator of my book *The Great Indian Novel* confesses his own subjectivity to his scribe, Ganapathi, and acknowledges the validity of alternative viewpoints on everything he has had to say:

> This is my story of the India I know, with its biases, selections, omissions, distortions, all mine. But you cannot derive your cosmogony from a single birth, Ganapathi. Every Indian must forever carry with him, in his head and heart, his own history of India.

I couldn't have put it better myself.

1

A Myth and an Idea

*I*ndia," Winston Churchill once barked, "is merely a geographical expression. It is no more a single country than the Equator." Churchill was rarely right about India, but it is true that no other country in the world embraces the extraordinary mixture of ethnic groups, the profusion of mutually incomprehensible languages, the varieties of topography and climate, the diversity of religions and cultural practices, and the range of levels of economic development that India does.

And yet India is more than the sum of its contradictions. It is a country held together, in the words of its first prime minister, Jawaharlal Nehru, "by strong but invisible threads. . . . About her there is the elusive quality of a legend of long ago; some enchantment seems to have held her mind. She is a myth and an idea, a dream and a vision, and yet very real and present and pervasive."

How can one approach this land of snow peaks and tropical jungles, with seventeen major languages and twenty-two thousand distinct dialects (including some spoken by more people than speak Danish or Norwegian), inhabited in the last decade of the twentieth century by nearly 940 million individuals of every ethnic extraction known to humanity? How does one come to terms with a country whose population is 51 percent illiterate, but which has educated the world's second largest pool of trained scientists and engineers, whose teeming cities overflow while four out of five Indians scratch a living from the soil? What is the clue to understanding a country rife with despair and disrepair, which nonetheless moved a Mughal emperor to declaim, "If on earth there be paradise of bliss, it is this, it is this, it is this . . .?" How does one gauge a culture that elevated nonviolence to an effective moral principle, but whose freedom was born in blood and whose independence still soaks in it? How does one explain a land where peasant organizations and suspicious officials attempt to close down Kentucky Fried Chicken as a threat to the nation, where a former prime minister bitterly criticizes the sale of Pepsi-Cola "in a country where villagers don't have clean drinking water," and which yet invents a greater quantity of sophisticated software for U.S. computer manufacturers than any other country in the world? How can one portray the present, let alone the future, of an ageless civilization that was the birthplace of four major religions, a dozen different traditions of classical dance, eighty-five political parties, and three hundred ways of cooking the potato?

The short answer is that it can't be done — at least not to everyone's satisfaction. Any truism about India can be immediately contradicted by another truism about India. The country's national motto, emblazoned on its governmental crest, is *Satyameva Jayate:* "Truth Always Triumphs." The question remains, however: Whose truth? It is a question to which there are at least 940-plus million answers — if the last census hasn't undercounted us again.

But that sort of answer is no answer at all, and so another answer to those questions has to be sought. And this may lie in a single insight: the singular thing about India is that you can only speak of it in the plural. There are, in the hackneyed phrase, many Indias. Everything exists in countless variants. There is no single standard, no fixed stereotype, no "one way." This pluralism is acknowledged in the way India arranges its own affairs: all groups, faiths, tastes, and ideologies survive and contend for their place in the sun. At a time when most developing countries opted for authoritarian models of government to promote nation-building and to direct development, India chose to be a multiparty democracy. And despite many stresses and strains, including twenty-two months of autocratic rule during a "state of emergency" declared by Prime Minister Indira Gandhi in 1975, a multiparty democracy — freewheeling, rambunctious, corrupt, and inefficient, perhaps, but nonetheless flourishing — India has remained.

One result is that India strikes many as maddening, chaotic, inefficient, and seemingly unpurposeful as it muddles through into the twenty-first century. Another, though, is that India is not just a country but an adventure, one in which all avenues are open and everything is possible. "All the convergent influences of the world," wrote E. P. Thompson, "run through this society: Hindu, Moslem, Christian, secular; Stalinist, liberal, Maoist, democratic socialist, Gandhian. There is not a thought that is being thought in the West or East that is not active in some Indian mind."

That Indian mind has been shaped by remarkably diverse forces: ancient Hindu tradition, myth, and scripture; the impact of Islam and Christianity; and two centuries of British colonial rule. The result is unique, not just because of the variety of contemporary influences available in India, but because of the diversity of its heritage.

Many observers have been astonished by India's survival as a pluralist state. But India could hardly have survived as anything else. Pluralism is a reality that emerges from the very nature of the country; it is a choice made inevitable by India's geography and reaffirmed by its history.

One of the few generalizations that can safely be made about India is that nothing can be taken for granted about the country — not even its name, for the word *India* comes from the river Indus, which flows in Pakistan. That anomaly is easily explained, for what is today Pakistan was part of India until the country was partitioned by the departing British in 1947. (Yet each explanation breeds another anomaly. Pakistan was created as a homeland for India's Muslims, but throughout the 1970s and 1980s there were more Muslims in India than in Pakistan.)

So the Indus is no longer the starting point for a description of India's geography, which underpins the national principle of variety. Instead one might start with the dimensions of the country. India is huge; it is the world's seventh largest country, covering an area of 1,269,419 square miles (3,287,782 square kilometers). It is also the second most populous nation on earth, with an estimated 1996 population of over 940 million against China's estimated 1 billion, but with its population — which grows annually by 13 million, equivalent to a new Australia every year — projected to overtake China's within three decades. Another indication of the immensity of India is the length of its coastline (3,533 miles, or 5,653 kilometers) and its land frontiers with its neighbors (9,425 miles, or 15,168 kilometers).

One figure is particularly revealing. India extends 2,009 miles (3,214 kilometers) from its mountainous northern border with China, in the state of Jammu and Kashmir, to the southernmost tip of the mainland, the rocky beach of Kanniyakumari (formerly Cape Comorin). Indeed, the Andaman and Nicobar Islands, also Indian territory, are hundreds of nautical miles farther to the southeast, in the Bay of Bengal, which flows into the Indian Ocean. India thus stretches from 38 degrees north latitude, well above the Tropic of Cancer and on a line with Atlantic City or Denver, Colorado, to 7 degrees above the equator, the same as Freetown, Sierra Leone, or Addis Ababa. Few countries on earth extend over so many latitudes.

Looked at longitudinally, the distances are only slightly less imposing. From west to east, India's western frontier with Pakistan, in the marshes of the Rann of Kutch, is 1,840 miles (2,944 kilometers) away from the thickly wooded hills of northeastern Assam, on the country's border with Myanmar (Burma). In between, the country of Bangladesh is embraced as an enclave between the Indian state of West Bengal (from which it was partitioned in 1947 as East Pakistan) and the northeastern states of Assam, Meghalaya, Mizoram, and Tripura.

The country's four extremes represent four dramatically different types of ecological systems, but there are still others within the subcontinent they enclose. These range from the Thar Desert of Rajasthan in the northwest, covering about 8 percent of India's land surface, to the lush alluvial plain of the Ganga River basin; and India also has the largest area in the world covered by snow and ice, outside the polar regions.

While the Himalaya mountains allowed a distinctive civilization to flourish in their shadows, they are remarkably penetrable. A number of passes, some more difficult than others, have allowed curious scholars, intrepid traders, and ambitious invaders to bring their own influences into India. If the phrase "ethnic melting pot" had been coined two thousand years ago, India would have had a fair claim to the title. The "indigenous people," around 1500 B.C., were probably dark-skinned Dravidians, with aboriginals of Negroid stock in many forests. Then came the great wave of Aryan migration from the Central Asian steppes. The Aryans were pale-skinned and light-eyed nomads whose search for a new homeland branched into three waves, one stopping in Persia, one sweep continuing on to Europe as far as Germany, and the other descending into India. (This common heritage explains why the Nazis in Germany used a variation of the swastika, an Aryan religious symbol still revered by Indian Hindus.) That was not all. Over the centuries, India witnessed the mingling of Greeks, Scythians, and Parthians; Mongols, Huns, and Chinese; and an assortment of mercenary warriors from Central Asia, Iran, Turkey, and even Ethiopia. As they intermarried with each other and with the local population, the Indian melting pot produced a people with a variety of skin colors and every physiognomic feature imaginable, as a look at any Indian cricket, hockey, or soccer team will confirm.

Immigrants, invaders, and visitors, whether their intentions were warlike or peaceful, usually made for the Gangetic plain, the fertile stretch of land that gave birth to the Indo-Aryan civilization over three thousand years ago. The people of "Aryavrata," the Hindi-speaking national heartland, serve as the stock image of the stereotypical "Indian." But there are dramatically visible differences among those who live within this "cow belt," as urbanized anglophones derisively call it, and further differences between it and the farmlands of what remains of the Indus's tributaries in the northwest of India. To the east, the

Ganga flows to the sea in Bengal, part of which is now the independent state of Bangladesh. Beyond Bangladesh rise the hills and valleys of India's northeast, most of whose people are physically shorter and have Mongoloid features akin to their neighbors in Southeast Asia. The seven states of the northeast — the "seven sisters" — embrace a wide diversity of cultural strains, from the tribal traditions of the Nagas and the Mizos to the mainstream Hinduism of Manipur, home of a major school of Indian classical dance. The people range from Bengali migrants in Tripura and Assam to the Christian hill folk of Nagaland, whose official state language is English; from anglicized tea planters to aborigines with bones through their noses. Tourist brochures usually call the northeast "picturesque," the kind of euphemism that accurately suggests both charm and underdevelopment.

But diversity does not end with the northern latitudes. The aged and weatherbeaten peninsula of the Deccan is host to an India of darker shades, hotter food, more rapid speech, and rounded scripts; there is Dravidian pride and a rich overlay of Sanskritic high culture. On both sides of the inverted southern triangle, coastal Indians have for millennia looked beyond their shores for trade and cultural contact with other lands. In the west, traces have been found of contact across the Arabian Sea with Iraq, Yemen, and East Africa going back three thousand years. Jews persecuted in the Babylonian conquest of Judea in the sixth century B.C. and Zoroastrians fleeing Islamic rule in Persia in the eighth century A.D. found refuge and established flourishing communities. Travelers ranged from Saint Thomas the Apostle in the first century A.D., who brought Christianity to the lush southwestern state of Kerala, to the Portuguese sailor Vasco da Gama in 1492, who took away calico (so named for the port of Calicut, where he landed) and spices. The enclave of Goa on the west coast was ruled by Portugal till 1961, and that of Pondicherry in the southeast by France; they still bear a different cultural character from the surrounding states.

Though the Aryans and later the northern rulers never penetrated so far into the south, South Indians cannot be easily stereotyped. Kerala hosts the oldest Jewish community in the world outside of the Middle

East, and a Christian community going back to the first decades after Christ (and therefore having a faith and rituals much older than those of the European missionaries who arrived centuries later). In the southeast the travel was all in the other direction, with traders and colonists a thousand years ago venturing to Sri Lanka and as far afield as Indonesia, but receiving virtually no visitors themselves from across the seas.

What makes so many people one people? One answer is the physical realities of the subcontinent — mountains to the north and northwest, water surrounding the rest — which have carved out a distinct geographical space for Indians to inhabit. Through the millennia, the peoples of India have moved freely within this space, the political and territorial boundaries within them ever shifting and always fungible; but they have rarely, if ever, ventured beyond these natural confines without being conscious of entering alien lands. A second, equally revealing, answer may be found in the attitude of generations of foreigners, from Alexander the Great to the first of the Great Mughals, Babur, who consistently saw the peoples of the land beyond the Indus — "Hindustan" — as one. Divided, variegated, richly differentiated, but one.

The history of each of the many peoples of India overlaps with each of the others, but only marginally with those outside the geopolitical space of the subcontinent. Their travails and triumphs, their battles and their blessings, their dreams and defeats, have all been shared with other Indians. History has bound them together as indissolubly as geography.

With diversity emerging from its geography and inscribed in its history, India was made for pluralism. It is not surprising, then, that the political life of modern India has been rather like traditional Indian music: the broad basic rules are firmly set, but within them one is free to improvise, unshackled by a written score.

·   ·   ·

The India that achieved its freedom at midnight on August 14–15, 1947, was the product of several thousand years of history and civilization and, more immediately, of just under two hundred years of British colonial rule. Learned British econometricians have tried to establish that the net result of this experience was neutral — that the British put about as much into India as they took out. The negative side of the ledger is easily listed: economic exploitation (often undisguised looting of everything from raw materials to jewels); stunting of indigenous industry (symbolized by the deliberate barbarity with which, on at least two occasions, the British ordered the thumbs of whole communities of Indian weavers chopped off so that they could not compete with the products of Lancashire); the creation of a landless peasantry (through land settlement acts that vested land ownership in a complaisant squirearchy of *zamindars* created by the British to maintain rural order); and general poverty, hunger, and underdevelopment. The pros to these cons are less obvious. It is true that the British brought in the railways, the post and telegraphs, a national administrative system with a well-planned capital city, libraries, museums, and the English language; but all were instruments of British imperialism, intended in the first place to facilitate and perpetuate British rule, and only secondarily to benefit those among whom these were introduced. It is also true that British rule gave India a political unity it had not enjoyed for centuries; but the British also sowed a variety of political disunity India had never experienced before in its long and tumultuous history, a disunity rooted in sectarianism.

Never throughout all the centuries of rule by Hindu, Buddhist, and Muslim kings had any section of the Indian people sought a different political order on the grounds of religion alone; even the most intolerant of Muslim kings, those who razed temples and exacted the *jaziya* tax on unbelievers, had had Hindu generals and ministers to serve them, including in wars against Muslim rivals. (And the Maratha king Shivaji, idolized by the eponymous but Muslim-hating Shiv Sena party, had Muslim officers in his army, too.) But the idea of dividing Indians by the manner in which they held out their hands to God was born in the wake of the unsuccessful, but multireligious, "mutiny" of 1857, when Hindus and Muslims rose together in revolt against the foreigner. The sight (and the dismaying prospect) of Indians of varying faiths and regions united in a shared struggle against alien rule struck more terror into the hearts of the British than their actual revolt, which was put down by the force of superior arms. Colonial administrators, needing to defend the imperial project, came up with the old Roman maxim *divide et impera* — "divide and rule." What the British euphemistically dubbed "communal feeling" was actively stoked; it became a tenet of colonial policy to encourage particularist consciousness among Indians, both religious (so that they would be Muslims or Sikhs first and Indians second, if at all) and regional (so that they would be Bengalis or Dogras rather than Indians). If the structures of British rule tended toward the creation of a united India for the convenience of the rulers, its animating spirit was aimed at fostering division to achieve the same ends. This seeming paradox (but in fact entirely logical construct) of imperial policy culminated in the tragic Partition of India upon independence — so that August 15, 1947, was a birth that was also an abortion.

But despite the mourning in many nationalist hearts at the amputation that came with freedom, despite the refusal of Mahatma Gandhi to celebrate an independence he saw primarily as a betrayal, despite the flames of communal hatred and rioting that lit the midnight sky as the new country was born, there was reason for pride, and hope. India's first prime minister, Jawaharlal Nehru, put it in words that still stir the soul:

> Long years ago we made a tryst with destiny, and now the time comes when we shall redeem our pledge, not wholly or in full measure, but very substantially. At the stroke of the midnight hour, when the world sleeps, India will awake to life and freedom. A moment comes, which comes but rarely in history, when we step out from the old to the new, when an age ends and when the soul of a nation, long suppressed, finds utterance. It is fitting that at this solemn moment we take the pledge of dedication to the service of India and her people and to the still larger cause of humanity.

It was typical of Nehru that, at this moment of unprecedented triumph and tragedy for the Indian nation, he should still spare a thought for the "larger cause of humanity." But this was not merely the soaring worldview of an overeducated visionary; India had always seemed, to the more thoughtful of its leaders, a crucible of human striving, one that offered, in its mistakes and failings as much as in its successes, lessons for all mankind.

.   .   .

The most striking feature of the first years of Indian independence was an absence. It was the absence of the man whom we all called (though he rejected the phrase) the Father of the Nation, the Mahatma (Great Soul — another term he detested) Gandhi, assassinated by a Hindu fanatic on January 30, 1948. Indian democracy was just five months old, and Gandhi died, with the name of God on his lips, in the capital of the new state he had done more than anyone else on earth to establish. The Mahatma was killed by a young man who thought Gandhi was too pro-Muslim; indeed, he had just come out of a fast he had conducted to coerce his own followers, the ministers of the new Indian Government of India, to transfer a larger share than they had intended of the assets of undivided India to the new state of Pakistan. Gandhi had also announced his intention to spurn the country he had failed to keep united and to spend the rest of his years in Pakistan, a prospect that had made the government of Pakistan collectively choke. But that was Gandhi: idealistic, quirky, quixotic, and determined, a man who answered to the beat of no other drummer, but got everyone else to march to his tune. Someone once called him a cross between a saint and a Tammany Hall politician; like the best crossbreeds, he managed to distill all the qualities of both and yet transcend their contradictions.

In 1983 the U.S. Academy of Motion Picture Arts and Sciences awarded a rare slew of eight Oscars to Sir Richard Attenborough's film *Gandhi*. Disgruntled supporters of the competition, which included Steven Spielberg's blockbuster *E.T.: The Extra-Terrestrial*, sourly remarked that the Academy was supposed to be rewarding cinematic excellence, not handing out the Nobel Peace Prize. But Gandhi, of course, had never won the Nobel Peace Prize (a distinction the Swedish Academy has since conferred on a series of self-proclaimed Gandhians, from Martin Luther King Jr. to Adolfo Perez Esquivel). His prize had been something less tangible. Publicity posters for the film proclaimed that "Gandhi's triumph changed the world forever." I saw the posters, enjoyed the film (despite its many historical inaccuracies), and rooted for it when the Oscars were handed out. But I never stopped wondering whether Gandhi had in fact triumphed at all.

Much of the international debate sparked by the film, of course, focused on the man rather than his message. There was the inevitable controversy over the portrayal of the Mahatma and the omission of facts and personalities who might have detracted from the celluloid hagiography. Yet amid both acclaim and accusation, few took Sir Richard Attenborough up on his frequent assertion of the film's contemporary relevance. Gandhi's life was, of course, his lesson. He was unique among the statesmen of the twentieth century in his determination not just to live his beliefs but to reject any separation between beliefs and action; in his life, religion flowed into politics; his public life meshed seamlessly with his private conduct. The claim emblazoned on those publicity posters for the film suggested that the lessons of his life had been learned and widely followed. But even for the man who swept aside the British Raj, Paul Newman, and *Tootsie* in his triumphal progress toward a shelf full of golden statuary, this was a difficult claim to sustain.

Mahatma Gandhi was the kind of person it is more convenient to forget. The principles he stood for and the way in which he asserted them are easier to admire than to follow. While he was alive he was impossible to ignore. Once he had gone he was impossible to imitate.

The screen depicted Gandhi as the extraordinary leader of the world's first successful nonviolent movement for independence from colonial rule. At the same time he was a philosopher who was constantly seeking to live out his own ideas, whether they applied to individual self-improvement or social change: his autobiography was typically subtitled *The Story of My Experiments with Truth*. No dictionary imbues truth with the depth of meaning Gandhi gave it. His truth emerged from his convictions: it meant not only what was accurate, but what was just and therefore right. Truth could not be obtained by "untruthful" or unjust means, which included inflicting violence upon one's opponent.

To describe his method, Gandhi coined the expression *satyagraha* — literally, "holding on to truth" or, as he variously described it, truth-force, love-force, or soul-force. He disliked the English term "passive resistance," because *satyagraha* required activism, not passivity. If you believed in Truth and cared enough to obtain it, Gandhi felt, you could not afford to be passive: you had to be prepared actively to suffer for Truth.

So nonviolence, like many later concepts labeled with a negation, from noncooperation to nonalignment, meant much more than the denial of an opposite; it did not merely imply the absence of violence. Nonviolence was the way to vindicate the truth by the infliction of suffering not on the opponent, but on oneself. It was essential to accept punishment willingly in order to demonstrate the strength of one's convictions.

This was the approach Gandhi brought to the movement for our independence — and it worked. Where sporadic terrorism and moderate constitutionalism had both proved ineffective, Gandhi took the issue of freedom to the masses as one of simple right and wrong, and gave them a technique to which the British had no response. By abstaining from violence, Gandhi wrested the moral advantage. By breaking the law nonviolently, he showed up the injustice of the law. By accepting the punishments imposed on him, he confronted his captors with their own brutalization. By voluntarily imposing suffering upon himself in his hunger strikes, he demonstrated the lengths to which he was prepared to go in defense of what he considered to be right. In the end he made the perpetuation of British rule an impossibility.

Of course, there was much more to Gandhism — physical self-denial and discipline, spiritual faith, a belief in humanity and in the human capacity for selfless love, the self-reliance symbolized by the spinning wheel, religious ecumenism, idealistic internationalism, and a passionate commitment to human equality and social justice (especially in our caste-ridden country). The improvement of his fellow human beings was arguably more important to him than the political goal of ridding India of the British. But it is his central tenet of nonviolence in the pursuit of these ends that represents his most significant original contribution to the world.

The case for the film's international relevance was typified by the declaration of Coretta Scott King, the widow of Martin Luther King Jr., the most famous of the many who claimed to have been inspired by the teachings of Mahatma Gandhi, that the film "will rekindle world-wide interest in nonviolence. . . . Gandhi's challenge to the world is once again before the public forum and it is up to all of us to translate it into action." One did not have to wait a decade to point to the utter futility of both the prediction and the hope that underlay it. But Mrs. King's comment was particularly interesting because it was her husband, more than anyone else, who had used nonviolence most effectively outside India, in breaking down segregation in the southern United States. King himself had declared that "the Gandhian method of nonviolent resistance . . . became the guiding light of our movement. Christ furnished the spirit and motivation and Gandhi furnished the method."

So Gandhism arguably helped to change the Deep South forever. But it is difficult to find many other instances of its success. India's independence marked the dawn of the era of decolonization, but many nations still came to freedom only after bloody and violent struggles. Other peoples have fallen under the boots of invading armies, been dispossessed of their lands, or been forced to flee in terror from their homes. Nonviolence has offered no solutions to them. It could work only against opponents vulnerable to a loss of moral authority — governments responsive to domestic and international public opinion, capable of being shamed into conceding defeat. In Gandhi's own day, nonviolence could have done nothing for the Jews of Hitler's Germany, who disappeared unprotestingly into gas chambers far from the flashbulbs of a conscience-stricken press.

The power of nonviolence rests in being able to say, "To show you that you are wrong, I punish myself." But that has little effect on those who are not interested in whether they are wrong and are already seeking to punish you whether you disagree with them or not. For them, your willingness to undergo punishment is the most convenient means of victory.

On this subject Gandhi sounds frighteningly unrealistic: "The willing sacrifice of the innocent is the most powerful answer to insolent tyranny that has yet been conceived by God or man. Disobedience to be 'civil' must be sincere, respectful, restrained, never defiant, and it must have no ill will or hatred behind it. Neither should there be excitement in civil disobedience, which is a preparation for mute suffering."

For many smarting under injustice across the world, that would sound like a prescription for sainthood — or for impotence. Mute suffering is all very well as a moral principle, but it has rarely brought about meaningful change. The sad truth is that the staying power of organized violence is almost always greater than that of nonviolence. And when right and wrong are less clear-cut, Gandhism flounders. The Mahatma, at the peak of his influence, was unable to prevent partition, even though, in his terms, he considered it "wrong." Gandhi believed in "weaning an opponent from error by patience, sympathy and self-suffering" — but if the opponent believes equally in the justice of *his* cause, he is hardly going to accept that he is in "error." Gandhism is viable at its simplest and most profound in the service of a transcendent principle like independence from foreign rule. But in more complex situations it cannot — and, more to the point, does not — work as well.

Gandhi's ideals had a tremendous intellectual impact on the founding fathers of the new India, who incorporated many of his convictions into the directive principles of state policy. Yet Gandhian solutions have not been found for many of the ills over which he agonized, from persistent interreligious conflict to the ill treatment of Untouchables (whom he renamed Harijans, or "Children of God," a designation its beneficiaries found patronizing, for were we not *all* Children of God? Today they prefer to be known as Dalits, meaning "the Oppressed.") Instead, his methods (particularly the fast, the *hartal,* and the deliberate courting of arrest) have been abused and debased by far lesser men in the pursuit of petty sectarian ends. Outside India, too, Gandhian techniques have been perverted by such people as terrorists and bomb-throwers declaring hunger strikes when punished for their crimes. Gandhism without moral authority is like Marxism without a proletariat. Yet few who wish to use his methods have his personal integrity or moral stature.

Internationally, Gandhi expressed ideals few can reject: he could virtually have written the United Nations Charter. But the decades after his death have confirmed that there is no escape from the conflicting sovereignties of states. Some 20 million more lives have been lost in wars and insurrections since his passing. In a dismaying number of countries, governments spend more for military purposes than for education and health care combined. The current stockpile of nuclear weapons represents over a million times the explosive power of the atom bomb whose destruction of Hiroshima so grieved him. Universal peace, which Gandhi considered so central to Truth, seems as illusionary as ever.

As governments compete, so religions contend. The ecumenist Gandhi, who declared, "I am a Hindu, a Muslim, a Christian, a Zoroastrian, a Jew," might find it difficult to stomach the exclusivist revivalism of so many religions and cults the world over. But perhaps his approach has always been inappropriate for the rest of the world. As one of his Muslim critics retorted, to his claim of eclectic belief, "Only a Hindu could say that."

And finally, the world of the spinning wheel, of self-reliant families in contented village republics, is even more remote today than when Gandhi first espoused it. Despite the brief popularity of intermediate technology and the credo "small is beautiful," there does not appear to be much room for such ideas in an interdependent world. Self-reliance is too often a cover for protectionism and a shelter for inefficiency in the Third World. The successful and prosperous countries are those who are able to look beyond spinning *chakras* to silicon chips — and who give their people the benefits of technological developments that free them from menial and repetitive chores and broaden the horizons of their lives.

But if Gandhism has had its limitations exposed in the years after

1947, there is no denying Gandhi's greatness. While the world was disintegrating into fascism, violence, and war, Gandhi taught the virtues of truth, nonviolence, and peace. He destroyed the credibility of colonialism by opposing principle to force. And he set and attained personal standards of conviction and courage that few will ever match. He was that rare kind of leader who was not confined by the inadequacies of his followers.

Yet Gandhi's Truth was essentially his own. He formulated its unique content and determined its application in a specific historical context. Inevitably, few in today's world can measure up to his greatness or aspire to his credo. No, Gandhi's "triumph" did not change the world forever. It is, sadly, a matter of doubt whether he triumphed at all.

The India of the first fifty years after independence was therefore a post-Gandhian India. It paid lip service to much of its Gandhian patrimony while striking out in directions of which Gandhi could not have approved. But its central challenges remained the ones Gandhi identified: those of overcoming disunity and discrimination, of ensuring the health and well-being of the downtrodden, of developing the capacity to meet the nation's basic needs, of promoting among Indians the integrity and commitment he labeled "Truth." These challenges, modified by the ways in which India has attempted to rise to them in the last fifty years, remain. They will continue to set the defining agenda of the next fifty years.

2

Two Assassinations and a Funeral
The Death of a Dynasty

*A*fter the general elections of 1996, as after those of 1991, the question on many Indian lips was a curious one: Will she or won't she?

As a minority government tenuously wielded power in the monsoon of 1991 after the inconclusive result of India's most violent general election ever, its future clouded by swirling speculation about the ambitions of rival leaders, the most avid speculation in New Delhi's political circles concerned a nonpolitician. The question was again asked in mid-1996, though in more muted terms, after a more tranquil contest that witnessed the repudiation of much of India's political establishment. Will Sonia Gandhi, the Italian-born widow of former prime minister Rajiv Gandhi, enter politics? And if she does, how long will it be before modern India's dominant political dynasty rules again?

On the face of it, the question was absurd. Not only was Sonia a "foreigner" (her Indian passport too recent in 1991 to have needed renewal) and a Roman Catholic (in a land where fewer than 2 percent of the population share her Christian faith), but she was reserved, intensely private, and famously antipolitical. The tales of her reluctance, tragically vindicated, to allow her late husband to entangle himself in India's murky public life were legendary. It was only on emotional and "familial" grounds that she acquiesced in Rajiv Gandhi's entry into politics when his mother, Prime Minister Indira Gandhi, was left bereft by the death in a plane crash of her younger son and political heir, Sanjay. And when Rajiv was precipitated into the highest office by Indira Gandhi's assassination, Sonia — who had cradled the dying prime minister in her arms — reportedly pleaded with him not to take the job. If anything, the killing of her husband in the midst of an election campaign justified her worst fears. Surely she wouldn't dream of putting herself and her children on the firing line again, for a cause that had already cost them so much?

Indeed, the persistence of the question seems, at one level, strange. The Congress Party bosses offered Sonia the crown of thorns within forty-eight hours of her husband's death. In the chaos and uncertainty following Rajiv Gandhi's murder by a suicide bomber from the Tamil Tiger terrorist movement in neighboring Sri Lanka, they unanimously voted her to the party's presidency. She was the only remaining adult symbol of the family that had ruled India for all but six of its forty-four years of independence, but Sonia, still devastated by grief and shock, turned them down flat. That, it had then seemed, was that: the end of the Nehru-Gandhi dynasty.

But it didn't quite work out that way. Calls for Sonia Gandhi to change her mind were made every day. One nominee to the first post-Rajiv federal Council of Ministers, Rudra Pratap Singh, refused to take his oath of office until Sonia announced her entry into politics. She did not oblige, and he was dropped from the government, but his stand struck a chord. An incessant stream of political visitors, from the new prime minister on down, flowed to her New Delhi residence every day. Within weeks of her husband's death, the political class stopped pretending that these were "condolence visits"; politicians wanted to seek her advice, her blessing, or at least her proximity, and critics began muttering darkly that the young widow was becoming "an extraconstitutional center of power."

As the compromise prime minister, P. V. Narasimha Rao, slowly but surely consolidated his grip on office, Sonia Gandhi edged out of contention, but not out of the limelight. She remained the most visible symbol of the Congress Party's link to its Nehruvian glory; she was invited to every function of national importance, from the Independence Day celebrations to the ceremonial "beating the retreat" by the massed bands of the Indian armed forces, and her presence or absence had the power to rock the government. Every political crisis, real or imagined, in Delhi was accompanied by calls for her to take on, at the very least, the presidency of the Congress Party. Five years after the chorus began, newspaper and magazine articles continued to suggest that, whatever Sonia's personal hesitations, the pressure on her was too great to resist indefinitely.

And then there is, after all, in true dynastic tradition, the need to think of the aspirations of the next generation. Her son Rahul, born in 1970, and his reputedly more ambitious sister, Priyanka, two years younger and described by admirers as a clone of Indira Gandhi, would not always be too young to enter Parliament. Their father's seat must, observers suggest, be kept warm for one of them — and who better to nurse the Amethi constituency he so successfully nurtured than Sonia herself?

Sonia Gandhi has sternly resisted such temptations, though no one doubts that if she runs for her late husband's seat in Parliament, she will win handily. But even without entering Parliament, she could be offered, it is said, the Congress Party presidency, held as of early 1997 by the octogenarian Sitaram Kesri. Such talk is more muted now, but it is not implausible to imagine that she could become prime minister herself one day, if she chooses, or decide who does, if she prefers.

A builder's daughter from Torino, without a college degree, with no experience of Indian life beyond the rarefied realms of the prime minister's residence, fiercely protective of her privacy, so reserved and unsmiling in public that she has been unkindly dubbed "the Turin shroud," leading 940 million Indians at the head of the world's most complex, rambunctious, and violent democracy? The prospect, improbable though it sounds, is proof again of the enduring appeal of the Nehru-Gandhi dynasty.

Politicians certainly have no doubt about that appeal. Congress Party members of Parliament whom I spoke to in 1991 were dismissive of Sonia's disqualifications for the post. "The *people* don't consider her a foreigner, or a Catholic, or otherwise unsuitable," declared Mani Shankar Aiyar, a close aide to Rajiv Gandhi and a member of Parliament from the southern state of Tamil Nadu. "They think of her as the nation's *bahu*, their collective daughter-in-law. I can't address a meeting anywhere in my constituency without someone getting up and calling for Sonia *Amma* [Mother Sonia] to take over the party. It's only the intellectuals who carp about dynastic rule. The Congress Party has always needed one unquestioned figure at the top where the buck stopped — a monarch, if you like, whose decisions were the last word. We don't have such a figure in the party today. But if Sonia came into politics, we would."

Aiyar is no country politico, but a former diplomat with a Cambridge degree and a rapier wit who is not known to suffer fools gladly. If people like him do not squirm at the prospect of pledging allegiance to a leader whose only qualification to lead is the name on her marriage certificate, obituaries for the dynasty are premature indeed.

• • •

It all began, like so much else that is good, bad, and ugly in modern India, under the British Raj. Motilal Nehru (1861–1931), a prosperous Kashmiri lawyer in the northern city of Allahabad, became a leading light of the Indian National Congress (the principal vehicle of the nationalist movement) and the first of four members of his family to ascend to its presidency. But even at his peak he was only one among several Congress leaders of comparable stature, all of whom were dwarfed by the towering figure of their generation, Mohandas ("Mahatma") Gandhi. When Motilal died at seventy, with Indian independence still a remote dream, he could scarcely have imagined he would one day be regarded as the founder of modern India's preeminent political dynasty.

He had, it is true, done everything possible to bring his Harrow- and Cambridge-educated son, Jawaharlal (1889–1964), a moody, idealist intellectual of Fabian socialist convictions, into the center of nationalist politics. Under his father's tutelage, Jawaharlal became the youngest member of the Working Committee of the Indian National Congress in 1918. But it was the Mahatma who, for all the difference in their worldviews, saw the younger Nehru's potential and made him his political protégé. Imprisoned for the first time in 1921, Jawaharlal spent eighteen years in British jails. In between he became Congress president in 1928, dominated the articulation of the party's political, economic, and foreign policies, and ascended unchallenged, as Mahatma Gandhi's nominee, to the prime ministry of an interim government in 1946, a post he retained upon full independence in 1947.

For the next seventeen years, Nehru *was* India. With the Mahatma's assassination at the hands of a Hindu fanatic in 1948, Jawaharlal Nehru became the keeper of the national flame, the most visible embodiment of the freedom struggle, the spirit of Indian independence incarnate. Despite his dreamy, abstracted air and occasional Brahminical imperiousness, the masses adored him, and it did not hurt that he, rather than any of the committed Gandhians who came to oppose him, was the Mahatma's chosen heir. Incorruptible, secular, a politician above politics, Nehru's stature in the country at large was so great that all he needed to do if anyone opposed him was threaten to resign. The dissenters quickly pleaded with him to stay, and swallowed their dissent. Nehru usually got his way.

But for all that, he was a convinced democrat, a man so wary of the perils of autocracy that he once authored an anonymous article warning Indians of the dangers of giving dictatorial temptations to Jawaharlal Nehru. As prime minister he carefully nurtured the forms and institutions of democracy. He was always careful to treat the party as his master rather than the other way around, and to defer to its elders, paying careful deference to the country's ceremonial presidency, writing regular letters to the chief ministers of India's states explaining his policies, subjecting himself to cross-examination in Parliament by a fractious opposition. But he did little to cultivate alternatives to himself: he was, in the celebrated Indian metaphor, the immense banyan tree in whose shade no other plant could grow. Independent India's policies, from nonalignment in the cold war to statist socialism at home, were thus unduly the reflection of one man's vision. He became identified with them, and they with him.

The worldview of the Nehru-Gandhi dynasty was shaped, in its essentials, during India's nationalist struggle against British rule, and was therefore founded above all on opposition to British (and, by extension, Western) imperialism. Whereas Motilal Nehru was an affluent lawyer, schooled in the institutions of the Raj, who fought — in the American phrase — for Indians to have "the rights of Englishmen," Jawaharlal based his nationalism on a complete rejection of the British and all their works. His letters from Harrow and Cambridge reveal greater sympathy for the "extremists" in the Indian National Congress than for the "moderates" with whom his father was then politically aligned. And though he became a protégé of Mahatma Gandhi, Jawaharlal Nehru's political beliefs owed far more to the Russian Revolution than to Gandhi's Hindu humanism.

Nehru, like many Third World nationalists, saw the imperialism that had subjugated his people as the logical extension of international capitalism, for which he therefore felt a profound mistrust. As an idealist deeply moved by the poverty and suffering of the vast majority of his countrymen under colonial capitalism, Nehru was inevitably more attracted to noncapitalist solutions for their problems. The ideas of Fabian socialism captured an entire generation of English-educated Indians; Nehru was no exception. In addition, the seeming success of the Soviet model — which Nehru admired for bringing about the industrialization and modernization of a large, feudal, and backward multinational state not unlike his own — appeared to offer a valuable example for India. Like many others of his generation, Nehru thought that central planning, state control of the "commanding heights" of the economy, and government-directed development were the "scientific" and "rational" means of creating social prosperity and ensuring its equitable distribution. Self-reliance was the mantra: the prospect of allowing a Western corporation into India to "exploit" its resources immediately revived memories of the British East India Company, which also came to trade and stayed on to rule.

In India, one of the lessons we learn from history is that history too often teaches the wrong lessons.

For all that, the political image of the Nehru dynasty was one of staunch anti-imperialism, a determination to safeguard India against foreign domination, and a commitment — at least in principle — to uplift the poorest sections of Indian society. In addition, the Nehrus were, by upbringing and conviction, completely secular. Not only did Indira Gandhi marry a Parsi, but her daughters-in-law were an Italian Christian and a Punjabi Sikh. The one strand of political opinion Nehru and his offspring abhorred was that of Hindu religious revivalism.

The Nehru legacy to India was thus a mixed one. It consisted of four major pillars — democratic institution-building, staunch secularism, nonalignment, and socialist economics. The first two were indispensable to the country's survival; the third preserved its self-respect and enhanced its international standing without bringing any concrete benefits to the Indian people (who arguably might have fared better in alliance with the West); the fourth was disastrous, condemning the Indian people to poverty and stagnation and engendering inefficiency, red-tapism, and corruption on a scale rarely rivaled elsewhere.

On his desk, Jawaharlal Nehru kept two totems — a gold statuette of Mahatma Gandhi and a bronze cast of the hand of Abraham Lincoln, which he would occasionally touch for comfort. The two objects reflected the range of his sources of inspiration. It says something about the narrowing of the dynasty's intellectual heritage that both ended up in a museum — and his heirs just kept the desk.

• • •

When Nehru died, broken by the China war into which he had blundered, there was no obvious successor. The Congress Party bosses picked the leader who was least disliked by a majority of them, the diminutive but shrewd Lal Bahadur Shastri (1904 – 1966). In his low-key manner, Shastri began to evolve a collegial style of governance, one that might in time have seemed the natural way to rule a pluralist state that was constitutionally supposed to be federal. But he couldn't see it through; less than two years after he assumed office, following a futile and bloody war thrust upon him by the military dictatorship in Pakistan, Shastri died of a heart attack in the Soviet city of Tashkent, where he had gone to make peace with Pakistan and signed away most of what his soldiers had won on the battlefield. Appalled by the pointlessness of the conflict and the waste of life and resources it involved, the good and decent Shastri died, quite literally, of a broken heart.

The Congress Party was thrown into confusion. None of the leaders rejected at the time of Shastri's election could be picked without rousing the ire of others with equal or better claims. Casting about for a compromise, the party stalwarts, known as the Syndicate, performed a masterstroke. There was one candidate available who benefited from national recognition, had held political office, and yet could be counted upon to take instructions from the party: Nehru's daughter.

Indira (1917–1984) had dropped out of college in Oxford and married a young Congress worker, Feroze Gandhi. Feroze was no relation to the Mahatma: indeed, he wasn't even a Hindu, but a member of the tiny Parsi minority, descended from Zoroastrian refugees who had fled Muslim persecution in Persia in the eighth century A.D. The Parsis settled originally in the coastal state of Gujarat, and many adopted Gujarati surnames, such as Gandhi or Patel. Others, however, took on surnames under the British that reflected their professions, so that there are Parsis called Engineer, Driver, Cooper, and Merchant, as well as Mistry (carpenter), Daruwalla, and Toddywalla (liquor traders both). Had Indira's Parsi husband been a Toddywalla rather than so conveniently a Gandhi, I sometimes wonder, might India's political history have been different?

The marriage soon foundered, however. Nehru, a widower, wanted his daughter to live with him as his official hostess and political aide. Feroze, a fiercely independent Congress MP and anticorruption crusader, felt politically and personally stifled, and moved out of the prime minister's residence. Indira chose her father over her husband, or, as she saw it, her duty to the nation over her loyalty to her marriage. She became Congress president for a year in 1959; Feroze suffered a heart attack at the wheel of his car and died young in 1960.

Indira served in Shastri's cabinet in the minor portfolio of Minister for Information and Broadcasting, but her principal political asset remained her pedigree. One member of the Syndicate that made her prime minister thought she would be a *goongi gudiya*, a "dumb doll," the presentable face of boss rule. For a year this indeed seemed to be the case, as Indira, inarticulate and tentative, overly reliant on advisers of dubious competence, stumbled badly in office. The party paid the price in the elections of 1967, losing seats around the country, and seeing motley opposition governments come to power in several states. The veteran Congress politician Morarji Desai (1896–1995) even challenged Mrs. Gandhi's right to continue as prime minister, and had to be accommodated as deputy prime minister. The dynasty's days appeared to be numbered.

At the brink of the abyss, Indira fought back. Many of the Syndicate had been defeated at the polls in the 1967 debacle; she now set about systematically reducing their influence in the party. Finding allies among socialists and ex-Communists, she engineered a split in the Congress in 1969 on "ideological" grounds (the two principal issues being the abolition of the subsidies paid to India's erstwhile maharajahs, and the nationalization of banks, both of which the old guard opposed as unconstitutional). Having established a populist image and expelled the old bosses, she led her wing of the Congress to a resounding victory in 1971, campaigning on the slogan *Garibi Hatao*: "Remove Poverty." This was swiftly followed by the decisive defeat of Pakistan in the Bangladesh War that year. Her popularity soared; India's leading modern painter, the Muslim M. F. Husain, depicted her as a Hindu

Mother Goddess. The imagery was appropriate: indeed, at her peak, Indira Gandhi was both worshiped and maternalized.

As Nehru's daughter and political heir, Indira Gandhi had imbibed his vision whole. As a child she was the recipient of his memorable letters from British jails that spelled out Nehru's convictions and taught her his view of world history. Perhaps unsurprisingly, she took great pride in the fact that she was born in the year of the Russian Revolution. "The birth and development of socialism in the Soviet Union has been a major factor in shaping the course of world history," she told a Moscow audience in 1975. "To many of us in the developing countries engaged in the task of consolidating political and economic freedom, your experience and success have been a stimulus." From her father she had learned to be skeptical of Western claims to stand for freedom and democracy when India's historical experience of colonial oppression and exploitation appeared to bear out the opposite. Nehru's conclusion was to see a moral equivalence between the two rival power blocs, a position that helped create nonalignment. Indira went further than her father: when I interviewed her in 1977 on the subject of her foreign policy, she argued that while the Soviets had helped liberation struggles from Angola to Bangladesh, the West was "not on the side of freedom. [They] were against the freedom struggle in all countries, so far as I know. . . . It's only when they thought that Russian influence was coming, and that freedom would come anyway, that they jumped in." These convictions fitted in with her domestic left-wing political strategy, her need for Soviet support on the subcontinent against a U.S.-backed Pakistan-China axis, and her dark suspicion, born more out of personal insecurity than of any hard evidence, that the CIA was out to destabilize her government as it had done Allende's.

Nonetheless, Indira Gandhi once memorably confessed to an American interviewer, "I don't really have a political philosophy. I can't say I believe in any ism. I wouldn't say I'm interested in socialism as socialism. To me it's just a tool."

But tools are used for well-defined purposes, and it was never clear that Indira Gandhi had any, beyond the political short term. The

1971 electoral and military triumphs — the first over a sclerotic and discredited political establishment at home, the second over a sclerotic and discredited martial-law establishment next door — saw the Nehru-Gandhi mystique at its pinnacle. But it was not to last. Mrs. Gandhi was skilled at the acquisition and maintenance of power, but hopeless at the wielding of it for larger purposes. She had no real vision or program beyond the expedient campaign slogans; "remove poverty" was a mantra without a method. Her genuine convictions, as one observer put it, were "somewhere to the left of self-interest." Prices, unemployment, and corruption rose; her standing in the nation fell. Mounting protests, led by the saintly Gandhian Jayaprakash Narayan, brought down one Congress state government and threatened others. As anarchy loomed, a high court judge in Allahabad convicted the prime minister, on a technicality, of electoral malpractice in her crushing 1971 victory. Mrs. Gandhi, it seemed, would have to resign in disgrace.

Instead, she struck back. Declaring a state of emergency, Indira Gandhi arrested opponents, censored the press, and postponed elections. As a compliant Supreme Court overturned her conviction, she proclaimed a "twenty-point program" for the uplift of the common man. (No one found it humorous enough to remark, as Clemenceau had done of Wilson's Fourteen Points, that "even the good Lord only had Ten.") Its provisions — which ranged from rural improvement schemes and the abolition of bonded labor to mass education and urban renewal — remained largely unimplemented. Meanwhile, her thuggish younger son, Sanjay (1946–1980), emphasizing two of the twenty points, ordered brutally insensitive campaigns of slum demolitions and forced sterilizations. The compact between the people and the dynasty was ruptured, even as a meretricious slogan spouted by a pliant Congress Party president proclaimed that "Indira is India and India is Indira."

.   .   .

For many Indians of my generation, the Emergency was the seminal event of their political maturation. I went to the United States on a graduate fellowship soon after it was declared, and found myself traveling an even longer route to political awareness.

At first, like most foreign students in the United States, I instinctively thought it my duty to explain and defend my country to my not-always-well-disposed hosts. Ironically, I had had a minor personal taste of the petty tyranny inaugurated by the Emergency; soon after it was imposed, the censors who had moved into newspaper offices spiked an innocuous short story of mine that had been accepted by a Calcutta youth magazine and was, as luck would have it, slated to appear the week after the Emergency was declared. It was a detective story with a trick ending, and it was called "The Political Murder"; but the very thought that anyone might be murdered for political reasons was anathema to the Emergency censors, who tended to make up in zeal what they lacked in judgment. A big red stamp was duly applied on the manuscript, banning its appearance.

Soon afterward I left for the United States, where I had a scholarship to pursue graduate studies at the Fletcher School of Law and Diplomacy, the world's oldest school of international affairs, administered by Tufts University in cooperation with Harvard. There I found myself being greeted, by liberals and conservatives alike, as if I had just arrived from Ceauşescu's Romania or Pinochet's Chile. A lot of their criticisms of the Emergency were excessively formalistic, or so it seemed to me at the time; they seemed much more concerned about what Mrs. Gandhi had done to the trappings of democracy — press, Parliament, judiciary — than about those whom democracy was meant to benefit, the common men and women of India. They assumed that as a newly banned writer breathing the air of American freedom, I would agree, but I found myself arguing (with the reflexive chauvinism that strikes most Indians when they first come abroad) that I was precisely the sort of Indian who was least entitled to object to the Emergency: I belonged to the tiny minority that could write and publish and be banned, whereas the Emergency — however cynical Mrs. Gandhi's reasons for imposing it — was working for the betterment of the vast, toiling multitudes for whom such rights meant little. Their bread was more important than my freedom.

I nearly convinced myself with this argument for a while, but I soon came to realize how hollow it was. My roommate at Fletcher was a journalist, and he brought me daily the wire service copy about the latest atrocities — the slum demolitions, the bulldozings of homes and livelihoods, the compulsory sterilization schemes and the arbitrary quotas assigned to them, the arrests and beatings, the torture in jail of young student activists. Travelers from India brought me copies of underground newsletters, cyclostyled or badly printed on cheap paper, their ink smudged but their message clear, eloquent testimony both to the people's despair and their defiance. (The very thought that India, famously overflowing with a free and irresponsible press, even *produced* "underground" literature shamed me utterly.) Most of the real victims of the Emergency were among the poorest classes of Indians — the ones who, I came to realize, most needed the protections of democracy. For all its chaos and confusion, our parliamentary system and its inefficient trappings were all that stood between them and the absolute power of the state — a state that could seize them in the bazaars or in the fields and cart them off to have their vas deferens cut off in a sterilization camp.

Middle- and upper-class Indians, except for the handful who sought to resist, largely carried on as before; their newspapers may have been blander, and opinions usually expressed at the tops of their voices may have had to emerge in stage whispers, but little really changed in their daily lives. If anything, many saw improvements: the proverbial trains ran on time, prices held steady as hoarders and black marketeers lay low, there were fewer strikes, demonstrations, and other disturbances, and the habitual absenteeism in government offices fell so dramatically that the bureaucracy suffered a crippling shortage of chairs and desks to accommodate the number of personnel who unexpectedly reported for work. For most Indians of the middle and upper classes, the Emergency was by and large a Good Thing. For me, living and studying in America, the discovery that my country, which had so proudly described itself as the world's largest democracy, was now descending into becoming the world's second largest banana republic was more than I could bear. I read about the outspoken Indian student in Chicago whose passport the embassy refused to renew because of his anti-Emergency activities, and burned with shame that the regime I had been defending had sunk to this: I had associated my Indian passport with the right to express myself freely on any subject I chose to, and now it was a document denied to one who had exercised that basic right of every Indian.

And so the Emergency became the defining experience of my political consciousness. By starting out defending it and then coming to realize why it was indefensible, I learned one more thing about what it was that I cherished about the country I had grown up in, and why I would never be able to accept that "Indira is India and India is Indira."

.   .   .

Sadly, Nehru's daughter betrayed her father's legacy. But his instincts reasserted themselves in her first big error of judgment. Blinded by the mirrors of her sycophants, deafened by the silence of the intimidated press, Mrs. Gandhi called an election in March 1977, expecting vindication in electoral victory. Instead she was routed, losing her own seat and the reins of office to an opposition coalition, the Janata (People's) Front, under her old nemesis Morarji Desai.

But the fractious Janata government could not hold together. By their mistakes, ineptitude, and greed (cynically, if artfully, exploited by Mrs. Gandhi and Sanjay), they opened the way for her improbable comeback. In January 1980, Mrs. Gandhi, having split the Congress once more and unembarrassedly renamed her faction after herself (as Congress-Indira, or "Congress-I") was prime minister of India again.

The rest of the story is more familiar, and all tragic. Sanjay, recklessly flying a stunt plane in defiance of local regulations (and shortly after engineering the dismissal of the upright director general of civil aviation, retired air marshal Zahir, who had tried to curb his illegal joyrides), killed himself within months of returning to power. One editor wrote trenchantly that had he lived, Sanjay would have done to the country what he did to the plane. Mrs. Gandhi, having systematically alienated, excluded, or expelled any leader of standing in her own party who might have been a viable deputy (and thus a potential rival) to her, drafted the only person she could entirely trust — her self-effacing, nonpolitical, and deeply reluctant elder son Rajiv (1944–1991) — to fill the breach.

Rajiv had barely begun to grow into the role when Mrs. Gandhi was assassinated by the forces of Sikh extremism, forces she had herself primed, along with Sanjay, for narrow partisan purposes. In 1977 the Congress Party had been ousted in Punjab by the Sikh Akali Dal Party, an ally of Janata; Mrs. Gandhi typically decided to undermine them from the quarter they least expected, by opponents even more Sikh than the Akalis. So she encouraged (and reportedly even initially financed) the extremist fanaticism of a Sikh fundamentalist preacher, Jarnail Singh Bhindranwale. Bhindranwale soon tired of assassinating clean-shaven Sikhs for their apostasy and instead took up the cause of an independent Sikh state, Khalistan. As the murders mounted, Mrs. Gandhi had little choice but to destroy the monster she had herself spawned, and she finally violated a basic tenet of the Indian state by sending armed troops into a place of worship, the historic Golden Temple in Amritsar, to flush out the terrorists holed up there. Bhindranwale and his immediate cohort of gunmen were killed in "Operation Bluestar," but so were a number of unarmed civilians trapped in what was, after all, the Sikhs' most important place of worship; great damage, not all of it repairable, was done to the temple itself. By the time she acted, Mrs. Gandhi probably had no choice (though many wished she could have starved the killers into submission rather than assaulting their sanctified stronghold), but her real fault lay in having created the problem in the first place and in letting it mount to the point where the destructive force of "Operation Bluestar" seemed the only solution.

The assault on the Golden Temple deeply alienated many Sikhs whose patriotism was unquestionable; the Gandhi family's staunchest ally in the independent press, the Sikh editor Khushwant Singh, returned his national honors to the government, and a battalion of Sikhs, the backbone of the army, mutinied. Two years earlier, when a Sikh deputy inspector general of police, A. S. Atwal, was murdered in the Golden Temple — shot in the back as he came out of the sanctum sanctorum after saying his prayers with his eight-year-old son by his side — the outrage within the Sikh community against Bhindranwale's thugs was so great (and the extent of his defenses in the temple so much more limited) that an appeal to Sikh soldiers and police to volunteer to cleanse their own shrine of these killers might have been enough to make a later Bluestar unnecessary. But Mrs. Gandhi, as ever tentative in wielding the power she was so skilled at acquiring, hesitated to respond to the Atwal killing, and the moment passed.

Mrs. Gandhi never understood the extent to which so many Sikhs saw Bluestar as a betrayal. She refused to draw the conclusions her security advisers did, and to her credit turned down their recommendations to remove Sikhs from her personal guard detail. Two of them, men sworn to protect her with their lives, turned their guns upon her instead. It was a cool Delhi morning in October 1984, when the sun had just begun to warm the crisp autumnal air, but her killing flamed hot in the streets of Delhi, in the horror of the anti-Sikh riots that followed it, which saw whole families burned alive for the sin of sharing the religion of her assassins.

Mrs. Gandhi's death reverberated through the country like an earthquake; but her martyrdom came at the end of an inglorious second term of office, at a time when the prospects of reelection looked remote. Yet her death, in these terrible circumstances, preserved her dynasty. Her son Rajiv was sworn in as prime minister within hours of her killing, to the dismay of those Indians who, like me, thought the nation could find someone more qualified than a forty-year-old airline pilot with no experience of government to rule us.

But the Congress, atrophied under Indira, had no one better. Certainly no other name could match the vote-catching potential of Rajiv Gandhi's. And the choice was ratified by the electorate in a sweeping sympathy vote that gave Rajiv a greater parliamentary majority than any Indian prime minister had ever had.

Then our dismay briefly turned to hope, as Rajiv proceeded to overturn all the drift and expedient cynicism that had marked his mother's era. For a year or so the winds of change blew across the country like a tropical cyclone. Rajiv was India's first purely technocratic politician. He led a generation that had hardly been aware of the British colonial presence in India but had become familiar with the West on its own terms. Education, language, and cultural affinities turned such Indians naturally westward; they admired Western technology, economic advancement, and political freedom, and had correspondingly fewer illusions about the Soviet system. (One should not overstate the importance of education, though: Rajiv dropped out of his engineering course at Cambridge; Sonia, the inheritor of his legacy, was in Cambridge to study English as a second language, not political philosophy.) Rajiv's initial enthusiasm for change and reform of India's bureaucratized statism foundered not on ideological grounds but as the result of a series of political compromises with the entrenched establishment.

At first Rajiv rode a wave of national enthusiasm not seen since the heady days of his mother's triumph in 1971. Then the rot set in; what was good for the nation was not necessarily good for the Congress Party, and Rajiv — a latecomer to politics, without the sureness of touch that comes from having climbed the ropes rather than having merely pulled them — soon decided politics was more important than statesmanship. Compromise followed sellout as New Delhi returned to business as usual. Charges of corruption in a major howitzer contract with the Swedish arms manufacturer Bofors tarnished the mystique of the dynasty: little children sang, *Galli-galli mein shor hai / Rajiv Gandhi chor hai:* "Hear it said in every nook / Rajiv Gandhi is a crook." The Rajiv regime's distance from the masses, both figurative (he remains to this day the only Indian prime minister ever to have been photographed in jeans and a Lacoste T-shirt) and literal (thanks to the overzealous security measures imposed upon him after his mother's assassination) exacted a further political price. The 1989 elections brought yet another anti-Congress coalition to power. And yet again it fell apart, seemingly paving the way for a resurrection of the dynasty.

But this time it was not to be.

•   •   •

Every assassination comes as a shock, but the bomb blast that murdered Rajiv Gandhi took more than his life and those of others around him. The elections in which he was running were briefly postponed, then rescheduled and held; Parliament sat, a new prime minister was sworn in, the business of governance went on; but in a real sense the killing disenfranchised Indians.

The India that killed Rajiv was not the India I grew up in. In April 1975, as a college student and freelance journalist of nineteen, I went to Parliament House in New Delhi to interview Prime Minister Indira Gandhi for a youth magazine. A friend from my college hostel asked whether he could accompany me; as his excuse, he carried a tape recorder in a shoulder bag. We strolled unchallenged past the guards and into the prime minister's outer office, where a cheerful shambles reigned.

Supplicants, officials, and hangers-on sat around, walked in and out, and brought tea and conversation to the private secretary, who told an irreverent anecdote about the uncannily plausible portrayal of an Indira Gandhi—like figure in a current Hindi film.

After a while, the press secretary, the reflective and erudite H. Y. Sharada Prasad, emerged from Mrs. Gandhi's inner sanctum to call me in. I asked if my friend could join me. "Why not?" he said, and we both walked into to the prime ministerial presence. The shoulder bag might have contained a bomb, but no one bothered to check. The thought wouldn't even have occurred to them. Despite the assassination of Mahatma Gandhi twenty-seven years before, Indians didn't order their affairs that way.

Within a decade of this encounter, religious and sectarian violence had inflamed India. When Rajiv ascended to power following his mother's assassination, he carried out his public duties clad noticeably in a bulletproof vest. He addressed crowds from behind a Perspex screen, a security cordon of Black Cat commandos around him.

In a country where any individual could join the breakfast throng at the prime minister's residence to seek a favor or benediction, even members of Parliament had to pass through intensive security checks. Some complained about how demeaning it was to be frisked before meeting their prime minister, but the complaints were muted. After what had happened to Indira Gandhi, security precautions became unavoidable.

And yet old habits die hard, and democracies, especially one as freewheeling as India's, are not instinctively good at protecting their leaders. Security became an issue in itself; the distance that safety considerations obliged Rajiv Gandhi to keep from the people cost him votes. The prime minister came to be seen as an aloof and remote figure. The trappings of security created, in many voters' eyes, an imperial prime ministry, occupied by an imperious prime minister. It was this, as much as anything, that cost him the 1989 election.

So it was hardly surprising that the next time around, in 1991, Rajiv Gandhi threw safety to the winds in his campaign. He reveled in casting his bodyguards aside and plunging into the throng; he asked the crowds to flock into the empty spaces in front of the podium that were sectioned off for security purposes. His every gesture reaffirmed the vital premise, so necessary to all democrats, that they are safest among their own people; that to be touched by the Indian masses was, for an Indian leader, to be in touch with the sources of his own power.

In India, as in all true democracies, elections legitimize the system not merely through the casting of votes, but through the process itself, the self-renewing exchange of hopes and promises, demands and compromises, that make up the flawed miracle of democracy.

India's voters had repeatedly proved — and were in the process of demonstrating again — that a democracy offers other ways of manifesting disagreements with one's leaders. Despite the spiraling violence, the growing criminalization of politics, the increasing number of fringe groups who found bombs more effective than debate, Indians had never ceased to believe in themselves. The bomb that killed Rajiv

Gandhi shook that self-belief by attacking its very basis: that Indians could choose their rulers, and preserve a way of doing things that offers meaning and value to that choice.

Soon after the killing, the platitudes flowed like blood: the end of a dynasty, a life cut short in its prime, the bullet's triumph over the ballot. I mourned, too, for the India I grew up in. I had no doubt that India would survive, that Indians would find the resilience to transcend one more national calamity. But it will never again be an India where freedom is untrammeled by fear, an India where a student can walk in uninvited upon his prime minister.

· · ·

I could not have voted for Rajiv Gandhi's party in the elections that took his life. But I grieved his loss. I grieved, of course, for his family, for a nation plunged again into mourning. I grieved for the hopes he had once raised in me, for the frustration and disappointment he had later evoked, for the potential he still represented till the moment of his passing. And I grieved because his death, and the manner of it, again shook, in a very different way from the Emergency, my sense of what, as an Indian, I could always take for granted.

Rajiv Gandhi had had no obvious qualifications for office, but in the frenzy and chaos that followed India's first major political assassination since that of Mahatma Gandhi in 1948, the Congress Party clamored for the stability and reassurance of a familiar vote-catching name at the helm. Its leaders chose Rajiv Gandhi not for himself, but for his lineage. His genes justified their ends.

So I was dismayed. But within weeks my dismay dissolved into hope. For the unexpected ascent of Rajiv Gandhi had brought to power the kind of Indian almost completely unrepresented in Indian politics. My kind of Indian.

There are many of us, but, among India's multitudes, we are few. We have grown up in the cities of India, secure in a national identity rather than a local one, which we express in English better than in any Indian language. We rejoice in the complexity and diversity of our India, of which we feel a conscious part; we have friends of every caste and religious community, and we marry across such sectarian lines. We see the poverty, suffering, and conflict in which a majority of our fellow citizens are mired, and we clamor for new solutions to these old problems, solutions we believe can come from the skills and efficiency of the modern world. We are secular, not in the sense that we are irreligious or unaware of the forces of religion, but in that we believe religion should not determine public policy or individual opportunity.

And, in Indian politics, we are pretty much irrelevant.

We don't get a look in. We don't enter the fray because we can't win. We tell ourselves ruefully that we are able, but not electable. We don't have the votes: there are too few of us, and we don't speak the idiom of the masses. Instead we have learned to talk about political issues without the expectation that we will be able to do anything about them.

Until Rajiv Gandhi, the accidental prime minister, came to power.

The only time I ever met Rajiv Gandhi was at a gathering of expatriate Indians in Geneva, Switzerland, in June 1985, six months after the election landslide that had vindicated his party's cynical faith in genealogy. He spoke softly but fluently, without notes, for forty-five minutes about the situation in India and his plans for the country. When he finished there was a light in even the most skeptical eye. I should know, for I was blinded by mine.

Rajiv Gandhi was unlike any Indian political figure I had ever met. He had nothing in common with the professional politicians we had taught ourselves to despise, sanctimonious windbags clad hypocritically in homespun who spouted socialist rhetoric while amassing private wealth through the manipulation of political favors. Instead of the visionless expediency that had been his mother's only credo, Rajiv offered transparent sincerity and conviction. Instead of the grasping opportunism of careerists who saw politics as an end in itself, he was a reluctant politician thrust unwillingly into public office but determined to make something of it — the very antithesis of his brother Sanjay.

For one exhilarating year, those of us who had thought ourselves alienated from the Indian political process were swept up in the unfamiliar excitement of having one of our own as prime minister. In every step Rajiv Gandhi seemed determined to stem the drift, to find urgent solutions to the perennial problems of India. He pledged to shed the shopworn socialist dogmas that had consigned the economy to stagnation and left workers and consumers alike to the mercy of the permit/license/quota-granting bureaucracy. In place of the tired reiteration of sterile slogans, he spoke of liberalization, of technology, of modernity, of moving India into the twenty-first century. He even chose the self-congratulatory occasion of the Congress Party's centenary celebrations in 1985 to assail the corruption and complacency that had made the party atrophy into an unresponsive behemoth.

Nor did the politicians themselves escape his cleansing fervor. He shunted aside the old-timers and the time-servers, brought in fresh professional faces from the private sector (including energetic entrepreneurs who had made their fortunes in the United States, but wished to serve their homeland), and outlawed the unprincipled "defections" that had made party labels a matter of convenience. Best of all, he made peace with rebellious Sikhs in Punjab, agitating students in Assam, and unreconciled guerrillas in Mizoram, bringing them back into an electoral process they had preferred to subvert. To Indians like me, this was heady stuff.

It was also too good to last. Rajiv Gandhi became the victim of his own success. His actions strengthened the country, but undermined his party. His peace accords, by bringing disaffected minorities into the mainstream, gave them power at the expense of the Congress. The veteran politicians rumbled in complaint: Rajiv Gandhi, they said, was indulging his personal predilections at the party's expense. And because he had not worked his way up the political ladder, Rajiv Gandhi was uniquely vulnerable to the charge, leveled by those who had, that his instincts were the wrong ones. He gave in.

Within two years of his coming to power, it was back to business as usual. Politics was elevated above performance, the national interest subordinated to the party interest. When a seventy-five-year-old divorced Muslim woman, Shah Banu, won a Supreme Court case obliging her husband of forty-three years to give her the equivalent of five dollars a month in alimony, Rajiv Gandhi bowed to outraged Muslim orthodoxy and sponsored a law officially named, with breathtaking cynicism, "The Muslim Women's (Protection of Rights Upon Divorce) Act," placing Muslim widows outside the purview of the country's civil codes. He had initially taken the opposite view, but was persuaded by the opportunists in his party that that would cost him "the Muslim vote." As compromise followed compromise, promises to Punjab were broken to appease neighboring Haryana; economic liberalization was stifled to preserve political control; resources that could have gone to providing clean drinking water and electricity to the villages of India flowed into arms purchases; the investigators of governmental corruption were fired rather than the corrupt. The fresh faces quickly faded away, the party hacks returned. Rajiv Gandhi was no longer one of us.

He was, instead, trying hard to be what he was not — a traditional Indian politician. In having to operate the levers of Indian democracy, he had lost sight of where he had intended the engine to go.

Is a democracy best served by leaders whose pulse throbs with the passions and prejudices of their people, or by those who transcend the limitations of their followers? Sitting on the sidelines, I had no doubt about the answer; caught in the vortex, Rajiv Gandhi couldn't even ask the question.

I learned the humbling lesson that the give and take of democracy does not always produce the results sought by its impatient observers. Rajiv Gandhi's charisma was no substitute for experience: where a veteran politician might have been able to trust his instincts and lead with vision, the tyro was pressured into retreat. And despite all his compromises, Rajiv Gandhi — isolated from his natural constituency, counseled into political opportunism, and protected from the public by a security phalanx — still lost the next election.

So I couldn't have supported him the next time; my disappointment still stuck too raw in my throat. But I was glad to have him in the fray, because I hoped that someday he might more effectively give voice to the convictions of his own upbringing. And at a time when casteists and religious fanatics were attempting to redefine India and Indianness on their own terms, I was proud to have an Indian leader who belonged to no single region, caste, or community, but to the all-embracing India I called my own. By simply being Rajiv Gandhi, he represented a choice it was vital for India to have.

An assassin's bomb deprived India of the right to exercise that choice. With Rajiv Gandhi's passing, there was no longer any Indian political leader of whom it could be said that his appeal was truly national, and in the spectrum of alternatives available to Indians, that loss was disenfranchisement indeed.

It was not true, of course, despite the fatuous pronouncements of some TV commentators in the sound-bite-ridden West, that the assassination demonstrated India's unfitness for democracy, any more than the shootings of John and Robert Kennedy and Martin Luther King Jr. made the United States an unsuitable place for freedom. Indian democracy survived, as it has survived other calamities. But though violence cannot destroy democracy, it can weaken its most vital premise: that democrats do not need to be shielded from their own people.

Rajiv Gandhi tried to overcome his literal and figurative distance from the people by mingling with the crowds in his campaign. His successors would now hesitate to do that; the bulletproof vest, the protective screen, the commando escort, the roads cleared before every VIP convoy, would become an ineluctable part of the Indian political scenery. And so barriers have come to be erected between India's leaders and her people — if not in the hustings, then intangibly, in every Indian mind. That, too, has disenfranchised India.

Perhaps the ultimate reflection of both the extent and the limitations of Rajiv Gandhi's appeal lay in the decision of his Congress Party to offer his place to his widow, Sonia. Behind the extraordinary selection of an Italian-born nonpolitician — and though she turned it down — lay the implicit judgment that Rajiv Gandhi's value as a leader lay not in his qualities but in his name. From the party he led to his death, this was an unworthy epitaph.

The assassination of Rajiv Gandhi took from Indians, of whatever political coloration, part of the glory of their Indianness. The knowledge of our freedom of opinion and choice was something that we lit inside ourselves like a flame. Now its glow was forever dimmed by the knowledge that, in the election of 1991, the most important verdict was delivered not in a ballot box, but in a coffin.

•   •   •

When Rajiv fell at the hands of Sri Lankan Tamil assassins, his party looked likely to emerge as the largest single political force in the new Parliament, but well short of a viable majority. Ironically, it was the outpouring of support after his assassination — Rajiv's death, psephologists estimate, swung some forty seats to his party — that enabled Congress even to form a minority government. Had he lived, as one aspiring prime minister among many, Rajiv might well have presided over the terminal decline of the dynasty. But in death he focused the minds of the nation again on the sacrifices made by his family, and so revived its mystique.

What, then, *is* this mystique made of, that it can make an Indian ruler out of an Italian whose only patrimony is matrimony?

Mystiques are, almost by definition, difficult to analyze, since they are suffused with a magic that is greater than the sum of their ingredients. Salman Rushdie saw the Nehru-Gandhi mystique as the stuff of myth: "We have poured ourselves into this story, inventing its characters, then ripping them up and reinventing them. In our inexhaustible speculations lies one source of their power over us." Perhaps Rushdie's is the best way to see the dynasty, as a sort of collective dream of all Indians, a dream from which the nation periodically seems about to wake, before fitfully relapsing into oneirodynia.

But there is more to the dynasty's appeal — more meat to the myth — than that. Perhaps the most important characteristic of the

Nehrus and the Gandhis is that, though their parliamentary seats may lie in the populous northern heartland around Allahabad, they are truly national figures. *The New York Times'* Abe Rosenthal reported about Jawaharlal's visits around the country that "it was always as if Nehru was looking into the eyes of India and India was just one soul." When Ved Mehta first met Nehru, he wrote, "I feel I am confronting Sanskrit, Mughal, and English India at the same time. . . . I feel the real secret of free India lies in the prime minister. His character reconciles the various Indias." Displaced Kashmiris to begin with, the Nehrus' family tree sports Parsi, Sikh, and now Italian branches, and its roots are universally seen as uncontaminated by the communal and sectarian prejudices of the Hindi-speaking "cow belt." Nehru himself was an avowed agnostic, as was his daughter until she discovered the electoral advantages of public piety. All four generations of Nehrus in public life remained secular in outlook and conduct. Their appeal transcended caste, region, and religion, something impossible to say of any other leading Indian politician.

Then there were the inestimable advantages of underdevelopment. In a country as vast, as multilingual, as illiterate, and as poorly served by communications as India, national name recognition is not easily achieved. Once attained, it is self-perpetuating; for any rival to catch up on decades of Nehru-Gandhi dominance is virtually impossible. The public mind has, since the heady days of the onset of independence, identified the family with Indian nationalism. It is a perception that gives any member of the dynasty a headstart over anyone else. Even Sanjay's teenage son, Feroze Varun Gandhi, whose mother, Maneka, is a bitter opponent of the Congress Party, is spoken of as a future political leader.

Nor can we forget the negative reasons for the lack of viable alternatives to the dynasty: Nehru's failure to groom a successor, Indira's ruthless elimination of rivals, and the desiccation of the Congress under her into a complacent instrument of dynastic despotism (there were no intraparty elections in the Congress for two decades: all the office-bearers were appointed by Indira, Sanjay, or Rajiv). If the Congress could not produce a convincing alternative, the opposition parties' collective failure has been worse: on the two occasions when the electorate has allowed them to supplant the dynasty, the non-Congress governments have collapsed in a partisan scramble for office. Rajiv's successor, the ostensibly colorless P. V. Narasimha Rao, surprised India as much as the world by leading a stable Congress government through its full term (1991–1996). But as the 1996 elections halved the Congress's parliamentary majority and its future seemed less and less certain, the calls arose again for Sonia Gandhi to take her rightful place at the helm of the party.

And so the mystique glows on. As early as at Rajiv's funeral, even the correspondent of the London *Sunday Times* could not resist praising the "dry-eyed fortitude" of the "so appealing" Priyanka Gandhi, "composed, dignified and beautiful in her grief." As a decent, competent, but uncharismatic prime minister bravely made the best of the difficult job of pulling India out of economic quicksand, talk of restoring the dynasty became more muted. Now he and the Congress are out of power, licking their wounds as they support an anti-Congress minority coalition government in Parliament. The party of Nehru and Indira Gandhi, reduced to less than a fourth of the seats in the lower House, sits literally at the margins of governance, a prop rather than a pillar of the polity of independent India.

The Congress, its supporters are convinced, deserves better than that. A Gandhi at the helm of affairs might lead a revival. Will Sonia Gandhi take the plunge? Her reluctance to do so has meant that the golden chariots are no longer beating a path to the door of the woman known in the Piedmont as the Cinderella of Orbassano. But they would the moment she signaled that they might be welcome. Except that Indian Cinderellas know only too well that fairy tales, like Hindu myths, don't always have a happy ending.

3

Unity, Diversity, and Other Contradictions

From the Milk Miracle to the Malayali Miracle

*M*y wife, Tilottama, and I have twin sons, born in June 1984. Though they first entered the world in Singapore, and though the circumstances of my life have seen them grow up in Switzerland and then the United States, it is India they have always identified with. Ask them what they are, and that's what they'll tell you: they're Indian. Not "Hindu" not "Malayali," not "Nair" not "Calcuttan," though they could claim all those labels too. Their mother is herself half Bengali and half Kashmiri, which gives them further permutative possibilities. They desire none. They are just Indian.

Yet they found themselves traveling back with us annually to visit (and in their case, often to spend two to three months in) an India in which that answer began to seem less and less adequate. As they began to take notice of the political world around them, they learned of a mosque destroyed, of a trust betrayed, and of the flames of communal frenzy blazing again across the land. The week before our departure for

India in December 1992, a howling mob of Hindus tore down a disused mosque, the Babri Masjid in Ayodhya, that they claimed had been built on the birthplace of the Hindu god Rama. Communal violence erupted across the country as a result of this wanton act of destruction. Headlines spoke of riots and killing, Hindu against Muslim, of men being slaughtered because of the mark on a forehead or the absence of a foreskin. This is not the India my wife and I had wanted our sons to inherit.

In the early 1990s, India's political culture underwent a change. It was not the kind of change that a traumatic event like the Emergency brings about. The Emergency suspended the rules of the polity and so demonstrated their value, but at the same time it was an event so sharply defined and distinct that the end of the Emergency also ended the threat it posed to the national consensus on governance. The change that occurred in the last decade of the twentieth century was not an event but a process. Arguably, though, it was an event — the destruction of the mosque — that was emblematic of the process. The real change involved something intangible, if as pervasive as smog. It was a change in the dominant ethos of the country, in the attitudes of mind that define what it means to be Indian.

My generation grew up in an India where our sense of nationhood lay in the simple insight I described in chapter 1: that the singular thing about India was that you could only speak of it in the plural. This pluralism emerged from the very nature of the country; it was made inevitable by India's geography and reaffirmed by its history. There was simply too much of both to permit a single, exclusionist nationalism.

We were brought up to take this for granted, and to reject the communalism that had partitioned the nation when the British left. In rejecting the case for Pakistan, Indian nationalism also rejected the very idea that religion should be a determinant of nationhood. We never fell into the insidious trap of agreeing that, since Partition had established a state for the Muslims, what remained was a state for the Hindus. To accept the idea of India you had to spurn the logic that had divided the country.

This was what that much-abused term *secularism* meant for us.

Western dictionaries defined secularism as the absence of religion, but Indian secularism meant a profusion of religions, none of which was privileged by the state. Religion was too pervasive in the popular culture for unreligion to become public policy, despite the open agnosticism of Nehru. But the notion that religion had no *place* in public policy was easily accepted in India, where the distinction between God and Caesar had been enshrined since time immemorial. In the traditional caste system, the priestly Brahmin class had its own unchallenged monopoly of matters metaphysical, while the kingly Kshatriya caste went about the physical business of ruling and fighting. (True, medieval India was less effective at keeping religion out of governance. Some Muslim kings tried to make their religion into public policy by taxing the idolaters they didn't behead; yet the most successful rulers among them were those who publicly praised the Lord but kept their fervor dry.)

Sanctified by tradition or not, the India born in 1947 firmly separated temple and state. Independent India was a country for everyone, since it had emerged from a struggle for freedom in which secularism was integral to nationalism. Secularism in India did not mean irreligiousness, which even avowedly atheist parties like the Communists or the southern Dravida Munnetra Kazhagam (DMK) found unpopular among their voters; rather it meant, in the Indian tradition, pluri-religiousness. In the Calcutta neighborhood where I lived during my high school years, the wail of the muezzin calling the Islamic faithful to prayer blended with the chant of the mantras at the Hindu Shiva temple and the crackling loudspeakers outside the Sikh *gurudwara* reciting verses from the Granth Sahib. Their coexistence was paradoxically made possible by the fact that the overwhelming majority of Indians were committed to what we so inappropriately called "secularism."

Throughout the decades after independence, the political culture of the country reflected these "secular" assumptions and attitudes. Though the Indian population was 82 percent Hindu and the country had been partitioned as a result of a demand for a separate Muslim homeland, two of India's first five presidents were Muslims; so were innumerable governors, cabinet ministers, chief ministers of states, ambassadors, generals, and Supreme Court justices and chief justices. When Prime Minister Indira Gandhi traveled abroad in the tense months before the 1971 Bangladesh War with Pakistan, the Council of Ministers was chaired by a Muslim, Fakhruddin Ali Ahmed; during that war, the Indian Air Force in the northern sector was commanded by a Muslim, Air Marshal (later Air Chief Marshal) Latif. (The 1971 war was a triumph for Indian secularism as much as for the force of arms: the army commander was a Parsi, General Sam Manekshaw, the general officer commanding the forces that marched into Bangladesh was a Sikh, General Jagjit Singh Aurora, and the general flown in to negotiate the surrender of the Pakistani forces in East Bengal, Major General J. F. R. Jacob, was Jewish.)

Yet the India I visited in December 1992, just after the destruction of the Babri Masjid in Ayodhya, no longer seemed to cherish that ethos. My family and I arrived the week after the demolition of the Masjid, when the echoes of the riots that followed had not yet begun to fade. We were in India during the horrors of the butchery that followed in Bombay, when at least some police connived as Hindu mobs attacked Muslims: indeed, I was visiting the office of the then editor of the *Times of India* as the bulletins were coming in of the murder and carnage taking place in what we used to think of as India's most cosmopolitan city. But India has survived violence before, and I had no doubt it would do so again. What I was unprepared for, even in the aftermath of Ayodhya, was the communalization of political discourse that I encountered, not only in the mass rallies and assaults, but in the living rooms of middle-class India. Educated people uttered thoughts that once they would not have considered respectable to formulate, let alone express.

In dozens of conversations in Delhi and Calcutta I heard the soon-familiar litany: Muslims are "pampered" for political ends ("look at the Shah Banu case and Muslim Personal Law" — the Indian term for laws on matters concerning worship, marriage, inheritance, and divorce); Muslims have four wives and are outbreeding everyone else ("soon they will overtake the Hindus"); Muslims are disloyal ("they set off firecrackers whenever Pakistan beats India at cricket or hockey"). Often such sentiments were expressed by people who had close professional or personal relationships with individual Muslims. But it was never Mohammed X or Akbar Y they objected to; what had occurred was the demonization of a collectivity. The national mind had been afflicted with the intellectual cancer of thinking of "us" and "them."

It was no consolation that such prejudices were only superficially held, and rarely stood up to much probing. I tried to argue the point at first, but found it almost too simple to do so. The Rajiv Gandhi government's action on the divorced Shah Banu was pure political opportunism; it was a sellout to Muslim conservatives, but a betrayal of Muslim women and Muslim reformers. Why stigmatize the community as a whole when many among them, too, lost out in the process? In any case, Personal Law covers only marriage, inheritance, and divorce; how does it affect those who are not subject to it? Even if some Muslims have four wives — and very few do — how does that increase the Muslim population, since the number of reproductive women remains unchanged? And by what statistical projection can 115 million Muslims "overtake" 700 million Hindus? If a handful of Muslims are pro-Pakistani, how can one label an entire community? Surely the family of the former Indian cricket captain Mohammed Azharuddin (or, for that matter, those of the nation's numerous Muslim hockey stars) isn't setting off firecrackers to commemorate Indian defeats by Pakistan? I never got straight answers to these questions, only a verbal shuffling of feet. But communalism thrives in the absence of specifics, and thriving it certainly seemed to be.

The sad irony is that India's secular coexistence was paradoxically made possible by the fact that the overwhelming majority of Indians are Hindus. It is odd to read today of "Hindu fundamentalism," because Hinduism is a religion without fundamentals: no organized church, no compulsory beliefs or rites of worship, no single sacred book. The name itself denotes something less, and more, than a set of theological beliefs. In many languages — French and Persian among them — the word for "Indian" is "Hindu." Originally, *Hindu* simply meant the people beyond the river Sindhu, or Indus. But, as noted, the Indus is now in Islamic Pakistan; and to make matters worse, the word *Hindu* did not exist in any Indian language till its use by foreigners gave Indians a term for self-definition.

Hinduism is thus the name others applied to the indigenous religion of India. It embraces an eclectic range of doctrines and practices, from pantheism to agnosticism and from faith in reincarnation to belief in the caste system. But none of these constitutes an obligatory credo for a Hindu; there are no compulsory dogmas.

I grew up in a Hindu household. Our home (and my father moved a dozen times in his working life) always had a prayer room, where paintings and portraits of assorted divinities jostled for shelf and wall space with fading photographs of departed ancestors, all stained by ash scattered from the incense burned daily by my devout parents. Every morning, after his bath, my father would stand in front of the prayer room wrapped in his towel, his wet hair still uncombed, and chant his Sanskrit mantras. But he never obliged me to join him; he exemplified the Hindu idea that religion is an intensely personal matter, that prayer is between you and whatever image of your maker you choose to worship. In the Indian way, I was to find my own truth.

Like most Hindus, I think I have. I am a believer, despite a brief period of schoolboy atheism (of the kind that comes with the discovery of rationality and goes with an acknowledgment of its limitations — and with the realization that the world offers too many wondrous mysteries for which science has no answers). And I am happy to describe myself as a believing Hindu, not just because it is the faith into which I was born, but for a string of other reasons, though faith requires no reason. One is cultural: as a Hindu I belong to a faith that expresses the ancient genius of my own people. Another is, for lack of a better phrase, its intellectual "fit": I am more comfortable with the belief structures of Hinduism than I would be with those of the other faiths of which I know. As a Hindu, I claim adherence to a religion without an established church or priestly papacy, a religion whose rituals and customs I am free to reject, a religion that does not oblige me to demonstrate my faith by any visible sign, by subsuming my identity in any collectivity, not even by a specific day or time or frequency of worship. As a Hindu, I subscribe to a creed that is free of the restrictive dogmas of holy writ, that refuses to be shackled to the limitations of a single holy book.

Above all, as a Hindu I belong to the only major religion in the world that does not claim to be the only true religion. I find it immensely congenial to be able to face my fellow human beings of other faiths without being burdened by the conviction that I am embarked upon a "true path" that they have missed. This dogma lies at the core of Christianity, Islam, and Judaism — "I am the Way, the Truth and the Life; no man cometh unto the Father [God], but by me" (John 14:6), says the Bible; "There is no God but Allah, and Mohammed is his Prophet," declares the Koran — denying unbelievers all possibility of redemption, let alone of salvation or paradise. Hinduism, however, asserts that all ways of belief are equally valid, and Hindus readily venerate the saints, and the sacred objects, of other faiths.

How can such a religion lend itself to fundamentalism? That devotees of this essentially tolerant faith have desecrated a shrine and assaulted Muslims in its name is a source of shame and sorrow. India has survived the Aryans, the Mughals, the British; it has taken from each — language, art, food, learning — and grown with all of them. To be Indian is to be part of an elusive dream we all share, a dream that fills our minds with sounds, words, flavors from many sources that we cannot easily identify. Muslim invaders may indeed have destroyed Hindu temples, putting mosques in their place, but this did not — could not — destroy the Indian dream. Nor did Hinduism suffer a fatal blow. Large, eclectic, agglomerative, the Hinduism that I know understands that faith is a matter of hearts and minds, not of bricks and stone. "Build Ram in your heart," the Hindu is enjoined; and if Ram is in your heart, it will little matter where else he is, or is not.

But the twentieth-century politics of deprivation has eroded the culture's confidence. Hindu chauvinism has emerged from the competition for resources in a contentious democracy. Politicians of all faiths across India seek to mobilize voters by appealing to narrow identities;

by seeking votes in the name of religion, caste, and region, they have urged voters to define themselves on these lines. Indians have been made more conscious than ever before of what divides us.

Two years before the demolition of the Babri Masjid in 1992, the country had suffered through the divisive trauma of the Mandal affair. In 1990 the minority Janata government of the famously incorruptible V. P. Singh approved the long-neglected report of the Mandal Commission, which had recommended that 27 percent of all government jobs be reserved for the politically influential "backward castes," in addition to the 22.5 percent already reserved for the "scheduled castes and tribes" (the former outcasts of Indian society). The Mandal recommendation had been ignored by previous governments because it would have brought the percentage of jobs "reserved" for specific quotas to nearly half the total, but the "backwards" were the backbone of Singh's electoral support, and he decided to implement the Mandal report. The upper and middle castes erupted in protest across northern India, with students immolating themselves at the prospect of the further shrinking of their employment horizons; twelve died, consumed quite literally in the flames of their outrage. The Bharatiya Janata Party (BJP) withdrew its support to Singh's Janata government and instead launched into the Ram Janmabhoomi agitation that led eventually to the destruction of the mosque and the rioting that followed.

Of course there is a reactionary element to the Mandal protests, the privileged defending generations of privilege; but Mandal posed ethical dilemmas even to the Indian liberal. This was not simply a case of affording opportunities to the underprivileged. The notion that government employment is an end in itself, unrelated to educational attainment or ability, is troubling for two reasons. First, because efficient and effective administration are seen as less important than granting access to the levers of government to some admittedly underrepresented communities: one "backward caste" friend acidly told me, "after all, if efficiency is more important than representation, we should never have asked the British to leave." Second, because it perpetuates a culture of overbureaucratized governance, where government jobs are seen as a means of wielding power in a state, and a society, where the government already intrudes in far too many areas of economic activity. Most troubling of all to me, however, is that when Mandal and Masjid elevate sectarianism to the level of public policy, we are defined by that which divides us, and it becomes more important to be a Muslim, a (tribal) Bodo, or a ("backward") Yadav than to be an Indian. Our politics have created a discourse in which the clamor goes up for Assam for the Assamese, Jharkhand for the Jharkhandis, Maharashtra for the Maharashtrians — but who, my father would ask, believes in an India for Indians?

Identities thus formed are asserted, sometimes through violence. I am prepared to concede that Hindu fanaticism — which ought to be a contradiction in terms, since we have no dogmas to be fanatical about — is partly a reaction to other chauvinisms. I am not among the Indian secularists whose opposition to the Babri Masjid agitation is based on a meticulously researched rejection of the historicity of their claim that the mosque stood on the site of the birth of the Hindu god-king Ram — because to me what matters is what most people believe, for their beliefs offer a sounder basis for public policy than the historians' footnotes. (Instead of saying to impassioned Hindus, "You are wrong, there is no proof this was Ram's birthplace, there is no proof that the temple Babur demolished to build this mosque was a temple to Ram, go away and leave the mosque in place," how much more effective might it have been to say, "You may be right, let us assume for a moment that there was a Ram Janmabhoomi temple here that was destroyed to make room for this mosque four hundred seventy years ago; does that mean we should behave in that way today? If the Muslims of the 1520s acted out of ignorance and fanaticism, should Hindus act the same way in the 1990s? By doing what you propose to do, you will hurt the feelings of the Muslims of today, who did not perpetrate the injustices of the past and who are in no position to inflict injustice upon you today; you will provoke violence and rage against your own kind; you will tarnish the name of the Hindu people across the world; and you will irreparably damage your own cause. Is this worth it?")

I also accept the reproach of those Hindus who see a double standard at work here. Muslims say they are proud to be Muslim, Sikhs say they are proud to be Sikh, Christians say they are proud to be Christian, and Hindus say they are proud to be . . . secular. It is easy to see why this sequence should provoke the scorn of those Hindus who declaim, *Garv se kahon hum Hindu hain:* "Say with pride that we are Hindus." But in what precisely are we to take pride? Hinduism is no monolith; its strength is found within each Hindu, not in the collectivity. As a Hindu, I take no pride in destroying other people's symbols, in hitting others on the head because of the cut of their beard or the cuts of their foreskins. I *am* proud of my Hinduism: I take pride in its diversity, in its openness, in religious freedom. Defining a "Hindu" cause may partly be a political reaction to the definition of non-Hindu causes, but it is a foolish one for all that. The rage of the Hindu mobs is the rage of those who feel themselves supplanted in this competition of identities, who think that they are taking their country back from usurpers of long ago. They want revenge against history, but they do not realize that history is its own revenge.

· · ·

Om maha Ganapathe namaha,
sarva vignoba shantaye,
om Ganeshaya namaha. . . .

Every morning, for longer than I can remember, I have begun my day with that prayer. I learned it without being fully aware of what all the Sanskrit words meant, knowing only that I was invoking, like millions of Hindus around the world, the name of the great elephant-headed god to bless all my endeavors to come.

Ganesh, or Ganapathi as we prefer to call him in the south, sits impassively on my bedroom shelf, in multiple forms of statuary, stone, metal, and papier-mâché. There is nothing incongruous about this; he is used to worse, appearing as he does on innumerable calendars, posters, trademarks, and wedding invitation cards. Paunchy, full-bodied, long-trunked (though with one broken tusk), attired in whatever costume the artist fancies (from ascetic to astronaut), Ganesh, riding his way across Indian hearts on a rat, is arguably Hinduism's most popular divine figure.

Few auspicious occasions are embarked upon without first seeking Ganesh's blessing. His principal attribute in Hindu mythology — a quality that flows from both his wisdom and his strength — is as a remover of obstacles to the fulfillment of desires. No wonder everyone wants Ganesh on his side before launching any important project, from starting a factory to acquiring a wife. My own courtship violated time-honored Indian rules about caste, language, region, age, and parental approval; but when we got married, my wife and I had an embossed red Ganesh adorning the front of our wedding invitations.

I have since developed an even more personal connection to Ganesh. The great two-thousand-year-old epic called the Mahabharata was supposedly dictated by the sage Vedavyasa to Ganesh himself; since then, many a writer has found it helpful to invoke Ganesh in his epigraph. When I recast the characters and episodes of the Mahabharata into a political satire on twentieth-century Indian history, *The Great Indian Novel,* I had it dictated by a retired nationalist, Ved Vyas, to a secretary named Ganapathi, with a big nose and shrewd, intelligent eyes, who enters with elephantine tread, dragging an enormous trunk behind him. Such are the secular uses of Hindu divinity.

For in my Hinduism the godhead is not some remote and forbidding entity in the distant heavens. God is immediately accessible all around us, and he takes many forms for those who need to imagine him in a more personalized fashion. The Hindu pantheon includes thousands of such figures, great and small. Ganesh is the chief of the *ganas,* or what some scholars call the "inferior deities." He is not part of the trinity of Brahma (the Creator), Shiva (the Destroyer), and Vishnu (the Preserver), who are the principal Hindu gods, the three facets of the Ultimate First Cause. But he is the son of Shiva, or at least of Shiva's wife, Parvati (one theory is that she shaped him from the scurf of her own body, without paternal involvement).

As a writer I have always been interested in the kinds of stories a society tells about itself. So part of the appeal of Ganesh for me lies in the plethora of stories about how this most unflappable of deities lost his (original) head and acquired his unconventional appearance.

The most widely held version is the one my grandmother told me when I was little — about the time that Parvati went to take a bath and asked her son to guard the door. Shiva arrived and wished to enter, but Ganesh was firm in his refusal. Enraged by this effrontery, Shiva cut off the boy's head. Parvati, horrified, asked him to replace it, and Shiva obliged with the head of the first creature he could find, an elephant.

This was a salutary lesson in the perils of excessive obedience to your parents, though I don't think my grandmother intended me to take it that way. My mother, who always tried unsuccessfully to resist the temptation to boast about her children, had another version: a vain Parvati asked Shani (Saturn) to look at her perfect son, forgetting that Shani's gaze would reduce the boy's head to ashes. Once again, an elephant's was the head that came to hand.

Growing up in an India where loyalty seems all too often on sale to the highest bidder, I could not but be impressed by Ganesh's rare quality of stubborn devotion to duty. However he may have lost his head, it was Ganesh's obduracy as a guard that, in my grandmother's telling, cost him a tusk. "The powerful avatar Parasurama," she recounted, as we little ones gathered round her at dusk, "possessor of many a boon from Shiva, came to call on the Great Destroyer at his abode of Mount Kailash. Once again, Ganesh was at the door, and he refused to let the visitor disturb the sleeping Shiva. Parasurama, furious, tried to force his way in, but found Ganesh a determined opponent." (My eyes widened in excitement at this part.) "Ganesh picked Parasurama up with his long trunk, swung him round and round till he was dizzy and helpless, and threw him to the ground. When his head cleared, Parasurama flung his ax at the obstinate Ganesh. Now, Ganesh could have avoided the ax easily, but he recognized the weapon as one of Shiva's. He could not insult his father by resisting his weapon. So he took the ax humbly upon his tusk." Ever since, Ganesh has been depicted with only one tusk.

The thrill of that story did not diminish for me when I learned the more prosaic version, which says that Ganesh wore down one tusk to a stub by using it to write down the epic verse of the Mahabharata. For this reason, the missing tusk signifies knowledge. As I grew older, I learned of more such symbols associated with Ganesh. Scholars of Hinduism tell us that Ganesh's fat body represents the hugeness of the cosmos, its combination of man and pachyderm signifying the unity of the microcosm (man) with the macrocosm (depicted as an elephant). Some suggest it has the less esoteric purpose of demonstrating that appearances mean little, and that an outwardly unattractive form can hide internal spiritual beauty. (In any case, his looks do not prevent Ganesh, in most popular depictions, from being surrounded by beautiful women, including his twin wives, Siddhi and Buddhi.) Further, Ganesh's trunk can be curled into the symbol for *Om*, the primal sound; and the snake found coiled around his waist represents the force of cosmic energy.

"But, Ammamma," I would ask my grandmother, "why does Ganesh ride a rat?" For in most of the pictures in our prayer room, the deity is shown on this unusual mount. At the simplest level, the sight of an elephantine god on a tiny mouse visually equates the importance of the greatest and smallest of God's creatures. And, as my grandmother explained, each animal is a symbol of Ganesh's capacities: "Like an elephant he can crash through the jungle, uprooting every impediment in his path, while like the rat he can burrow his way through the tightest of defenses." A god who thus combines the attributes of elephant, mouse, and man can remove any obstacle confronting those who propitiate him. No wonder that many worship him as their principal deity, despite his formally more modest standing in the pantheon.

And what is the secret of his appeal to a late-twentieth-century urbanite like me? As his unblinking gaze and broad brow suggest, Ganesh is an extremely intelligent god. When I was very young, I heard the story of how Parvati asked her two sons, Ganesh and Kartikeya, to go around the world in a race. Kartikeya, the more vigorous and martial-minded of the two, set off at once, confident he would encircle the globe faster than his corpulent brother. Ganesh, after resting awhile, took a few steps around his mother and sat down again. Parvati reminded him of her challenge. "But you are my world," Ganesh replied disarmingly, "and I have gone around you." Needless to say, he won the race — and my unqualified admiration.

So it is no surprise that Ganesh is worshiped in India with not just reverence but enthusiasm. Sometimes this can be carried to extremes, as when Ganesh devotees in western India in the 1890s allowed the bubonic plague to take many lives rather than cooperate with a British campaign to exterminate the rats that carried it (for the rats were also, after all, Ganesh's mounts).

In late September 1995, word spread around the world that statues of Ganesh had begun drinking milk. In some cases, statues of his divine parents, Shiva and Parvati, were also reported to be imbibing these liquid offerings, but Ganesh it was who took the elephant's share. Early on Thursday, September 21, the rumors started in Delhi that the gods were drinking milk; it was said that an idol of Ganesh in a suburb of the capital had swallowed half a cup. Within hours the frenzy had spread around the globe, as reports came in of temples and private domestic shrines in places as far removed as Long Island and Hong Kong witnessing the same phenomenon. At the Vishwa temple in London's Indian-dominated Southall district, a fifteen-inch statue was said to be drinking hundreds of spoons of milk offerings; the august London *Times* reported on its front page that "in 24 hours 10,000 saw it drink." At the Geeta Bhavan temple in Manchester, prodigious quantities were ingested by a three-inch silver statue of Ganesh. Hard-bitten British tabloid journalists, looking for a fraud to debunk, filmed and photographed the phenomenon and professed themselves flabbergasted. " I gazed in awe," confessed the man from the *Daily Star;* his rival from the *Sun* "gasped in disbelief."

In India, the rationalists were quick to react. It was, they averred, a matter of simple physics. Molecules on the rough stone and marble surfaces of the statues had created a "capillary action" that sucked in the droplets of milk. These were not really absorbed into the statue, but formed a thin layer of droplets on the surface that would be visible if the statue were dark. A team of government scientists proceeded to demonstrate this on television, placing green powder in the milk and showing a green stain spreading over the face of a white marble statue. Mass hysteria was alleged; Indian priests (who live off the offerings of devotees in the temples) were merely trying to whip up more custom, said some; it was all politics, said others, pointing to the need for the flagging Hindutva movement to attract the credulous to their credo. Delhi's *Pioneer* newspaper published a photograph of a spout emerging from the back of a temple from which milk poured into a bucket; the implication was that it was chicanery, not divine ingestion, that accounted for the disappearing milk in the temples.

The rationalists and the believers were probably both right. That is in the nature of faith; scientific faith, no less than religious, tends to confirm itself. I was traveling when the story broke, and when it was reported that the milk-drinking had ceased in most places on Friday afternoon the day after it began, I thought I had missed the miracle altogether. A week later, in Texas, I was told of a house in a Houston suburb where the phenomenon had persisted. Slightly skeptical but decidedly curious, I went to see it for myself, and was driven there in a Mercedes by a worldly Sikh businesswoman who had neither a religious nor a pecuniary interest in seeing the miracle vindicated. We drew up at an ordinary middle-class Indian home; ropes had been strung outside to control the throngs, but there were none on this day, it being the eighth day after the phenomenon had first been reported, and a working day to boot. The lady of the house took us to her little shrine, an unremarkable *puja* room like so many in Hindu homes around the world. She had a number of statues and portraits, but only one was drinking milk: a tiny terra-cotta statue of Ganesh, no more than two and a half inches high. My Sikh friend, with trembling hand, extended her spoon toward the miniature trunk of the statue, and we both watched the milk disappear into the little Ganesh. It was now my turn; with callous incompetence I held the spoon firm and level, and the milk held steady. "Tilt it a bit," our hostess urged, and when I did the milk duly disappeared into the statue. It was not as if I had poured the milk out, because then it would have flowed differently; nor was the milk simply spilled, though a couple of drops fell to the floor. Instead there seemed to be a gentle drawing out of the milk by an unknown force, perhaps capillary action. *(Om capillary actioneyeh namaha?)* The statue, we were told, had been "fed" some 180 times a day for eight days; surely its capillary channels and overall absorptive capacity would have been exhausted by now? As we stood mulling these thoughts, a young Indian woman in T-shirt and jeans, evidently part of the new generation of subcontinental Americans, came to take her turn before the statue. Ganesh drank willingly from her extended spoon.

The lady of the house took no money, accepted no offerings. Her husband was neither a priest nor a Hindu revivalist; he held a senior executive position in a Houston computer firm. When we spoke to her she exuded the simple religiosity of so many middle-class women; she was touched by what was happening in her own home, she believed implicitly in the miracle, she did not question its nature or purpose, she sought nothing from it (indeed, she put up with considerable inconvenience because of it) except vindication of her own personal faith. Every night she bathed the little statue and put it "to bed" in a little golden throne, swaddled in muslin; the next morning Ganesh was back on the low pedestal in the *puja* room, as thirsty as ever.

I did not know how to react to what I had just seen. I had come out of curiosity, not to explore or affirm belief. The milk-drinking was essentially irrelevant to "my" Hinduism; my faith was neither strengthened nor exalted by the sight of a statue drinking milk, nor would it have been shaken or diluted if Ganesh had refused to imbibe. I was prepared to believe that there might be a fully rational explanation for the event, but I was equally willing to accept that a miracle might have occurred, one not readily susceptible to the demystification of scientists. I believe the world has more questions to pose than science has yet found answers for, and so have no intellectual difficulty with a notion of the supernatural. Nor, more to the point, do the millions of devotees who flocked to temples worldwide, who saw in the phenomenon a simple message from the heavens that the gods remained interested in the affairs of ordinary mortals.

But Hindus have always believed that to be the case; the "milk miracle" merely reinforced an unstated assumption about the nature of the Godhead. Our gods crowd the streets, smile or frown on us from the skies, jostle us for space on the buses; they are part of our daily lives, as intimate and personal as the towels in which we wrap ourselves after a bath. If they push us out of our beds tomorrow, there will always be scientists pointing to a geological fault, but Hindus will accept the divine intent to arouse them, just as they accepted the miracle of the milk.

So the intrusion of the gods into our lives through the milk-drinking episode is no great aberration. They are part of our lives anyway; we see ourselves in them, only idealized. My own affection is for Ganesh himself, a god who — overweight, long-nosed, broken-tusked, and big-eared — cheerfully reflects our own physical imperfections. After all, a country with many seemingly insurmountable problems needs a god who can overcome obstacles.

When I was a child in Bombay, I was enraptured once a year by the city's great Ganesh Chathurthi festival, in which India's bustling commercial capital gives itself over to celebration of this many-talented deity. Hundreds of statues of Ganesh (and of his beautiful wives) are made, decorated, and lovingly dressed; then they are taken out across the busy city streets in a procession of more than a million followers, before being floated out to sea in a triumphant gesture of release. As a little boy I stood on the beach watching the statues settle gradually into the water while the streams of worshipers dispersed. It was sad to see the giant elephant head disappear beneath the waves, but I knew that Ganesh had not really left me. I would find him again, in my wall calendars, on my mantelpiece, at the beginning of my books — and in the prayers with which I would resume my life the morning after the festival:

> Om, I invoke the name of Ganapathi;
> Bringer of peace over all troubles,
> Om, I invoke the name of Ganesh. . . .

.   .   .

So, yes, I am a believer, with the blend of piety and practicality, faith and irreverence, that characterizes much of Hindu belief. It is an attitude toward religion that helps sustain Indian secularism.

I came to my own secularism through my Kerala roots. My parents were both born in Kerala of Malayali parents, speakers of Malayalam — the only language in the world with a palindromic name in English — the language of that remarkable sliver of a state in southwest India. Non-Malayalis who know of Kerala associate it with its fabled coast, gilded by immaculate beaches and leafy lagoons (both speckled nowadays with the more discerning among India's deplorably few foreign tourists). But my parents were from the interior of the state, the rice-bowl district of Palghat, nestled in the last major gap near the end of the mountain chain known as the Western Ghats, which runs down the western side of the peninsula like a subsidiary spine. Palghat — or Palakkad, as it is now spelled, to conform to the Malayalam pronunciation — unlike most of the rest of Kerala (which was ruled by maharajahs of an unusually enlightened variety), had been colonized by the British, so that my father discovered his nationalism at a place called Victoria College. The town of Palghat itself is unremarkable, even unattractive; its setting, though, is lushly beautiful, and my parents both belonged to villages an hour away from the district capital, and to families whose principal source of income was agriculture. Their roots lay deep in the Kerala soil, from which has emerged the values that I cherish in the Indian soul.

It is not often that an American reference seems even mildly appropriate to an Indian case, but a recent study established some astonishing parallels between the United States and the state of Kerala. The life expectancy of a male American is seventy-two years, that of a male Keralite seventy years. The literacy rate in the United States is 95 percent; in Kerala it is 99 percent. The birth rate in the United States is sixteen per thousand; in Kerala it is eighteen per thousand, but it is falling faster. The major difference is that the annual per capita income in Kerala is around $300 to $350, whereas in the United States it is $22,500, about seventy times as much. Kerala has, in short, all the demographic indicators commonly associated with "developed" countries, at a small fraction of the cost.

Kerala's demographics are unique. It has the highest population density of any Indian state, its women outnumber its men (there are 1,040 women to every 1,000 men), and it has a higher rate of literacy than the United States, including two districts where every resident above the age of six is literate. Its working men and women enjoy greater rights and a higher minimum wage than exist anywhere else in India. It was the first place on earth to democratically elect a Communist government, remove it from office, reelect it, vote the Communists out, and bring them back again. When the Italian political system saw the emergence of a Communist Party willing to play by the rules of liberal democracy, the world spoke of Euro-Communism, but Kerala had already achieved Indo-Communism much earlier, subordinating the party of proletarian revolution to the ethos of political pluralism. Malayalis are highly politically aware: when other Indian states were electing film stars to Parliament or as chief ministers, a film star tried his political luck in Kerala and lost his security deposit. (Ironically, the first Indian film star to become the chief minister of a state was a Malayali, Marudur G. Ramachandran, known to all as "MGR" — but he was elected in the neighboring state of Tamil Nadu, where he had made a career as a Tamilian film hero.) Malayalis rank high in every field of Indian endeavor, including in their ranks many top national civil servants, eminent editors, innovative writers, and award-winning film-makers.

More important, Kerala is a microcosm of every religion known to the country; its population is divided into almost equal fourths of Christians, Muslims, caste Hindus, and Scheduled Castes (the former Untouchables), each of whom is economically and politically powerful. The Christians of Kerala belong to the oldest Christian community in the world outside Palestine, converted by Jesus' disciple Saint Thomas (the "Doubting Thomas" of biblical legend). Islam came to Kerala not by the sword, as it was to do elsewhere in India, but through traders, travelers, and missionaries. And Jews fleeing Babylonian attacks and later Roman persecution found refuge, and acceptance, in Kerala. Kerala's outcasts — one group of whom, the Pariahs, gave the English language a term for their collective condition — suffered discrimination every bit as vicious and iniquitous as in the rest of India, but overcame their plight far more successfully than their country-men elsewhere. A combination of enlightened rule by far-thinking maharajahs, progressive reform movements within the Hindu tradi-tion (especially that of the remarkable Ezhava sage Sree Narayana Guru), and changes wrought by a series of left-dominated legislatures since independence have given Kerala's Scheduled Castes a place in society that other Dalits (former Untouchables) across India are still denied.

Part of the secret of Kerala is its openness to the external influ-ences — Arab, Roman, Chinese, British; Islamist, Christian, Marx-ist — that have gone into the making of the Malayali people. More than two millennia ago Keralites had trade relations not just with other parts of India, but with the Arab world, with the Phoenicians, and with the Roman Empire. From those days on, Malayalis have had an open and welcoming attitude to the rest of humanity. When Saint Thomas brought Christianity to Kerala (well before it reached Europe), he made converts among the highborn elite. After the early Jewish refugees es-caping Babylon six hundred years before Christ, Jews fleeing Roman persecution found refuge in Cranganore in A.D. 68 and flourished there until Europeans (the Portuguese) came to Kerala to persecute them 1,500 years later, at which point they found a new welcome in another Kerala town, Cochin. As for Islam, not only was it peacefully embraced, but it found encouragement in attitudes and episodes without parallel elsewhere in the non-Islamic world: in one example, the all-powerful Zamorin of Calicut asked each fisherman's family in his domain to bring up one son as a Muslim, for service in his Muslim-run navy. It was prob-ably a Malayali seaman, one of many who routinely plied the Arabian Sea between Kerala and East Africa, who piloted Vasco da Gama, the Portuguese explorer and trader, to Calicut in 1496. (Typically, he was welcomed by the Zamorin, but when he tried to pass trinkets off as valuables, he was thrown in prison for a while. Malayalis are open and hospitable to a fault, but they are not easily fooled.)

In turn, Malayalis brought their questing spirit to the world. The great Advaita philosopher, Shankaracharya, was a Malayali who trav-eled throughout the length and breadth of India on foot in the eighth century A.D. laying the foundations for a reformed and revived Hinduism. To this day, there is a temple in the Himalayas whose priests are Namboodiris from Kerala. In the fifth century A.D. the Malayali astronomer Aryabhatta deduced, a thousand years before his European successors, that the earth is round and that it rotates on its own axis; it was also he who calculated the value of pi (3.1614) for the first time. But a recitation of names — for one could invoke great artists, musicians, and poets, enlightened kings and learned sages, throughout history — would only belabor the point. Kerala took from others, everything from Roman ports to Chinese fishing nets, and gave to the rest of India everything from martial arts and systems of classical dance to the skills of its hardworking labor force.

Keralites never suffered from inhibitions about travel: an old joke suggests that so many Keralite typists flocked to stenographic work in Bombay, Calcutta, and Delhi that "Remington" became the name of a new Malayali subcaste. In the nation's capital, the wags said that you couldn't throw a stone in the Central Secretariat without injuring a Keralite bureaucrat. Nor was there, in the Kerala tradition, any prohibition on venturing abroad, none of the ritual defilement associated in parts of north India with "crossing the black water." It was no accident that Keralites were the first, and the most, to take advantage of the post-oil-shock employment boom in the Arab Gulf countries; at one point in the 1980s, the largest single ethnic group in the Gulf sheikhdom of Bahrain was reported to be not Bahrainis but Keralites. The willingness of Keralites to go anywhere to do anything remains legendary. When Neil Armstrong landed on the moon in 1969, my father's friends laughed, he discovered a Malayali already there, offering him tea.

All this speaks of a rare and precious heritage that is the patrimony of all Malayalis — a heritage of openness and diversity, of pluralism and tolerance, of high aspirations and varied but considerable accomplishment. To be a Malayali is also to lay claim to a rich tradition of literature, dance, and music, of religious diversity, of political courage and intellectual enlightenment. With all this, Keralites tend to take pride in their collective identity as Malayalis; our religion, our caste, our region, come later, if at all. There is no paradox in asserting that these are qualities that help make Malayalis good Indians in a plural society. You cannot put better ingredients into the melting pot.

So Kerala embodies the "Malayali miracle": a state that has practiced openness and tolerance from time immemorial; that has made religious and ethnic diversity a part of its daily life rather than a source of division; that has overcome caste discrimination and class oppression through education, land reforms, and political democracy; that has honored its women and enabled them to lead productive, fulfilling, and empowered lives. Not everyone is equally laudatory of the "Kerala model"; economists point out that it places rather too much emphasis on workers' rights and income distribution, and rather too little on production, productivity, and output. But its results are truly remarkable; and as a Keralite and an Indian, I look forward to the day when Kerala will no longer be the exception in tales of Indian development, but merely the trailblazer.

Having raised my Kerala roots, I am obliged to indulge in a small digression. Though I am a Malayali and a writer, I have no claims to be considered a Malayali writer; indeed, despite setting some of my fictional sequences in Kerala and scattering several Menons through my stories, I could not have written my books in Malayalam because I cannot write my own mother tongue.

And yet I am not inclined to be defensive about my Kerala heritage, despite the obvious incongruities of an expatriate praising Kerala from abroad and lauding the Malayali heritage in the English language. I have felt vindicated in my Malayaliness ever since I received an unusual endorsement of it, unusual in that it was unintended. It came to me when I was living and working in Singapore. A leading member of the expatriate Malayali community there, a prominent doctor, met me casually one evening and mentioned that he had just read a short story of mine in the *Illustrated Weekly of India*. Since I was young and very proud of the story, which was called "The Death of a Schoolmaster," I did something no author should ever do — I asked him how he had liked it. He was not exactly effusive in his reaction. "Oh, it was all right," he said grudgingly, "but you just seem to have recorded the story of your own upbringing in Kerala — there was not much fiction in it."

At that point we were interrupted. But I could see he was startled by the look of sheer delight that crossed my face on hearing these less than complimentary words. Since I was called away soon afterward, I never had a chance to explain to him why his mild criticism had pleased me as if it were the most generous praise. The reason was simple: I had never had an upbringing in Kerala. I was born in London, brought up in Bombay, went to high school in Calcutta, attended college in Delhi, and received my doctorate in the United States. My short story was entirely fiction. But the Malayali doctor's reaction suggested that I had succeeded in evoking village Kerala — a Kerala he knew far better than I did — convincingly enough for him to consider it authentic.

As a child of the city, my only experience of village Kerala had been as an initially reluctant vacationer during my parents' annual trips home. For many non-Keralite Malayali children traveling like this, there was often little joy in the compulsory rediscovery of their roots, and many saw it more as an obligation than a pleasure. For many, Kerala was a world of private inconveniences and mosquito bites; when I was ten I told my father that this annual migration to the south was strictly for the birds. But as I grew older, I came to appreciate the magic of Kerala: the extraordinary natural beauty of the land, its lagoons, its forests, its beaches, and above all the startling, many-hued green of the paddy fields, with palm trees swaying in the gentle breeze that whispers everywhere in Kerala. As a Malayali, this beauty is bred into my soul; but there is much more to the Kerala experience. In my own lifetime I have seen remarkable transformations in Kerala society, with land reform, free and universal education, and dramatic changes in caste relations. But I had seen all this as an outsider.

In meeting expatriate Indians in Singapore, London, Geneva, and the United States, I have seen much of the predicament of the Malayali who is, geographically, no longer a Keralite. Indian Malayalis outside Kerala have the same problem of living in a society that is not fully their own. Modern communications and jet travel have made our situation both easier and more difficult than in the past. It is easier, because we are always able to renew our contact with the home, the family, the village. It is also more difficult, because it is precisely this tantalizing access that complicates the agonizing conflict between adjustment to the world around us (wherever we happen to live) and loyalty to our cultural legacy — a loyalty that fades with each succeeding generation born in exile.

We are, for the most part, conscious — some would say inordinately proud — of our Malayali cultural heritage. But as we are cut off from its primary source, the source of daily cultural self-regeneration — Kerala itself — we have to evolve our own identities by preserving what we can of our heritage and merging it with those of the others around us, whether Americans in Queens or a pan-Indian potpourri in Delhi. As we grow up outside Kerala, we know that we are not the Malayalis we might have been if our parents had never left Kerala. In due course, Onam becomes only as much a part of our culture as any other holiday, and we are as likely to give a younger relative a Christmas present as a *Vishukkaineettam* (New Year's gift). It gets worse with each succeeding generation. Your father, as an Indian Malayali outside Kerala, may consider himself a Malayali, but as long as he does not live in his home state he remains on the outside, looking in. We, his descendants — Malayalis without our *Mathrubhumi* or *Manorama* newspapers, who do not understand the *Ottamthullal* folk dance and have never heard of the great poet Kumaran Asan — are, when we come to visit Kerala, foreigners in our own land.

I am such a Malayali — and in towns and cities around India and across the world, thousands more are growing up like us. Our very names are often absurdities in Kerala terms. In my case, my father's *veetu-peru* (house name, the family name handed down from his mother and her female forebears in the Nair matrilineal tradition) has been transmuted into a surname. We speak a pidgin Malayalam at home, stripped of all but the essential household vocabulary, and cannot read or write the language intelligibly. I tried to teach myself the script as a teenager on holidays in Kerala, gave up on the *Koottaksharams* (joined letters), and as a result can recognize only 80 percent of the letters and considerably fewer of the words. (When an Indian ambassador in Singapore wanted to inform me discreetly of his imminent replacement by a Kerala politician, he passed me a clipping from a Malayalam newspaper and was startled at my embarrassed incomprehension of the news.) Our parents consider it more important that we master English and do well in the prevailing second language, whether Hindi or one of the "regional" languages (Bengali in Calcutta, perhaps Spanish in New York); so no serious attempt is made to teach us to be literate in our mother tongue. Malayalam books and magazines may be found at home, but they are seen by us as forlorn relics of an insufficiently advanced past and are ignored by the younger generation, whose eager eyes are on the paperbacks, comics, and textbooks of the impatient and westernized future.

Even the Keralite liberality and adaptiveness, such great assets in facilitating Malayali emigration and good citizenship anywhere, can serve to slacken, if not cut, the cords that bind non-Keralites to their cultural assumptions. I remember one trivial episode during my student theater days at Bombay's Campion School, which helped make the point. I was a ten-year-old representing the sixth grade in an interclass theatrical event at which the eighth grade's sketch featured Chintu (Rishi) Kapoor, younger son of the matinee idol and producer Raj Kapoor, and later to become a successful screen heartthrob in his own right. I had acted, elocuted a humorous poem, and MC'ed my class's efforts to generous applause, and the younger Kapoor was either intrigued or disconcerted, for he sought me out the next morning at school.

"Tharoor," he asked me at the head of the steps near the bathroom, "what caste are you?"

I blinked my nervousness at the Great Man. "I — I don't know," I stammered. My father, who had shed his caste name for nationalist reasons in his Victoria College days and never mentioned anyone's religion, let alone caste, had not bothered to enlighten me on such matters.

"You don't *know?*" the actor's son demanded in astonishment. "What do you mean, you don't know? Everybody knows his own caste." I shamefacedly confessed I didn't.

"You mean you're not a Brahmin or something?"

I couldn't even avow I was a something. Chintu Kapoor never spoke to me again. But I went home that evening and extracted an explanation from my parents, whose eclectic liberality had left me in such ignorance. They told me, in simplified terms, about the Nairs; and so it is to Chintu Kapoor, celluloid hero of the future, that I owe my first lesson about my genealogical past.

That was not untypical, because Keralites tend to be the chameleons of India, adjusting to the circumstances they see around them. The children of Keralites outside Kerala generally tend to be well adjusted and increasingly deracinated. Even growing up in India, our music was the eclectic mix of all cosmopolitan living rooms, from Madonna to Mozart, rather than the fifteen minutes of All-India Radio's Malayalam "Vividh Bharati" to which my mother avidly listened. Even when we turn to "Indian pop," our film philistinism bears the voice of Bollywood's Lata Mangeshkar, not Kerala's P. Susheela, and the national superstar Amitabh Bachchan means more to us than the Kerala screen legend Mammooty. We may eat *idli*s at home if we are lucky, but most of our food would be unrecognizable in Kerala, and our wardrobes are largely bereft of the distinctive white waistcloths, the *mundu*s, which are the standard attire of the Malayali male. In the process Kerala becomes a remote place, an ancestral homeland long since abandoned, associated with family but not friends, a repository of other people's memories. Our visits to what our parents continue to refer to as "home" are increasingly the self-distancing trips of tourists. "Home" is, after all, where our parents are, not where their parents used to be.

It is all too easy to slip into this mindset. My parents were both born in little towns that had barely outgrown village status, but having lived all my life in concrete metropolises, I felt the experience of their upbringing only secondhand. When, on our annual visits to Kerala, I overcame the initial childish condescension of the city-bred for village life and genuinely tried to understand and to belong, I met with the most unexpected resistance from my Keralite relatives themselves. It was not just that my world was seen by my cousins as impossibly removed from theirs. What was worse, in a curious kind of inverted snobbery, they delighted in my difference from them. "He doesn't speak Malayalam, only *English*," they would boast in perverse pride to their neighbors, before I could voice an embarrassed (and no doubt ungrammatical) disclaimer in Bombay Malayalam.

What does it mean, then, for a non-Keralite Malayali like myself to lay claim to my Malayali heritage? In many ways my sense of being Malayali is tied up with my sense of being Indian. I may not be able to quote from Vallathol or understand the whirling dance of the village *vellichapad,* but what my Kerala roots have given me is a sense of the infinite variety of humankind and the vital importance of engaging openly with all of it. And so the Indian identity that I want, in my turn, to give my half-Malayali sons imposes no pressure to conform. It celebrates diversity: if America is a melting pot, then to me India, like Kerala, is a *thali,* a selection of sumptuous dishes in different bowls. Each tastes different, and does not necessarily mix with the next, but they belong together on the same plate, and they complement each other in making the meal a satisfying repast. And the important thing is that Mathai and Mohammedkutty and Mohanan still sing the same songs and dream the same dreams together, preferably in Malayalam.

It may seem paradoxical that I am advocating a vision of a pluralist but united India while singing the praises of a single Indian state. In fact the contradiction is more apparent than real. Western students of nationalism, most recently Michael Ignatieff, have tended to suggest that group identities breed conflict, and that the only solvent for the intolerance and hatred of competing chauvinisms is the replacement of group identification by raging individualism. As a Keralite and an Indian I have profound difficulties with that view, though I yield to no one in my respect for individual rights and in my assertion of my own individuality. The Kerala experience suggests to me that the best antidote to unhealthy group-think is *healthy* group-think. If you want to discourage Indians from mobilizing themselves principally as Hindus and Muslims hostile to each other, you can do worse than to instill in them pride in identities that transcend the Hindu-Muslim difference, including regional and cultural identities founded on the same pluralism you want to promote across India. A Malayali Hindu feels instinctively closer to a Malayali Muslim than he does to a Punjabi Hindu, and there is no harm in that, in and of itself — unless, of course, the regional identity becomes the source of a different sort of chauvinism, the kind that has led to separatism among some Indian groups. There is no danger of that from Kerala, both because of the pluralist traditions of Keralite culture and because Malayalis have always understood that there are far too many of us who would have to cope with far too little space if Kerala did strike out on its own. Keralites see the best guarantee of their own security and prosperity in the survival of a pluralist India. It is a belief that exists, if in smaller measure, throughout the rest of India — and one that must be extended further and deeper if it is to be self-fulfilling.

The Malayali ethos is the same as the best of the Indian ethos — inclusionist, flexible, eclectic, absorptive. The central challenge of India as we enter the twenty-first century is the challenge of accommodating the aspirations of different groups in the national dream. The ethos that I have called both Keralite and Indian helped the nation meet this challenge. It is an ethos rooted in our native tradition, and therefore in what, for lack of a better word, we can call Hinduism — or at least one kind of Hinduism. The battle for India's soul will thus be between two Hinduisms, the secularist Indianism of the nationalist movement and the particularist fanaticism of the Ayodhya mob. The danger of neo-Hinduism, of "us" and "them," is that the cancer will spread; there will be new "us's" and new "thems." It was no accident that Bombay's Shiv Sainik rioters in early 1992 particularly targeted South Indian Muslims: the Shiv Sena had first acquired attention and notoriety by attacking South Indian migrants in Bombay, irrespective of their faith. Today it is "Hindus" and "Muslims"; tomorrow it could be Hindi-speakers against Tamils, upper castes against "backwards," north versus south.

We are all minorities in independent India. No one group can assert its dominance without making minorities of the majority of Indians. If upper-caste Hindus agitate for Hindutva, a majority of Hindus are not upper caste; if North Indians in the cow belt clamor for Hindi to be the "national language," a majority of Indians do not speak it as their mother tongue; and so on. India's strength is that it is a conglomeration of minorities using democratic means to ascertain majority opinion on the crucial questions of the day.

This is why the change in the public discourse about Indianness is so dangerous, and why the old ethos must be restored. An India that denies itself to some of us could end up being denied to all of us. This would be a second Partition — and a partition in the Indian soul would be as bad as a partition in the Indian soil. For my sons, the only possible idea of India is that of a nation greater than the sum of its parts. That is the only India that will allow them to continue to call themselves Indians.

4

Scheduled Castes, Unscheduled Change

I was about eight or nine when I first came across Charlis.
A few of us children were kicking a ball around the dusty courtyard of my grandmother's house in rural Kerala, where my parents
took me annually on what they called a holiday and I regarded as a cross
between a penance and a pilgrimage. (Their pilgrimage, my penance.)
Balettan, my oldest cousin, who was all of thirteen and had a bobbing
Adam's apple to prove it, had just streaked across me and kicked the ball
with more force than he realized he possessed. It soared upward like
a startled bird, curved perversely away from us, and disappeared over
our high brick wall into the rubbish heap at the back of the neighbor's
house.

"Damn," I said. I had grown up in Bombay, where one said things
like that.

"Go and get it, *da*," Balettan commanded one of the younger
cousins. *Da* was a term of great familiarity, used especially when
ordering young boys around.

A couple of the kids, stifling groans, dutifully set off toward the
wall. But before they could reach it the ball came sailing back over their
heads toward us, soon followed over the wall by a skinny, sallow youth

with a pockmarked face and an anxious grin. He seemed vaguely familiar, someone I'd seen in the background on previous holidays but not really noticed, though I wasn't sure why.

"Charlis!" a couple of the kids called out. "Charlis got the ball!"

Charlis sat on the wall, managing to look both unsure and pleased with himself. Bits of muck from the rubbish heap clung to his shirt and skin. "Can I play?" he asked diffidently.

Balettan gave him a look that would have desiccated a coconut. "No, you can't, Charlis," he said shortly, kicking the ball toward me, away from the interloper who'd rescued it.

Charlis's face lost its grin, leaving only the look of anxiety across it like a shadow. He remained seated on the wall, his leg — bare and thin below the grubby *mundu* he tied around his waist — dangling nervously. The game resumed, and Charlis watched, his eyes liquid with wistfulness. He would kick the brick wall aimlessly with his foot, then catch himself doing it and stop, looking furtively at us to see whether anyone had noticed. But no one paid any attention to him, except me, and I was the curious outsider.

"Why can't he play?" I finally found the courage to ask Balettan.

"Because he can't, that's all," replied my eldest cousin.

"But why? We can always use another player," I protested.

"We can't use *him*," Balettan said curtly. "Don't you understand anything, stupid?"

That was enough to silence me, because I had learned early on that there was a great deal about the village I didn't understand. A city upbringing didn't prepare you for your parents' annual return to their roots, to the world they'd left behind and failed to equip you for. Everything, pretty much, was different in my grandmother's house: there were hurricane lamps instead of electric lights, breezes instead of ceiling fans, a cow in the barn rather than a car in the garage. Water didn't come out of taps but from a well, in buckets laboriously raised by rope pulleys; you poured it over yourself out of metal vessels, hoping the maidservant who'd heated the bathwater over a charcoal fire had not made it so hot you'd scald yourself. There were the obscure indignities of having to be accompanied to the outhouse by an adult with a gleaming stainless-steel flashlight and of needing to hold his hand while you squatted in the privy, because the chairlike commodes of the city had made you unfit to discharge your waste as an Indian should, on his haunches. But it wasn't just a question of these inconveniences; there was the sense of being in a different world. Bombay was busy, bustling, unpredictable; there were children of every imaginable appearance, color, language, and religion in my school; it was a city of strangers jostling one another all the time. In my grandmother's village everyone I met seemed to know one another and be related. They dressed alike, did the same things day after day, shared the same concerns, celebrated the same festivals. Their lives were ordered, predictable; things were either done or not done, according to rules and assumptions I'd never been taught in the city.

Some of the rules were easier than others to grasp. There were, for instance, complicated hierarchies that everyone seemed to take for granted. The ones I first understood were those relating to age. This was absolute, like an unspoken commandment: everyone older had to be respected and obeyed, even if they sent you off on trivial errands they should really have done themselves. Then there was gender: the women existed to serve the men, fetching and carrying and stitching and hurrying for them, eating only after they had fed the men first. Even my mother, who could hold her own at a Bombay party with a cocktail in her hand, was transformed in Kerala into a dutiful drudge, blowing into the wood fire to make the endless stacks of thin, soft, crisp-edged *dosas* we all wolfed down. None of this had to be spelled out, no explicit orders given; people simply seemed to adjust naturally to an immutable pattern of expectations, where everyone knew his place and understood what he had to do. As someone who came from Bombay for a month's vacation every year, spoke the language badly, hated the bathrooms, and swelled up with insect bites, I adjusted less than most. I sensed dimly that the problem with Charlis, too, had something to do with hierarchy, but since he was neither female nor particularly young, I couldn't fit him into what I thought I already knew of Kerala village life.

We finished the game soon enough, and everyone began heading indoors. Charlis jumped off the wall. Instinctively, but acting with the casual hospitability I usually saw around me, I went up to him and said, "My mother'll be making *dosa*s for tea. Want some?"

I was puzzled by the look of near panic that flooded his face. "No, no, that's all right," he said, practically backing away from me. I could see Balettan advancing toward us. "I've got to go," Charlis added, casting me a strange look as he fled.

"What's the matter with him?" I asked Balettan.

"What's the matter with *you?*" he retorted. "What were you saying to him?"

"I just asked him to join us for some *dosa*s, that's all," I replied. Seeing his expression, I added lamely, "you know, with all the other kids."

Balettan shook his head in a combination of disgust and dismay, as if he didn't know whether to be angry or sad. "You know what this little foreigner did?" he announced loudly as soon as we entered the house. "He asked Charlis to come and have *dosa*s with us!"

This was greeted with guffaws by some and clucks of disapproval by others. "Poor little boy, what does he know?" said my favorite aunt, the widowed Rani-*valiamma*, gathering me to her ample bosom to offer a consolation I hadn't realized I needed. "It's not his fault."

"What's not my fault?" I asked, struggling free of her embrace. The Cuticura talcum powder in her cleavage tickled my nose, and the effort not to sneeze made me sound even more incoherent than usual. "Why shouldn't I invite him? He got our ball back for us. And you invite half the village anyway if they happen to pass by."

"Yes, but which half?" chortled Kunjunni-*mama*, a local layabout and distant relative who was a constant presence at our dining table and considered himself a great wit. "Which half, I say?" He laughed heartily at his own question, his eyes rolling, a honking sound emerging from the back of his nose.

I couldn't see why anyone else found this funny, but I was soon sent off to wash my hands. I sat down to my *dosa*s feeling as frustrated as a vegetarian at a kebab-shop.

"Who *is* Charlis, anyway?" I asked as my mother served me the mild chutney she made specially since I couldn't handle the fiery spiced version everyone else ate.

"I don't know, dear, just a boy from the village," she responded. "Now finish your *dosa*s, the adults have to eat."

"Charlis is the Prince of Wales, didn't you know?" honked Kunjunni-*mama*, enjoying himself hugely. "I thought you went to a convent school, Neel."

"First of all, only girls go to convent schools," I responded hotly. "And anyway the Prince of Wales is called Charles, not Charlis." I shot him a look of pure hatred, but he was completely unfazed. He soaked it in as a paddy field would a rainstorm, and honked some more.

"Charlis, Charles, what's the difference to an illiterate Untouchable with airs above his station? Anyway, that's how it sounded in Malayalam, and that's how he wrote it. Charlis. So you see how the Prince of Wales was born in Vanganassery." He exploded into self-satisfied mirth, his honks suggesting he was inhaling his own pencil-line mustache. I hadn't understood what he meant, but I vowed not to seek any further clarification from him.

My mother came to my rescue. I could see that her interest was piqued. "But why Charles?" she paused in her serving and asked Kunjunni-*mama*. "Are they Christians?"

"Christians?" Kunjunni-*mama* honked again. "My dear *chechi*, what do these people know of religion? Do they have any culture, any traditions? One of them, that cobbler fellow, Mandan, named his sons Mahatma Gandhi and Jawaharlal Nehru. Can you imagine? The fellow didn't even know that 'Mahatma' was a title and 'Nehru' a family surname. His brats were actually registered in school as M. Mahatma Gandhi and M. Jawaharlal Nehru. So of course when this upstart scavenger shopkeeper has to name *his* offspring, he went one better. Forget nationalism, he turned to the British royal family. So what if they had Christian names? So what if he couldn't pronounce them? You think Charlis is bad enough? He has two sisters, Elizabeth and Anne. Of course everyone in the village calls them Eli and Ana."

This time even I joined in the laughter: I had enough Malayalam to know that *Eli* meant "rat" and *Ana* meant "elephant." But a Bombayite sense of fairness asserted itself.

"It doesn't matter what his name is," I said firmly. "Charlis seems a nice boy. He went into the rubbish heap to get our ball. I liked him."

"Nice boy!" Kunjunni-*mama's* tone was dismissive, and this time there was no laughter in his honk. "Rubbish heaps are where they belong. They're not clean. They don't wash. They have dirty habits."

"What dirty habits?" I asked, shaking off my mother's restraining hand. "Who's *they?*"

"Eat your food," Kunjunni-*mama* said to me, adding, to no one in particular, "and now this Communist government wants to put them in our schools. With our children." He snorted. "They'll be drinking out of our wells next."

.   .   .

A few days later, the kids at home all decided to go to the local stream for a dip. On earlier Kerala holidays my mother had firmly denied me permission to go along, sure that if I didn't drown I'd catch a cold; but now I was older, I'd learned to swim, and I was capable of toweling myself dry, so I was allowed the choice. It seemed a fun idea, and in any case there was nothing better to do at home: I'd long since finished reading the couple of Biggles books I'd brought along. I set out with a sense of adventure.

We walked through dusty, narrow lanes, through the village, Balettan in the lead, half a dozen of the cousins following. For a while the houses we passed seemed to be those of relatives and friends; the kids waved cheerful greetings to women hanging up their washing, girls plaiting or picking lice out of each other's hair, bare-chested men in white *mundus* sitting magisterially in easy chairs, perusing the day's *Mathrubhumi*. Then the lane narrowed and the whitewashed, tile-roofed houses with verdant backyards gave way to thatched huts squeezed tightly together, their interiors shrouded in a darkness from which wizened crones emerged stooping through low-ceilinged doorways, the holes in their alarmingly stretched earlobes gaping like open mouths. The ground beneath our feet, uneven and stony, hurt to walk on, and a stale odor hung in the air, a compound of rotting vegetation and decaying flesh. Despair choked my breath like smoke. I began to wish I hadn't come along.

At last we left the village behind, and picked our way down a rocky, moss-covered slope to the stream. I didn't know what I'd expected, but it wasn't this, a meandering rivulet that flowed muddily through the fields. At the water's edge, on a large rock nearby, women were beating the dirt out of their saris; in the distance, a man squatted at a bend in the stream, picking his teeth and defecating. My cousins peeled off their shirts and ran into the water.

"Come on, Neel," Balettan exhorted me with a peremptory wave of the hand. "Don't be a sissy. It's not cold."

"Just don't feel like it," I mumbled. "It's okay. You go ahead. I'll watch."

They tried briefly to persuade me to change my mind, then left me to my own devices. I stood on the shore looking at them, heard their squeals of laughter, then looked away at the man who had completed his ablutions and was scooping water from the river to wash himself. Downstream from him, my cousins ducked their heads underwater. I quickly averted my gaze.

That was when I saw him. Charlis was sitting on a rocky overhang, a clean shirt over his *mundu,* a book in his hand. But his eyes weren't on it. He was looking down at the stream, where my cousins were playing.

I clambered over the rocks to him. When he spotted me he seemed to smile in recognition, then look around anxiously. But there was no one else about, and he relaxed visibly. "Neel," he said, smiling. "Aren't you swimming today?"

I shook my head. "Water's dirty," I said.

"Not dirty," he replied in Malayalam. "The stream comes from a sacred river. Removes all pollution."

I started to retort, then changed my mind. "So why don't you swim?" I asked.

"Ah, I do," he said. "But not here." His eyes avoided mine, but seemed to take in the stream, the washerwomen, my cousins. "Not now."

Bits of the half-understood conversation from the dining table floated awkwardly back into my mind. I changed the subject. "It was nice of you to get our ball back for us that day," I said.

"Ah, it was nothing." He smiled unexpectedly, his pockmarks creasing across his face. "My father beat me for it when I got home, though. I had ruined a clean shirt. Just after my bath."

"But I thought you people didn't —" I found myself saying. "I'm sorry," I finished lamely.

"Didn't what?" he asked evenly, but without looking at me. He was clearly some years older than me, but not much bigger. I wondered whether he was scared of me, and why.

"Nothing," I replied. "I'm really sorry your father beat you."

"Ah, that's all right. He does it all the time. It's for my own good."

"What does your father do?"

Charlis became animated by my interest. "He has a shop," he said, a light in his eyes. "In our part of the village. The Nair families don't come there, but he sells all sorts of nice things. Provisions and things. And on Thursdays, you know what he has? The best *halwa* in Vanganassery."

"Really? I like *halwa*." It was, in fact, the only Indian dessert I liked; Bombay had given me a taste for ice cream and chocolate rather than the deep-fried *laddoo*s and bricklike *Mysoor-paak* that were the Kerala favorites.

"You like *halwa?*" Charlis clambered to his feet. "Come on, I'll get you some."

This time it was my turn to hesitate. "No, thanks," I said, looking at my cousins cavorting in the water. "I don't think I should. They'll worry about me. And besides, I don't know my way about the village."

"That's okay," Charlis said. "I'll take you home. Come on." He saw the expression on my face. "It's really good *halwa*," he added.

That was enough for a nine-year-old. "Wait for me," I said, and ran down to the water's edge. "See you at home!" I called out to the others.

Balettan was the only one who noticed me. "Sure you can find your way back?" he asked, as my cousins splashed around him, one leaping onto his shoulders.

"I'll be okay," I replied, and ran back up the slope as Balettan went under.

.   .   .

Charlis left me at the bend in our lane, where all I had to do was to walk through a relative's yard to reach my grandmother's house. He would not come any farther, and I knew better than to insist. I walked slowly to the house, my mind full of the astonishment with which his father had greeted my presence in his shop, the taste of his sugary, milky tea still lingering on my palate, my hands full of the orange-colored wobbling slabs of *halwa* he had thrust upon me.

"Neel, my darling!" my mother exclaimed as I walked in. "Where have you been? I've been so worried about you."

"Look what I've got!" I said proudly, holding out the *halwa*. "And there's enough for everyone."

"Where did you get that?" Balettan asked, a white *thorthumundu*, a thin Kerala towel, in his hand, his hair still wet from his recent swim.

"Charlis gave it to me," I said. "I went to his father's shop. They —"

"You did *what?*" Balettan's rage was frightening. He advanced toward me.

"I — I —"

"Went to Charlis's shop?" He loomed over me, the towel draped over his shoulder making him look even older and more threatening. "Took food from Untouchables?" I began to shrink back from him. "Give that to me!"

"I won't!" I snatched the *halwa* away from his hands, and as he lunged, I turned and ran, the precious sweet sticky in my grasp. But he was too fast for me; I had barely reached the yard when he caught up, seized me roughly by the shoulders, and turned me around to face him.

"We don't do this here, understand?" he breathed fiercely. "This isn't Bombay." He pried my hands apart. The *halwa* gleamed in my palms. "Drop it," he commanded.

"No," I wanted to say, but the word would not emerge. I wanted to cry out for my mother, but she did not come out of the house.

"Drop it," Balettan repeated, his voice a whiplash across what remained of my resistance.

Slowly I opened my hands outward in a gesture of submission. The orange slabs slid reluctantly off them. It seemed to me they took an age to fall, their gelatinous surfaces clinging to the soft skin of my palms until the last possible moment. Then they were gone, fallen, into the dust.

Balettan looked at them on the ground for a moment, then at me, and spat upon them where they lay. "The dogs can have them," he barked. He kicked more dust over them, then pulled me by the arm back toward the house. "Don't you ever do this again."

I burst into tears then, and at last the words came, tripping over themselves as I stumbled back into the house. "I hate you! All of you! You're horrible and mean and cruel and I'll never come back here as long as I live!"

.   .   .

But of course I was back the next year; I hardly had any choice in the matter. For my parents, first-generation migrants to the big city, this was the vital visit home, to their own parents and siblings, to the friends and family they had left behind; it renewed them, it returned them to a sense of themselves, it maintained their connection to the past. I just came along because I was too young to be left behind, indeed too young to be allowed the choice.

In the year that had passed since my last visit, there had been much ferment in Kerala. Education was now universal and compulsory and free, so all sorts of children were flocking to school who had never been able to go before. There was talk of land reform, and giving title to tenant farmers; I understood nothing of this, but saw the throngs around men with microphones on the roadside, declaiming angry harangues I could not comprehend. None of this seemed, however, to have much to do with us, or to affect the unchanging rhythms of life at my grandmother's house.

My cousins were numerous and varied, the children of my mother's brothers and sisters and also of *her* cousins, who lived in the neighboring houses; sometimes the relationship was less clear than that, but as they all ran about together and slept side by side like a camping army on mats on the floor of my grandmother's *thalam*, it was difficult to tell who was a first cousin and who an uncle's father-in-law's sister's grandson. After all, it was also *their* holiday season, and my parents' return was an occasion for everyone to congregate in the big house. On any given day, with my cousins joined by other children from the village, there could be as many as a dozen kids playing in the courtyard or going to the stream or breaking up for cards on the back porch. Sometimes I joined them, but sometimes, taking advantage of the general confusion, I would slip away unnoticed, declining to make the effort to scale the barriers of language and education and attitude that separated us, and sit alone with a book. Occasionally someone would come and look for me. Most often, that someone was my aunt Rani-*valiamma*.

As a young widow, she didn't have much of a life. Deprived of the status that a husband would have given her, she seemed to walk on the fringes of the house; it had been whispered by her late husband's family that only the bad luck her stars had brought into his life could account for his fatal heart attack at the age of thirty-six, and a whiff of stigma clung to her like a cloying perfume she could never quite wash off. Remarriage was out of the question, nor could the family allow her to make her own way in the world; so she returned to the village house she had left as a bride, and tried to lose herself in the routines of my grandmother's household. She sublimated her misfortune in random and frequent acts of kindness, of which I was a favored beneficiary. She would bring me well-sugared lime-and-water from the kitchen without being asked, and whenever one of us brought down a green mango from the ancient tree with a lucky throw of a stone, she could be counted upon to return with it chopped up and marinated in just the right combination of salt and red chili powder to drive my taste buds to ecstasy.

One day Rani-*valiamma* and I were upstairs, eating deviled raw mango and looking out on the kids playing soccer below, when I saw something and nearly choked. "Isn't that Charlis?" I asked, pointing to the skinny boy who had just failed to save a goal.

"Could be," she replied indifferently. "Let me see — yes, that's Charlis."

"But he's playing in our yard! I remember last year —"

"That was last year," Rani-*valiamma* said, and I knew that change had come to the village.

But not enough of it. When the game was over, the Nair kids trooped in as usual to eat, without Charlis. When I asked innocently where he was, it was Balettan, inevitably, who replied.

"We play with him at school, and we play with him outside," he said. "But playing stops at the front door."

I didn't pursue the matter. I had learned that whenever any of the Untouchable tradespeople came to the house, they were dealt with outside.

With each passing vacation, though, the changes became more and more apparent. For years my grandmother, continuing a tradition handed down over generations, had dispensed free medication (mainly aspirins and cough syrup) once a week to the poor villagers who queued for it; then a real clinic was established in the village by the government, and her amateur charity was no longer needed. Electricity came to Vanganassery: my uncle strung up a brilliant neon light above the dining table, and the hurricane lamps began to disappear, along with the tin cans of kerosene from which they were fueled. The metal vessels in the bathroom were replaced by shiny red plastic mugs. A toilet was installed in the outhouse for my father's, and my, convenience. And one year, one day, quite naturally, Charlis stepped into the house with the other kids after a game.

No one skipped a beat; it was as if everyone had agreed to pretend there was nothing unusual. Charlis stood around casually, laughing and chatting; some of the kids sat to eat, others awaited their turn. No one invited Charlis to sit or to eat, and he made no move himself to do either. Then those who had eaten rose and washed their hands and joined the chatter, while those who had been with Charlis took their places at the table. Still Charlis stood and talked, his manner modest and respectful, until everyone but he had finished eating, and then they all strolled out again to continue their game.

"Charlis hasn't eaten," I pointed out to the womenfolk.

"I know, child, but what can we do?" Rani-*valiamma* asked. "He can't sit at our table or be fed on our plates. Even you know that."

"It isn't fair," I said, but without belligerence. What she had stated was, I knew, like a law of nature. Even the servants would not wash a plate off which an Untouchable had eaten.

"You know," honked Kunjunni-*mama*, tucking into his third helping, "They say that boy is doing quite well at school. Very well, in fact."

"He stood first in class last term," a younger cousin chimed in.

"First!" I exclaimed. "And Balettan failed the year, didn't he?"

"Now, why would you be asking that?" chortled Kunjunni-*mama* meaningfully, slapping his thigh with his free hand.

I ignored the question and turned to my aunt. "He's smarter than all of us, and we can't even give him something to eat?"

Rani-*valiamma* saw the expression on my face and squeezed my hand. "Don't worry," she whispered. "I'll think of something."

She did; and the next time Charlis walked in, he was served food on a plantain leaf on the floor, near the back door. I was too embarrassed to hover near him as I had intended to, but he seemed to eat willingly enough on his own.

"It's just not right!" I whispered to her as we watched him from a discreet distance.

"*He* doesn't mind," she whispered back. "Why should you?"

And it was true that Charlis probably ate on the floor in his own home.

When he had finished, a mug of water was given to him on the back porch, so that he could wash his hands without stepping into our bathroom. And the plantain leaf was thrown away: no plate to wash.

We returned to the game, and now it was my turn to miskick. The ball cleared the low wall at one end of the courtyard, hit the side of the well, teetered briefly on the edge, and fell in with a splash.

It had happened before. "Go and get it, *da*," Balettan languidly commanded one of the kids. The well was designed to be climbed into: bricks jutted out from the inside wall at regular intervals, and others had been removed to provide strategic footholds. But this was a slippery business: since the water levels in the well rose and fell, the inside surface was pretty slimy, and many of those who'd gone in to retrieve a floating object, or a bucket that had slipped its rope, had ended up taking an unplanned dip. The young cousin who had received Balettan's instruction hesitated, staring apprehensively into the depths of the well.

"Don't worry," Charlis said quietly. "I'll get it." He moved toward the edge of the well.

"No!" There was nothing languid now about Balettan's tone; we could all hear the alarm in his voice. "I'll do it myself." And Charlis, one half-raised foot poised to climb onto the well, looked at him, his face drained of expression, comprehension slowly burning into his cheeks. Balettan ran forward, roughly pushing aside the boy who had been afraid to go, and vaulted into the well.

I looked at Rani-*valiamma*, who had been watching the game.

"Balettan's right," she said. "Do you think anyone would have drunk water at our house again if Charlis had gone into our well?"

.   .   .

Years passed; school holidays, and trips to Kerala, came and went. Governments fell and were replaced in Kerala, farm laborers were earning the highest daily wage in the country, and my almost toothless grandmother was sporting a chalk-white set of new dentures under her smile. Yet the house seemed much the same as before. A pair of ceiling fans had been installed, in the two rooms where family members congregated; a radio crackled with the news from Delhi; a tap made its appearance in the bathroom, though the pipe attached to it led from the same old well. These improvements, and the familiarity that came from repeated visits, made the old privations bearable. Kerala seemed less of a penance with each passing year.

Charlis was a regular member of the group now, admitted to our cardplaying sessions on the porch outside, joining us on our expeditions to the cinema in the nearest town. But fun and games seemed to hold a decreasing attraction for Charlis. He was developing a reputation as something of an intellectual. He would ask me, in painstaking textbook English, about something he had read about the great wide world outside, and listen attentively to my reply. I was, in the quaint vocabulary of the villagers, "convent-educated," a label they applied to anyone who emerged from the elite schools in which Christian missionaries served their foreign Lord by teaching the children of the Indian lordly. It was assumed that I knew more about practically everything than anyone in the village; but all I knew was what I had been taught from books, whereas they had learned from life. Even as I wallowed in their admiration, I couldn't help feeling their lessons were the more difficult, and the more valuable.

Balettan dropped out of school and began turning his attention to what remained of the family lands. It seemed to me that his rough edges became rougher as the calluses grew hard on his hands and feet. He had less time for us now; in his late teens he was already a full-fledged farmer, sitting sucking a straw between his teeth and watching the boys kick a ball around. If he disapproved of Charlis's growing familiarity with all of us, though, he did not show it — not even when Charlis asked me one day to go into town with him to see the latest Bombay blockbuster.

I thought Charlis might have hoped I could explain the Hindi dialogue to him, since Keralites learned Hindi only as a third language from teachers who knew it, at best, as a second. But when we got to the movie theater, Charlis was not disappointed to discover the next two screenings were fully sold out. "I am really wanting to talk," he said in English, leading me to an eatery across the street.

The Star of India, as the board outside proclaimed, was a "military hotel"; in other words, it served meat, which my grandmother did not. "I am thinking you might be missing it," Charlis said, ushering me to a chair. It was only when the main dish arrived that I realized that I was actually sitting and eating at the same table with Charlis for the first time.

If he was conscious of this, Charlis didn't show it. He began talking, hesitantly at first, then with growing fluency and determination, about his life and his ambitions. His face shone when he talked of his father, who beat him with a belt whenever he showed signs of neglecting his books. "You can do better than I did," he would say before bringing the whip down on Charlis. "You will do better."

And now Charlis was aiming higher than anyone in his family, in his entire community, had ever done before. He was planning to go to university.

"Listen, Charlis," I said gently, not wanting to discourage him. "You know it's not going to be easy. I know you're first in class and everything, but that's in the village. Don't forget you'll be competing for places with kids from the big cities. From the — convents."

"I am knowing that," Charlis replied simply. Then, from the front pocket of his shirt, he drew out a battered notebook filled with small, tightly packed curlicues of Malayalam lettering in blue ink, interspersed with phrases and sentences in English in the same precise hand. "Look," he said, jabbing at a page. "The miserable hath no other medicine / But only hope. — Shakespeare, *Measure for Measure*, III.i.2," I read. And a little lower down, "Men at some time are masters of their fates; / The fault, dear Brutus, is not in our stars, / But in ourselves, that we are underlings." Charlis had underlined these words.

"Whenever I am reading something that inspires me, I am writing it down in this book," Charlis said proudly. "Shakespeare is great man, isn't it?"

His Malayalam was of course much better, but in English Charlis seemed to cast off an invisible burden that had less to do with the language than with its social assumptions. In speaking it, in quoting it, Charlis seemed to be entering another world, a heady place of foreign ideas and unfamiliar expressions, a strange land in which the old rules no longer applied.

"'For the Colonel's Lady an' Judy O'Grady,' " he declaimed at one point, "'are sisters under their skins!' — Rudyard Kipling," he added. "Is that how you are pronouncing it?"

"Rudyard, Roodyard, I haven't a clue," I confessed. "But who cares, Charlis? He's just an old imperialist fart. What does anything he ever wrote have to do with any of us today, in independent India?"

Charlis looked surprised, then slightly averted his eyes. "But are we not," he asked softly, "are we not brothers under our skins?"

"Of course," I replied, too quickly. And it was I who couldn't meet his gaze.

The following summer, I was sitting down to my first meal of the holiday at my grandmother's dining table when Rani-*valiamma* said, "Charlis was looking for you."

"Really?" I was genuinely pleased, as much by Charlis's effort as by the fact that it could be mentioned so casually. "What did he want?"

"He came to give you the news personally," Rani-*valiamma* said. "He's been admitted to Trivandrum University."

"Wow!" I exclaimed. "That's something, isn't it?"

"Untouchable quota," honked the ever-present Kunjunni-*mama*, whose pencil-line mustache had gone from bold black to sleek silver without his ever having done a stroke of work in his life.

"Reserved seats for the Children of God. Why, Chandrasekhara Menon's son couldn't get in after all the money they spent on sending him to boarding school, and here Charlis is on his way to University."

"The village *panchayat* council is organizing a felicitation for him tomorrow," Rani-*valiamma* said. "Charlis wanted you to come, Neel."

"Of course I will," I responded. "We must all go."

"All?" snorted Kunjunni-*mama*, who was incapable of any action that could be called affirmative. "To felicitate Charlis? Speak for yourself, boy. If you want to attend an Untouchable love-in organized by the Communists who claim to represent our village, more's the pity. But don't expect to drag any members of the Nair community with you."

"I'll come with you, Neel," said a quiet voice by my side. It was Rani-*valiamma*, her ever-obliging manner transformed into something approaching determination.

"And me," chirped a younger cousin, emboldened. "May I go too, Amma?" asked another. And by the next evening I had assembled a sizable delegation from our extended family to attend the celebration for Charlis.

Kunjunni-*mama* and Balettan sat at the table, nursing their cups of tea, and watched us all troop out. Balettan was silent, his manner distant rather than disapproving. As I passed them, I heard the familiar honk: "Felicitation, my foot."

The speeches had begun when we arrived, and our entry sparked something of a commotion in the meeting hall, as Charlis's relatives and the throng of well-wishers from his community made way for us, whispers of excitement and consternation rippling like a current through the room. I thought I saw a look of sheer delight shine like a sunburst on Charlis's face, but that may merely have been a reaction to hearing the *panchayat* president say, "The presence of all of you here today proves that Charlis's achievement is one of which the *entire* village is proud." We applauded that, knowing our arrival had given some meaning to that trite declaration.

After the speeches, and the garlanding, and Charlis's modest reply, the meeting broke up. I wanted to congratulate Charlis myself, but he was surrounded by his own people, all proud and happy and laughing. We made our way toward the door, and then I heard his voice.

"Neel! Wait!" he called out. I turned, to see him pulling himself away from the crush and advancing toward me with a packet in his hands. "You mustn't leave without this."

He stretched out the packet toward me, beaming. I opened it and peered in. Orange slabs of *halwa* quivered inside.

"It's the last bag," Charlis said, the smile never fading from his face.

"My father sold the shop to pay for me to go to university. We're all moving to Trivandrum." I looked at him, finding no words. He pushed the *halwa* at me. "I wanted you to have it."

I took the bag from him without a word. We finished the *halwa* before we got home.

· · ·

Years passed. Men landed on the moon, a woman became prime minister, wars were fought; in other countries, coups and revolutions brought change (or attempted to), while in India elections were won and lost and things changed (or didn't). I couldn't go down to Kerala every time my parents did; my college holidays didn't always coincide with Dad's leave from the office. When I did manage a visit, it wasn't the same as before. I would come for a few days, be indulged by Rani-*valiamma*, and move on. There was not that much to do. Rani-*valiamma* had started studying for a teacher's training diploma. My grandmother spent most of her time reading the scriptures and chewing areca, usually simultaneously. Balettan, tough and taciturn, was the man of the house; now that agriculture was his entire life, we had even less to say to each other than ever. My cousins were scattered in several directions; a new generation of kids played football in the yard. No one had news of Charlis.

I began working in an advertising agency in Bombay, circulating in a brittle, showy world that could not have had less in common with Vanganassery. When I went to the village the talk was of pesticides and irrigation, of the old rice-levy and the new, government-subsidized fertilizer, and, inevitably, of the relentless pace of land reform, which was taking away the holdings of traditional landlords and giving them to their tenants. It was clear that Balettan did not understand much of this, and that he had not paid a great deal of attention to what was happening.

"Haven't you received any notification from the authorities, Balettan?" I asked him one day, when his usual reticence seemed only to mask ineffectually the mounting level of anxiety in his eyes.

"Some papers came," he said in a tone whose aggressiveness betrayed his deep shame at his own inadequacy. "But do I have time to read them? I'm a busy man. Do I run a farm or push papers like a clerk?"

"Show them to Neel," Kunjunni-*mama* suggested, and as soon as I opened the first envelope I realized Balettan, high-school dropout and traditionalist, had left it too late.

"What are these lands here, near Kollengode?"

"They're ours, of course."

"Not anymore, Balettan. Who's T. Krishnan Nair, son of Kandath Narayananunni Nair?"

"He farms them for us, ever since Grandfather died. I farm here at Vanganassery, and Krishnan Nair takes care of Kollengode, giving us his dues after each harvest. It's the only way. I can't be at both places at the same time, can I?"

"Well, it says here he's just been registered as the owner of those lands. You were given fourteen days to show cause as to why his claim should not have been admitted. Why didn't you file an objection, Balettan?"

We were all looking at him. "How can they say Krishnan Nair owns our land? Why, everybody knows it's our land. It's been ours ever since anyone can remember. It was ours before Grandmother was born."

"It's not ours anymore, Balettan. The government has just taken it away."

Balettan shifted uneasily in his chair, a haunted, uncomprehending look on his face. "But they can't do that," he said. "Can they?"

"They can, Balettan," I told him sadly. "You know they can."

"We've got to do something," honked Kunjunni-*mama* with uncharacteristic urgency. "Neel, you've got to do something."

"Me? What can I do? I'm a Bombay-wallah. I know less about all this than any of you."

"Perhaps," admitted Kunjunni-*mama*. "But you're an educated man. You can read and understand these documents. You can speak to the Collector. He's the top IAS man in the district, probably another city type like you, convent-educated. You can speak to him in English and explain what has happened. Come on, Neel. You've got to do it."

"I don't know," I said dubiously. The advertising life had not brought me into contact with any senior Indian Administrative Service officers. I hadn't the slightest idea what I would say to the Collector when I met him.

And then I saw the look in Balettan's eyes. He had grown up knowing instinctively the rules and rituals of village society, the cycles of the harvest, how to do the right thing and what was never done. He could, without a second thought, climb trees that would make most of us dizzy, descend into wells, stand knee-deep in the slushy water of a paddy field to sprout grain into the world. But all these were skills he was born with, rhythms that sang in his blood like the whisper of his mother's breath. He wore a *mundu* around his waist, coaxed his buffalo across the fields, and treated his laborers and his family as his ancestors had done for thousands of years. He was good at the timeless realities of village India; but India, even village India, was no longer a timeless place. "Don't you understand anything, stupid?" he had asked me all those years ago; and in his eyes I saw what I imagined he must have seen, at that time, in mine.

"I'll go," I said, as Balettan averted his eyes. In relief, perhaps, or in gratitude. It didn't matter which.

.   .   .

The Collector's office in Palghat, the district capital, was already besieged by supplicants when I arrived. Two greasy clerks presided over his antechamber, their desks overflowing with papers loosely bound in crumbling files held together with string. Three phones rang intermittently, and were answered in a wide variety of tones, ranging from the uncooperative to the unctuous, depending on who was calling. People crowded round the desks, seeking attention, thrusting slips of paper forward, folding hands in entreaty, shouting to be heard. Occasionally a paper was dealt with and a khaki-uniformed peon sent for to carry it somewhere; sometimes, people were sent away, though most seemed to be waved toward the walls where dozens were already waiting, weary resignation on their faces, for their problems to be dealt with. All eyes were on the closed teak door at the corner, bearing the brass nameplate

M. C. THEKKOTE, I.A.S., behind which their destinies were no doubt being determined.

"It's hopeless," I said to Balettan, who had accompanied me. "I told you we should have tried to get an appointment. We'll be here all day."

"How would we have got an appointment?" Balettan asked, reasonably, since we did not yet have a phone in the village. "No, this is the only way. You go and give them your card."

I did not share Balettan's faith in the magical properties of this small rectangular advertisement of my status, but I battled my way to the front of one of the desks and thrust it at an indifferent clerk.

"Please take this to the Collector-*saare*," I said, trying to look both important and imploring. "I must see him."

The clerk seemed unimpressed by the colorful swirls and curlicues that proclaimed my employment by AdAge, Bombay's smartest new agency. "You and everyone else," he said skeptically, putting the card aside. "Collector-*saare* very busy today. You come back tomorrow, we will see."

At this point Balettan's native wisdom asserted itself. He insinuated a five-rupee note into the clerk's palm. "Send the card in," he said. "It's important."

The clerk was instantly responsive. "I am doing as you wish," he said grudgingly. "But you will still have to wait. Collector-*saare* is so so very busy today."

"You've told us that already," I replied. "We'll wait."

A peon wandered in, bearing tea for the clerks. Once the man at the desk had satisfied himself that his tea was sugared to his taste, he added my card to the pile of papers he gave the peon to take in to the Collector. "It will take some time," he added curtly.

It didn't. Soon after the door had closed behind the peon, the black phone on the clerk's desk jangled peremptorily. "Yes, saar. Yes, saar," he said, perspiring. "No, saar. Not long. Yes, saar. At once, saar." He had stood up to attention during this exchange, and when he replaced the receiver there was a new look of respect in his eyes. "Collector-*saare* will be seeing you now, saar," he said, with a *salaam*. "You didn't explain who you were, saar." The five-rupee note re-emerged in his hand. "You seem to have dropped this by mistake, saar," he said shamefacedly, handing it to Balettan.

"Keep it," Balettan said, as mystified as I by the transformation in the man's attitude. But the clerk begged him to take it back, and bowed and scraped us toward the imposing doorway.

"Obviously Bombay's ad world counts for more than I thought with these government-wallahs," I whispered to Balettan.

"He's just happy to be able to speak English with someone," Balettan suggested.

The clerk opened the door into a high-ceilinged office. The Collector rose from behind a mahogany desk the size of a Ping-Pong table, and stretched out a hand. "It's so good to see you again, Neel," he said.

It was Charlis.

"Charlis!" I exclaimed, astonishment overcoming delight. "B-but — the name — the IAS —"

"You never did know my family name, did you? After all these years." Charlis spoke without reproach. "And yes, I've been in the IAS for some time now." The Administrative Service, too, I found myself thinking unworthily, offered one more of the quotas Kunjunni-*mama* liked to complain about. "But this is the first time I've been posted so close to Vanganassery. I've barely got here, but once I've settled in, I'm planning to visit the village again soon." He added casually, "It's part of my district, after all. That'd make it an official visit, you see."

He seemed to enjoy the thought, and I found myself looking at Balettan. I didn't know what I expected to find in his expression, but it certainly wasn't the combination of hope, respect, and, yes, admiration with which he now regarded the man across the desk.

Charlis seemed to catch it, too. "But what is this? We haven't even asked Balettan to sit down." He waved us to chairs, as tea appeared. "Tell me, what can I do for you?"

We explained the problem, and Charlis was sympathetic but

grave. The law was the law; it was also just, undoing centuries of absentee landlordism. In our case, though, thanks to Balettan's inattention (though Charlis didn't even imply that), it had been applied unfairly, leaving Balettan with less land than his former tenant. Some of this could be undone, and Charlis would help, but we would not be able to get back all the land that had been confiscated. Charlis explained all this carefully, patiently, speaking principally to Balettan rather than to me. "Some changes are good, some are bad," he concluded, "but very few changes can be reversed."

"Shakespeare or Rudyard Kipling?" I asked, only half in jest, remembering his little notebook.

"Neither," he replied quite seriously. "Charlis Thekkote. But you can quote me if you like."

Charlis was as good as his word. He helped Balettan file the necessary papers to reclaim some of his land, and made sure the files were not lost in the bureaucratic maze. And the week after our visit, knowing I would not be staying in Vanganassery long, Charlis came to the village.

I will never forget the sight of Charlis seated at our dining table with the entire family bustling attentively around him: Rani-*valiamma*, on leave from the school where she was now vice-principal, serving him her soft, crisp-edged *dosa*s on Grandmother's best stainless-steel *thali*; Kunjunni-*mama*, honking gregariously, pouring him more tea; and half the neighbors, standing at a respectful distance, gawking at the dignitary.

But the image that will linger longest in my memory is from even before that, from the moment of Charlis's arrival at the village. His official car cannot drive the last half-mile to our house, on the narrow paths across the paddy fields, so Charlis steps down, in his off-white safari suit and open-toed sandals, and walks to our front door, through the dust. We greet him there and begin to usher him into the house, but Balettan stops us outside. For a minute all the old fears come flooding back into my mind and Charlis's, but it is only for a minute, because Balettan is shouting out to the servant, "Can't you see the Collector-*saare* is waiting? Hurry up!"

I catch Charlis's eye; he smiles. The servant pulls a bucketful of water out of the well to wash Charlis's feet.

.   .   .

This story is about change, democratic change, the kind that India has sought to promote for fifty years since independence. It has worked better in Kerala — where successive Communist governments have sublimated their revolutionary zeal in favor of evolutionary change — than elsewhere, but change has occurred all over India. Some seventy of India's 365 districts are headed by IAS administrators who, like Charlis, belong to the Scheduled Castes or Tribes. And the most striking change in my story is in the one institution that most foreigners still associate with India, caste.

Caste, like *Hindu* and *curry*, is a word invented by outsiders to describe what Indians understand without precise definition. This ancient system of dividing society was rejected by Mahatma Gandhi and the Indian nationalist movement as entrenching discrimination, but it has persisted in Indian society nonetheless. Caste began, quite simply, as apartheid; the original term for it, *varna*, meant "color" in Sanskrit, and the caste system was probably invented by the light-skinned Aryans who invaded north India in about 1500 B.C. to put down the darker-hued indigenes. A verse of the Rig Veda enshrines the original fourfold caste division: when God made Man, the verse says, the learned, priestly Brahmin emerged from his forehead, the warrior Kshatriya from his arms, the farmer-merchant Vaishya from his thighs, and the laborer-artisan Sudra from his feet. The Untouchables lay even beyond this caste classification, and were therefore literally outcasts; one outcast group, the Parayans of Kerala, gave the English language the word that best defines their condition — *pariah*. (And, to make matters more complicated, within each caste are innumerable subcastes, for instance subcastes of potters, of scribes, of tanners, and so on.)

Over centuries of intermixing, which have given India perhaps the world's most hetero-hued population (with skin color often varying startlingly even within a single family), color gave way to occupation as the determining factor of caste. Members of the same caste usually worked in the same profession, married and ate within their caste groups, and tended to look down (or up, depending on their place on the social ladder) on other castes. Caste rules acquired rigidity over millennia: Brahmins would not eat food cooked by non-Brahmins; Untouchables, who performed such "polluting" tasks as disposing of waste or handling carcasses, could not draw water from wells reserved for the upper castes, or live in upper-caste areas; Brahmins would feel obliged to bathe afresh if the shadow of an Untouchable fell across them; only caste Hindus could worship at the village temples; in some states, only upper-caste men could twirl their mustaches upward; in others, lower-caste women had to bare their breasts before their betters. Intimate contact, let alone marriage, across caste lines became unthinkable, except in the context of a master-servant relationship.

The lower castes also tended to be exploited (for their labor, their services, and sometimes their bodies) by the higher ones, who taught them that their inferior status was part of the natural order of things, that conformity and good behavior might lead to their being reborn in a higher caste in their next life, and that in the meantime they were to do as they were told. This was their *dharma*, the code of right conduct in accordance with which each Hindu must live. Only by honoring caste rules and fulfilling the *dharma* his caste enjoined upon him could a good Hindu hope to be reincarnated in a better life. Interpreted literally by the unimaginative, this would mean that caste oppression was good because it upheld the natural order.

Looking at the prohibitions imposed by caste, and the prejudice and discrimination it permitted, it is easy to see why Gandhi and the more enlightened of India's nationalists, anxious to unite the country against the foreign colonizer, campaigned passionately against the caste system. They were hardly new in this: Siddhartha, the Buddha, had preached against the iniquities of caste in 500 B.C. But caste survived his attempts at reform as it did those of Mahavira, the founder of Jainism, and two thousand years later the efforts of Nanak, the founder of Sikhism. Even Christian missionaries found themselves adapting to the realities of caste: Portuguese churches in Goa reputedly have two doors, one for Brahmin Christians, the other for lower-caste converts. Reform movements within Hinduism ranged from the Brahmo Samaj of Rammohan Roy in the early 1800s to the lower-caste spiritualism of Kerala's Sree Narayana Guru nearly a century later; Gandhi crusaded against caste, and Ambedkar, himself an Untouchable, outlawed Untouchability as the principal drafter of free India's constitution. But still it has persisted, though its hold on educated urban Indians is slipping.

Most educated Indians, proud of their country's record in opposing racial discrimination in South Africa and elsewhere, are embarrassed by a part of their heritage that enshrines bigotry. Today a significant proportion of the matrimonial advertisements placed in India's English-language newspapers state that "caste [is] no bar" to an otherwise suitable alliance (looks, finances, career prospects, and class have outstripped caste among the considerations favored by the spouse-hunting middle class). In any case, India's teeming cities offer inconvenient ground for the petty prohibitions of caste; it is hardly possible to know the caste of the straphanger rubbing shoulders with you on the bus or jostling past you on the street, or for that matter of the cook who made the meal you ate in an anonymous restaurant. Modern life obliges you to shake the hands of, lunch with, and (thanks to India's extraordinary affirmative-action program) take orders from people of lower castes, or of no caste at all. Education and economics, not caste, account for today's inequalities, and the stigma of caste is disappearing more rapidly in Indian cities than that of race in the United States. (As the Indian sociologist André Béteille once pointedly told an American interviewer, "Your blacks are visible. Ours are not.") Urban India — and India is increasingly urbanized; some 26 percent of the population live in cities today, a more than 50 percent increase since 1961 — has made giant strides toward achieving Gandhi's dream of a casteless society.

Which is not to say that the crushing reality of caste oppression has disappeared from the Indian countryside. Despite fifty years of freedom, well-trained and enlightened administrators, and politically correct rhetoric at all levels, caste continues to enslave village society. Each week brings a new horror story into the national press. A Dalit woman is stripped and paraded naked through the streets of her village because her son dared to steal from an upper-caste Thakur; she is then forced to have sex with the offending boy before a sneering audience of Thakurs. A highborn Jat girl falls in love with an Untouchable boy and is caught trying to elope with him; they and their accomplice, another Untouchable, are caught, beaten, tortured in front of their families, and hanged, and their bodies are then burned (the girl is not immediately killed by her noose, and is still alive when the fire is lit; she tries to crawl out, but is thrown back into the flames). In one village, twenty-two "uppity" Untouchables are gunned down in an upper-caste massacre; in another, four hundred Dalit families are burned out of their huts for daring to demand the legal minimum wage for their labors. These are not isolated incidents, in that dozens like them are reported every year. But on the other hand they are not cause for despair about the prospects of social change in rural India. Indeed, they are evidence of resistance to change rather than of the impossibility of it. The victims of these crimes had dared to challenge the proscriptions of the traditionalists; they had tried to lift the dead weight of the ages off their backs. As political equality, guaranteed by the vote, brings democratic clout, the lower castes are inevitably demanding social equality as well, and increasingly obtaining it. For each one who fails, a dozen, across India, are succeeding in casting off their shackles.

At the same time, it is important to realize that the incidents I have described are not simple acts of criminality committed by people from whom society should be protected. In fact, the greater horror lies in the fact that they are people who might not otherwise commit any crime and who believe that, by their actions, they are upholding society rather than endangering it. Such people must be brought to justice and punished for their crimes, but the real solution to the attitudes they represent lies in their increasing irrelevance. Change has already come to India, and it is accelerating. A recent seven-year-long study by the the Anthropological Survey of India has strikingly demonstrated the extent to which the link between caste and occupation has been broken in independent India.

At the same time, politics has inevitably transformed caste. It is amusing for an Indian to follow the impassioned debates about affirmative action in America, when all it involves is a pale shadow of the world's first and most rigorous affirmative-action program, written into the Indian Constitution by a former Untouchable, the Columbia University–educated lawyer and statesman Dr. B. R. Ambedkar. (Ambedkar himself led his followers in a mass conversion to Buddhism, to escape the stigma of Untouchability within Hinduism.)

Independent India's determination to compensate for millennia of injustice to its social underclasses meant that, from the very first, the "Scheduled Castes and Tribes" (so called because the eligible groups of Dalits and aboriginals were listed in a "schedule" annexed to the Constitution) were granted guaranteed admissions to schools and colleges even where their grades would not have justified it; 22.5 percent of all government jobs, both in officialdom and in the public-sector industries, were reserved for them; and, uniquely, they were assured representation in Parliament, where 85 seats out of 545 are set aside for members of the Scheduled Castes and Scheduled Tribes to ensure their representation in the legislature. This last is an extraordinary provision in the annals of democracy, because it means that a caste Hindu (or, for that matter, a Muslim or a Christian) from an area that falls into a reserved constituency cannot seek to represent his own neighbors in Parliament, because only Scheduled Caste candidates are eligible to contest the seat.

The Scheduled Tribes, also known as the Adivasis, or "original inhabitants," include some four hundred aboriginal communities, mainly inhabiting remote and forested areas of the country. In the 1991 census they amounted to some 66 million people, just under 8 percent of India's population. The Scheduled Castes were twice that number, and occupied the lowest economic and social strata of Indian society, living in segregated areas in many villages, and suffering discrimination and oppression. The newest beneficiaries of affirmative action, the "Other

Backward Classes" (known to everyone, with the Indian penchant for acronyms, as the OBCs), are as numerous as the Scheduled Tribes and Scheduled Castes combined — indeed, depending on who is doing the counting, they may constitute a majority of the Indian population. (No one can be entirely certain, since castes have not been counted by Indian census takers since 1931, i.e., in the last seven censuses). The OBCs are the thrusting lower middle castes of Indian society, whose claim on reservations (quotas) and similar benefits was supported by the Mandal Commission in 1980 and upheld by the Supreme Court in a land-mark judgment in 1992. The decision of the V. P. Singh government to implement the Mandal recommendations in 1990 sparked a wave of upper-caste protests and self-immolations that was as intense as it was short-lived. Today the Mandal recommendations are state policy, and the protests are forgotten, except by the grieving relatives of the protesters. And "backward" and Dalit politicians have not just come to power in an unprecedented number of states — with an Untouchable woman, Mayawati, of the Dalit Bahujan Samaj ("Majority People's") Party, briefly ruling India's most populous and tradition-bound state, Uttar Pradesh, in the Gangetic heartland — but they also control the central government for the first time. The twenty-one-member cabinet of United Front prime minister H. D. Deve Gowda (himself a "back-ward" of the Vokkaliga or ploughman subcaste, who herded sheep as a child and learned his lessons by candlelight) contains only two members of the upper castes.

India's brand of affirmative action guarantees outcomes, not just opportunities, and yet it has aroused far less open hostility within the country (prior to the anti-Mandal agitation) than the far more mod-est, and far more recent, American equivalent. Indeed, so complete was the country's acceptance of the principle of affirmative action that the clamor to join the bandwagon of reservations grew, and led to more and more groups wanting reservations of their own. The addition of the "backward classes" as recommended by the Mandal Commission has now taken the total of reserved jobs in the federal government and national governmental institutions to 49.5 percent, and in several states the local reservations are even higher, extending to some 69 percent in Tamil Nadu. Increasing literacy is making its own contribution: if the lower castes are only 35 percent literate, that is still more than triple the figure in the 1961 census, and reservations at schools and colleges continue to raise those figures.

Despite these constitutional protections, inequalities persist between the upper castes and the former Untouchables. Affirmative action, perhaps inevitably, benefited a minority of Dalits who were in a position to take advantage of it; independent India has witnessed the creation of privileged sections within formerly underprivileged groups, as the sons and daughters of rich and influential Scheduled Caste leaders get ahead on the strength of their caste affiliation. Caste Hindus have increasingly come to resent the offspring of cabinet ministers, for instance, benefiting from reservations and lower entry thresholds into university and government that were designed to compensate for disadvantages these scions of privilege have never personally experienced. Even the Supreme Court has muttered its disquiet about the benefits hogged by the so-called creamy layers at the top of the bottom ranks of society. But since the objective of the affirmative-action program is justice and representation in an almost cosmic sense, rather than equity here and now, such resentment can be, and is, disregarded by the authorities.

This has been augmented by the increasing importance of caste as a factor in the mobilization of votes. Candidates are picked by their parties with an eye to the caste loyalties they can call upon; often their appeal is overtly to voters of their own caste or subcaste, urging them to elect one of their own. (In India the workings of democracy have meant that the quest for social advancement has become inextricably linked with the pursuit of political power.) "Do not look at which party will get to rule after the elections," former prime minister V. P. Singh told journalists after the 1996 polls. "Try to see the people [who have been elected] within all the parties and you will find a deep social change has taken place." The lower castes have used their numerical strength in the Indian electorate to acquire political office: in the states of Bihar and Uttar Pradesh, for instance, Yadav-dominated coalitions of the underprivileged, including Muslims and Untouchables, have acquired a stranglehold on power at the expense of the old Brahmin and Thakur elites. Upper-caste Indians have found themselves, for the first time in millennia, subordinates and supplicants to those whom they traditionally regarded as menials. The traditionally upper-caste-dominated national parties, especially the Congress and the Hindu-chauvinist Bharatiya Janata Party (BJP), have bowed to the reality of electoral mathematics and promoted unprecedented numbers of low-caste members to leadership positions.

The result of this politically led social revolution has been a phenomenon the leaders of the anti-British nationalist struggle would never have imagined, however inevitable it seems in retrospect: the growth of caste consciousness and casteism throughout Indian society. In a recent conversation, an uncle of mine by marriage, who was born just before independence, put it ironically: "In my grandparents' time, caste governed their lives: they ate, socialized, married, *lived*, according to caste rules. In my parents' time, during the nationalist movement, they were encouraged by Gandhi and Nehru to reject caste; we dropped our caste-derived surnames and declared caste a social evil. As a result, when I grew up, I was unaware of caste; it was an irrelevance at school, at work, in my social contacts; the last thing I thought about was the caste of someone I met. Now, in my children's generation, the wheel has come full circle. Caste is suddenly all-important again. Your caste determines your opportunities, your prospects, your promotions. You can't go forward unless you're a Backward."

The emphasis on reservations and quotas as the most effective means of promoting affirmative action flies in the face of the constitutional provisions in favor of equal opportunity and equality under the law; it is never easy to reconcile "special opportunities for some" with "equal opportunity for all." Reserving parliamentary seats for Dalits and Adivasis is one thing, holding places in medical colleges for OBCs quite another. Not all federal or state institutions lend themselves equally well to the argument that representation is more important than efficiency:

whereas legislatures must obviously be representative of the populations they govern, the same is not necessarily true of a research laboratory (the government runs several) or a public-sector hospital. Nor are reservations in themselves a magic solution to all ills. A dissenting judge in the Supreme Court case quoted the sociologist André Béteille:

> The problems of the backward classes are too varied, too large and too acute to be solved by job reservation alone. . . . [T]he masses of Harijans and Adivasis are too poor and too lonely even to be candidates for the jobs that are reserved in their names.

Yet Béteille has been positive, elsewhere, about what affirmative action has done for India's downtrodden:

> [T]here are now untouchables and tribals serving as vice-chancellors at universities, as doctors, airline pilots and lawyers. Positive discrimination has brought about considerable changes in how individuals define their own personal horizon of possibilities. You see this clearly in the contrast between the expectations and ambitions of younger untouchables and those of their parents.

In other words, if you think Charlis has made it, wait till you meet his son.

5

Of Indians and Other Minorities

So we are, as I have already observed, all minorities in India. A Hindi-speaking Hindu male from the Gangetic plain state of Uttar Pradesh might cherish the illusion that he represents the "majority community," to use an expression much favored by the less industrious of our journalists. But he does not. As a Hindu he belongs to the faith adhered to by some 82 percent of the population, but a majority of the country does not speak Hindi; a majority does not hail from Uttar Pradesh; and if he were visiting, say, Kerala, he would discover that a majority is not even male. Worse, our archetypal UP Hindu has only to step off a train and mingle with the polyglot, polychrome crowds thronging any of India's five major metropolises to realize how much of a minority he really is. Even his Hinduism is no guarantee of majorityhood, because his caste automatically places him in a minority as well: if he is a Brahmin, 90 percent of his fellow Indians are not; if he is a Yadav, 85 percent of Indians are not, and so on.

To make this point is not to dismiss perceptions of "majority" and "minority" on the part of Indians, but to place them in some sort of perspective. Current estimates (1997) for India's nearly 940 million people divide them roughly as follows: 700 million Hindus, 115 million Muslims, 70 million "tribals" (largely animist in their worship), 21 million Christians, 17 million Sikhs, some 11 million Buddhists and Jains, half a million Parsis (followers of the Zoroastrian faith), and smatterings of Jews, Baha'is, atheists, and only-God-knows-whats.

How useful is it to extrapolate notions of minorities from such figures? Muslims, just over 12 percent of the population, are a majority in only one state and a minority in 24; however, they are the majority in several districts within states in which they are a minority; and they are politically influential in many districts where they are not a majority, because their votes hold the balance between rival elements of the "majority" population. In six states they account for more than 15 percent of the electorate, rising to 22 percent in Kerala, numbers significant in India's "first past the post" electoral system, where a winning candidate in a divided field may have no more than 35 to 40 percent of the votes cast. In addition, Muslims are proportionately more urbanized than Hindus, and constitute a third of the population in many Indian cities. As a result of all this, Muslim chief ministers have held power in a number of states in which Muslims are numerically a modest minority, including Bihar, Gujarat, Kerala, Maharashtra, and Rajasthan.

Or take language. The Constitution of India recognizes seventeen (three, including the language of the Pakistani province of Sind, having been added to the original list of fourteen in response to political pressure). In fact, there are thirty-five Indian languages that are spoken by more than a million people — and these are *languages*, with their own scripts, grammatical structures, and cultural assumptions, not just dialects (and if one were to count dialects within these languages, there are more than 22,000). Each of the native speakers of these languages is in a linguistic minority, for none enjoys majority status in India. Thanks in part to the popularity of Bombay's Hindi cinema, Hindi is understood, if not always well spoken, by nearly half the population of India, but it is in no sense the language of the majority; indeed, its locutions, gender rules, and script are so unfamiliar to most Indians in the south or northeast that any attempt to impose it as a truly "national" language would destroy the country's unity. English, on the other hand, is spoken by a minority estimated by the 1991 census at 2 percent of the population (almost certainly a severe undercount, since a far larger proportion — by my reckoning, at least 10 to 15 percent — have a basic acquaintance with the language, including reading and writing it). But this minority is scattered throughout the country, and the Indian professional elite is educated in English, so that English has a far more genuine "national" existence: it is the language in which two Indian government officials would naturally converse, in which two teenagers might discuss cricket or music, in which a Madras journalist might instinctively address a Bombay businessman, and in which the "national media" (those publications aiming at a countrywide audience) are published. It is undoubtedly the language of a small minority, but its speakers feel no "minority complex" at all.

Ethnicity further complicates the notion of a majority community. Most of the time an Indian's name immediately reveals where he is from and what his mother tongue is; when we introduce ourselves we are advertising our origins. The difference this reflects is often more apparent than the elements of commonalty. A Karnataka Brahmin shares his Hindu faith with a Bihari Kurmi, but feels little identity with him in respect to appearance, dress, customs, tastes, language, or political objectives. There would similarly be little in common between a Jharkhand tribesman in north India and a Bodo tribesman of Assam despite their aboriginal identities; between a Kashmiri Muslim and a Moplah of Malabar, who both owe allegiance to the Islamic faith; between a Naga Pentecostalist and a Syrian Orthodox Keralite, both Christians separated by thousands of miles and nearly as many shades of complexion. At the same time a Tamil Hindu would feel that he has far more in common with a Tamil Christian or Muslim than with, say, a Haryanvi Jat with whom he formally shares a religion.

Affinities between Indians span one set of identities and cross into another. I am simultaneously Keralite (my geographical state of origin), Malayali (my linguistic-cultural affiliation), Hindu (my religious faith), Nair (my caste), Calcuttan (as a result of my schooling and by marriage), Stephanian (because of my education at Delhi's St. Stephen's College), and so on, and in my interactions with other Indians, each or several of these identities may play a part. Each, while affiliating me to a group with the same label, sets me apart from others; but even within each group, few would share the other identities I also claim, and so I find myself again in a minority within each minority.

If I stress this point, it is because I believe it dangerous to draw the wrong conclusions from the ostensibly crushing majority that "Hindus" appear to represent in the Indian population. Yes, there is a sense in which all Hindus have the broad elements of a common faith, but it would be impossible to list the basic beliefs to which we all swear adherence. We have, within Hinduism, different ways of worshiping God, and prefer to do so in different forms in different parts of the country, even naming our deities differently; there are major variations in the theological underpinnings of our faith, in which scriptures we emphasize, in the rituals we conduct, and in which (if any) of the 333,000 divine manifestations of God we choose to place our faith. Because of these multiplicities of approach, the clearly defined (and restrictive) consciousness of collective faith typical of Christianity, Islam, or Judaism never evolved in Hinduism. The fourteenth-century religious philosopher Madhavacharya identified sixteen fundamentally different Hindu schools of thought in his celebrated treatise *Sarva Darshana Samagrha*. Nor are rituals, cultural practices, ecclesia, or social customs universally held in common by all Hindus. One cannot say, for instance, that a Hindu is someone who prays to Ram, worships at a Shiva temple, believes in caste and in reincarnation, reads the Vedas, treats the Bhagavad Gita as holy writ, heeds the injunctions of the Shankaracharya of Kanchipuram, considers the cow sacred, abjures beef, wears ash on his forehead, and washes away his sins in the holy Ganga, because it is possible to do none of those things and still consider oneself a Hindu.

This laxness at the heart of the practice of Hinduism, this failure to require conformity, troubles many Hindus today. Today's votaries of Hindutva have, in reaction, begun asserting a self-conscious collective identity, facilitated, many suggest, by the televising of Hindu myths and epics like the Ramayana and the Mahabharata, which attracted over a hundred million viewers each across the country. But other Hindus find this kind of "national Hinduism" artificial; some have suggested that such movements are attempting to "Semitize" the Hindu faith, which lacks the dogmas, doctrines, and moral absolutism characteristic of the Semitic creeds. The proponents of Hindutva argue, however, that in rejecting such "Semitization," liberals are also rejecting the collective self-consciousness without which the faith will stagnate or decline. It is precisely by denying what Hindus have in common, they say, that secular Hindus have made it impossible for Hindus as a whole to hold their own in a world where others, notably (in the subcontinental context) Muslims, have proudly asserted their own religious identity, whether as a minority or a majority.

One of the intellectual godfathers of Hindutva, the Rashtriya Swayamsevak Sangh's V. D. "Veer" Savarkar, described a Hindu as "a person who regards this land . . . from the Indus to the Seas as his fatherland as well as his Holyland." The definition is simultaneously territorial (though Savarkar's reference to the Indus predated Partition), atavistic (the reference to "fatherland" suggesting the continuity of bloodlines), and religious. The last element raises the question: What about those whose faiths originated outside India, and for whom India cannot therefore be their "holy" land? The Hindutva ideologues' response is that they should "assimilate," as others before them have assimilated, into Hindu India. The reaction of many members of minority faiths, particularly Muslims, is to assert their distinctiveness rather than their assimilability.

The result of this sort of thinking is that, fifty years after Partition and independence, religion has again become a key determinant of political identity. It was the phenomenon of Indian Muslims beginning to think of themselves, politically, as Muslims first and Indians second that facilitated Britain's "divide and rule" policy, gave the country separate electorates, promoted communal representation, impelled the separatist politics of the Muslim League, and led finally to Partition. With the creation of Pakistan, it might have been hoped that the Muslims remaining in India would relegate religion to a secondary place in their political life; indeed, with the emigration to Pakistan of much of the Muslim middle class (and upper middle class), the community was shorn of leadership at a time when many felt collective guilt over the breakup of the country. Not only has the emigration option now dried up — because of new Pakistani laws discouraging it, because of anti-Mohajir [immigrant] violence in Pakistan, and because the Pakistani economy no longer offers the attractive prospects of the immediate post-Partition days, when jobs and business vacated by Hindus could be had for the asking — but net Muslim migration in the subcontinent is *to* India, particularly from Bangladesh. Nonetheless, the trauma of Partition appears to have left most Muslims with an enhanced sense of their minorityhood, underscored by the conversion of so many of their co-religionists into foreigners.

Despite the prominence of Muslim leaders in all the major political parties of the country, Muslim Indians found themselves unable to escape the politics of identity. Their leaders have tended to mobilize the community on three collective issues: identity first and foremost, as on the issue of Muslim Personal Law and in the major efforts made to construct schools, colleges, theological institutions, and clinics for Muslims; security, no small matter when Muslims account for a disproportionate number of deaths in communal rioting; and public-sector employment, where Muslims hold fewer jobs than their share of the population warrants, but probably less owing to discrimination than as a consequence of the skewed demographics of the community following the departure of most of its educated members to Pakistan. An additional factor, as always, is economics. Poverty has made many Indian Muslims insecure and conservative. A community that falls behind in the competition for economic advancement tends to cling all the more to its atavistic identity, in turn accentuating its separateness from the rest of the nation.

There were notable exceptions — Muslim leaders whose standing had nothing whatsoever to do with their imagined place in their community, or their ability to win the allegiance and the votes of their fellow Muslims. The eminent Bombay jurist, diplomat, and statesman Mohammed Currim Chagla was one of them: a man of intellect, conviction, and style, who served as ambassador in Washington and London, foreign minister, and education minister, and characteristically resigned over an issue of principle unconnected with his faith (a faith he wore as lightly as did his former friend and comrade Mohammed

Ali Jinnah). But his was a rare case. When a successful career diplomat with a socialist past, Syed Shahabuddin, resigned his ambassadorial post in 1977 to contest parliamentary elections as a Janata candidate, some of us expected the emergence of a left-wing Chagla, a figure of eminence in his field who would transfer his expertise to the political arena. It was not to be: within a short while Shahabuddin stopped writing well-informed exegeses on foreign policy and became instead a narrow-minded spokesman for Muslim sectarian interests, achieving literary notoriety as the man instrumental for the Indian government's ban on Salman Rushdie's *Satanic Verses*.

That ban was a classic instance of Muslim politics at work in India: passions inflamed over a book its critics had not read ("I do not need to wade in a gutter to know it is filthy," Shahabuddin said memorably), the self-appointed "leaders" of the Muslim community presuming to speak for all their co-religionists, a government acting in its own political self-interest for fear of losing the "Muslim vote." Had the government not caved in and preemptively banned the book, some Muslim leaders might well have provoked angry demonstrations that could have turned violent, so that in the end the dictates of public order might well have provided a rationalization for a ban, but the calculations on both sides had less to do with law and order than with the political manipulation of communal identities.

Years before the Rushdie affair, I called on Mr. Shahabuddin once at his parliamentarian's bungalow in Delhi to discuss foreign policy, but all he wanted to talk about was the percentage of Muslims in the Uttar Pradesh Provincial Armed Constabulary. Yet briefly the secular Indian diplomat emerged: "My daughter asks me," he admitted, "Daddy, how can you even *think* like this?" Quite. But Shahabuddin *did* think like that, and at one point lost what little credibility he had with secular liberals by calling for a Muslim boycott of India's Republic Day celebrations ("unki jumhooriyat," he was quoted as saying: "*their* republic"). Though not all Muslim politicians have felt obliged to tread so sectarian a path, for the most part Muslim political leaders have derived their strength and influence from their position *as* Muslims, i.e., as members and representatives of a minority community.

This was, of course, not true in other fields of endeavor: religion was irrelevant in the advancement of military, business, sports, and cultural figures from the Muslim community. Air Chief Marshal Latif could not have risen to the top rank in the country's air forces except by being a superb general officer; Mohammed Azharuddin's seven-year-long captaincy of the Indian cricket team was a tribute to his indispensability as a player; the cinematic triumphs of a variety of unrelated Khans was based entirely on their box-office appeal; and M. J. Akbar became India's youngest editor on the strength of his journalistic brilliance. The extraordinary Zaki family, which in the early 1990s boasted three generals in the Indian army and a senior air force officer as well, proudly speaks of its eight generations of soldiering; and the scientist who developed India's first long-range missiles and continues to lead this most sensitive defense program is also a Muslim, A. P. J. Abdul Kalam. In such cases, Indian pluralism worked neutrally, by ensuring that religion was not a handicap or an obstacle to career advancement — indeed, that it was no factor at all.

Politicians from other religious minorities in India usually transcended their confessional identity: the Christian George Fernandes built his career as a socialist firebrand, his Christianity irrelevant in all respects, while the Parsis Minoo Masani and Piloo Mody articulated free-enterprise views devoid of any explicit Zarathustran inspiration or content. And some subsections of Indian Muslims have not, generally speaking, fallen prey to communal politics: the Dawoodi Bohras, a prosperous community of traders and professionals, is famed for being largely apolitical. Nonetheless, the fact that a substantial religious minority of Muslims, projecting its political hopes and fears on the national scene in the wake of Partition, developed a communitarian identity was not in itself surprising. What is curious today is that, in Hindutva, a credible political movement (and one can speak of *a* Hindutva movement, despite its fragmentation into many rival organizations) has sprung up that seeks to convert the religion of the "majority" into an identity for mass mobilization. It is the result not just of mass sentiment but of diligent organizational work by the Rashtriya Swayamsevak Sangh, Shiv Sena, and the Vishwa Hindu Parishad, particularly the first, which has abandoned the traditional Hindu emphasis on self-realization for a collective operational Hinduism of early-morning drills in khaki shorts, social service, and volunteer work after natural and man-made disasters.

Such a movement has arisen, at least in part, as a reaction to Muslim resurgence and Sikh militancy, which has seen the killing and expulsion of Hindus from parts of Kashmir and Punjab; but it has become *possible* because of the nature of the strategy pursued by the Indian state since independence on the identity question. Indian federalism is based on the recognition of linguistic identity; the states were reorganized in 1956 to group the speakers of each language together into a political unit. The issue of caste identity was, as we have seen, dealt with through the world's oldest and most far-reaching affirmative-action program. And the same willingness to shore up identity was manifest in relation to India's religious communities.

Thus the ostensibly secular Indian state granted major concessions to its minority religions, organized not just as religions but as social communities. "Personal law" was left to the religious leaders of each community to maintain and interpret; the state passed no law to alter or abridge Muslim Personal Law, even though Parliament, through the Hindu Code Bill, radically transformed Hindu society in these areas as early as 1956. Educational and cultural institutions of religious minorities are subsidized (in some cases almost entirely funded) by state grants; these include even explicitly religious schools. Muslim divines and preachers routinely receive government grants, and the government disburses considerable sums annually on arranging for them to travel on the annual Haj pilgrimage to Mecca. Indeed, despite the fact that a political party organized on religious lines had partitioned the country, the government did nothing to discourage political mobilization on the basis of religion, so that the rump of Jinnah's Muslim League not only continued to be active in independent India, but even became an electoral ally of the Congress Party.

If Muslim politicians developed a vested interest in minorityhood, the Indian state evolved a vested interest in its perpetuation: support the leaders of the minority, pre-empt their radicalization vis-à-vis the state by giving them no cause to fear it, and so co-opt them into the national consensus. When objections were voiced on religious grounds, as over the Shah Banu alimony case, the state rushed to appease the most conservative elements in the minority community. Instead of keeping an "equal distance" from all religions, successive Indian governments came to "equal engagement" with each of them, offering subventions both financial and political to their leaders. This was not particularly secular in any sense of the term, but secularism is what we — not knowing any better — called it for fifty years.

As the eminent Harvard economist Amartya Sen put it, "Secularism as it is practiced in India . . . reflects the sum of the collective feelings of intolerance of the different communities and is not based on combining their respective capacities for tolerance." Perhaps inevitably, some Hindus have begun to see the disadvantages of their "majority" status. The secular state, they say, openly favors minorities but remains neutral (or, as with the Hindu Code Bill, interventionist) in regard to the majority; so what price majorityism? The classic instance of this realization was the request of the Ramakrishna Mission, an active group of Hindu missionaries who both perform social service and provide theological guidance, to be classified as a minority institution under the tax laws. Arguably it was another government policy — the approval of the Mandal proposal for reservations for the "backward classes" — that gave impetus to the agitation that led to the destruction of the Babri Masjid at Ayodhya, as Hindu leaders sought to put *mandir* (temple) before Mandal. The secular Indian state has come to be seen by many Hindus as an instrument to control, divide, and rein in the Hindus, while perpetuating the self-assertion of the minorities (and by this is almost always meant one particular minority, the Muslims). Atal Behari Vajpayee, the BJP leader who briefly became prime minister after the 1996 elections but failed to win a majority in Parliament, put it bluntly to *The New York Times*: "If you go on talking about 'Muslims, Muslims,' and 'minorities, minorities,' you injure the Hindu psyche. People start asking, 'Is it going to be a crime to be a Hindu in this country?'"

Liberal Indians can well say, as I have often done, that the Hindutva reaction to Muslims as a *community* is misplaced, because most believing Muslims are also patriotic Indians, and because one cannot tar a collectivity in reaction to the excesses of a few. But the problem is that the good intentions of the Indian state — by granting privileges and exceptions to the Muslims as a *community*, and thereby treating the community politically as if it were a monolith — have made such a reaction possible. Too many Hindus now fail to draw a distinction between the bearded Muslim priest preaching sectarianism or even separatism on religious grounds and the bearded Muslim priest who merely sees his faith as a vital personal anchor in a troubled world. Both are objectified politically in the same way, and the nationalist discourse suffers accordingly.

To some degree, the workings of Indian democracy, which remains the best guarantee of Indian pluralism, have served to create and perpetuate India's various particularisms. The Hindu-Muslim divide is merely the most visible, but that within Hinduism, between caste Hindus and the former Untouchables and now between the upper castes and the lower intermediate castes — the "backwards" — is actually transforming Indian society in ways the founding fathers did not anticipate. The uses of caste as an index of eligibility for affirmative action and as an instrument of political mobilization have, in particular, made today's Indians more caste-conscious than ever before.

This damaging consequence of well-intentioned social and political engineering means that, in the five decades since independence, we have failed to create a single Indian community. Instead we have become more conscious than ever of what divides us: religion, region, caste, language, ethnicity. What makes us, then, a nation? At a time when, across the world, more and more ethnic, religious, and cultural groups agitate for separation from larger political entities that subsume them with groups unlike themselves, this question is particularly relevant.

Amid the popular ferment that made an Italian nation out a congeries of principalities and statelets, the nineteenth-century Italian novelist Massimo Taparelli d'Azeglio wrote memorably, "We have created Italy. Now all we need to do is to create Italians." Oddly enough, no

Indian nationalist succumbed to the temptation to express the same thought: "We have created India; now all we need to do is to create Indians." Such a sentiment would not, in any case, have occurred to the preeminent voice of Indian nationalism, Jawaharlal Nehru, because he believed in the existence of India and Indians for millennia before he gave words to their longings; he would never have spoken of "creating" India or Indians, merely of being the agent for the reassertion of what had always existed but had been long suppressed. Nonetheless, the India that was born in 1947 was in a very real sense a new creation: a state that had made fellow citizens of the Ladakhi and the Laccadivian for the first time, that divided Punjabi from Punjabi for the first time, that asked the Travancore peasant to feel allegiance to a Kashmiri Pandit ruling in Delhi, also for the first time. Nehru would not have written of the challenge of "creating" Indians, but creating Indians was what, in fact, his nationalist movement did.

Nations have been formed out of varying and different impulses. France and Thailand are the products of a ruthless and unifying monarchy, while Germany and the United States are those of a sternly practical and yet visionary modernizing elite. Italy and Bangladesh are the results of mass movements led by messianic figures, Holland and Switzerland the creation of discrete cantons wishing to merge for their mutual protection. But it is only recently that race or ethnicity has again been seen as the basis of nationhood, as has become apparent in the breakup of the former Yugoslavia.

Most modern nations are the product of a fusion of population groups over the centuries, to the point where one element is indistinguishable from the next. The nineteenth-century French historian Ernest Renan pointed out, for instance, that "an Englishman is indeed a type within the whole of humanity. However, [he] . . . is neither the Briton of Julius Caesar's time, nor the Anglo-Saxon of Hengist's time, nor the Dane of Canute's time, nor the Norman of William the Conqueror's time; [he] is rather the result of all these." We cannot yet say the same of an Indian, because we are not yet the product of the kind of fusion that Renan's Englishman represents: despite some intermarriage at the elite levels in the cities, Indians still largely remain endogamous, and a Bengali is easily distinguished from a Punjabi.

So India cannot claim ethnicity as a uniting factor, since what we loosely have in common with one another as a generally recognizable "type" we also have in common with Pakistanis, Bangladeshis, Sri Lankans, Maldivians, and Nepalese, with whom we no longer share a common political identity. Looking again at foreign models of the nation-state, many scholars have pointed out that the adoption of Christianity by both conquerors and conquered helped the creation of the Western European nations, since it eliminated the distinction between ethnic groups in the society on the basis of their religion. But this is not an answer to the Indian predicament, for most of India's Bengalis and Punjabis share a common faith, and are still distinct; and equally important, more than 150 million Indians do not share the faith of the majority, and would be excluded from such a community (as non-Christian minorities among immigrants in Europe feel excluded today from full acceptance into their new societies).

A third element that has, historically, served to unite nations in other parts of the world is language. In Europe, conquerors and conquered rapidly came to speak the same language, usually that of the conquered. In India, attempts by Muslim conquerors to import Persian or Turkic languages never took root; instead, the hybrid camp language called Urdu or Hindustani evolved as the language of both rulers and ruled in most of north India. But Hindi today has made very limited inroads into the south, east, and northeast, so linguistic unity remains a distant prospect (all the more so, given that languages like Bengali, Malayalam, and Tamil have a far richer cultural and literary tradition than the Hindi that seeks to supplant them). One of the more remarkable political events of 1996 was the sight of Prime Minister Deve Gowda, a southerner with no knowledge of Hindi, delivering his Independence Day address from the traditional ramparts of Delhi's sixteenth-century Red Fort in that language — the words having been written for him in his native Kannada script (in which they, of course, made no sense). Such an episode is almost inconceivable elsewhere, but it represents the best of the oddities that help make India India:

the fact that the country can be ruled by a man who does not understand its "national language," the fact that he would make the effort to speak it nonetheless, and the nature of the solution found to enable him to do so. One of Indian cinema's finest "playback singers," the Keralite K. J. Yesudas, sung his way to the top of the Hindi charts with lyrics in that language written in the Malayalam script for him to read, but to see the same practice elevated to the prime ministerial address on Independence Day was a startling affirmation of Indian pluralism.

Language and religion have, around the world, proved themselves an inadequate basis for nationhood. More than eighty countries profess Christianity, but they do not seek to merge with one another; the Organization of the Islamic Conference has more than fifty members, who agree on many issues but do not see themselves as a single nation. As for language, Arabic makes meetings of the Arab League more convenient, no doubt, but has hardly been a force for political unity; Spanish has not melted the political frontiers that vivisect Latin America; and England and the U.S.A. remain, in the famous phrase, two countries divided by a common language.

A more poetic suggestion made by Renan, in his famous 1882 speech "What Is a Nation?" is that historical amnesia is an essential part of nation-building, that nations need to forget the horrible price they have paid in the distant past for their unity (the union of northern France with the Midi in the thirteenth century, he pointed out, followed from a period of warfare, massacres, and terror that lasted nearly a hundred years, and yet France is an archetypal nation, one whose people are almost unanimously conscious of being French). "The essence of a nation," Renan wrote, "is that all individuals [in it] have many things in common, and also that they have forgotten many things." That *is* true of India, though we Indians are not as good at forgetting as we should be. We carry with us the weight of the past, and because we do not have a finely developed sense of history and historicism, it is a past that is still alive in our present. We wear the dust of history on our foreheads, and the mud of the future on our feet.

Indian nationalism is a rare animal indeed. It is not based on language (since we have at least seventeen or thirty-five, depending on whether you follow the Constitution or the ethnolinguists), geography (the "natural" frontiers of India have been hacked by the Partition of 1947), ethnicity (the "Indian" accommodates a diversity of racial types in which many Indians have more in common with foreigners than with other Indians), or religion. Indian nationalism is the nationalism of an idea, the idea of an ever-ever land. This land imposes no procrustean exactions on its citizens: you can be many things *and* one thing. You can be a good Muslim, a good Keralite, and a good Indian all at once. Our founding fathers wrote a constitution for a dream; we have given passports to our ideals. Where Freudians note the distinctions that arise out of "the narcissism of minor differences," in India we celebrate the commonalty of major differences. To stand Ignatieff on his head, we are a land of belonging rather than of blood.

Ultimately, what matters in determining the validity of a nation is political will: the will among the inhabitants of a nation to work together within a single political framework. Such a political will may not necessarily be unanimous, for there will always be those who reject the common framework for narrow sectarian ends, and every state has a duty to defend itself against such elements. Democracy rests on the premise that government occurs with the consent of the governed, but in the face of sectarianism and secession — the attempt to obtain political sovereignty for an ethnic community — no nation can allow its strongest principles of democracy to become its weakest link. But if the overwhelming majority of the people share the political will for unity, and if they can look back to both a past and a future, a nation can indeed be said to exist whatever the diversity it comprises. This is the case with India.

Renan argued that a "nation is a spiritual principle, the outcome of profound complications of history." Nehru, as we have seen, echoed this vision in his own discovery of India. Renan also spoke of "the desire to live together, the will to perpetuate the value of the heritage one has received," as the animating principle of a nation. Though his views were first expounded more than a century ago, a fact that his vocabulary sometimes betrays, it is worth citing Renan again:

The nation, like the individual, is the culmination of a long past of endeavors, sacrifice and devotion. . . . A heroic past, great men, glory . . . , this is the social capital upon which one bases a national idea. To have common glories in the past and to have a common will in the present; to have performed great deeds together, to wish to perform still more — these are the essential conditions for being a people. . . . More valuable by far than common customs posts and frontiers conforming to strategic ideas is the fact of sharing, in the past, a glorious heritage and regrets, and of having, in the future, [a common] program to put into effect, or the fact of having suffered, enjoyed and hoped together.

This is very similar to José Ortega y Gasset's argument that a nation is not really a nation unless it has both a past that influences it inactively and a valid historical project that is capable of animating dissimilar spirits within the community and of giving unity and transcendence to the efforts of its individual members. Nehru tried to find such a unifying project in the challenges of modernization and economic development; but his task is incomplete. India, with its glorious heritage and its many regrets (most recently, of course, the collective national trauma of Partition), meets the test of history; it must now rise to the challenge of the future.

Nehru articulated a vision of India as pluralism vindicated by history:

India . . . was like an ancient palimpsest on which layer upon layer of thought and reverie had been inscribed, and yet no succeeding layer had completely hidden or erased what had been written previously. . . . Though outwardly there was diversity and infinite variety among our people, everywhere there was that tremendous impress of oneness, which had held all of us together for ages. . . . [India] was a world in itself, a culture and a civilization which gave shape to all things. Foreign influences poured in . . . and were absorbed. Disruptive tendencies gave rise immediately to an attempt to find a synthesis. Some kind of a dream of unity has occupied the mind of India since the dawn of civilization. That unity was not conceived as something imposed from outside, a standardization of externals or even of beliefs. It was something deeper and, within its fold, the widest tolerance of belief and custom was practiced and every variety acknowledged and even encouraged.

Nehru went on to argue that the unity of India was apparent from the outside: every Indian, whatever his differences from other Indians, was seen by foreigners as an Indian first, rather than as a Christian or Muslim, even though he might share his religion with those foreigners.

For Nehru, the "Indian people" have a timeless quality, emerging from history and stretching on the future. The present is merely a point of observation. Octavio Paz, writing about Mexico, asked a somewhat different pair of questions that are implicit in my consideration of India:

> What are we, and how can we fulfill our obligations to ourselves as we are? The answers we give to these questions are often belied by history, perhaps because what is called the "genius of a people" is only a set of reactions to a given stimulus. The answers differ in different situations, and the national character, which was thought to be immutable, changes with them. . . . To become aware of our history is to become aware of our singularity. . . . But why search history for an answer that only we ourselves can give?

There is no question but that Indians today have to find answers themselves to the dilemmas of running a plural nation. "A nation," wrote the Zionist visionary Theodor Herzl, "is a historical group of men of recognizable cohesion, held together by a common enemy." The common enemy of Indians is an internal one; it lies in the forces of sectarian division that would, if unchecked, tear the country apart. There lies the common historical project sought by Ortega y Gasset. We have to return to the pluralism of the national movement. While this involves turning away from the strident calls for Hindutva that would privilege a doctrinaire view of Hinduism at the expense of the minorities, it also requires the rejection of the pseudo-secularism that has made the state hostage to the most obscurantist religious figures among the minorities. India must find its own formula, transcending the thralldom of minority and majority.

It is not entirely paradoxical to suggest that Hinduism, India's ancient home-grown faith, can help in ways that the proponents of Hindutva have not understood. In one sense Hinduism is almost the ideal faith for the twenty-first century: a faith without apostasy, where there are no heretics to cast out because there has never been any such thing as a Hindu heresy, a faith that is eclectic and nondoctrinaire, responds ideally to the incertitudes of a postmodern world. Hinduism, with its openness, its respect for variety, its acceptance of all other faiths, is one religion that should be able to assert itself without threatening others. But this cannot be the Hinduism that destroyed a mosque, or the Hindutva spewed in hate-filled speeches by communal politicians. It has to be the Hinduism of Swami Vivekananda, who, a century ago, at Chicago's World Parliament of Religions in 1893, articulated best the liberal humanism that lies at the heart of his and my creed:

> I am proud to belong to a religion which has taught the world both tolerance and universal acceptance. We believe not only in universal toleration, but we accept all religions as true. I am proud to belong to a nation which has sheltered the persecuted and the refugees of all religions and all nations of the earth. I am proud to tell you that we have gathered in our bosom the purest remnant of the Israelites, who came to southern India and took refuge with us in the very year in which their holy temple was shattered to pieces by Roman tyranny. I am proud to belong to the religion which has sheltered and is still fostering the remnant of the grand Zoroastrian nation. I remember having repeated a hymn from my earliest boyhood, which is every day repeated by millions of human beings: *"As the different streams having their sources in different places all mingle their water in the sea, so, O Lord, the different paths which men take through different tendencies, various though they appear, crooked or straight, all lead to Thee."* . . . [T]he wonderful doctrine preached in the Gita [says]: *"Whosoever comes to Me, through whatsoever form, I reach him; all men are struggling through paths which in the end lead to me."*

Vivekananda went on to denounce the fact that "sectarianism, bigotry, and its horrible descendant, fanaticism, have long possessed this beautiful earth." His confident belief that their death-knell had sounded was sadly not to be borne out. But his vision — summarized in the Sanskrit credo *Sarva Dharma Sambhava:* "All religions are equally worthy of respect" — is, in fact, the kind of Hinduism practiced by the vast majority of India's Hindus, whose instinctive acceptance of other faiths and forms of worship has long been the vital hallmark of Indianness. Vivekananda made no distinction between the actions of Hindus as a people (the granting of asylum, for instance) and their actions as a religious community (tolerance of other faiths): for him, the distinction was irrelevant because Hinduism was as much a civilization as a set of religious beliefs. In a different speech to the same Chicago convention, Vivekananda set out his philosophy in simple terms:

> Unity in variety is the plan of nature, and the Hindu has recognized it. Every other religion lays down certain fixed dogmas and tries to force society to adopt them. It places before society only one coat which must fit Jack and John and Henry, all alike. If it does not fit John or Henry, he must go without a coat to cover his body. The Hindus have discovered that the absolute can only be realized, or thought of, or stated through the relative, and the images, crosses, and crescents are simply so many symbols — so many pegs to hang spiritual ideas on. It is not that this help is necessary for everyone, but those that do not need it have no right to say that it is wrong. Nor is it compulsory in Hinduism. . . . The Hindus have their faults, but mark this, they are always for punishing their own bodies, and never for cutting the throats of their neighbors. If the Hindu fanatic burns himself on the pyre, he never lights the fire of Inquisition.

It is sad that this assertion of Vivekananda's is being contradicted on the ground by those who claim to be reviving his faith in his name. Of course, it is true that, while Hinduism as a faith might espouse tolerance, this does not necessarily mean that all Hindus behave tolerantly. Nor should we assume that, even when religion is used as a mobilizing identity, all those so mobilized act in accordance with the tenets of their religion. Nonetheless it is ironic that even the Maratha warrior-king Shivaji, after whom the Shiv Sena is named, exemplified the tolerance that Hinduism lays claim to. In the account of a contemporary critic, the Mughal historian Khafi Khan, Shivaji "made it a rule that wherever his followers were plundering, they should do no harm to the mosques, the book of God, or the women of any one. Whenever a copy of the sacred Quran came into his hands, he treated it with respect, and gave it to some of his Mussalman followers."

But the misuse of Hinduism for sectarian minority-bashing is especially unfortunate, since Hinduism provides the basis for a shared sense of common culture within India that has little to do with religion. Hindu festivals, from Holi (when friends and strangers of all faiths are sprayed with colored water in a Dionysian ritual) to Deepavali (the festival of lights, firecrackers, and social gambling) have already gone beyond their religious origins to unite Indians of all faiths as a shared experience. Festivals, *melas*, *lila*s, all "Hindu" in origin, have become occasions for the mingling of ordinary Indians of all backgrounds; indeed, for generations now, Muslim artisans in the Hindu holy city of Varanasi have made the traditional masks for the annual Ram Lila (the dance-drama depicting the tale of the divine god-king, Rama), because Hindu respect for their artisanal skills transcends religious considerations. Religion lies at the heart of Indian culture, but not necessarily as a source of division; such religious myths as the Ramayana and the Mahabharata provide a common idiom, a shared matrix of reference, to all Indians, and it was not surprising that when national television broadcast a fifty-two-episode serialization of the Mahabharata, the script was written by a Muslim poet, Dr. Rahi Masoom Raza. Hinduism and Islam are intertwined in India; both religions, after all, have shared the same history in the same space, and theirs is a cohabitation of necessity as well as fact. In the Indian context today, it is possible to say that there is no India without Islam, and no Islam without India. The saffron and the green both belong on the Indian flag.

Both Hindus and Muslims throng the tombs and *dargah*s of Sufi Muslim saints. Hindu devotional songs are magnificently sung by the Muslim Dagar brothers. Muslim sociologists and anthropologists have argued that Islam in rural India is more Indian than Islamic, in the sense that the faith as practiced by the ordinary Muslim villagers reflects the considerable degree of cultural assimilation that has occurred between Hindus and Muslims in their daily lives. The Muslim reformist scholar Asghar Ali Engineer has written that "rural Islam . . . [is] almost indistinguishable from Hinduism except in the form of worship. . . . The degree may vary from one area to another; but cultural integration between the Hindus and Muslims is a fact which no one, except victims of misinformation, can deny." The American scholars Susanne Hoeber Rudolph and Lloyd I. Rudolph recounted a story that they had heard from an Indian Muslim friend:

> As a child in India, she was once asked to participate in a small community drama about the life of Lord Krishna. Krishna is the blue "Hindu" god adored by shepherdesses, who dance for his pleasure. They exemplify through their human passion the quest of the devout soul for the lord. Not exactly a Muslim monotheist's theme. She was invited to dance as a shepherdess with other schoolgirls. Her father forbade it: Muslims don't dance. In that case, said the drama's director, we will cast you as Krishna. All you have to do is stand there in the usual Krishna pose, a flute at your mouth. Her father consented. She played Krishna.

To some degree, India's other minorities have found it comfortable to take on elements of Hindu culture as proof of their own integration into the national mainstream. The tennis-playing brothers Anand, Vijay, and Ashok Amritraj all bear Hindu names, but they are Christian, the sons of Robert and Maggie Amritraj, and they played with prominent crosses dangling from their necks, which they were fond of kissing in supplication or gratitude at tense moments on court. But giving their children Hindu names must have seemed to Robert and Maggie more nationalist in these postcolonial times, and quite unrelated to which God they were brought up to worship. I would not wish to make too much of this, because Muslim Indians still feel obliged to adopt Arab names in deference to the roots of their faith, but the Amritraj case (repeated in many other Christian families I know) is merely an example of Hinduism serving as a framework for the voluntary cultural assimilation of minority groups, without either compulsion or conversion becoming an issue.

It is possible to a great extent to speak of Hinduism as culture rather than as religion (a distinction the votaries of Hindutva reject or blur). The inauguration of a public project, the laying of a foundation stone, or the launching of a ship usually starts with the ritual smashing of a coconut, an auspicious practice in Hinduism, but one that most Indians of other faiths cheerfully accept in much the same spirit as a teetotaler acknowledges the role of champagne in a Western celebration. Interestingly, similar Hindu customs have survived in now-Muslim Java and now-Buddhist Thailand; Islamic Indonesians still cherish the Ramayana legend, now shorn (for them) of its religious associations. For the people of Java, heirs to a syncretic tradition of Islam superimposed on ancient Hindu and Buddhist beliefs, culture is uniquely able to transcend religion. I visited the Shiva temple on Indonesia's Hindu island of Bali once with the daughter of a Jakarta Qazi, a Muslim divine, and was astonished to see her praying before the idol, the Shivalingam. When I asked her about it, she was wide-eyed in her innocence: the Hindu gods were also a part of her cultural heritage, and she saw no incompatibility between her obeisance and the purist faith rigorously preached by her father. Such a scene is still impossible to imagine in India, but it hints at intriguing potentialities for mutual interchange — when each community feels secure enough in itself to acknowledge its debt to the others.

Lapsed Hindus have continued to recognize the value of Hindu cultural symbols even when they are no longer fully rooted in faith. India's most famous agnostic, Jawaharlal Nehru, a man who openly despised temples and was never known to have worshiped at any Hindu shrine in his long life, asked in his will to be cremated, like other Hindus, and to have his ashes scattered from the air over the country, to mingle with the Indian earth, except for a portion of them, which would be immersed in the sacred river Ganga at Allahabad. This last would not have been a surprising request from a devout man, but Nehru's reasons, spelled out in his will, had little to do with religion:

> The Ganga, especially, is the river of India, beloved of her people, round which are intertwined her racial memories, her hopes and fears, her songs of triumph, her victories and her defeats. She has been a symbol of India's age-long culture and civilization, ever-changing, ever-flowing, and yet ever the same Ganga. She reminds me of the snow-covered peaks and the deep valleys of the Himalayas, which I have loved so much, and of the rich and vast plains below, where my life and work have been cast. Smiling and dancing in the morning sunlight, and dark and gloomy and full of mystery as

the evening shadows fall, a narrow, slow and graceful stream in winter and a vast, roaring thing during the monsoon, broad-bosomed almost as the sea, and with something of the sea's power to destroy, the Ganga has been to me a symbol and a memory of the past of India, running into the present, and flowing on to the great ocean of the future. And though I have discarded much of past tradition and custom, and am anxious that India should rid herself of all shackles that bind and constrain her and divide her people, . . . I do not wish to cut myself off from the past completely. I am proud of that great inheritance that has been, and is, ours, and I am conscious that I too, like all of us, am a link in that unbroken chain which goes back to the dawn of history in the immemorial past of India.

In this reading, the most sacred river of Hinduism becomes a force for cultural unity, a torrent that unites history with hope. There is nothing in Nehru's use of the Ganga as symbol that could alienate an Indian Muslim or Christian. By narrowly appropriating such powerful national metaphors for a dogmatic version of their faith, the advocates of Hindutva are denying themselves and their co-religionists the all-embracing potential of a culture that truly can incorporate Indian non-Hindus into a common civilizational space.

The economist Amartya Sen made a related point in regretting

the neglect by the Hindu leaders of the more major achievements of Indian civilization, even the distinctly Hindu contributions, in favor of its more dubious features. Not for them the sophistication of the Upanishads or the Gita, or of Brahmagupta or Sankara, or of Kalidasa or Sudraka; they prefer the adoration of Rama's idol and Hanuman's image. Their nationalism also ignores the rationalist traditions of India, a country in which some of the earliest steps in algebra, geometry, and astronomy were taken, where the decimal system emerged, where early philosophy — secular as well as religious — achieved exceptional sophistication, where people invented games like chess, pioneered sex education, and began the first systematic study of political economy. The Hindu militant chooses instead to present India — explicitly or implicitly — as a country of unquestioning idolaters, delirious fanatics, belligerent devotees, and religious murderers.

Sen is right to stress that Hinduism is not simply the Hinduism of Ayodhya; it has a religious, philosophical, spiritual, and historical track record that gives meaning to the reflexive language of secularism. At a more mundane level, Hinduism's own accommodations to other faiths have involved interesting compromises, not the least of which is the flourishing success of Christian missionary schools across the country, overwhelmingly to educate the Hindu middle class without any serious attempt to achieve their formal conversion to the faith of the Bible. A brief digression from my own childhood experience may help illuminate one of the many striking aspects of this oddly secular interpenetration.

Christmas did not mean a great deal to me and my largely non-Christian classmates at our Jesuit school in Bombay, except that, for those of us of a theatrical bent, it provided the excuse for our Christmas play.

Our school, Campion, was, like its eponymous Elizabethan martyr, a Catholic institution, one of many through which the Jesuits fulfilled their considerable talent for educating the privileged of the Third World. It was a not wholly successful vocation, for the Jesuits were uncomfortably elitist and the elites enthusiastically Jesuitical. But perhaps because of its academic limitations, Campion encouraged the idea that there was more to school than studies. It offered a variety of extracurricular activities that helped you to find yourself outside the classroom even if you had lost yourself inside it.

Foremost among these was the stage. There were frequent opportunities for participating in what was called (with no pun intended) interclass dramatics; and Campion offered, uniquely, optional afterschool instruction in drama from one of the most talented, vibrant, and experienced figures of the Bombay stage, Pearl Padamsee — born Jewish, married first to a Hindu and then to a Muslim, a small, bouncing bundle of barely repressed energy who transformed several classloads of self-conscious, awkward schoolboys into confident, compelling actors and directors. Pearl's classes were great fun, and they also led to bigger things — not just drama competitions at school, but extravagant public productions in overflowing Bombay theaters where people with no connection to Campion paid for standing-room-only tickets to watch us perform.

Inevitably, theater at Campion sometimes taught us about matters that had nothing much to do with the theater. One instructive occasion came when a bunch of us seventh graders were to perform in that staple of Catholic schooling, the Christmas play.

On this occasion the play, a longish one-acter, was called *The Boy Who Wouldn't Play Jesus,* and had been written by an American with a social conscience. It was unusual in several respects, including that it was *meant* to be performed by schoolchildren; the cast were to portray themselves in the course of rehearsing a Christmas play. All is good-natured chaos until the hero, a good hamburgers-and-root-beer American kid, decides that, as long as there's so much suffering and injustice in the world, he won't play Jesus. So he leads the cast off the stage and into the audience, collecting funds for — remember, this was a 1960s American play — the hungry children of Bombay.

So here we were, privileged Bombay kids, performing *The Boy Who Wouldn't Play Jesus* (with me in the title role). The play was written to be easily adapted to any group of children, for they were all to use their own names and "be themselves," but Pearl took the adaptation process a stage further. We too would protest injustice and suffering by refusing to play Jesus; but the issue that roused the Indian cast of Campion's Christmas play, that prompted them to walk into the aisles shouting slogans, would not be India's starving but Vietnam's.

This was 1967, and the Vietnam War was a favorite theme of the anti-American left, but Pearl was no radical, and Campion no training ground for revolutionaries. She had no political message to deliver to the audience of parents, teachers, and VIP invitees in our seething hot-bed of social rest. All she was trying to do in changing the script was avoid offending Bombayites.

Eleven years old at the time, I gave it no more than a passing thought. We were all aware of the change from our cyclostyled scripts, and I believe we all thought it was justified: after all, *we* were children of Bombay and we weren't starving, were we? It was only very much later that I realized what I had lent my innocence to. It was the Christmas after the Bihar famine, when thousands had lost their lives to hunger less than a day's train ride from Bombay, and massive infusions of food aid were being shipped in to keep Indian children alive. But we, insulated in the security of our Campion existence, and too young to pay attention to the front pages of our parents' papers, remained unaware of our own people's plight.

We could have changed "Bombay" in the script to "Bihar," or even "Calcutta," and the play might have had a startling relevance to its audience. But a pointed reminder of the reality outside our ivoried bower would only have proved embarrassing to our distinguished well-wishers. We needed an alien cause — popular with the educated class we were being trained to join, but far enough from our daily lives to cause no discomfort — to provoke our carefully rehearsed outrage.

And so we stepped off our Bombay stage in accordance with our script, refusing to play Jesus out of solidarity with starving children in Vietnam. We declaimed a Christmas message of caring and compassion to our largely non-Christian audience — a message they were meant to understand didn't really apply to them.

It was, I suppose, another Jesuit compromise between conviction and conformity, another sort of Christmas message. It showed how the Christian gospel could be propagated in a largely non-Christian world without endangering its votaries or undermining their vocation. The play was a huge success; the enthusiastically applauding parents, with hardly a Catholic among them, made record donations to the school fund. Perhaps that was ultimately the play's vindication. Or perhaps, more simply, that is how Catholic schools the world over ensure that they will continue to have Christmases to celebrate.

So India's minorities have found their own ways of adjusting to plural India. In turn, India absorbed them: the widespread calls for Sonia Gandhi to take over the Congress reflect not merely the political penury of those making such appeals but the eclecticism of Hindu India, into which this Roman Catholic would be seamlessly incorporated just as Hinduism itself has incorporated so many deities and external influences over the millennia. In such a culture the acceptance of difference is not difficult because cultural self-definition is remarkably elastic and absorptive. And yet I do not wish to underestimate the risk that Hinduism can pose to the pluralism of which it is the best example.

Paradoxically, I saw this risk at close hand, not in India but in that unlikely hotbed of Hindu chauvinism, the United States.

. . .

To explore that, we will go abroad in the next chapter. It is worth stressing again that only an all-inclusive pluralism will guarantee the survival and success of the Indian nation. India's minorities will succeed if they see themselves as Indians first and minorities second; and this will happen only if the India that grants them membership is an India in which they see themselves as equal in every respect to those of the real or imagined majority.

One way of making pluralism work in practice as a force for progress rather than confrontation is to harness its diversity for common endeavors. The way in which different communities have come together for "secular" ends — whether in ecological movements like the Himalayan agitations against deforestation, or in the social work of Baba Amte, or in the cinema industry of Bollywood — points to the potential for cooperative rather than divisive mobilization. Where members of different communities, according to evidence gathered by Harvard professor Ashutosh Varshney, are used to working together in civic associations like unions, clubs, or business partnerships, communal riots either do not occur or are rapidly defused. It is when groups have stayed apart, and failed to interact in secular activities, that their communal identities prevail; the lack of brotherhood guarantees their "otherhood." And then conflict, hatred, and violence erupt.

The existence of consent — not just to be ruled, but to strive together with other communities — is crucial to my understanding of nationhood; a nation's existence, Renan said a century ago, was a daily plebiscite. Two decades before Renan, a British historian and politician enunciated what at the time seemed a self-evident proposition. "A state which is incompetent to satisfy different races condemns itself; a state which does not include them is destitute of the chief basis of self-government," wrote Lord Acton in 1862. His words remain just as true of India today as they were of the British Empire then.

6

NRIs

"Never Relinquished India" or "Not Really Indian"?

On August 6, 1993, some fifteen thousand largely Indian expatriates assembled at the Washington Hilton and the Omni Shoreham Hotel for a "Global Conference" grandly titled "World Vision 2000." A glossy brochure promoting the conference described it as "a grand effort to bring [together] youths from across the U.S.A. and around the world" to "deliberate on the Vision of Wholeness for the future of life on our planet." Under a blazing headline, "Look Who Is Comming [*sic*] to the Global Conference!" one could find, in boldface, the names of President Clinton and the Dalai Lama and, in more modest type, Bill Moyers and Carl Sagan. Careful scrutiny, however, revealed that these luminaries had — no surprise — not actually accepted their invitations. And that those "dignitaries and spiritual leaders" who were in fact going to "guide the Global Conference" represented — surprise, surprise — most of the pantheon of India's Hindu extremist fringe.

For this seemingly innocuous event, it turned out, was not just another idealist, woolly-minded potlatch of the let's-preach-to-the-youngsters-to-keep-their-minds-off-sex-and-drugs variety. You could have been fooled, though, by the ersatz glossiness of the brochure, on which the Washington Monument and the U.S. Capitol shared covers with a suitably Saganesque depiction of the cosmos, and whose elaborate registration instructions were complemented by alluring photographs of "the inside of a room at the five-star Omni Shoreham Hotel" (complete with a postcoital Caucasian couple in bathrobes). The "Global Conference" was timed for the centenary of the appearance at Chicago's World Parliament of Religions of the brilliant Hindu humanist Swami Vivekananda, and its breathless blurbs sought to appropriate his luster. But its organizers had no claim to the all-embracing tolerance and wisdom of the late sage. They were the Vishwa Hindu Parishad, whose "Vision" (*their* capital V) extended most famously so far to the destruction of the Babri mosque at Ayodhya in northern India in December 1992, an act that unleashed violence and rioting on a scale not seen in India since independence.

The VHP, which enjoyed the rare distinction of being considered more extremist than the Rashtriya Swayamsevak Sangh, the party of Mahatma Gandhi's assassin, has made something of a specialty of incitements to hatred. Under its benevolent auspices during the Bombay pogroms of January 1993, Muslims were abused, attacked, turned out of their homes, deprived of their livelihoods, butchered in the streets. Its more articulate sympathizers have expressed admiration for Hitler's way with inconvenient minorities. This was the happy crew of moral and spiritual guides to whom fifteen thousand Indian émigré youngsters, some no doubt inveigled by the prospect of hearing the Dalai Lama and the president, entrusted their Washington weekend. When the brochure proclaimed "a variety of high quality programs to raise the awareness of human beings about their future directions," one's natural tendency to yawn was replaced by a shudder down a slowly chilling spine.

Washington was certainly an unlikely setting for a celebration of Hindu fanaticism. And yet it was not such an improbable venue after all. For there seems to be something about expatriation that breeds extremism. The American ethnic mosaic is full of imported bigotry, from the Muslim fundamentalists who have been trying with commendable ineptitude to blow up New York, to Miami's many incarnations of Attila the Cuba-Hun. Indian Americans have done their best to compete with these Fidelios of the foreign fringe. A coven of well-heeled Hindu professionals from Southern California swamped newspapers in India with a post-Ayodhya advertising campaign designed to counteract the bleeding-heart "pseudo-secularism" of the appalled liberals like myself who published denunciations of the destruction of the mosque and its aftermath. The ads — a farrago of ahistorical half-truths calling upon Indians in India to "awake," for otherwise "India and Hindus are doomed" — were merely the latest evidence that exile nurtures political extremists. The "Global Conference" therefore continued in a hoary tradition.

The strident chauvinism of these American Hindus is, after all, only one more installment in a long saga of zeal abroad for radicalism at home. We have already had expatriate Sikhs pouring money, weapons, and organizational skills into the cause of a "pure" (tobacco-free and barberless) "Khalistan"; Irish Americans supporting, willfully or otherwise, IRA terrorism in Northern Ireland; Jaffna Tamils in England financing the murderous drive for "Eelam" in Sri Lanka; and lobbying groups of American Jewry propounding positions on Palestinian issues that are far less accommodating than those of the Israeli government itself (at least in its Rabin and Peres incarnations).

The irony of political extremism being advocated from distant ivory towers of bourgeois moderation is only the most obvious of the contradictions of this phenomenon. The more visible Khalistanis of North America may have carefully regroomed their beards and thrown away their cigarettes, as enjoined upon them by the Sikh scriptures, but they derive sustenance almost entirely from clean-shaven expatriate coreligionists largely unfamiliar with the prohibitions and injunctions of their faith. And the Hindu chauvinists of Southern California flourish in a pluralist melting pot whose every quotidian experience is a direct contradiction of the sectarianism they trumpet in the advertisement pages of newspapers in India.

The explanation for this evident paradox may lie in the very nature of expatriation. Most of the contemporary world's emigrants are people who left their homelands in quest of material improvement, looking for financial security and professional opportunities that, for one reason or another, they could not attain in their own countries. Many of them left intending to return: a few years abroad, a few more dollars in the bank, they told themselves, and they would come back to their own hearths, triumphant over the adversity that had led them to leave. But the years kept stretching on, and the dollars were never quite enough, or their needs mounted with their acquisitions, or they developed new ties (career, wife, children, schooling) to their new land, and then gradually the realization seeped in that they would never go back. And with this realization, often only half-acknowledged, came a welter of emotions: guilt at the abandonment of the motherland, mixed with rage that the motherland had somehow — through its own failings, political, economic, social — forced them into this abandonment. The attitude of the expatriate to his homeland is that of the faithless lover who blames the woman he has spurned for not having sufficiently merited his fidelity.

That is why the support of extremism at home is doubly gratifying: it appeases the expatriate's sense of guilt at not being involved in his homeland, and it vindicates his decision to abandon it. (If the homeland he has left did not have the faults he detests, he tells himself, he would not have had to leave it.) But that is not all. The expatriate also desperately needs to define himself in his new society. He is reminded by his mirror, if not by the nationals of his new land, that he is not entirely like them. In the midst of racism and alienation, second-class citizenship and self-hatred, he needs an identity to assert — a label of which he can be proud, yet which does not undermine his choice of exile. He has rejected the reality of his country but not, he declares fervently, the essential values he has derived from his roots. As his children grow up "American" or "British," as they slough off the assumptions, prejudices, and fears of his own childhood, he becomes even more assertive about them. But his nostalgia is based on the selectiveness of memory; it is a simplified, idealized recollection of his roots, often reduced to their most elemental — family, caste, region, religion. In exile among foreigners, he clings to a vision of what he really is that admits no foreignness.

But the tragedy is that the culture he remembers, with both nostalgia and rejection, has itself evolved — in interaction with others — on its national soil. His perspective distorted by exile, the expatriate knows nothing of this. His view of what used to be home is divorced from the experience of home. The expatriate is no longer an organic part of the culture, but a severed digit that, in its yearning for the hand, can only twist itself into a clenched fist.

.   .   .

India is probably the only country in the world that not only has given official recognition to its expatriates, but has even devised a formal acronym for them. NRI, or Non-Resident Indian, is a term that, over the last decade, has found a firm place in the national vocabulary, though it is yet to be reflected in any dictionary. And NRIs as a breed have been granted an extraordinary range of special concessions by the government of India, ranging from privileged rates of interest on their hard-currency deposits in Indian banks, to exclusive housing colonies, to the opportunity to import Hollywood films onto India's screens. As the nation's economists look for solutions to India's balance-of-payments difficulties, there is only one point on which both government and opposition seem to be agreed — that a vital element in any equation will be the well-heeled, and still patriotic, NRI, one for whom the acronym could well mean "Never Relinquished India."

Non-Resident Indians have certainly come a long way since the days when Indian prime ministers sanctimoniously urged them to be loyal to the foreign countries in which they had settled. As late as 1974, an Indian foreign minister told Parliament that "overseas Indians," as they were then known, had chosen to live abroad and so were responsible for their own condition: the government of India had no obligation toward them. But since then New Delhi has developed expectations of its NRIs, and a reciprocal sense of obligation, too, has followed. Today NRIs are seen as people on whom the motherland — and its elected representatives — have a legitimate claim. It is a claim willingly conceded by many NRIs; for every extremist or secessionist abroad, there are a dozen who continue to demonstrate a remarkable degree of interest in, and commitment to, the land of their birth (or of their forebears).

The law defines NRIs in broad terms — not just as Indian citizens resident abroad, but as persons of Indian "origin" irrespective of their current nationality. "A person shall be deemed to be of Indian origin," the government explains in a promotional brochure, "if: (i) he, at any time, held an Indian passport; or (ii) he or either of his parents or any of his grandparents was an Indian and a permanent resident of undivided India at any time." New Delhi's anxiety to define the category as broadly as possible has led to some interesting terminological calisthenics. Not only can anyone with one Indian grandparent declare himself an NRI and claim the benefits of that designation, but the "wife of a citizen of India, or of a person of Indian origin, *shall also be deemed to be of Indian origin though she may be of non-Indian origin.*" (Italics added. The semantic sexism is quite deliberate: the rules do not apply in reverse, to the foreign husbands of female NRIs.)

These criteria, though liberal by international standards, still omit some who are visibly of Indian origin. One obvious problem, of course, is that if the NRI definition is interpreted literally, practically every citizen of Pakistan and Bangladesh would qualify as being of "Indian" descent. (The authorities have got around the implications of this by specifically requiring Pakistani and Bangladeshi nationals to obtain the prior permission of the Reserve Bank of India before seeking to avail themselves of any NRI facilities.) The NRI definition also disqualifies descendants of some of the earlier waves of Indian migration, mainly in the last century, to such far-flung outposts of Empire as Malaya and Mauritius, Ghana and Guyana, Singapore and Suriname. In most cases, nationals of those countries, though manifestly of Indian origin, are descended from migrants of earlier generations, higher up the family tree than their grandparents. Some of those expatriate communities did, however, renew their links to their ancestral lands through marriage with Indians from India, and so have the right to the NRI designation. But the vast majority of eligible NRIs are products of more recent migrations, mainly in the latter half of the twentieth century.

Their stories vary. Many of the first Indian emigrants to Britain, for instance, went in search of an education and stayed on to work. Then, from the 1950s on, came less educated members of the working class, attracted by the liberalization of British entry laws during the labor shortages of the postwar boom years. A third wave of Indians came in the 1970s via East Africa, from where many were expelled in the xenophobic fervor that swept some African states after independence. All three groups, and their offspring, have acquired a reputation for hard work, business sense, and ethnic clannishness. Their success and, paradoxically, their failure to assimilate fully into British society have made them ideal NRIs — still owing residual loyalty to their Indian past, and usually well off enough to do something about it. This has appealed to all those in India who wish to court their support, not only the government but those opposed to it. It is no accident, of course, that some of the mother country's extremist and secessionist movements have found aid, comfort, and hard cash from NRIs.

The first Indian immigrants to the United States and Canada came as early as the 1890s, when shiploads of Sikhs settled on the Pacific coast and established thriving farming communities in British Columbia and California. Racist entry legislation — prompted by such events as anti-Indian riots in the state of Washington in 1907 — prevented them from adding to their numbers, however, and it was only a thin trickle of students who came to the United States from India after the 1920s. (As late as 1935, signs on the doors of certain California establishments declared, "No Jobs for Japs or Hindus.") The number of Indian students began to increase after independence, and an increasing proportion of them stayed on, bringing high levels of academic attainment and valuable scientific and engineering skills to their new country. By the early 1970s the small but influential Indian minority was estimated as having the highest per capita income of any ethnic group in the United States. (As early as 1980 the median family income of the Indian American, according to the U.S. census of that year, was $25,644 per annum — at a time when the median income of white American citizens was $20,800.)

It was the more liberal Immigration Act of 1965 that opened the sluice-gates to the United States. But while the trickle of Indian professionals became a stream, in more recent years it is illegal immigration that has swelled the flow into a torrent. Working-class Indians found their way into the United States for the first time in the late 1970s and early 1980s, toiling on construction sites, taking over newspaper kiosks on street corners, operating rundown motels, cooking and serving in Indian restaurants, and driving taxicabs. A pair of "amnesties" gave them the legal status they needed to bring their families over, and today this "third wave" of Indian immigrants accounts for about half of the estimated one million Indians in the United States.

That figure is almost certainly an undercount, omitting as it does those who are still illegal and those who trace their direct descent from another center of the Indian diaspora, such as the Caribbean. But allowing for the approximations that are inevitable in such an exercise, there are major populations of Indian descent outside India, including over a million in Malaysia, Sri Lanka, and South Africa; nearly as many in both Great Britain and the United States; and about half a million each in Mauritius, Trinidad and Tobago, and Guyana, with smaller but significant numbers in the United Arab Emirates, Oman, Singapore, Yemen, and Suriname. There are, of course, tiny Indian minorities in a variety of countries, from some twenty thousand in Hong Kong to a solitary couple in El Salvador — and (until his premature death in 1994) one lone Indian, Bezal Jesudason, on the last outpost before the North Pole, running a base camp and provision store for Arctic explorers in the wilds of the aptly named and remote Canadian settlement of Resolute. In a statement in Parliament in May 1988, the government of India estimated that there were some 10 million Indians living in 155 countries around the world, including eight in Iceland, four in Kampuchea, and one in the Pacific island state of Vanuatu. But the government's figures conflated Indian passport-holders with known ethnic minorities of Indian descent, and its total of 10 million, though not an unreasonable guesstimate, cannot be arrived at by adding up the officially available statistics.

Though the available numbers are not therefore entirely reliable, one area where the figures are more easily verified is that of the financial contribution made by NRIs to their motherland. Throughout the second half of the 1980s, remittances home from NRIs — primarily the diligent Indian workers in the countries of the Arab/Persian Gulf — averaged some five thousand crores of rupees ($1.5 billion) a year. As a source of foreign exchange, this amounted to 40 percent of India's annual merchandise exports, or some 3 to 4 percent of the GNP. (In the state of Kerala, these remittances were responsible for generating a remarkable boom in the real estate and construction businesses, as money was poured into new housing for NRIs, and land values tripled in some areas.) In addition, NRI depositors placed over nine thousand crore rupees (nearly $3 billion) in external deposit accounts of Indian banks during the period 1976–88. Though the levels of these contributions may change from time to time, it is easy to understand why a government strapped for hard currency enthusiastically woos the NRI.

What are the elements with which the NRI can be wooed? The obvious financial incentives — special terms on bank deposits, offers of government securities, and the facilitation of direct investment by NRIs in Indian industry — have already been among the principal features of the Indian government's approach. But NRIs want more. One increasingly vocal demand has been for dual citizenship: Indian laws oblige an NRI who takes on the passport of his country of residence to give up his Indian nationality. NRIs have long argued that this is iniquitous, because while adopting a foreign country's citizenship may be a matter of convenience (and sometimes of necessity), giving up Indian citizenship is an assault on their faith and pride. New Delhi's official rules are based largely on the sound though increasingly outdated principle that one cannot owe one's loyalty to two sovereigns. NRIs argue that in today's world of large-scale and rapid migrations, the passport one holds is no proof of one's fundamental affinities and loyalties. Though not everyone's motives are entirely idealistic, most NRIs who clamor for dual citizenship do so for reasons that have more to do with emotional identification than with practical advantage. In late 1991 the government of India provided some indications that this was a demand it was prepared to consider more sympathetically than in the past. But despite carefully hedged supportive words from Prime Minister Narasimha Rao, the idea dribbled away into the dry desert sands of the Indian bureaucracy, where it has remained half-buried, to be brought out occasionally whenever NRIs need to be wooed.

An even more thorny issue is that of the right to vote. NRIs who are Indian citizens have made the point that while they are invited, indeed expected, to make a contribution to the country's development and its balance of payments, they are allowed no role in influencing the policies of the country as voters. India is one of the few democracies in the modern world that has developed no tradition of absentee balloting for national elections, with the result that citizens living abroad are, in effect, disenfranchised. In 1991 the Kerala High Court even admitted a petition challenging India's electoral laws, but the case went nowhere. If NRI citizens are indeed given the right to vote, the politics of Kerala — a state with more than a million Malayalis working abroad, and whose election results are often decided by margins of a thousand votes or fewer — would be dramatically affected. But this is not a question that is likely to be settled quickly; legal experts suggest the principles involved will probably take the issue all the way to the Supreme Court.

Meanwhile, the NRI continues to make his way abroad, primarily on the strength of qualities regarded as "typically Indian" — hard work, discipline, self-sacrifice, and thrift. The way in which Indians have taken over unprofitable motels across the United States, and run newsstands in New York City or late-night groceries in London, is widely seen as reflective of those qualities. One American newspaper wholesaler told *The New York Times* that the Indians "basically replaced the old Jewish and Italian merchants and they've filled a tremendous void because nobody will put in the fourteen and sixteen-hour days that they do quite willingly and that you have to put in when running a news-stand." A Londoner who discovers at midnight that she has run out of milk cheerfully decides to "go down to the local Indian." A shopper in Hong Kong prefers to make her purchases at the Indian shops, rather than those run by the colony's Chinese majority, because "you always get a better deal from the Indians. They're willing to accept a smaller margin of profit than the others." Not all the comments are entirely positive. "If you have a toxic dump to clean up," wrote *The Wall Street Journal*, "there is a good chance than an Indian engineer's company will do it. Not many U.S. firms want such dirty work."

By 1986 it was estimated that 28 percent of the 53,629 motels and small hotels in the United States were owned by Indians, largely Indians named Patel. "In Anaheim and along San Francisco's Route 1 and in sections of Georgia, Oklahoma and Texas," wrote an American journalist, James P. Sterba, "it is hard to find one that isn't." Sterba's explanation was that "the Patels were security-conscious savers, eager to own property," who took advantage of low prices and generous mortgage financing in the early 1970s. "A motel," Sterba pointed out in the *The Wall Street Journal*, "provided property, home, business and employment for a large extended family." Those motivations are widely considered representative of the new Indian approach to business opportunity abroad—a stark contrast to the earlier image of the studious Indian graduate who went from being every American professor's favorite research assistant to becoming the hardest-working salaried employee of banks, laboratories, and research corporations. Though there are still Indian doctors and scientists of considerable renown (including two Nobel Prize–winning American scientists who were born, raised, and educated in India), the new wave of Indian immigrants is demonstrating that they, too, have the entrepreneurial spirit and are prepared to take the risks that their predecessors in the professional classes largely did not.

A list of successful NRIs ranges from the likes of Dr. Hargobind Khorana, Nobel Prize–winning geneticist, and Dr. Subrahmanyan

Chandrashekhar, Nobel Prize–winning astrophysicist, to the Oscar-winning actor Ben Kingsley (born Krishna Bhanji), the millionaire British industrialist Lord Swraj Paul, and the conductor Zubin Mehta, and embraces both self-help guru Deepak Chopra and the United States' biggest peach farmer, Didar Singh Bains. Salman Rushdie has a claim to the designation (and recently sued for the restitution of property his father had owned in India). Most of India's nationalist leaders, from Jawaharlal Nehru to the anti-Emergency opposition leader Jayaprakash Narayan, were NRIs at one time, though the term had not been invented while they lived abroad.

With increasing affluence and visibility, the NRI is also beginning to develop political clout, though not yet at a level comparable to his new-found political clout in India. In Britain's House of Commons, there are only three members of parliament of Indian origin, two of whom were not born in India (Keith Vaz, who was born in Aden, and Nirj Deva, born in Sri Lanka of Indian parents). The unelected House of Lords has a handful of nominated NRI members. In the United States there is no Indian member of Congress, though an American of Indian descent, Dalip Singh Saund, did serve three terms in the United States House of Representatives in the early 1960s, representing a Los Angeles constituency. (Indians have sought the nominations to Congress of the major parties in recent years, without much success.) But if NRIs are not yet elected holders of national office, their influence on those who are is mounting. The hostility to India of certain American congressmen, particularly on the issues of Punjab and Kashmir, is directly attributable to the views — and the financial backing — of NRIs from their constituencies who are active in the "Khalistan" and Kashmiri separatist movements. Conversely, the sympathy for the Indian government's positions usually extended by the highly regarded former congressman Stephen J. Solarz of Brooklyn was directly connected to the help and support he regularly received from well-heeled Indians in his New York district. Solarz frequently conducted direct-mail solicitation campaigns for contributions to his reelection that were targeted at voters of Indian origin.

Nonresident Indians thus represent a growing force, increasing in numbers and financial strength, beginning to flex their political muscle and widely seen as a national resource for the regeneration of their homeland. What is often overlooked in India, though, is that as individual human beings NRIs face a range of social problems implicit in the immigrant condition: alienation, anxiety about their identity, dilemmas about the values in which to bring up their children. Are NRIs just what the term implies, Indians who happen not to be resident in India, or are they Americans, Britons, or Tanzanians of a different ethnicity than the majority of their new compatriots? Issues of discrimination in employment and housing, social and racial conflicts, differing levels of language skills, and varying degrees of social acceptance complicate the response to this question. And whatever passports they may currently hold, their loyalties are easily impugned in their new countries: in Britain, a former Conservative minister, Norman Tebbit, pointed out that Indian Britons at international cricket matches still supported the Indian team. (This was briefly undercut in June 1996 when England fielded, in their eleven for the first Test against India, no fewer than three players of Indian origin; but two of them soon lost their England places.) Salman Rushdie has written eloquently of the dilemma of the divided self, a dilemma all NRIs, to a greater or lesser extent, live with every day.

This can manifest itself in ugly ways, even when it does not transform itself into support for extremism. Some years ago a Malaysian friend sent me a clipping from the Singapore *Straits Times* with the provocative title "How India Changed Me." It might not have been worthy of a second glance were it not for two things: its prominence (it occupied most of the editorial page of the paper) and what its contents revealed about the overseas Indian syndrome. The article purported to be the account of a journey in India and the lessons learned from it by the author, who sported an Indian name, P. N. Balji, and presumably a Southeast Asian passport. Balji began by confessing that he is usually "embarrassed" to talk about his visits to India, but that after his "recent trips" there, he is no longer so, "for I have discovered a new India. An

India that jolts my conscience, helps me to educate my eight-year-old daughter, reminds me of the things I take for granted and that money cannot buy everything."

Unexceptionable so far? Perhaps, but Balji's "new India" is not the India of industrial self-sufficiency, scientific research, or agricultural progress, or even the home of an ancient cultural heritage or profound spiritual values, all inferences that might reasonably flow from his earlier observation. It is an India that, if it bore the slightest resemblance to empirical truth, he and everyone else should indeed be embarrassed to talk about. Balji's "rediscovery" starts at "the stuffy terminal building" of Madras airport, where "lean and hungry-looking porters wait watchfully at strategic corners." Note the pejorative buildup to this startling story: "Suddenly a group of them descended on a helpless and unsuspecting woman passenger, who had a wailing baby in one hand and a handbag in the other. The result was probably a big hole in her purse or the loss of some items."

"Probably"? Balji advances no grounds for his supposition that the porters were motivated by criminality rather than the pursuit of custom. But the message is clear, and is underscored a couple of paragraphs later when "four scruffy-looking middle-aged men" aid him uninvited to secure his bags to the roof of a taxi and the driver suggests they should be tipped. "Weren't these people working in cahoots?" speculates Balji. "The Mafia, Madras-style, perhaps." This is preposterous; Balji could have simply told the men he didn't need their help, or tied the bags to the roof of the car himself; everywhere else in the world, he would be expected to pay for services rendered.

Balji seems to have had an enviably easy passage through customs (which he attributes with apparently characteristic gaucherie to his "nonchalance and a touch of the Englishman's accent plus some pomp and style"), but this does not prevent him from launching into an excruciating litany of the harassment to which he might have been subjected had he been less sophisticated. The rest of his journey — and his article — proceeds in the same spirit. A rushing porter on a crowded railway platform barges into his daughter; Balji abuses and hits him.

Indian railways "offer many lessons for me and my daughter," says Balji. "The filthy toilets in the trains, the push-and-hit crowds, the children who eat leftovers thrown from the train. My daughter's experience on the train journey disturbs her sometimes — when she has her meals or when I remind her of it. Looking out she saw girls and boys of her age, with runny noses, flies all over their bodies, eating leftover food thrown out by passengers. Back home, when she does not finish her dinner and when I remind her of that scene, she makes an effort not to leave anything on her plate."

So that is supposed to be the edifying experience with which India helped "educate" the girl. Of course there's no denying that poverty, squalor, and misery exist in India; but surely exposure to them should teach an eight-year-old compassion, not self-righteousness. The inability to distinguish between the "horrors" of filthy toilets and those of hungry children is a lamentable enough failure of sensibility in an adult; to use it to teach a "lesson" to an eight-year-old is appallingly crass and smug. Bias and conjecture are supplemented by ignorance and inaccuracy. Balji writes of meeting a "talented" lawyer who fails for six years to find a job because he is a "former communist sympathizer"(this in a country where half a dozen Communist parties flourish, where Communists have held ministerial office and Supreme Court judgeships, and have run the governments of three states.). He goes on to meet a Singaporean now settled in India, living in "palatial" comfort but "not enjoying his life" because he cannot get ballpoint pens and writing paper (this in a country where there is a profusion of writing implements available and whose decorated notepaper is a successfully exported gift item). "I smiled," reports Balji in triumph. He would.

So why is this silly article important? The answer is distressingly simple. The Baljis of this world abound across the globe, not only in Singapore and Malaysia but in Kenya, in Nigeria, in Britain. They (or their ancestors) have left India, but their mirrors and their identity cards limit the extent of their escape. They look Indian; most have Indian names; despite their current passports, they cannot flee the crippling bonds of their ethnicity. To outsiders they might even be Indian. Their reaction is to protest their rejection of India, to find comfort in echoing the most superficial of India's critics. In doing so they are curiously reassured: they have vindicated their emigration; they are better off than if they had remained.

So the India that emerges in the Balji article is the India that most overseas Indians want to congratulate themselves on having left behind. It is an India where porters are crooks and customs men are venal, where a pseudo-Englishness alone can open doors, where life is cheap and property is not respected, where toilets are filthy and garbage is food, where the able are unemployed and even the rich do not have access to pen and paper. That this bears no relation to a complete or accurate picture of India is entirely irrelevant. Its real purpose is to reaffirm the prejudices of an expatriate community, remind them of the deprivation they have escaped, and so vindicate their emigration. Balji's title was disingenuous. India can never change someone like him.

The Baljis of the world know, but prefer to overlook the fact, that India is, after all, a developing country (or, as I once wrote, a highly developed country of the past, in an advanced state of decay). It is also an overpopulated nation. If its airports have more porters than the workload justifies, travelers should surely prefer their importunate offers of service to the alternative of heaving their own baggage to the taxi-rank. As for the customs, no Indian who has voyaged abroad will seek to defend the *modus operandi* of these gentlemen, but we have to remember that they operate within laws designed to curb imports, which they apply with more zeal than judgment. On unemployment, no one could suggest that the country is teeming with unfilled job vacancies, since the curbs on investment and the pressure of numbers have resulted in applicants vastly exceeding available posts; but what is untenable is Balji's suggestion that qualified persons are denied opportunities on purely political grounds, because India tolerates a diversity of political opinion rarely found in the countries to which Indians have emigrated.

Indians are ordinary human beings like Americans or Europeans (or even Singaporeans), but unlike these others they have to struggle to attain and maintain the standards that NRIs like Balji are able to take for granted. To some degree that struggle has been imposed upon them by nature, but they are aware that a lot of their problems are man-made, and they are trying through a democratic constitutional system to overcome them. When your children ask about Indian poverty and dirt, I want to say to NRIs, tell them about the lack of resources, the historical iniquities from feudalism to colonialism, the misguided policies of post-independence bureaucrats; and tell them also of the attempts to evolve Indian answers to these Indian problems, of land reform and Dalit rights, of free elections and a free press. Your outrage at injustice or suffering is echoed in thousands of Indian voices; and if you want to do your bit to help overcome these Indian evils, there are dozens of Indian organizations that would welcome your time, your efforts, and your remittances. But what India does not need, as it tries to rise to its challenges, is the contempt and the contumely of those who have left India.

Yet it keeps coming: a different sort of India-hating NRI syndrome exists as well. It has become customary in recent years for the Indian media in particular and Indian opinion-makers in general to take up the cudgels on behalf of Indian immigrants abroad, especially in Britain. Whether it was the notorious practice, now abandoned, of British immigration officials in effect peering up the saris of Indian women to establish their virginity at Heathrow Airport (the British thought "virginity tests" were the best way of establishing the authenticity of the claims of immigrant brides), or the somewhat less objectionable stipulation that Sikh motorcyclists in Southall must crown their turbans with helmets, we in India have always granted our ex-compatriots publicity and sympathy. The presumption has largely been that they are flesh of our flesh, and that their humiliation should therefore provoke our outrage.

In this vein, a significant proportion of the limited amount of space available in Indian publications for foreign news has been devoted to tales of the defenestration of subcontinental immigrants — the Gillingham Gujarati wife unceremoniously ejected from England after her divorce, the Birmingham Bengali woman expelled from Britain following the death of her husband (in each case the lady's claim to residence in the U.K. was based on her marriage, and expired with it). Such tales are (sometimes) undoubtedly moving, though I for one failed to find anything especially tragic in principle in the return of either lady to what is after all her homeland. But one instance of the application of the official British boot to a displaced Indian posterior led me emphatically to question where, indeed, our sympathies as Indians ought to lie.

The case was that of Rodney Pereira, or perhaps one should refer to him as Rodney Pereira, Esquire, late of Bishop's Waltham, Hampshire, an undistinguished little hamlet near Southampton. Pereira arrived in England as a twenty-six-year-old Indian engineer on board a merchant navy ship in 1977, and didn't leave. He found work as a salesman in a local double glazing firm, was soon joined by an Indian girlfriend, Gail, whom he married in England, and their union was blessed by the arrival of a daughter, Keira, three years later.

The only problem was that Pereira had no business to be in England in the first place, and the Home Office finally told him so, in 1982. But at this point the wonderful inconsistency of the British people asserted itself; the good villagers of Bishop's Waltham rose in protest. It seems that during their years of illegal residence the Pereiras had been, in the words of a neighbor, "model citizens." They had regularly attended church, charming Gail had always spoken politely to the grocer; little Keira, an angel in human shape, was taking ballet lessons; and Rodney himself — I loved this touch — had played Santa Claus every Christmas at Yuletide celebrations in his daughter's nursery school. Fortified by public meetings, the support of their parish priest (who declared they were "very much part of the community"), and mass petitions to the Queen and the home office, the Pereiras refused to leave Bishop's Waltham. They embarked instead on the long series of appeals permitted by Britain's civil procedures. (It is one of the lesser ironies of international affairs that illegal immigrants are invariably so inexhaustibly litigious.) The technical details of the appeals themselves need not concern us here; for the record, the Pereiras were rebuffed by two separate Immigration Appeals Tribunals, both of which upheld the Home Ministry's deportation order.

What struck me, however, is what the Pereiras began saying publicly in order to stir popular sympathy in Britain to their side. India, according to one petition, is "a country that has nothing at all for them." A commentary on the recession or on widespread unemployment? Not a bit of it. "As English-speaking Roman Catholics," claimed Pereira, "we would face prejudice in India." (This, incidentally, from a man who grew up in India, embarked on his merchant navy career there, and actually had relatives living in Bombay.) The former seaman claimed he would not be re-employed by India's merchant navy (hardly surprising, since he had deserted it when he jumped ship in England), and as for his new profession, there was not much call for double glazing in India. But wait for the main reason: "We do not want to be sent back to a country whose language [*sic*] we do not speak." Poor Pereira: "We have nothing to go back to — except hostility and prejudice because we are Catholics and cannot speak the Indian language."

Of course this is absurd and appalling, but it is far from atypical. Whether it is a small-time sailor on the make, willing to lie about conditions in his country in order to persuade white Christians that he is really one of them, or an organized tour group of Sikhs claiming political asylum in Canada or Germany on the grounds that they are "persecuted" in India for their religion, Indians have proved themselves unhesitatingly able to put self-interest before principle abroad. If distorting, concealing, attacking, and deliberately misrepresenting the truth about Indian social and political tolerance can deliver a laminated green card or a Caucasian passport, some Indians will not hesitate to drag their own country through the mud. National loyalty, when seen from an economic, standard-of-living point of view, is hardly a sterling virtue. When it comes to personal material advancement, we are individualists par excellence.

The only "hostility and prejudice" Pereira might have encountered in India would not have been for his Catholicism or his linguistic limitations, but for his cheap attempt to deny an identity he could not lose unless he shed his skin. There are Pereiras and Baljis all over the world, whose hatred for their motherland is an essential condition of their ability to live with themselves in their new countries. (They, of course, qualify for the NRI label but are unlikely to lay claim to it.)

There are thus both positives and negatives in the NRI condition: grounds for fear and loathing, directed at both India and the NRI himself, as well as opportunity to exercise influence on India's behalf, contribute to India's development, and profit from India's growth. In an emotional sense, NRIs are the prodigal sons of a motherland they have left but not forgotten, clinging to a sense of nationhood they cannot define but will not surrender. Many would argue that, especially given the Indian government's open doors in the "liberalization" era (of which more later), NRIs have the best of both worlds. As the United States–based physicist E. C. G. Sudarshan put it, describing the unique situation of the NRI in relation to his home country and his country of adoption: "If you look at the world with two eyes, you see more. It is possible to live in two worlds."

. . .

It might seem an odd digression, to have been discussing India's minorities and then to find oneself looking at Indians who are minorities elsewhere. But they are linked phenomena, and as an NRI myself (one who has Never Relinquished India), I am conscious of the enormous potential for constructive contribution that NRIs represent, and the difference they can make to India — just as I am aware that for some other NRIs the acronym could as well stand for "Not Really Indian." The involvement of NRIs with the Indian predicament is, however, to me symptomatic of the perpetual pull of the motherland: whatever you feel about her, Mother India never really lets go.

7

The Hindu Rate of Growth, and Other Agnostic Legacies

*F*or most of the five decades since independence, India has pursued an economic policy of subsidizing unproductivity, regulating stagnation, and distributing poverty. We called this socialism.

The moment of truth about Indian economic policy — the moment when even its guardians had to accept that the old ways had not worked and could be sustained no longer — came in early 1991 when a large part of the nation's gold reserves had to be flown out to London as collateral for a $2.2-billion emergency IMF loan. Without the loan, India would have had to default on its international debt, and the economy would, for all practical purposes, have collapsed.

The country's foreign exchange reserves, which stood at just under a billion dollars in January 1991, would have covered just two weeks of imports; the Gulf War increased India's oil bills at precisely the time that Indian workers were fleeing the area and depriving Indian banks of their remittances. This left the government no choice but to raise money to service its debts — against the country's gold reserves.

One cannot imagine a greater psychological shock to the average Indian. We have, for millennia, placed our trust in gold as the ultimate security. In Indian culture, the woman of the house — the embodiment of the family's honor — treasures her gold jewelry both as her soundest asset and as the symbol of her status. The notion that the country was, in effect, pawning its collective jewelry abroad in order to keep paying the rent sent shock waves through the polity.

Experts had long said it would take a real crisis to crystallize the growing impetus for economic reform. The gold crisis did it. This event — more than any abstract figures in budgetary calculations — drove home the indispensability of serious change in economic policy. Things simply couldn't go on as they had.

The road to disaster was, as usual, paved with good, even noble, intentions. In 1954, Prime Minister Nehru, moved by the desperate plight of the Indian masses, got the Congress Party to agree to work toward the creation of a "socialist pattern of society." Within a year his principal economic adviser, the Strangelovian P. C. Mahalanobis, came up with the Second Five-Year Plan. This enshrined industrial self-sufficiency as the goal, to be attained by a state-controlled public sector that would dominate the "commanding heights" of the economy. This public sector would be financed by higher income, wealth, and sales taxes on India's citizenry. India would industrialize, Indians would pay for it, and the Indian government would run the show.

The logic behind this approach, and for the dominance of the public sector, was a compound of nationalism and idealism: the conviction that items vital for the economic well-being of Indians must remain in Indian hands — not the hands of Indians seeking to profit from such activity, but the disinterested hands of the state, that father-and-mother to all Indians. It was sustained by the assumption that the public sector was a good in itself; that, even if it was not efficient or productive or competitive, it employed large numbers of Indians, gave them a stake in worshiping at Nehru's "new temples of modern India," and kept the country free from the depredations of profit-oriented capitalists who would enslave the country in the process of selling it what it needed. In this kind of thinking, performance was not a relevant criterion for judging the utility of the public sector: its inefficiencies were masked by generous subsidies from the national exchequer, and a combination of vested interests — socialist ideologues, bureaucratic management, self-protective trade unions, and captive markets — kept it beyond political criticism.

But since the public sector was involved in economic activity, it was difficult for it to be entirely exempt from economic yardsticks. Yet, in 1992–93, of the 237 public-sector companies in existence, 104 had losses, amounting to some 40 billion rupees of the Indian taxpayers' money. (Most of the remaining 133 companies made only a marginal profit. The figures have undoubtedly worsened: according to a report in *Time* magazine in March 1996, the country's public-sector electric utilities alone lost $2.2 billion in the preceding twelve months, or 70 billion rupees a year. Other public-sector industries that experienced losses were not far behind.) Several of the state-owned companies are kept running merely to provide jobs — or, less positively, to prevent the "social costs" (job losses, poverty, political fallout) that would result from closing them down. In 1994, one British journalist, Stefan Wagstyl of the *Financial Times,* reported in disbelief from the government-owned Hindustan Fertilizer factory in Haldia, West Bengal, which employs 1,550 workmen but has produced no fertilizer since it was set up at a cost of $1.2 billion (and after seven years of construction) in 1986:

> There is a canteen, a personnel department, and an accounts department. There are promotions, job changes, pay rises, audits, and in-house trade unions. Engineers, electricians, plumbers and painters maintain the equipment with a care that is almost surreal. . . .

In a series of newspaper articles a decade earlier, right-of-center congressman Vasant Sathe had pointed out that the public-sector steel industry in India employed ten times as many people to produce half as much steel as the South Koreans (according to 1986 figures not yet available to Sathe, the facts were even worse: the Steel Authority of India paid 247,000 people to produce some 6 million tons of finished steel, whereas 10,000 South Korean workers employed by the Pohan Steel Company produced 14 million tons that same year). The home-grown product that emerged from this labor-intensive process was uneconomically expensive: India's finished steel cost $650 a ton, so it found few buyers abroad, since world prices were between $500 and $550 a ton. Ironically, India's raw material — iron ore — was cheap enough to be imported by foreign steel manufacturers, who used Indian iron ore to manufacture their own finished steel cheaper than India could. Sathe pointed out that if India had been able to make steel efficiently to world standards and at the world price, it would be earning four thousand rupees a ton in profit from exporting finished steel, whereas it was now exporting iron ore and making just seventy-five rupees a ton. This was, ironically, what had happened under colonialism — India being used as a source of raw material by countries that did their own manufacturing abroad. Now the same thing was being done in a spirit of anticolonialism: we were doing it to ourselves.

Sathe was an influential political figure and such views were increasingly common among thinking Indians, but governmental attitudes were slow to change. The rooting of economic policy in political atavism made change difficult; wary of opening the economy to foreign business for fear of repeating the experience of the East India Company, whose merchants had become rulers, India relied on economic self-sufficiency as the only possible guarantee of political independence. The result was extreme protectionism, high tariff barriers (import duties of 350 percent were not uncommon, and the top rate as recently as 1991 was 300 percent), severe restrictions on the entry of foreign goods, capital, and technology, and great pride in the manufacture within India of goods that were obsolete, inefficient, and shoddy but recognizably Indian (like the clunky Ambassador automobile, a revamped 1948 Morris Oxford produced by a Birla quasi-monopoly, which had a steering mechanism with the subtlety of an oxcart, guzzled gas like a sheik, and shook like a guzzler, and yet enjoyed waiting lists of several years at all the dealers).

The mantra of self-sufficiency might have made some sense if, behind these protectionist walls, Indian business had been encouraged to thrive. Despite the difficulties placed in their way by the British Raj, Indian corporate houses like those of the Birlas, Tatas, and Kirloskars had built impressive business establishments by the time of independence, and could conceivably have taken on the world. Instead they found themselves being hobbled by regulations and restrictions, inspired by socialist mistrust of the profit motive, on every conceivable aspect of economic activity: whether they could invest in a new product or a new capacity; where they could invest; how many people they could hire, whether they could fire them; what sort of new product lines they could develop; whether they could import any raw materials; where they could sell what, and for how much. Initiative was stifled, government permission was mandatory before any expansion or diversification, and a mind-boggling array of permits and licenses was required before the slightest new undertaking. And if a business employing more than a hundred people failed, it could not be closed without government permission, which was usually not forthcoming.

"What's your father doing these days?" I asked a Calcutta friend whose family had moved to Delhi in 1971. "Oh, he's very busy," replied the friend. "His job is to figure out ways by which his company can invest its profits at home without falling afoul of the various rules and regulations of the government preventing private-sector companies from expanding." That such a job existed in a country that was crying out for productive investment was horrifying enough, but worse was the fact that the government justified its restrictions in the name of socialism, as if socialism had nothing to do with the members of society who could have gained productive employment and food in their bellies from the investments the capitalists were not allowed to make. It is sadly impossible to quantify the economic losses inflicted on India over four decades of entrepreneurs frittering away their energies in queuing for licenses rather than manufacturing products, paying bribes instead of hiring workers, wooing politicians instead of understanding consumers, "getting things done" through bureaucrats rather than doing things for themselves.

The patriarch of the Kirloskar family, not without bitterness, compared his situation with that of Japan's Toyota. In 1947 S. L. Kirloskar, despite the obstacles thrown in his way by the British Raj, was already a manufacturer of some consequence, with a couple of factories, using imported machinery, and a market whose potential seemed limitless. According to Kirloskar, Kiichiro Toyoda, at that time, ran a Ford dealership in Tokyo. Within three decades Toyota had become one of the world's largest and commercially most successful automobile makers, with a brand name recognized around the world, while Kirloskar, struggling to grow under the stifling constraints imposed upon his like by the Indian government, had held his place as one of India's leading industrialists but had no claim to being mentioned in the same breath as his Japanese contemporary. Toyota had been helped, encouraged, and abetted by the government of Japan and its Ministry of International Trade and Industry; Kirloskar had had to fight his government all the way to expand. Ironically, Mahatma Gandhi's links with Indian businessmen during the nationalist movement suggest that a similar partnership between business and government, as in Japan, could have been possible, indeed might have been encouraged by a Vallabhbhai Patel (the pragmatic deputy prime minister who died within three years of independence). Nehru, who regarded capitalists with distaste and admired the great achievements of the socialist Soviet state, headed in another direction, and Mr. Kirloskar and his ilk had to run hard to stay in the same place. In an ironic footnote to the story, Kirloskar's heirs announced in August 1996 that they would participate in a joint venture to manufacture a subcompact car in India; their partner in the venture was Toyota.

Regulations and socialist-inspired restrictions on capital were only part of the problem. India taxed its businesses into starvation, and its citizens into submission; at one point the cumulative taxes on some Indians totaled more than 100 percent of their income. Taxation was meant to finance government overspending, but its yield — especially as extortionate rates drove more and more individuals and companies into tax evasion — could not keep pace with the voraciousness of the government's appetite. When it could not tax any more, the government borrowed money, piling up higher and higher deficits. Concomitantly, it tried to control more and more of the economy. Prime Minister Indira Gandhi nationalized the country's banks and insurance companies in 1969, and briefly even tried to take over the wholesale trade in food grains (though this proved disastrous and was quickly shelved).

Bank nationalization achieved the political objective of burnishing Mrs. Gandhi's socialist credentials and giving the government a ready source of money for essentially political purposes, with few questions asked; but it failed to fulfill either of the objectives it was ostensibly about, namely to serve the Indian masses better and to channel their savings efficiently into socially productive investments. Instead the government obliged the nationalized banks to make bad loan after bad loan to "priority sectors" designated for political purposes, reducing most nationalized banks to near insolvency, while basic services were provided in a manner that would be unacceptable anywhere in the democratic world.

The Janata Party government that briefly replaced Mrs. Gandhi between 1977 and 1980 proved no better, mainly because their dominant ethos was a combination of the Congress's Nehruvian old guard and the fiery (if wholly impractical) idealism of the former Socialist Party. Janata rule saw no changes in the basic patterns of the Indian economy, and was best known for the departures from India of IBM and Coca-Cola (the latter because the government insisted that the company reveal its secret formula). Heedless of the signal these exits sent to the rest of the world — whose brief hopes that a change of government might have led to a more welcoming investment climate were poured down the same drain as the Coke — the Janata ministers chose to celebrate the departures of these multinational corporations as a further triumph for socialism and anti-imperialist self-reliance. (One good thing, though, about the departure of Coca-Cola was the development of two competing Indian brands, Thumbs Up and Campa-Cola. I am not alone in believing that both were better than the "Real Thing," and when Coke returned to the country in 1995, it bought the Thumbs Up brand and kept it going for a loyal and discriminating Indian clientele.)

The combination of internal controls and international protectionism gave India a distorted economy, underproductive and grossly inefficient, making too few goods, of too low a quality, at too high a price. The resultant stagnation led to snide comments about what Indian economist Raj Krishna called the "Hindu rate of growth," which averaged some 3.5 percent in the first three decades after independence (or, to be more exact, between 1950 and 1980) when other countries in Southeast Asia were growing at 8 to 15 percent or even more. Exports of manufactured goods grew at an annual rate of 0.1 percent until 1985; India's share of world trade fell by four-fifths. Per capita income, with a burgeoning population and a modest increase in GDP, anchored India firmly to the bottom third of the world rankings. The public sector, however, grew in size though not in production, to become the largest in the world outside the Communist bloc.

Some economists argued that by protecting public-sector industry, the government actually damaged rural India, since the Mahalanobis plans completely neglected the agricultural sector, and the higher cost of manufactured goods in effect reduced the purchasing power of agricultural incomes. But these sins were compounded by a policy of generous subsidies to farmers, and an exemption from taxation on agricultural incomes, that gave the country's agrarian elites the same sort of vested interest in economic policy as the public-sector workers whose jobs would disappear if common sense dawned on the government. Meanwhile, income disparities persisted, the poor remained mired in a poverty all the more wretched for the lack of means of escape from it in a controlled economy, the public sector sat entrenched on the "commanding heights" and looked down upon the toiling, overtaxed middle class, and only bureaucrats, politicians, and a small elite of protected businessmen flourished from the management of scarcity.

As handouts drained the budget and restrictions hampered growth, there was an almost culpable lack of attention to the country's infrastructure (with the solitary exception of the railways, whose development has been a rare triumph). The country's overcongested roads, ports, bridges, and canals have fallen into disrepair, and few have been upgraded beyond the standards of the 1940s; goods sit (and sometimes rust or rot) at the docks because the harbors can no longer cope with the volume of cargo they need to handle; irrigation and power generation have made little or no progress (and power has actually taken several steps back, as demand has long since outstripped capacity, and ubiquitous power cuts have made the euphemism "load-shedding" a familiar cliché.) Communications was the worst of the list; the woeful state of India's telephones right up to the 1990s, with only 8 million connections and a further 20 million on waiting lists, would have been a joke if it wasn't also a tragedy — and a man-made one at that. The government's indifferent attitude to the need to improve India's communications infrastructure was epitomized by Prime Minister Indira Gandhi's communications minister, C. M. Stephen, who declared in Parliament, in response to questions decrying the rampant telephone breakdowns in the country, that telephones were a luxury, not a right, and that any Indian who was not satisfied with his telephone service could return his phone — since there was an eight-year waiting list of people seeking this supposedly inadequate product.

Mr. Stephen's statement captured perfectly everything that was wrong about the government's attitude. It was ignorant (he clearly had no idea of the colossal socioeconomic losses caused by poor communications), wrong-headed (he saw a practical problem only as an opportunity to score a political point), unconstructive (responding to complaints by seeking a solution apparently did not occur to him), self-righteous (the socialist cant about telephones being a luxury, not a right), complacent (taking pride in a waiting list the existence of which should have been a source of shame, since it pointed to the poor performance of his own ministry in putting up telephone lines and manufacturing equipment), unresponsive (feeling no obligation to provide a service in return for the patience, and the fees, of the country's telephone subscribers), and insulting (asking long-suffering telephone subscribers to return their instruments instead of doing something about their complaints). It was altogether typical of an approach to governance in the economic arena that assumed that the government knew what was good for the country, felt no obligation to prove it by actual performance, and didn't, in any case, care what anyone else thought.

This is not merely a gratuitous attack on one minister, who was by no means the worst of his breed. Rather, it is intended to raise the question of attitude as an issue in itself, in understanding India's disastrous persistence in an economic policy that was misconceived from the start and had clearly outlived its usefulness by the mid-1960s. The governmental attitudes of a C. M. Stephen underlay an approach that shackled the creative energies of the Indian people. One of the commonly asked questions of the 1970s and 1980s was how it was that *India* plodded along under its "Hindu rate of growth" when *Indians* thrived so spectacularly wherever they were given a chance abroad. The astonishing successes of the "Non-Resident Indians" or NRIs — the émigrés who, arriving penniless, soon broke into the ranks of the millionaires in Britain, and constituted the ethnic group with the highest per capita income in the United States — point to the Indian capacity for enterprise and hard work, a capacity that was stunted and frustrated at home, but flourished under systems that rewarded effort. Of course, some would argue that, merely by virtue of their expatriation, India's NRIs were already more ambitious and hardworking than their compatriots back home, but I have seen too much evidence of toil and striving being obstructed or unrewarded in India to accept that argument. The only real difference between Indians in India and Indians abroad is that abroad their energies are not extinguished by the system. Instead they are tangibly rewarded. Once, after a particularly nationalistic column in an Indian magazine in which I poured contempt on the India-bashing of ignorant NRIs, I received a flurry of letters from Indian emigrants. One that particularly moved me contained the painfully honest words of a Mr. Bal Krishan Sood of Ilford, Essex:

> Over 90 per cent of us left India with "third division" matriculation [a barely passing grade] and no training whatsoever in any profession. When we arrived in other countries we could not find the other people around us, whether it was Europe or America, any better than us, yet [they were] living a better, cleaner and happier life than us in India. . . . We observe that we Indians outside, within a reasonable period, find ourselves owning a house, a car and many other luxuries of life, whereas the likes of us in India are left to live without ordinary necessities and amenities. And we on our visits fail to find a better life for those who were far better educated and trained [than us]. We ask, why? Do you know, why?

Another, equally pointed, was from a clerk in Bristol: "In India I worked hard, did overtime, lived honestly and could not make ends meet. Here, with much less effort, I have a good salary, a car and a house and my children have a future to look forward to. And I do not have to ask anyone for favors or pay any bribes. How do you expect me not to be angry when I think of India?"

This was a healthy anger, the anger of one who knew it did not have to be that way. Senator Daniel Patrick Moynihan, known for his outspoken candor when he was the U.S. ambassador in New Delhi in the mid-1970s, used to enjoy comparing the port cities of Singapore, Rangoon, and Calcutta. In the late 1940s they were much alike: bustling, thriving ports, with the usual Third World combination of prosperity, poverty, and political agitation. By the 1970s, Singapore was a gleaming, modern city, the second largest port in the world, a haven of social peace and economic development; Calcutta was rundown, the port corrupt and failing, the city paralyzed by political violence, the homeless begging in the streets; and Rangoon was a forgotten, isolated backwater. I assume Moynihan's point was to compare economic systems and choices, not political ones. But though his image is evocative, comparisons of India with countries like Singapore, Taiwan, and South Korea are, on the face of it, invidious. There are obvious differences in the scale of the problems confronted, the size of the population, and the political systems adopted (autocracy drove economic growth in all three cases, but at a price that pluralist India could not pay). Nonetheless, Indians should not deflect the comparison. Our problems may have been larger in scale, but large problems could have been tackled as aggregates of small problems (by greater decentralization of economic decision-making to the states, for instance); and in any case, countries like Malaysia and Indonesia also grappled with comparable problems of overpopulation, ethnic diversity, and political conflict, while managing to spur economic growth. And Malaysia, in particular, did so with a democratic political system not significantly different from that which India enjoyed during the decades of Congress Party dominance. There is no getting away from the conclusion that the main difference with all these countries is not size, scale, or system, but substance — the substance of the economic policy that we chose, or that our elected rulers chose for us, self-righteously convinced that they were right.

Even Rajiv Gandhi, the first (and so far only) prime minister from the generation that grew up frustrated by, and impatient with, the sclerotic socialism practiced in India, did little to tinker with the economic system. In 1985 he introduced a "new economic policy," which (rather like the Holy Roman Empire) was neither new nor economic nor a policy; it amounted to little more than a relaxation of the old license-permit-quota regulatory system, without actually abolishing it. The regulations themselves remained largely untouched; their philosophical underpinnings were not contested; the rules were just as oppressive, but a larger number of exceptions were now permitted to them. This had the effect, simply, of enhancing the discretionary powers of the government, so that its stranglehold on the economy actually grew while it was able to point to the changes as evidence of reform. Aside from a minor boom in consumer goods (a pale parallel of what was occurring in the Western world at the same time), the Rajiv years left India's fundamental economic problems essentially unaltered.

So, for most of its existence, the government of independent India was proudly self-sufficient, independent of the dominance of world capital, rhetorically devoted to using the state to better the lot of the poor, and politically disinclined to debate the self-evident virtue of these propositions. By mid-1991, it was also virtually broke.

Back, then, to the national humiliation of the pawning of the gold reserves, which occurred just before the General Elections of 1991, the elections in which the assassination of Rajiv Gandhi swung enough sympathy votes to the Congress to permit it to form a minority government. As the election results were streaming in, inflation was galloping at 14 percent (unofficial estimates placed it higher), the rupee was trading in the black market at 25 percent lower than its official rate, foreign exchange reserves had dwindled to nothing, and India had become yet another debt-ridden developing country, the third-largest debtor in fact, its dues of $71 billion exceeded only by those Latin American paragons, Brazil and Mexico. (The internal debt was just as bad: interest payments on the government's borrowings within the country stood at 20 percent of the government's budget.) India's four-decade-old economic policy had never looked more thoroughly discredited. It was clearly time to let sweeping dogmas die.

In a symbol of his departure from politics as usual (and from the usual politicians), the new Congress prime minister, P. V. Narasimha Rao, appointed a nonpolitical figure, the economist Manmohan Singh, as his finance minister. Together they embarked on an immediate series of dramatic reforms. Gone was the old phobia about external capital: foreign investment was now permitted in thirty-four major areas from which non-Indian capital had been excluded in the past (ranging from food processing to power generation); the private sector was allowed entry into areas hitherto reserved for the state, such as aviation and roadbuilding; foreign investors were granted the right to acquire majority shareholdings in Indian companies; tariffs were slashed (in phases, down from 300 percent in 1991 to 50 percent by 1995) and external competition welcomed; and the rupee was made convertible on the trade account. Strikingly, there followed the dramatic devaluation of the rupee by 22 percent , in defiance of the conventional political wisdom; a 5 percent devaluation in 1967 had almost brought the government down, but now everyone seemed to accept there was no choice. In place of the old mantra of self-sufficiency, India was to become more closely integrated into the world economic system.

The immediate impact of the Rao-Singh reforms was positive. Capital began to flow in from abroad, into productive investments as well as into the stock exchanges, some $4 billion in the first four years of the reforms. The list of areas into which it was welcomed lengthened, to cover power, telecommunications, and even that bugbear of the economic nationalists, oil exploration. The foreign exchange reserves rose from $1 billion to $20 billion in two years (and somewhat more slowly to $22 billion in mid-1996). The budget deficit was reduced, as were tariffs; quotas were eliminated or liberalized. If my Calcutta friend's father hadn't already retired he might have lost his job, because the restrictions on private-sector expansion were quickly dissolved.

Despite this, overall growth was relatively slow, and not generally better than in the pre-liberalization 1980s. (With the population still increasing by about 2 percent a year, per capita growth is decidedly unimpressive.) Yet there were a number of individual success stories, like that of the Madras automotive components manufacturers Sundram Fasteners, who took advantage of both the lifting of restrictions on the import of machinery and the devaluation of the rupee to become the principal maker and supplier of General Motors radiator caps around the world. General Electric, whose total investments in India now exceed $300 million, meets a third of its worldwide software manufacturing requirements from its Indian operations.

The figures are impressive. In 1995 industrial production rose by nearly 11 percent, and some 7.2 million new jobs were created, a 50 percent improvement on the average annual rate of increase in the 1980s. Direct foreign investment in 1996 was expected to reach $2 billion (more than the grand total of all foreign capital invested in India between 1947 and 1991, which added up to $1.5 billion); in addition, foreign institutional investments in Indian portfolios rose to over $5 billion. Exports rose by 21 percent (April 1995–February 1996), and the gross domestic product grew 6.2 percent, five times more than it had done in that seminal year of 1991. In its annual economic survey in 1996, the Finance Ministry was able to claim "strong economic growth, rapid expansion of productive employment, a reduction of poverty, a substantial boom in exports, and a marked decline in inflation." Overall, however, the growth rate was half that of China (and foreign investment only a fraction of that country's), the export figures lower than Malaysia's, the job creation statistics not as good as in Indonesia. India had not yet joined the ranks of the Asian Tigers.

And, inevitably in a highly politicized society, the economic reforms raised vociferous, and sometimes thoughtful, objections across the country. The first major revolt was that of the workers in the public sector, who for the preceding four decades had been all but unfireable. The days of overmanning and underproductivity seemed numbered, and from their point of view that was not necessarily a good thing. More surprisingly, many Indian capitalists were also anxious about the impact of liberalization on their well-being; after decades of sheltering behind high tariffs, generous subsidies, and secure licenses, several got together to complain that foreign capital would drive them out of business. (A sophisticated variation of this argument came from the director of the Confederation of Indian Industry, a business lobby group, in a startling attack in April 1996 on the role of multinational corporations in India. He accused them of not being committed to India in the long term, of not bringing in state-of-the-art technology, and of an overreliance on imported components rather than Indian-made ones.) And then there were the vast numbers of Indians, particularly in the rural areas, who were largely untouched by the changes and saw little benefit in them — but who could be swayed by rhetoric declaiming that the government was providing Pepsi-Cola for the rich while it had failed to provide drinking water for the poor. The two were hardly incompatible, but the Indian voter might not see it that way.

Politically, Prime Minister Rao took care not to seem to go too far, too fast. Before announcing any new reform in the contentious areas of taxation, financial services, and the public sector, he appointed committees to explore each issue and to make recommendations; though these were not far removed from the prescriptions of the World Bank and the International Monetary Fund, they emerged from an Indian body as recommendations debated and agreed by Indians. The prime minister was also highly sensitive to the impact of reform on India's voters; his instincts were driven by politics, not economics. Ever since the "delinking" in 1971 of state assembly polls from those to the national Parliament, some state or the other is constantly going to the polls and Indian governments face, in effect, constant judgments at the tribunal of public opinion. Rao felt that an electoral setback even in one state could be interpreted as a verdict against the economic reforms nationwide; he therefore downplayed them as much as possible, and avoided making reforms that might have been politically costly in the short term, such as laying off public-sector workers, privatizing or closing down inefficient factories, reducing subsidies, or taxing agricultural income. Despite this, when electoral defeats came in states like Karnataka and Andhra Pradesh, political stalwarts were quick to ascribe them to the reforms, alleging that the masses at large had derived no benefit from them.

This is all the more ironic because a chronic problem of the Indian economy remains the desire of Indian governments, whether in New Delhi or in the states, to spend more than they earn, mainly on keeping alive inefficient state-sector industries and in subsidies to farmers (who remain untaxed). Deficit financing had become a routine method of running the government before the reforms; bringing the annual deficit down was supposed to be one of the objectives of the new economic policies. After a couple of austere budgets that were aimed at having that effect, Rao and Singh abandoned the objective, and deficits rose again. (In early 1996 they stood at 10.5 percent of the gross domestic product, no better than in 1991.) This in turn meant higher interest payments on the borrowed money: interest on India's public debt consumes some 47 percent of all the government's revenues. Farmers were paid higher prices for their crops than market conditions would justify, especially given the availability of a large buffer stock of food grains (28 million tons in mid-1996). Public-sector companies running at a loss were kept running at an even greater loss. The government has been unable to break out of the vicious circle of overexpenditure, leading to high deficits, which require higher interest rates and prevent lower taxes.

No government responsive to public opinion, and accountable to the mass of voters at the polls, can easily break out of this vicious circle. The reforms for which Prime Minister Rao receives full marks — those that liberalized the regimes governing industry, investment regulation, and trade and exchange rates — arguably hurt only overprotected businessmen and their corrupt partners in the bureaucracy, and so were not politically risky to undertake. Cutting off life support to the public sector and ending agricultural subsidies are another matter altogether. On issues like privatizing the nationalized banks — whose workers, entrenched in their ways, would resist and could bring the economy to a standstill — or taking on the public-sector unions, the government gingerly felt its way forward, came up against bumps in the road, and hastily reversed course.

There is no doubt that economic reform faces serious political obstacles in democratic India. Resources have to be generated, investment privileged above consumption, higher prices paid for many goods, sacrifices endured in the hope of later rewards, and all this while some segments of society reap the immediate benefits. In India the combination of liberalization and inflation has meant that a small group of businessmen and merchants, and their less savory cousins the hoarders, blackmarketeers, and speculators, have visibly profited while the woman in the street has found she can no longer afford her favorite foods at the bazaar. As one trenchant critic, Sundeep Waslekar, put it:

> [A] few million urbanites, white collar workers, trade union leaders, large farmers, blackmarketeers, politicians, police officers, journalists, scholars, stockbrokers, bureaucrats, exporters and tourists can now drink Coke, watch Sony television, operate Hewlett Packard personal computers, drive Suzukis and use Parisian perfumes, while the rest of the people live in anguish.

The social consequences of exclusion — of the growth of feelings of deprivation on the part of those newly unable to share in the conspicuous consumption of imported or foreign-brand-name goods — have yet to be measured, but no government can afford to be unaware of them. A former member of the country's Planning Commission, L. C. Jain, declared in August 1996 that liberalization had not yet helped the 88 percent of the economy that lay in the "unorganized sector." At the same time, the threat to the public sector makes politically powerful enemies of the large and well-organized labor unions attached to the country's leading political parties; the competition engendered by foreign investment hurts some protected Indian capitalists who have previously bankrolled the ruling party; the deregulation of interest rates removes one of the few advantages that small businessmen had over big industry (in 1994, 2.8 million "small-scale enterprises" launched a noncooperation movement against the government); the shift to market pricing for agricultural procurement (if it ever happens) would end major subsidies to farmers; and so on. It is easy to see that various segments of Indian society would have reason to be apprehensive of, and sometimes downright hostile to, the process of economic reforms.

Prime Minister Rao's strategy was to take all this into account, and to undertake only those reforms that would be politically acceptable to the public at large: as *The Economist* put it, he appears to have "reckoned that shock therapy would create losers straightaway, while creating winners only in the medium turn, and decided to leave some reforms to later, when winners had emerged." As a result, for instance, while deregulating the economy, Rao and Singh were careful to control the administered prices of essential commodities, notably oil and petroleum products, in order to avoid hurting the ordinary voter and provoking inflation. This cautious approach has had its critics, notably among foreign economists, but it had the merit of avoiding the massive job losses, inflation, and human suffering that came to be associated with the early stages of economic liberalization in many countries in Africa and Latin America.

It is an approach that has been understood with greater sympathy by governments in the West than by international business. Former

Clinton Administration official Jeffrey Garten recalled a visit to India
with the late U.S. commerce secretary Ron Brown:

> [When he met Prime Minister Narasimha Rao,] Brown had a thick briefing
> book filled with all the usual American trade and investment complaints.
> But from the moment the two men finished shaking hands, it was clear that
> Rao wanted to talk about something else. "Mr. Secretary," he said, "tell me
> what I should say to millions of countrymen who experience no discernible
> benefit from all the painful economic reforms we have undertaken these past
> few years, and who are convinced that they are being hurt as we remove sub-
> sidies and let in foreign competition." Later in the trip, Brown addressed a
> group of students in a town hall meeting. . . . Almost all the questions were
> variants of what the prime minister had asked.

Brown understood that there were no easy answers; Rao knew that
the mere questions carried a political price. There is also the larger
philosophical question — particularly relevant in a country that got
used to calling itself "socialist" (a term Prime Minister Indira Gandhi
even wrote into the Constitution in 1976) — about distributive justice.
Whenever economic growth has occurred, it has benefited some more
than others. The fabled "Green Revolution," for instance, when miracle seeds transformed the harvests in India's agrarian northwest, was
of course good for the country as a whole (it produced more food generally, and better yields for most farmers). But it helped Punjab more
than other states, helped wheat farmers more than rice farmers, helped
those with larger holdings more than those with smaller ones (ironically, where land reform had been effective and large holdings broken
up, the economic benefits of the Green Revolution were reduced), and
helped those in areas of better infrastructure (especially cheap water
and electricity) above those reliant on traditional methods of farming.
Yet there was no political backlash to the Green Revolution; farmers
everywhere in India have sought to emulate their Punjabi compatriots,
and agricultural extension officers in villages across the country find re-
ceptive audiences for their seeds, fertilizer, and pesticides, as well as for
the technical advice that goes with them. What economic liberalization

needs, if it is to succeed, is something similar: a general acceptance that the reforms are for the general good, that they might seem to help some more than others, but that in the long run everyone will benefit from them. Such an attitude is far from being realized.

Instead, Indian democracy is the arena for a brand of populist politics rarely practiced with comparable chutzpah elsewhere. A striking example of this came in the Andhra Pradesh state elections of November 1994. These were politically crucial for Prime Minister Rao, since Andhra is his home state; but he was facing a comeback attempt by the film star (and former chief minister) N. T. Rama Rao (no relation), whose principal campaign promise was that his Telugu Desam Party would offer rice to poor Andhraites for two rupees a kilo (about three U.S. cents a pound). Combined with pledges to increase the subsidy on electricity for farmers and to give up liquor-tax revenues by introducing prohibition (a major vote-winner with women voters in many Indian states, since Indian peasants have a not-undeserved reputation for gurgling away their monthly pay packet on drink before their wives get to see any of it), the Telegu Desam's promises would have done away with 15 percent of the state's annual revenues, some 15 billion rupees ($440 million). Not to be outdone, the Congress Party all but matched those campaign promises, and made others that were almost equally spendthrift: *their* plans would have cost the exchequer twelve billion rupees a year. The voters, faced with two alternative programs of fiscal irresponsibility, chose the more irresponsible: they voted for Rama Rao. Not only did the improvident Telugu Desam win handily, but the Congress's defeat was then promptly interpreted as a vote against Narasimha Rao's brand of economic reform.

Of course voters will vote for rice at two rupees a kilo if politicians do not explain to them what the other costs of such a giveaway are; but the Andhra elections were a sober reminder to Prime Minister Rao, and to anyone else watching, of the dangerous short-termism that dominates Indian political calculations. The risk of this kind of populist Micawberism is that it could fuel inflation, drive the government to bankruptcy, or both. Parties regularly campaign on pledges to forgive agricultural debt, lower the already highly subsidized costs of water and electricity for farmers, and provide rice (or school meals) to the poor. They have no idea how they are going to pay for their promises, but they make — and even keep — them anyway.

At least for a while. In July 1996 the Telugu Desam government, which had meanwhile become a constituent of the new United Front coalition ruling in Delhi, raised the price of rice from two rupees a kilo to three and a half, quintupled the subsidized electricity rates for farmers, and instituted a new water tax on agriculture. These politically unpopular steps had become unavoidable because the party's election-winning measures had drained the state's exchequer. Now it was the Congress opposition's turn to decry the Andhra Pradesh government's "anti-people" policies (short-term opportunism knows no political boundaries).

For now, the danger is that economic reforms will be supported only by those who stand to gain immediately and directly from it, which by definition is bound to be only a minority of the nation's population. Many Indian capitalists who feared foreign competition have made their peace with the devil, entering into foreign collaborations and joint ventures that marry their expertise in local market conditions with the entrepreneurial thrust, high technology, management skills, and brand-name recognition of the international firm. (Sometimes the pact is almost Faustian: after a bitter battle with Pepsi-Cola, in which he deployed every conceivable political argument and tool against the entry of multinationals into the soft-drink business in India, Ramesh Chauhan, owner of India's largest soft-drink company, sold his business lock, stock, and bottle cap, to Coca-Cola.) The graduates of India's excellent management schools now command salaries their parents would not have dreamed of; service industries catering to the newly affluent elite have created legions of prosperous restaurateurs, bankers, computer technicians, beer-parlor owners, and clothing and interior designers. But all these add up to a pretty small slice of Indian society, and their votes wouldn't, to coin a phrase, capture a booth in the polls.

Arrayed against them are the impressive forces of reaction, grouped largely under the banner of economic nationalism. During the years of the Rao government, the right-wing, pro-trader BJP party joined forces with the Communists and socialists to attack the economic reforms on a nativist platform. The slogans of *swadeshi* self-reliance suited both the right and left parties. Foreign companies, they argued, should not be allowed to make profits by manufacturing goods that Indian companies were already making. Foreign consumer goods, especially such symbols of Western decadence as McDonald's, Kentucky Fried Chicken, and Coca-Cola, should not be allowed in, they averred, both because they weren't "needed" by most Indians and because they represented an assault on the values and lifestyle of the nation. Finally, and most potently, they argued that the reforms had also weakened India's political independence because it had mortgaged the country's economic policy to the World Bank and the International Monetary Fund — both headquartered, of course, in that arch neo-imperialist city, Washington. (Ironically, the collapse of the Soviet Union and the penury of Cuba has left socialism as a truly authentic Indian ideology, owing no credible allegiance to exemplars abroad.)

The opportunism of these arguments was manifest in that they were being made by opposition parties who had the least reason to be wedded to the license-permit-quota-subsidy-tariff system entrenched by successive Congress governments. But because the government had seen the light, and taken steps that in the short term were bound to be politically unpopular, the opposition parties saw an opportunity to score short-term political points on the cheap, while sounding self-righteously nationalist in the bargain. Ironically, they were in effect lending aid and comfort to the vested interests maintaining the failures and iniquities of the system, including the nexus between bureaucrats, politicians, and businessmen who paid, patronized, and profited from each other's ability to manipulate the system for personal ends. (Even more ironically, their position enabled a Congress cabinet minister, Manmohan Singh, to attack the policies his own party had pursued for four decades. "Those who oppose foreign consumer goods companies are enemies of Indian consumers," he told a press conference during the election campaign in May 1996. "They want people to be content with shoddy goods as for the last forty-five years, and only help smugglers to thrive.")

The problem with economic nationalism of this variety is that it is neither good economics nor true nationalism. Its advocates claim to be speaking for India, and in particular for the Indian poor, but the policies they hark back to reduced India's standing in the world economy since 1947, and did far less to alleviate poverty or to increase the purchasing power of the poor than the liberal-internationalist economics of, say, Indonesia or Malaysia. The stark reality is that rules and restrictions ostensibly designed to protect the poor in fact protected the prosperous and the influential, whereas an open economy that brought in investment and created productive employment (as South Korea, Taiwan, and later China demonstrated) would have brought more people out of poverty than did the "socialist" economic policies followed before 1991.

A sounder critique of the Rao-Singh reforms, voiced by reasonable left-wing economists (even if that sounds like a contradiction in terms), is that they have not produced the growth they were supposed to, did little to improve the country's international credit rating, failed to upgrade the technological levels of Indian industry, did not make the huge dents in the unemployment figures that would be their principal social justification, and did not have an immediate discernible impact on the country's mass poverty. The only answer to such criticism is "give it time," but Indian politicians, dominated by the expedient and the short-term, and in all too many cases anxious to preserve their deniability should the reforms misfire, have not been saying this with either conviction or consistency.

At the same time the potency of economic nationalism as a force in India should not be underestimated, as became apparent once again in the hue and cry that erupted over the Uruguay round negotiations of the General Agreement on Tariffs and Trade (GATT), which culminated in the establishment of the World Trade Organization (WTO). Indians fearful that free trade would involve surrender to foreign imperialist interests made common cause with protected industries anxious about new patent rules (notably the pharmaceutical industry, which would no longer be able to copy a Western drug by patenting an alternative process of making it — the product itself could not be patented in India) and were supported by idealists dreading the effects of GATT on the common man (for instance, the end of affordable medication for the Indian poor). Of course many of the fears were exaggerated, but the calls for India to pull out of the treaty were genuine, even if ill-informed (and would have been calamitous for the country, since it would have cost India the Most Favored Nation trading status it enjoys with all WTO members).

The politically generated controversy over the "Enron deal," India's single largest foreign investment to date, illustrates both the opportunism and futility of economic nationalism in operation. The agreement between the Indian state of Maharashtra and a consortium led by the Houston-based Enron Corporation power company to construct India's largest power project was signed by a Congress government and therefore bitterly opposed by the Hindu-nationalist Shiv Sena and Bharatiya Janata parties, who decried it as a sellout to Western interests. They argued that Enron had received unduly favorable terms from a government that had obtained kickbacks, while Indian consumers would have to pay extortionate rates for their power. Though these charges were unsupported by any evidence and denied by all concerned, the nationalists promptly abrogated the agreement when they swept into power in the state, inviting a lawsuit from Enron and much headshaking from the international economic community, which began muttering about the unreliability of investing too many eggs in such a volatile political basket. Indian attitudes were hardly encouraging: a critic in the *Times of India* suggested that "India's status will be enhanced, not lowered, if it tells the world that it is no pushover, no banana republic ready to accept an atrocious deal." After much chest- and table-thumping, the agreement was quietly restored, with some largely cosmetic changes to enable the new government to claim it had negotiated a better deal than the old one. In the meantime, precious months, and millions of dollars, were wasted; India's reputation as the next great place to invest in was severely dented (reports said that, as a direct result of the Enron imbroglio, two American negotiations collapsed, and several other Western companies exploring investments in India pulled out); and much-needed power generation for India's largest industrial state was needlessly delayed, in a country where work-hours lost because of inadequate power generation remains the biggest single drag on productivity.

Economic and cultural nationalism combined in the Kentucky Fried Chicken drama, in which the first two Indian outlets of the fast-food chain came under political and physical assault from a coalition of right-wing chauvinists and left-wing farmers. The KFC store in Banga-lore, capital of India's new high-tech software industry (the city and its environs have been dubbed "Silicon Plateau" by ex-Californians), was trashed by a farmers' mob, which burst in after well-publicized protests and ransacked the premises. Subtler techniques were used in Delhi, where, in response to a legal complaint, the outlet was closed by a mag-istrate because two flies were found buzzing around the kitchen (many Indians thought an award should be given to KFC for having only two, far below the national average for restaurants). Eventually the police and the courts were needed in both Bangalore and Delhi to overcome such efforts to close the KFC outlets, and both are flourishing, albeit to a limited affluent clientele.

On the face of it the protests are puzzling, because it is not clear whom KFC hurts: they pay Indian poultry farmers good prices for In-dian chickens, cook them in India with Indian accompaniments, and employ Indian chefs and waiters. They will also make a very modest dent in the Indian fast-food market (chicken was already the most ex-pensive nonvegetarian fare, and only a tiny minority of Indians will be able to afford KFC's menu). The hostility to KFC is less, there-fore, about real economic damage to Indians than it is about politics. An American fast-food store is, to the likes of the farmers' leader Nanjundaswamy, a symbol of surrender to forces he fears: foreign pen-etration of the Indian economy made literal by foreign penetration of the Indian alimentary canal. The enemies of Kentucky Fried Chicken are decrying not their sales but the sellout, by the Indian government, to Western influences. That is the real reason they need to be taken seriously. But not too seriously, for no Indian government wanting to welcome foreign investment can afford to let its economic policy be wrecked by the excesses of a misguided mob.

Political caution and nationalist backlash are not the only impediments to effective economic reform. Bureaucratic inertia and some old-fashioned inefficiency have also played their part in the shambolic process of privatizing India's telecommunications sector, the lack of guidelines on the privatization of infrastructure (especially roadbuilding and power transmission and distribution), the failure to inject speed into bankruptcy proceedings (three bankruptcy cases recently marked their fiftieth anniversaries in court, a golden jubilee for the law firms concerned, but a disgrace to the legal system), and avoidable delays in clearing new projects for investment. Legal reform, and an Indian equivalent of U.S. vice president Gore's regulation-slashing program of "reinventing government," are essential if the reform policy is to succeed.

The new telecommunications saga was worthy of the C. M. Stephen days. The government learned little from its attempts in 1992 to privatize cellular-phone service in four major cities, which had ended in court after controversies over the process for selecting the private operators who would provide the service. In 1995, tenders were issued for privatizing basic telephone service in twenty zones across the country; after the bids were opened, the rules were changed, limiting the number of zones each company could have, and then highly unrealistic minimum price levels were set, which took a number of major firms out of the bidding (in eight of the twenty zones, no bids were received at all). A friend representing a German telecommunications company in Delhi was in despair about the unpredictability and irrationality of the process: decisions about telecoms privatization were being made by officials who, he said, didn't have a clue either about telecoms or about privatization. Parliament erupted in an uproar about alleged corruption involving the then minister of communications, Sukh Ram; in August 1996, when he was out of office following the Congress Party's defeat in the elections, the police found a million dollars in Indian rupee notes in two of his residences, and Sukh Ram himself, appropriately enough, went out of communication range by disappearing abroad. Meanwhile, the telephone system remained unreliable and out of date, and more potential investors packed their bags and decided to look elsewhere.

. . .

The United Front government that replaced the Congress in 1996 (after an eleven-day interregnum while the Hindu-oriented BJP party unsuccessfully sought coalition partners) surprised many, given the dominance of the thirteen-party coalition by socialist and other left parties (including two Communist parties), when it did not repudiate the economic reforms. The Congress party had pledged, in Manmohan Singh's words, to "expand liberalization, involve the private sector in infrastructure development, cut the fiscal deficit, reform the insurance sector and the tax structure, and cut government expenditure," a program staunchly opposed in the platforms of the parties constituting the United Front. This suggests that the liberalization of economic policy is indeed, as Prime Minister Narasimha Rao used to aver without conviction, irreversible. Indeed, the fact that practically every Indian political party of any consequence has run or is running a state government somewhere has injected a harsh dose of economic realism into the thinking of the national political establishment. In Delhi, their role was to oppose; in the states, their task was to govern. So they all know, from direct experience, that private investment, both domestic and foreign, is essential because both national and state governments are broke and cannot afford to go back to the bad old ways. (Indeed, the hospitability of the Communist state government in West Bengal to foreign private capital is now a byword, though the annual trips of its aging Marxist chief minister, Jyoti Basu, to England and the United States "to promote foreign investment in West Bengal" may have more to do with his wish to escape the heat of the Calcutta summer than the persistence of neo-imperialist interest in his state's investment climate.)

Nonetheless, the indications from Finance Minister P. Chidambaram's carefully balanced first budget are that the economy will be opened only slowly, and that the political costs will be carefully measured in doing so. There were several positive signs that cheered the reformers, including tax cuts (in capital gains, as well as in import and excise duties) aimed at generating economic growth of 7 percent and attracting five times the level of foreign capital than ever before — an estimated $10 billion. If this seemed unduly ambitious, the government struck an encouraging note by clearing $1.7 billion worth of foreign investment proposals just before the budget was declared. Due emphasis was, for the first time, placed on infrastructure development; agriculture and the basic services were also declared to be priorities. But that was the extent of the good news. A new minimum tax on companies previously exempt (a tax largely justified both by the government's revenue needs and by the fact that legal loopholes had brought corporate taxes as a proportion of pre-tax profits down to a record low of 14 percent in 1995–96 from nearly 30 percent three years earlier) rocked the stock market; a surcharge applied on all imports offset the impact of some tariff cuts and effectively raised the maximum tariff rate to 52 percent when it had been expected to be lowered below 50 percent ; and total public-sector borrowing remained above 10 percent of GDP. With new subsidies to state governments, the budget deficit remained high and the treasury seemed likely to have to meet interest payments to the tune of 47 percent of all government revenue (the figure had stood at 39 percent when the last government took office in 1991).

The new national consensus on economic reform is beset with what some see as compromise and hesitation, and others judge as political wisdom: liberalization yes, politically painful dismissals and cuts no. The much-touted "exit policy" of the early reform period — the intention of closing down unprofitable public-sector firms and laying off unproductive personnel — shows no signs of being implemented; the "entry policy" — letting in more foreign investment and increasing imports while lowering tariff barriers — continues, but more warily. Populist subsidies will continue, which means that budget deficits will not be reduced. (The wisecrack about deficits in New Delhi's political circles is that "any government that lives within its means lacks imagination.") The real problem with deficits is not the external balance of payments (which, through sensible exchange-rate management and a modicum of fiscal discipline, does not appear likely to become critical in the foreseeable future), but the domestic expenditures arising from internal political constraints. When Mr. Chidambaram briefly suggested that public-sector firms would have to justify their existence by contributing a minimum dividend to the national exchequer, he was forced to back down by howls of protest from his coalition partners.

Indian politicians have not yet accepted that public-sector companies are essentially holding hostage more than half the industrial capital at India's disposal. Subsidies to public-sector workers come at the expense of India's poor — they amount to five times what the government spends on health — yet their continuation is sought to be justified in the name of socialism. But one should not underestimate the popular support for the public sector: a public opinion poll in 1996 established that opposition to the privatization of the public sector vastly outstripped support for it among all sections of society. The irony is that where a governmental monopoly has ended, as with the deregulation of India's domestic airline services, the consumer has tangibly and visibly benefited, in better service, improved availability, and wider choice; yet the lesson is not being applied to other sectors. Divestment is not a word that has entered the official economic vocabulary, even though the government of India is still engaged in a number of businesses it has no business to be in — from running five-star hotels to manufacturing wristwatches.

At the same time, if the reform policy is not to suffocate from hesitancy, progress is clearly required in a number of areas. Not all the strangulating regulations have been taken off the books: the Companies Act still restricts mergers, takeovers, and intercorporate investments, and there are some fifty laws that apply to the treatment of the workforce and the settlement of labor disputes. Rules on privatization of ailing public-sector units, or of the telecommunications industry, have yet to be issued. Many clearances are still required, and oblige investors to run to more than one regulatory agency.

It is odd, too, that tariffs remain on trade in agricultural goods and consumer items — both to protect the domestic producers. ("It defies any economic logic and runs counter to the whole idea of an open internationally competitive economy," wrote the economists Vijay Joshi and I. M. D. Little recently. "If Mahalanobis had not been a Hindu [and therefore cremated when he died] he would be turning in his grave knowing that soft drinks are more protected than heavy machinery.") It would make more sense to help, for instance, the domestic handloom industry by subsidizing it directly, rather than restricting cotton exports as an indirect means of protecting the cottage industry in handlooms. It is a measure of the challenge facing India's reformers that though tariff relief is one of the successes of the new economic policy, the current tariffs, after five years of reductions, are still higher than in all the viable economies of the world. They will have to come down.

As for resource allocation, Indian planners from Nehru on down may have erred, to borrow a metaphor from Indian-American communications wunderkind Satyen "Sam" Pitroda, in putting greater emphasis on the "hardware" (the factories, dams, and steel mills that Nehru called the "new temples" of modern India) than on the operative "software" (education, health, communications). Subsidies to the inefficient private sector amount to five times the national expenditure on health; and the literacy rate of 52 percent stands in stark contrast to Sri Lanka's 93 percent and China's 77 percent. The economists Amartya Sen and Jean Dreze have pointed out that it is also far short of the 71 percent South Korea already had when it embarked upon its rise to industrialization in 1960; a literate workforce is far better able to meet the demands of high-technology companies than uneducated and unskilled labor, and the correlation between literacy and productivity needs no explanation. Lester C. Thurow, in his 1996 book *The Future of Capitalism*, has argued that we live in "an era dominated by man-made brainpower industries," in which natural resources and financial strength are less important than human skills, "the only source of long-run sustainable competitive advantage." The software engineers of Bangalore, sitting in offices in India's Silicon Plateau and beaming their software to

Texas and California by satellite, are in the vanguard of a revolution in human skills that could take India ahead of many developing countries in the race to economic well-being in the twenty-first century.

Provided, of course, that resources are allocated to developing such skills. It could be argued that maintaining the world's third-largest standing army — entirely justified, no doubt, by the state of tensions with two well-armed neighbors, China and Pakistan — has come at the expense of other national developmental priorities. There can, of course, be no development without national security; but without development, the army would have little worth protecting.

The same concern about priorities applies to some national expenditures that seem difficult to justify in purely economic terms. To take a favorite example of some of India's critics, the 1982 Asian Games in Delhi cost, according to unofficial estimates, 6 to 10 billion rupees; official figures admitted to 3.6 billion rupees, at a time when the national government's total budget receipts were Rs 140 billion (against expenditures of Rs 150 billion, the difference being made up by deficit financing). By way of comparison, the total investment in village development during the same fiscal year stood at Rs 2.7 billion. On the face of it, this seems spendthrift, even feckless; but I am not so sure. I do not wholly subscribe to the defense that the presence of competitors and dignitaries from fifty-two states, with their media and their television cameras, instilled a pride in the nation and in its capital that cannot be quantified; I think that pride was felt by too small a minority of Indians to be worth citing. More important to me were the practical consequences of the lavish expenditure. The Games left the capital with a legacy of development — highway overpasses, stadiums, housing complexes, hotels, restaurants, and roads — that have been of immeasurable value to the city. Yet there is little doubt that the political will, the financial resources, and the sheer energy required to construct these in record time simply would not have been found without the incentive and the deadline that the Games imposed. Sometimes seemingly mistaken priorities, executed in haste for short-term ends, can produce results that far-seeing planners might not have been able to ensure.

The Asian Games improved New Delhi's infrastructure, but the country's remains appalling. The infrastructural problems I described earlier are the result both of woefully inadequate investment in such sectors as communications and power generation, and the usual habit of controlling prices artificially for political purposes. The scale of the problem is now such that it is literally beyond the government's capacity to solve. India needs some 170,000 megawatts of additional power-generation capacity by the year 2010, a 200 percent increase in current generating capacity; an indication of the cost is that Enron will have to invest over $3 billion to produce just 2,400 megawatts in its newly restored project. India needs to upgrade its congested ports and create new ones along its magnificent coastline, but just meeting existing and foreseeable needs would, according to the Confederation of Indian Industry, cost some $137 billion in new investment over the next five years (and this is essential: port delays and high cargo-handling charges reduce and sometimes eliminate the cost advantage Indian exporters enjoy over their foreign competitors). In communications, it would cost some $150 billion to $175 billion to bring India up to the current developing-country average of six telephones for every hundred people (from its current figure of 0.8 telephones per hundred people); but a growing economy will need to do better than the average developing country, and economist Prem Shankar Jha suggests India will need another 40 million to 50 million telephone connections at a cost of a further $30 billion. To improve India's road system and create a network of highways, current estimates require $35 billion for 14,000 kilometers of roads. The kind of money required to upgrade the country's infrastructure — Jha puts it at $15 billion a year for the next ten years; Western economists have spoken of $500 billion by the year 2000 — simply cannot be found in the public treasury.

It will therefore have to come from the private sector. The 1996 budget recognizes this, though little has yet been done to frame the rules governing private-sector entry. The government has proceeded in fits and starts in areas like telecommunications, more as a result of ineptitude than of political hesitation; it has to do better, drawing up clear, investor-friendly rules and promulgating them quickly, if the clarion call by Finance Minister Chidambaram is to be heeded by private capital. But there will be a downside: if the private sector comes in, it will charge for its services, so that uneconomically cheap electricity or toll-free roads may no longer be feasible. And while the private sector may well be enthusiastic about building major new highways, it is not much interested in the rural roads government must develop and maintain but has no money for.

Agriculture cannot indefinitely remain exempt from the reform process either, especially considering that much of India's urban poverty is a direct overflow from rural poverty, as peasants unable to make a living from the land migrate to the sidewalks and shanties of the cities. At the moment farmers are not taxed, and their inputs (power, water, seeds, fertilizer) are uneconomically subsidized; but, equally, the prices of their produce are kept artificially low and farmers are still obliged to sell a fixed portion of their produce to the government at government-established rates. Since the government simply cannot afford to subsidize them forever, it may be worth exploring whether free trade in agricultural produce might not make up for a reduction in (if not an elimination of) subsidies. (The Common Minimum Program, or CMP, agreed upon by the United Front declares that "all controls and regulations that stand in the way of increasing the incomes of farmers will be reviewed immediately and abolished wherever found necessary." But it is less bold in giving up the subsidies and other benefits farmers have enjoyed for decades.) The nationalized banks are still being obliged to make unviable loans at artificially low interest rates to "priority sectors"; this practice represents yet another subsidy that the government cannot indefinitely afford to keep paying. The continuing habit of writing off agricultural loans wins votes but undermines the rural credit system. (Reforms in the banking and credit sectors require political will, which clearly does not exist now and may take some time to form.)

"No strategy of economic reforms and regeneration," the CMP declared, "can succeed without sustained and broad-based agricultural development." In a country where two-thirds of the population still derives its livelihood from agriculture, which is therefore still the single largest sector of the economy, this may seem a self-evident proposition. Agricultural output must grow as part of the country's overall economic growth, and farmers must feel better off if the reforms are to acquire and retain the support of India's rural majority. For most farmers, though, the reforms mean little if they do not improve the availability of water and electricity, and reduce the cost of inputs; fertilizer prices, for instance, have tripled over the last three years while the wheat grown with it earns the farmer only 8 percent more. Can the government reduce subsidies on the former and remove price controls on the latter without causing enormous social disruption? On the other hand, can it afford not to?

It is striking how dependent Indian agriculture remains on good monsoons; we have had eight since 1988, the quantity and distribution of rainfall contributing directly to better-than-expected agricultural production. But our luck with the weather cannot last indefinitely; structural reforms to improve per-worker agricultural productivity are essential. These do not necessarily have to be "liberal"; in Communist-ruled West Bengal, land reforms and decentralized development have improved efficiency and generated agricultural growth above the national average, and there may be lessons here for other states. The proportion of India's Gross Domestic Product derived from agriculture has declined from 55 percent to 30 percent as a result of the economic reforms, but there has not been a parallel decline in the percentage of Indians dependent for their livelihoods on farming. Economist L. C. Jain, a critic of the reforms, has argued that though 70 percent of Indian workers are in agriculture, only 5 percent of the new investment is being channeled to them. Paradoxically, of course, an increase in investment will happen only if the very reforms he opposes succeed.

On the other hand, if economic reforms are to be fully accepted in a country where change has always come slowly, perhaps it is just as well that no sudden shocks are inflicted on the voters. Any Indian government will have to ensure that the short-term negative consequences of liberalization are kept at bay by efficient economic management. Effective measures must include curbing inflation (since price rises are what many tend to see as the most directly visible consequence of economic reform); maintaining adequate and dependable supplies of food and other essentials (including buffer stocks for the inevitable bad monsoon); and guaranteeing that liberalization is not accompanied by short-term catastrophes for the more vulnerable sections of the population, because any Latin American–style disaster for the rural or urban poor and lower middle class would make reform politically impossible for a generation.

Controlling prices is the biggest challenge: the 1996 budget was preceded by a steep 25 percent rise in the price of gas and petroleum products (cut back, following protests, on diesel) and a less steep, but not inconsiderable, increase in railway fares and freight charges. These are costs that hit everybody's pocket; at least, they hurt everybody who has a pocket. As the inevitable inflationary consequences are predicted, an immediate political clamor has gone up within the ruling coalition for increased subsidies, particularly for the poorest of the poor: Indian politicians congenitally prefer to manage poverty rather than to create a system that enables poor people to break free of their poverty. Full employment is going to be a chimera for a long time, even if population control makes more progress than it has done so far, because the young people entering the job market of the twenty-first century have already been born. According to Mr. Chidambaram, India needs to create 8 million new jobs a year to keep its burgeoning population adequately employed. More must be done to generate revenue, either by increased taxation (on real-estate transactions, on speculative trading, on the incomes of the super-rich, or on undertaxed corporations; the ratio of tax revenues to GDP has fallen by 1 percent in the last five years) or by a more aggressive attempt to soak the underground economy, which by some estimates runs at 30 percent of GDP. When he was finance minister under Rajiv Gandhi, V. P. Singh used a shrewd combination of amnesty, incentives, and enforcement to bring significant sums of undeclared assets into the tax system. Something similar has to be tried again.

Equally important, much more needs to be done to persuade the public at large of the purpose and benefits of the reforms. "While Prime Minister Narasimha Rao speaks nine languages," commented *Time's* Rahul Jacob acidly just before Rao's electoral defeat, "he has not made a loud enough case in any of them for the liberalization that is his government's most notable achievement." The result of this sort of silence is that though the case is known to (and largely accepted by) the country's political establishment, the general population has not been given any corrective to decades of socialist rhetoric, which continues to be echoed by critics of the reforms alleging that India is being opened up to foreign exploitation and that westerners will profit "on the backs of India's poor." When the director of the Davos World Economic Forum told the New Delhi press in October 1996 that "India is becoming a key player in the region and more and more it will become a key player in the world," she felt obliged to add that "India's two major weaknesses . . . are that it has no clear agenda and that there is a lack of transparency." With weaknesses like that, strengths don't look as strong anymore.

Nonetheless, as Manmohan Singh put it in a 1996 speech, "there has been a sea change in the minds of Indians in the past four years . . . there is a new India in the making." Indeed, India's governmental track record for managing change is rather impressive, and its experience in preventing disastrous economic failures has become even better in recent years. In 1987 the monsoon failed and India reeled under one of the worst droughts it had suffered in a century. Two decades earlier, a similar meteorological catastrophe had led to a tragic famine, with the skeletal bodies of women and children littering the parched earth of states like Bihar. Nothing of the sort occurred this time. India had learned its lessons: the government had built up an impressive system of storage and distribution to tide its people through the consequences of the inevitable bad harvest. The Famine That Wasn't was the great unwritten news story of the 1980s. The grim Latur earthquake of 1994 also witnessed an exemplary and effective response by the authorities. Thanks to the government's efforts, the Indian people have come to believe they will not be left helpless in the great changes that are slowly sweeping the country. Even if nature or human error bring about setbacks in the progress of economic reform, there is reason to hope that the disaster stories won't need to be written.

For now, the signs are modestly hopeful that the economic reforms are taking root in Indian minds and hearts. In late 1996 the magazine *India Today* published the findings of an extensive public opinion poll conducted by the Delhi-based Center for the Study of Developing Societies, together with the Indian Council of Social Science Research; interestingly, the findings were compared with those of a similar poll conducted in 1971. Twenty-five years ago, in response to the question "Are you satisfied with your current financial condition?" 60 percent had replied in the negative, 29 percent were "somewhat satisfied," and only 11 percent answered with an unqualified yes. Today, 28 percent were satisfied, 42 percent somewhat satisfied, and only 30 percent, half the percentage of 1971, expressed themselves as dissatisfied with their lot. Asked what their expectations were for the future, 48 percent thought their financial condition would improve (up from 39 percent in 1971), 27 percent thought it would remain the same (against 21 percent in 1971), and only 9 percent forecast that they would fare worse (compared with 19 percent in 1971). Here was proof that the reforms have engendered some optimism among the Indian people.

Whatever headway India makes in reforming its economy, however, the biggest enemy of the country's economic progress — corruption — must be tackled. It is important to stress that the sight of a small minority in positions of privilege conspicuously consuming undeclared assets — even though this is a phenomenon that precedes liberalization — is not a good advertisement for the policy of economic reform; indeed, it is likely to create a sense of alienation from the market among people who feel they are denied access to it. Indian economists have estimated that only 15 percent of governmental expenditure actually reaches the intended target beneficiaries. It is impossible to overstate the importance of eradicating, with all the ruthlessness of the law, governmental corruption if the economic reforms are to succeed, because only people who are convinced that they hold within their own hands the capacity for self-advancement will create the savings and production that the reforms aim to generate. And as long as the ordinary citizen of India believes that only those who know how to cheat and deceive, who have the means to bribe and suborn, and who have bureaucratic access or political clout, can succeed, that faith will never take root in the mass of the population.

It is in this context that the issue of globalization arises; and globalization is, at the risk of sounding tautological, a worldwide phenomenon. Whereas not very long ago, 90 percent of the developing nations — members of the "Group of 77" that went on to comprise over a hundred United Nations member states — ran closed economies, today only Burma (and that, too, not entirely) resists the siren call of the global marketplace. In every country around the world, trade barriers are being lowered, imports and exports increased, foreign capital avidly sought; legal systems are being brought into line with the needs of international business, tax and property laws are being reexamined against foreign standards, and restrictive rules and regulations are being scrapped. More and more economies are being "plugged in" to the global system in what is a self-reinforcing process.

At the same time, as the economic journalist Prem Shankar Jha has pointed out, India has little choice regarding globalization. India needs to export an additional $2 billion to $3 billion worth of goods each year to service the $15 billion of foreign investment it needs in infrastructure; these exports would have to come out of the increased production made possible by infrastructure development. Export orientation requires openness to the global economy. Questioning the economic nationalism of Atal Behari Vajpayee's BJP, Jha asks, "With a full 65 percent of all global trade being undertaken between various branches and affiliates of multinationals (and a far higher percentage of all trade in sophisticated manufactures), just how far does Mr. Vajpayee think India will be able to go if it does not become part of the net?"

This is not to agree with those advocates of globalization who blithely suggest that we have moved from a world dominated by superpowers to a world dominated by supermarkets (a formulation attributed to *The New York Times*'s foreign affairs columnist, Thomas L. Friedman). That is a rather Occidental view of the world. Most Indians are still far removed from the supermarket shelves of the American globalizers, groaning under their cheery packages of overprocessed food and offering five Western brands for every imagined need. Though Friedman no doubt meant to include stock markets in his aphorism, it is true that globalization, to its most ardent exegetes, often seems to mean little more than the dominance of Western brand-name consumer products over territories abroad. The archetypal image was spelled out by the British magazine *The Economist* in a futuristic portrait of China published in early 1996:

> In 2006 the better-off Chinese consumer will get up, wash her hair with Procter & Gamble shampoo, brush her teeth with Colgate toothpaste and apply a little Revlon lipstick. As her Toyota grinds to [a] halt in yet another traffic jam, she will light up a Marlboro, glance at a copy of the Chinese edition of *Elle* magazine on the passenger seat and try to find her Motorola phone to call her secretary. At work she will put down her can of Pepsi by her Compaq computer and load up Windows 06.

The Economist, as an inveterate advocate of liberal competition, was quick to explain that foreign consumer-goods companies would do well because "the quality of their products is usually much higher, and their marketing far more professional, than their local rivals'." But whatever the reason, this portrait of "Coca-colonization" — of a country so taken over by foreign consumer products that it no longer has any national economic identity to call its own — is not one that any self-respecting Indian wants to see painted of his country. The difference with China, though, is that India already has excellent, affordable equivalents of all these products, some made with foreign collaboration and many not, and for the most part, given the advantages of culture, habit, and cost, these should be able to hold their own against their more expensive foreign competitors. *The Economist*'s portrait, if rewritten for India today rather than for the China of 2006, might read like this:

In 1996 the better-off Indian consumer gets up, puts Swastik hair oil on her head, brushes her teeth with Vicco Vajradanti toothpaste (which describes itself as "Ayurvedic medicine for teeth and gums" and uses ingredients recommended by the sages for three thousand years) and applies a little Lakmé lipstick. As her Maruti grinds to a halt in yet another traffic jam, she will light up an India Kings, glance at a copy of *India Today* magazine (or *Femina*, or *Stardust*, or *Society*, or another of the dozens of glossy magazines that offer a relevance no *Elle* or *Cosmopolitan* can provide) on the passenger seat. At work she will put down her bottle of Thumbs Up by her HCL computer; and when she goes to lunch, she will walk past the local Kentucky Fried Chicken outlet and instead stop at her favorite snack bar for a *masala dosa*.

So what does globalization mean in the Indian context? Not, I believe, an inundation of foreign goods driving out Indian ones, but principally more choice for a few, and more jobs for the many. As Harvard economist Jeffrey Sachs has suggested, the main reason developing countries have not caught up more rapidly with developed ones is that they were closed to the world economy and therefore to the benefits of increased trade and foreign investment. This was understandable in the postcolonial context, because India's closed and statist economic policies were principally a political and cultural reaction to imperialism. Indian self-reliance combined a Nehruvian concern for distributive social justice with a profound mistrust of the international economic forces that had enslaved the country for two hundred years; as citizens of a newly independent nation, Indians pursued economic autarchy out of both pride ("We can do it too") and suspicion ("We cannot rely on others to supply what we need when we need it, so we must make everything ourselves"). Economic self-reliance thus became an axiomatic corollary of independence itself, and became seen as synonymous with it. The most significant proof of India's maturity as an independent country is the willingness of its leadership to realize, at long last, that economic interdependence is not incompatible with political independence.

8

"Better Fed Than Free"

The Emergency and Other Urgencies

*T*o understand the crucial debate about Indian democracy — to attempt to respond to the question of whether India's democratic institutions can, quite literally, deliver the goods to the Indian people — it is important to examine the actual workings of Indian politics in the democratic system. This can be done from many angles: scholars might look at specific aspects of the country; reporters might travel through it; a social anthropologist could study the way in which the poorest Indians in the most humble villages have experienced democracy; and area specialists could analyze governmental actions, economic development, or human rights. All of these approaches would be valid, but there are many others better qualified than me to undertake them. My concern here is with institution building, since democracy is an engine rather than a vehicle; it is the engine that powers the vehicle of state. That vehicle stalled for a while in the Emergency of 1975–77, but it has been chugging on steadily since, a creaky, rattling, rusty machine taking the Indian people noisily on into the twenty-first century.

The Emergency framed the "bread versus freedom" debate in India; it took the argument out of the salons and into the country's actual political experience. When Prime Minister Indira Gandhi declared a state of national emergency in India on June 26, 1975, analysts in the Western world wrote almost unanimously of their regret that a great experiment had come to an end — the experiment of India's development within a pluralist democratic framework. Mrs. Gandhi's suspension of civil liberties, her arrests of opposition leaders, her attempts to amend the Constitution, and her postponement of scheduled national elections appeared to confirm liberal fears that an era of authoritarianism had dawned in India.

Mrs. Gandhi and her governmental colleagues, however, had a totally different interpretation of the situation at hand. Democracy, they said, had failed in India, at least as it was conventionally practiced. Instead of providing the mechanism for the establishment of a progressive national consensus, democracy had disintegrated into an expensive luxury, with effects that were divisive to the nation and detrimental to its development. Events had reached a point where the choice was clear: democracy or social justice — democracy for the elite few, or social justice for the downtrodden many. With such a choice before them, Mrs. Gandhi declared, the government had no doubt where to cast its lot.

Though Mrs. Gandhi briefly attempted to mend her public-relations fences with the West by claiming democracy had only been "temporarily" suspended, her basic argument was that the excesses of Indian democracy, as she declared in her nationwide radio broadcast, "weaken[ed] the capacity of the national government to act decisively inside the country," and "the threat to internal stability also affect[ed] production and the prospects of economic development." The thrust of the political changes the government attempted to introduce during the Emergency, culminating in the fifty-nine-clause Forty-second Amendment to the Constitution, also suggested there was nothing temporary about the transformation she was trying to bring about. They confirmed that Mrs. Gandhi intended to establish a system with fewer institutional impediments to the implementation of governmental directives. The traditional checks and balances of independent India — an unrestrained opposition, a free and critical press, an independent judiciary — were all severely curbed. The new emphasis was not on the individual's rights against the state, but on the community's duties toward it. Effective official action was made easier than before.

Despite the fact that the Emergency appeared to many to vindicate the fears expressed in India's Constituent Assembly when emergency provisions were proposed, some scholars were not unduly perturbed by its imposition, viewing the crisis as only the most severe of many that had arisen since 1947 in a polity unsuited to a developing nation. "Put bluntly," one noted American expert argued, " . . . when the per capita annual income is approximately one-hundred dollars a year, how can one expect anything other than 'emergencies' to occur from time to time?" The question reflected a perception of priorities that was most tellingly epitomized in the words of a government official defending the continuation of the emergency: "We are tired of being the workshop of failed democracy. The time has come to exchange some of our vaunted individual rights for some economic development." *Newsweek* put it aphoristically: "In India, it is more important to be fed than to be free."

Indeed, the Emergency came at a time when the political situation had disintegrated to a point where the very viability of the system had been called into question. By early 1975, as much of the country was paralyzed by the mass movement for "Total Revolution" led by the saintly Gandhian Jayaprakash "JP" Narayan, observers wrote of "a growing belief that the democratic process was failing to meet the needs of the masses" and of an increasing "distaste for democracy." Though the actual declaration of the emergency was principally determined by the political threat to Mrs. Gandhi after the Allahabad High Court judgment, it was explicitly coupled with a sense of the failure of the nation's traditional democratic system to deliver the goods to the Indian people.

Despite the Nehruvian enthusiasm for democracy, its inadequacies had long been the subject of debate within and outside India. It was not long after independence that India's leaders began to express publicly their irritation with "politically motivated" and "unrealistic and impractical" demands made by special interests ranging from refugee associations to trade union and peasant leaders. During the 1950s things began to get worse. As the eminent American political scientist Myron Weiner described it:

> In place of a growing sense of national unity, caste, tribal, religious, and linguistic bodies multiplied. Instead of being dedicated to increased production, trade unions, under leftist control, were launching strikes. Harmony was not growing in the countryside — the Communists and Socialists were busy fomenting class struggle. Young people did not seem determined to increase their technical skills, but instead student "indiscipline" increased. And instead of uniting to work as a single force to rally the country, the Congress Party became increasingly split by factionalism. From the point of view of the national leadership, it was "politics" — in the sense of narrow ambitions for power and the parochial loyalties of small men — which threatened national unity, economic development, and political order.

As India coped with these pressures, observers expressed doubts about democracy as a suitable system for a country facing such overwhelming challenges. Political scientists wedded to "modernization" bemoaned the relatively poor productivity of democratic systems; in countries like India, many argued, the challenges of mobilizing labor, of changing traditional practices, and of obliging people to postpone their material expectations and make sacrifices could not be met democratically, and rapid industrialization was impossible under governments that needed to compromise among different groups. The Swedish sociologist Gunnar Myrdal termed India a "soft state" that required "extraordinarily little" of its citizens. In turn, Indians, too, protested the limitations their democracy imposed upon them. The economist and cabinet minister C. D. Deshmukh suggested that India suffered

> economic and sociological handicaps in the establishment of a democracy. The old feudal or colonial regimes were destructive of the dignity of the individual and made no efforts to raise it by education. The average citizen is therefore uninformed and in a poor state of readiness to exercise the franchise. Often there is not a large informed middle class to acquire enlightened

views and influence others. Moreover, whatever independence of opinion there is can soon be corrupted in an environment of near destitution for the bulk of the population. The few that climb to leadership sometimes lack ordinary correctives and learn to serve themselves rather than the people.

Not surprisingly, India's democratic system, with its emphasis on gradualism and consensus, was perceived as being ineffective in developing the country, especially when contrasted with its totalitarian but economically more successful neighbor China. "What is crucial," according to the American historian Robert Heilbroner, "is that communism, as an ideology and as a practical political movement, is prepared to undertake the revolutionary reorganization of society — a task before which the noncommunist governments shrink." Given these circumstances, declared Heilbroner, "I opt for . . . 'total' change. . . . If I had to take my chances here and now as an anonymous particle of humanity in [India] . . . I would unhesitatingly choose the Communist side."

Apprehensions about this kind of reasoning frequently threw India on the defensive in international forums in the first decades of independence. One senior civil servant, B. K. Nehru, confessed to "a consciousness of the presence of China," which had adopted "a pattern of development different from that which the noncommunist world has adopted" and was progressing "at a rate more rapid than that of democratic India. We are not indulging in a race with China," he hastened to add, "we want to develop at our own pace, but the fact of the matter is that . . . people . . . do make comparisons."

Some of those comparisons helped create an entire field of scholarship that investigated the correlations between democracy and underdevelopment. Predictably enough, the conclusions differed widely. Most initial analyses suggested that a high level of economic development was a prerequisite for pluralist political democracy to work (which excused those developing countries, notably in Latin America and Southeast Asia, that said a little dictatorship was necessary to raise per capita income and that democracy would come later). In reaction, some commentators cited India's low GNP in refutation of that thesis (arguing that poverty and democracy *could* go together). Others insisted that there was no correlation at all between rates of growth and types of political systems. Then scholarly emphasis shifted from economic growth to social equity, and here the findings tended to be no more uniform. Some suggested, looking at the figures, that the effects of democracy on social equality were actually negative: in a democracy, influential elites prevented social change that benign dictators could have imposed. The eminent American scholars Samuel P. Huntington and Joan Nelson disagreed, writing in a highly influential study that while "greater economic participation does not lead to greater political participation," there is "some evidence that greater political participation tends to lead to a more egalitarian distribution of the national product."

So by 1975 there was a lively debate, but no consensus, on whether democracy actually helped or hindered development. At any rate, Mrs. Gandhi's suspension of the most cherished freedoms of Indian democracy occurred at a time when critics were already asking, What was the point of India's democracy if it couldn't adequately feed, clothe, and shelter Indians?

.   .   .

At the same time, some posed the argument differently. India, they said, was not really democratic; "the lofty spirit of the Constitution," as *The New Yorker* put it, "has touched mostly [those] who have the literacy and the economic means to avail themselves of the letter of the Constitution." India's Constitution was, in many ways, an ideal constitution — certainly it was the world's longest and most comprehensive — and in many ways it was an idealistic one, conferring rights and freedoms born of high principle, so much so that Britain's most famous constitutional expert, Sir Ivor Jennings, declared that it "is impregnated with the idea that law and government are dangerous and ought to be kept in concentration camps." Certainly it was arguable whether such a magnificently democratic document, despite being prefaced by its socialistic "directive principles of state policy," could facilitate the kind of effective governmental action a developing country of India's magnitude needed. Sir Ivor believed it would "benefit only the country's largest industry — litigation." By the time of the Emergency, Indians who prided themselves on their democratic political system had operated their Constitution for thirty-six years, but found it necessary, when its provisions seemed inconvenient, to amend it no fewer than forty-one times.

The leading Indian constitutional lawyer Nani Palkhivala identified the nine essential features he believed made up the "basic structure of the Constitution": the sovereignty of India; the integrity of the country; the republican form of government; the "democratic way of life" as distinct from "mere adult franchise" (in other words, the existence of fundamental rights, such as due process, judicial redress, and others that you need lawyers to help you exercise); no state religion; a free and independent judiciary; the dual structure of the Union and the states; and the maintenance of a balance among the legislature, the executive, and the judiciary. The Indian political system based on this Constitution was, accordingly, a product of the liberal tradition of Locke and Mill, the Fabian socialism of the London School of Economics, the checks and balances of Jefferson and Madison, and the pluralist theolatry of Hindu culture, overlaid with a desire on the part of the founding fathers to enjoy fully the political rights of Englishmen, which the Englishmen had for so long denied them.

During the Emergency, the government sought to institutionalize changes in an altered Constitution incorporating the basic elements of the new order. Law Minister H. R. Gokhale argued that the Constitution was "not only a legal document, [but] a political and social document. It must reflect the aspirations and wishes of the people and it must be an effective instrument for carrying out those changes which are necessary for effecting a socio-economic revolution." The Constitution's earlier preoccupation with liberty and fundamental rights thus needed to be replaced with a concern for social equity and "fundamental duties." The "statement of objects and reasons" appended to the Forty-second Amendment explained that democratic institutions "have been subjected to considerable stresses and strains and that vested interests have been trying to promote their selfish ends to the great detriment of the public good." One clause sought "to spell out expressly the high ideals of socialism, secularism and the integrity of the nation to make the directive principles more comprehensive and give them precedence over those fundamental rights which have been allowed to be relied upon to frustrate socio-economic reforms for implementing the directive principles." Another raised the number of judges required to invalidate legislation in order "to strengthen the presumption in favor of the constitutionality of legislation." The entire thrust of the constitutional changes was ostensibly to facilitate the attainment of socioeconomic progress, which had hitherto, it was implied, been thwarted by the existence of a flourishing democracy.

How had democracy prevented economic development and social justice? One answer lay in the highly developed protections of the Constitution, and another in the federal structure, which granted substantial powers to the states, especially in the crucial fields of education, agrarian reform, and land revenue. Frequent fears of subnational particularism, and occasional fears of Balkanization, were expressed in the early years of independence (a 1964 survey found that only 8 percent of the people showed "nationally oriented loyalties"). The main political threat from the states, however, lay in the risk of their obliging the subordination of national interests, plans, and goals to state problems and desires, a process that began with the election campaigns in which "national" parties had to respond to state-specific concerns. Victorious Congress governments themselves made difficult demands on the central government, not infrequently in contradiction of declared national policies or plans. Mrs. Gandhi claimed, "I don't really have a lot of power because in every state the chief minister has much more power than I have. I cannot do anything in a state. All I can do is to try to persuade the chief minister or the others. . . . But all the work, or whatever decisions, are his or hers."

This was a somewhat self-serving assertion, but when opposition governments were in power in the states, there was no doubt that difficulties had arisen with the Center. One prime area of state influence was in the allocation of national resources; states lobbied for favored treatment from the government, and obtained it even when such treatment was not justified on objective economic grounds. State governments also tended to be more profligate than the Center in embracing deficit budgets to buy popular support; in taking actions that aggravated the national food distribution problem by restricting grain trading in their state; and in seeking to increase the number of development projects in their own state while simultaneously minimizing the taxes they would levy within the state.

The requirements of political responsiveness were, the argument went on, not always in tune with the requirements of economic progress: thus, increasing direct taxes on agriculture, extension of cooperative farming, enforcement of land reform, and other types of agrarian change became politically, and therefore practically, unfeasible. Politicians who demand sacrifices don't usually win elections, but those who make rash promises that will bankrupt their successors are warmly remembered for their own tenures. As Marxist economists argued, the Indian ruling class's mass base was in conflict with its class interest; they were spouting socialist rhetoric but discovering that you can't have democracy and preserve your privileges at the same time. The result was deadlock, with slow and uneven growth that was simply insufficient to eradicate poverty or even reduce unemployment.

In his now classic *Asian Drama*, Gunnar Myrdal wrote that "the combination of radicalism in principle and conservatism in practice, the signs of which were already apparent in the Congress before independence, was quickly woven into the fabric of Indian politics. Social legislation pointed the direction in which society should travel, but left the pace indeterminate. Many of these laws were intentionally permissive." Others were passed, at the behest of Nehru and other idealists, by politicians who had no intention of implementing them. There was a schizophrenia at the heart of the system: the ruling party was attempting to transcend the limitations of its own support in order to achieve ends that negatively affected the interests of many of its own backers, and to attain this objective through the democratic means of pluralist bargaining. There were, undoubtedly, conflicts inherent in such an enterprise. And, some critics suggested, some cynicism as well; in Barrington Moore's words:

> Some students of Indian affairs have expressed surprise that India's small Western-educated elite has remained faithful to the democratic idea when they could so easily overthrow it. But why would they wish to overthrow it? Does not democracy provide a rationalization for their failure to overhaul, on any massive scale, a social structure that maintains their privileges?

Perhaps democracy was a rationalization (though subsequent social change has undermined Moore's argument). But it was true that democracy did not favor swift change; one had to bring the various political forces along, and one might be dependent for votes on those most resistant to change. Where economic growth was possible as a result of governmental action, local elites utilized their hold on the machinery of state government to preserve most of the gains for themselves, so that economic development in the first decades of independence ended up, in effect, promoting social injustice. India's socialist-inspired Five-Year Plans rarely benefited the poor directly. The urban-rural dichotomy meant that farmers sought more for their produce while city-dwellers demanded affordable food; the government needed both agrarian political support and urban political tranquillity. The result, again, was compromise, temporizing, half-measures: agricultural subsidies in the countryside, cheap food distributed at ration shops in the cities, no possibility of focusing agricultural production toward economic growth.

And then there was the nature of Indian democracy itself: freewheeling, user-friendly, but completely divorced from anything resembling a performance orientation. Just three months before the Emergency was proclaimed, *The New York Times*'s correspondent Bernard Weinraub reported in the *The Atlantic Monthly:*

In the troubled state of Bihar, in the midst of demonstrations and violence, Indian and foreign journalists drop into the office of the chief minister without appointments and are offered sweet, milky tea and some gossip. It may be an innocent, chaotic, and unproductive way of running a government, but it is also zealously democratic.

Mrs. Gandhi's supporters could, and did, point precisely to that sort of practice as typifying all that was wrong with the way the country was being run: better give up the innocence and the chaos, they said, in the interests of being a little more productive. Weinraub himself had been careless enough to write, in the same article, that "India's sad and ironic fate is that the brutality and repressive discipline that dictated development in China and the Soviet Union are wholly impossible in this democracy." Within three months, "impossible" would seem a hollow word indeed.

The formal processes of democracy were eloquently attacked by the Emergency's advocates. Many a weary Indian bureaucrat or governmental leader argued that most political criticism seemed to fail to understand governmental problems as real challenges that needed to be solved. All too frequently it was criticism unaccompanied by clear or workable prescriptions for feasible implementation. After one parliamentary debate, even Nehru declared memorably:

> There has been criticism of our policy. But we have waited in vain these two days for one concrete suggestion. . . . Brave words? Yes; forensic eloquence? Yes; melodrama? Yes; but no concrete suggestion.

During the crises with Pakistan that led to war in 1965, the opposition's badgering of the cautious Shastri had led one commentator to note that it had yet to discern the difference between being a watchdog and a bloodhound. There was undoubtedly some merit in the government's charge that opposition was very frequently conducted for its own sake, and that negativism was a major feature of its approach. As Mrs. Gandhi told the opposition in 1976:

When we used to meet [in Parliament House] before the draft outline of the [Five-Year] Plan was ready, we were told: "Why have you called us? What is there to discuss when the government had not made up its mind?" All right, then we draw up the draft outline and call them. We were asked: "Why have you called us? The draft outline is ready. What can we do now?" We have been through many such episodes.

Objective commentators did not find the charges too far exaggerated. "Some of the opposition parties," wrote one independent editor, "seem to have been more interested in creating scenes and getting publicity in the press rather than [in] contribut[ing] to informed discussion on vital issues." Another recalled:

That Parliamentary democracy is government by discussion was forgotten and invective and shouting often took the place of argument and reasoning. Parliamentary privilege was repeatedly and wantonly abused.

Mrs. Gandhi said she found "the abuse, the shouting, the threats, the intimidation" a "constant feature" of parliamentary life, with the opposition's "obstructive defeatism" going so far as to make cooperation impossible.

The opposition's frustration was at least partially a function of its own fragmentation, which to some degree conditioned its ineffectiveness. Mrs. Gandhi noted that the opposition groups "ridicule[d] and contradict[ed] each other" and that consultations would continue to be bogged down in procedural trivialities unless they resolved their differences. Until then, she implied, she could hardly take their opposition seriously:

In a motion of no-confidence [in the government] . . . we look for some alternative policy. . . . But when we find not one alternative policy but as many alternative policies as there are parties and sometimes as there are members in the same party, then I very humbly submit that there is not much sense in such no-confidence motions.

All too frequently the divided opposition, unable to make headway, manifested its frustration through frequent walkouts.

In such a climate, and given the overwhelming need to overcome poverty, disease, and suffering, many wondered whether a democratic multiparty system could play anything other than a diversionary or obstructive role. One leading Indian politician, the Socialist Asoka Mehta, in the early 1960s articulated the view that the opposition's role should be "corrective" rather than competitive, but he carried that position to its logical extreme by joining the ruling party. Frequently in developing countries, opposition itself was seen as an illegitimate activity; as Lucian Pye explained, "The broad and diffuse interests of the ruling elites make it easy for them to maintain that they represent the interests of the entire nation. Those seeking power are thus often placed in the position of appearing to be, at best, obstructionists of progress and, at worst, enemies of the country. . . . This situation is important in explaining the failure of responsible opposition parties to develop."

Irresponsibility had indeed become a characteristic of politics in India. Students, labor unions, and political parties raised the politics of protest to the status of a new art form. There were demonstrations; strikes; fasts, often "unto death"; *bandhs,* or general strikes; *gheraos,* or virtual imprisonment of authorities by picketing their offices and prohibiting their exit; *dharnas,* or agitations at the premises of the institution being protested. Despite the havoc they often wreaked, these practices were resorted to by politicians of all ideological hues, and were even defended by government ministers as exercises in public education. Yet extrasystemic pressure like this, when freely resorted to, can become a serious threat to the system, imposing strains on the polity that often paralyze its ability to act in other arenas of public importance. Thus, when the "JP movement" for "Total Revolution" reached its peak in 1974–75, budgetary allocations for the police had to be doubled, major governmental and educational institutions in Bihar were either closed or guarded at considerable expense, and journalists speculated that "the country is being forced . . . away from democracy." When the Emergency was declared, all Mrs. Gandhi needed to do was to point an accusing finger at the chaos of Indian politics to justify its imposition.

What about that part of the polity least vulnerable, at least in theory, to the limitations of democracy — the Indian bureaucracy? The Indian political system, it has been said, is characterized by centralized policy-making and decentralized policy administration. The importance of the bureaucracy, therefore, as the actor effecting the implementation of developmental policy, was considerable. I incurred much good-humored wrath some years ago by describing bureaucracy as simultaneously the highest of Indian art forms and the most crippling of Indian diseases. Evolved over centuries, under successive empires, Indian administration is usually precise, rule-bound, laborious, and slow; it has also been accused of being "an autocratic Anglo-Brahmin structure created to run a static economy," whose bias "in allocating favors is always inegalitarian and conservative."

"Politics," Woodrow Wilson wrote, "sets the tasks for administration." It also creates some of administration's greatest problems. Independent India soon discovered that structures established during an imperial and then a colonial past, when governments were expected to rule rather than to respond to public demands, were not easy to transform into agents of popular democracy. The attempts to inject some degree of responsiveness into the system created complications both when they failed and when they succeeded. Since administrative systems were far more developed than political ones, the latter were ill-equipped either to determine the appropriate goals of administration or to maintain the integrity of the administrative system. When democratic demands that the bureaucracy be responsive to popular political currents were implemented, however, Indians found their administration becoming "politicized" — so that rural economic elites used their political power to modify governmental policy by trying to influence its implementation by the administration. With the growing strength of the democratically elected politician, especially in regard to appointments and transfers — the strongest levers over a bureaucrat — politicization became, to the higher levels of administration, what corruption was to the lower.

Ironically, where the bureaucracy was relatively independent (in places where the political leadership was either highly principled or weak), it tended toward autonomy and self-aggrandizement, serving its own interests, protecting its own powers, and resisting the growth of democratic politics and institutions; but where the bureaucracy was subject to the influence of politics and interference from politicians in its day-to-day work, it became corrupt and inconsistent, retreating into itself, seeking to avoid responsibility for fear of political reprisals, and placing the preferences of politicians above the dictates of policy or the regulations. Either way, the workings of Indian democracy did not prove a fertile breeding ground for bureaucratic efficiency or effectiveness. And at the lower levels of the bureaucracy, where posts were all too frequently filled at the behest of political patrons, the system engendered delays, nonperformance, petty bribe-taking, an obsession with routine, and inordinate amounts of paperwork and file-pushing to generate the impression of usefulness.

Bureaucracy was not the only force upholding the status quo. Independent India inherited a hierarchical caste system from its forebears and an iniquitous class system from the British. The colonial rulers had preserved (and in some cases created) a secure aristocracy and squirearchy across the country, whether one already existed or not, and relied on these "traditional" (or invented) oligarchies to maintain order and stability. Nehru saw the hierarchical structure of rural relations as a major obstacle to progressive change. Nevertheless, he embarked on the "modernization" of India with great hope, in the knowledge that the Congress Party had emerged from the independence movement as an authoritative voice of the nation as well as its legitimate agent of self-criticism and change. Under Nehru, the Congress remained more a nationalist movement than a political party, embracing every ideological tendency and every religious, regional, class, or caste interest within it. If development and social justice were to come to India through democratic means, the Congress Party seemed to be the ideal tool to bring it about.

The Congress Party's proudest characteristic, however, and one that had sustained it throughout its heyday as a nationalist movement, was that, instead of a tightly knit, ideologically committed, political party, it was an eclectic agglomeration; my metaphor of choice would be not the "big tent" of American political cliché but rather a Hindu temple, housing many gods and goddesses, hearing many different rituals and chants. To continue to be an influential agent in Indian society it had to stay that way, building up and maintaining its structures of support across the various divisions of society, organizing to fight and win elections throughout the country. In the process, the intellectuals, social reformers, and idealists who formulated policies lost power within the party to the rural elites who could deliver the votes and the businessmen who could fill the campaign coffers. The party mobilized support for aims that the very exercise of mobilization helped defeat, because the acquisition of power required the party to rely on those whom the utilization of power might otherwise hurt.

The process of democratic bargaining, compromise, and consensus-building inevitably slowed down the government. The need to "carry the party" resulted in concessions to the traditional elites and power brokers. The process was unavoidable and perhaps endemic to all democratic polities. As Myron Weiner explained, "In its efforts to win, Congress adapts itself to the local power structures. It recruits from among those who have local power and influence. It trains its cadres to perform political roles similar to those performed in the traditional society before there was party politics. It manipulates factional, caste, and linguistic disputes, and uses its influence within administration to win and maintain electoral and financial support." As a result, as Francine Frankel demonstrated in the late 1960s, "The major beneficiaries of electoral democracy were the most prosperous sections of the dominant land-owning castes, individuals who could exploit a wide network of traditional caste, kinship, rank, and economic ties to organize a large personal following." On the other hand, for many years the rate of politicization of low-caste members was very low. They did not act independently in making demands on the political system; rather, they related to the political process largely, if not exclusively, through the dominant caste leadership. The same pattern of hierarchical mobilization prevailed in the cities, where Congress leadership also came from the prominent figures in their own localities — merchants, contractors, and factory owners.

Political reliance on the traditional structure of society for mobilization purposes introduced an extra dimension to the process: the organization of caste, community, and tribal associations to press for group interests within the political framework. American political scientists, who pioneered research into this development, waxed enthusiastic about it, for they saw these as equivalents of American interest-group politics. But critics of the Indian system alleged that they overestimated the beneficial effects of such forms of democratic participation on the lowest sections of society. For one thing, caste and other particularism placed intolerable strains on the distribution capabilities of the system, as demonstrated by the attempts of motley groups to get themselves classified as "backward" in order to qualify for various kinds of preferential treatment. For another, the successes of lower castes often benefited only the elites among them, the privileged among the underprivileged. And the challenges of national integration and economic development became more difficult as more and more caste associations entered the political arena solely to advocate their own narrow, parochial interests.

Those problems were magnified when aggregated at the national level. "National integration," the *Hindustan Times* editorialized before the Emergency, "is still a matter of debate and the very leaders who publicly condemn communalism, casteism, and regionalism are often seen to woo communal, caste and regional elements for personal and party gain. . . . Many of the problems which vitiate our national life are the product of party politics conducted at a very low level." Expedient alliances between national parties and ethnic interest groups have led to situations in which nativist groups have been able to apply pressure on local authorities to restrict the migration of skilled labor to their areas and often to exclude or expel them altogether, even though what is thus politically expedient may not be economically beneficial to the area, the state, or the nation. Yet, before the Emergency, Mrs. Gandhi rationalized the Congress's adherence to such counterproductive styles of functioning as unavoidable:

> In a country as large as ours, where pluralism is a basic fact of life, a political party has to be not only concerned with ideology but also with effective methods of harmonizing smaller and larger loyalties. Therefore, a national party in a country like India has an additional reason to aim at carrying with it as large a number of people as possible in every region.

The irony is that Mrs. Gandhi had split the Congress Party in 1969 because she considered its organization an obstacle to reform; now her very success in attracting the bulk of the old Congress to her side guaranteed her failure. The very interests Congress sought to assimilate had been mobilized all too often for negative ends, that is, to *preventing* government from pursuing some course of action otherwise mandated by policy.

Nor were the grassroots institutions of popular democracy built up; stress continued to be laid on the acquisition and maintenance of political power. By 1973 Mrs. Gandhi was forced to concede:

> I am afraid our performance is disappointing. The party continues to function in a rather flabby way. It devotes too much attention to elections at the cost of solid fieldwork which alone builds the party's base. It lacks the apparatus which could enable it to do systematic work among young and rural people, industrial labor and other workers, women and the intelligentsia.

She mentioned "industrial labor," and this was no accident, for this was the one section of society that could be said to have benefited from the Indian ruling class's rhetorical attachment to socialism. Trade unions organized a small percentage of India's workers, but they won them considerable benefits — better salaries, benefits, and living conditions, coupled with fewer obligations to work hard or be productive, the bargain enforced by a startling willingness to go on strike at the drop of an ultimatum. This despite the fact that democratic India had, to borrow a metaphor from C. D. Deshmukh, to "achieve industrialization with its hands tied behind its back . . . whereas nearly all the Western countries completed their industrialization unencumbered by strict labor laws and often unhindered by considerations of international ethics."

Most of these charges were equally applicable to the political opposition, which failed to offer a more prepossessing alternative. In reacting similarly to the prevailing social forces, the Indian opposition revealed a remarkable tendency to imitate the Congress both in the issues it championed and in the manner in which it sought to construct its support. As the magnetic pull of nationalism faded, loyalty to the Congress as an institution declined, and politicians who had been (or could have been) Congressmen turned to the opposition to pursue their ambitions. This was not surprising: given a secure rural base, it rarely mattered to a politician which political party he belonged to; if his patron-client nexus was strong and he belonged to the right caste or social group, he could even run — and win — as an independent. Party affiliations then became a matter of convenience, and since, in general, the object of politics was not to overturn the old order but rather to gain entry into it, political defections from one party to another for political gain became astonishingly frequent. In the first twelve months after the 1967 general elections, there were as many as 438 defections in the state assemblies; one Haryana legislator, Gaya Ram, crossed the floor so many times in the expectation of office from one party or another that his name lent itself to a celebrated Hindi pun, *Aaya Ram, Gaya Ram:* "Ram came, Ram went."

So India's political democracy, its critics argued, had nothing to do with performance, and everything to do with power. What about its watchdogs, the press? Freedom of the press had always been one of India's proudest practices: the journalist Khushwant Singh even used the occasion of Montreal's international Expo '67 to tell the world:

We are free, our press is free. We speak our minds without having to look over our shoulders or having to lower our voices. I am emboldened to say that of the many countries of Asia and Africa which achieved freedom in the last twenty years, this is true only of one country, India.

Despite being free, though, the print media (radio and, when it came, television were for a long time government monopolies) was a target of the left-wing critics of Indian democracy. Many "progressives" saw the press as a reactionary institution intimately linked to the "moneybags" of big business who owned the newspapers and journals that dominated public discourse among the educated classes. Their criticism of Mrs. Gandhi's "socialist" actions and sympathy for opposition parties led them to be dubbed elitist and hostile to the masses.

. . .

"Much is written, even more spoken, every day about India's politics and policies," commented a former Indian diplomat toward the close of Prime Minister Indira Gandhi's reign. "In Delhi, in particular, dons, area specialists, and others wax eloquent on these subjects. They participate in public seminars, give radio and television talks and interviews, and publish articles. Their zeal for educating the public and drawing attention to themselves is astonishing." Even more astonishing, perhaps, is how little that zeal actually mattered. Intellectual activity in relation to Indian politics remained startlingly barren, seemingly unrelated to the empirical realities of Indian policy-making, and virtually unable to make the slightest dent in the armor of the political establishment. It was striking that, despite the prolific punditry, the only "abstract thinkers" whom our politicians bothered to consult were their astrologers.

Our sociocultural heritage had only served to reaffirm the divorce between India's intellectuals and her rulers. Indian intellectuals were heirs to one of the most elitist intellectual traditions of the world. The Brahmins of the post-Vedic era in India enjoyed exclusive intellectual distinction in principle, and the caste system confirmed their elitism in practice. To be an intellectual was to be a member of a caste of the learned, a caste that axiomatically desired nothing other than to *be* learned. Kings and warriors enjoyed temporal power, but they bowed before their gurus, who did not: intellectual distinction was thus an end in itself, and the Brahmins prided themselves on being above politics. In ancient India, this was no problem, because they were still eagerly sought out for their wisdom, and being above politics did not prevent them from giving sage political advice, which was almost invariably heeded. Increasingly, however, this Brahminical elitism became a hallmark of all Indian intellectualism. The search for knowledge, and in turn the entire realm of ideas, was detached from the everyday concerns of the rest of society. Over the years — from the earliest simple divisions between the Brahmins (as the intellectual and priestly caste) and the Kshatriyas (as the warrior and ruling caste), to the gulf that separates the twentieth-century academic from the politician — intellectuals abandoned worldly affairs to those qualified to act rather than to analyze.

In modern India, too, intellectuals remained aloof from the quotidian concerns of governmental policy, but this distance no longer reflected a Brahminical superiority. Instead, intellectuals were a deprived breed, shorn of that which made their elitist forebears respected — influence over the wielders of power. Power was in the hands of the state, and as the institutions of the state had grown in importance in independent India, an increasingly populist politics and a career bureaucracy had taken over the symbols of state authority. The spread of education had ended the Brahminical monopoly on intellectualism, but learning was now a means to an end, and the end that mattered was power. Anyone could be an intellectual, but only a few could exercise real authority. The intellectual had correspondingly been reduced to irrelevance. In the new formulation, those who could, did; those who could not, theorized.

The value preferences of middle-class India inevitably reflected those norms. "Society" had come to accord more respect (measured by any yardstick, including that of the price commanded in the marriage market) to the most junior Administrative Service officer — or, indeed, to the customs or tax official — than it did the most qualified academic or journalist. Intellectuals, therefore, formed a segment of the educated class from which spring the country's rulers, but they were not members of what Gaetano Mosca would have called the "ruling class." Many intellectuals had come to regret this. In independent India they sat in judgment all too frequently on those whose seats they would gladly have occupied, had they been given the opportunity. Far from advising kings or even constituting a jury of peers in a people's court on governmental performance, intellectuals were — as the subjects of their prescriptions realized — by and large passing verdicts on their betters. Sentenced to a lower social status, his livelihood often subsidized by government grants, the Indian intellectual was a poor relative of the Indian bureaucrat, and he knew it.

Indian intellectuals, torn between the pull of an ancient tradition and the attractions of the modern world, schooled in Western ideas but conscious that those ideas to some degree obliged them to commit cultural and spiritual matricide, already felt they were one step removed from the rest of their countrymen. Worse, by their very acquisition of the attributes of intellectualism, they had lost the direct mass contact that alone would have enabled them to influence either rulers or ruled. For many, their status as intellectuals symbolized privilege, and made them acutely conscious of their distance from the concerns of the masses — as well as vulnerable to attack because of this distance.

Nor did Indian intellectuals have any other support base. Their audience was limited by language, literacy, communications problems, socioeconomic factors, and a simple shortage of resources, which severely reduced the numbers of those with the time, the inclination, or the learning to support intellectual life. Even today, in a country with a literate population of 400 million, a book that sells four thousand copies is already a best-seller. The only exception is textbooks, but textbooks have to be government-approved, and non-textbooks hardly sell. Not surprisingly, therefore, intellectuals had not developed a significant audience among the general public. Such a situation both resulted in and perpetuated a tragic paucity of sophisticated literature on political ideas. The sheer struggle for economic survival, even among the educated middle economic class, had underscored the low priority of book-reading in Indian culture. Indian intellectuals therefore had no constituency but themselves. No wonder they apologetically accused themselves of being "out of touch with the people."

What was the outcome of this self-conscious divorce from the masses? In many cases, reflexive guilt drove intellectuals to mortgage themselves to the most visible self-proclaimed representative of the masses — the government. To some, support of the government's socialist goals appeared to elitist intellectuals as a low-risk gambit to salve their consciences on the cheap. Abject conformism followed, masquerading as "commitment" to a more progressive society. Those who thought they were sitting in an ivory tower felt they had no right to challenge the premises of those who claimed to be toiling in the slums.

In this climate the elite public opinion represented by Indian intellectuals often bore little relation to analyses of reality, and even less to prospects for action. While opinions were expressed, it was usually without expectation that policy change would result. As the one-time U.S. ambassador to India, John Kenneth Galbraith, dryly recalled: "I had been long in Delhi before I realized how urgent could be the discussion of economic planning, village development, schemes for health and educational betterment, development of village crafts and, of course, family planning, and how slight would be the consequences."

Yes, Indian intellectuals discussed policies, intensely and avidly. But they learned, like the British about their weather, not to expect anything to be done about it. Discussion was an art form in India, an egocentric ritual of simulated conviction or, at best, a secondhand expression of conscience. Its vitality was attenuated by its own irrelevance.

Thus the terrain of the intellectual had been cheerfully abandoned by the politician. The intellectual dealt with ideas, principles, analyses; the politician thought of power, and chose his party only as a means to it. Indian politicians changed parties the way a *filmi* dancer changed skirts, as often as it was expedient and as long as it appealed. The rhetoric did not change, since the party label reflected nothing more than opportunism. Who needed an intellectual articulating convictions when the only conviction a politician needed was in himself?

．　　　．　　　．

The irrelevance of the Indian intellectual was felt most keenly in that bastion of the educated, the Indian press. Khushwant Singh, when he was the editor of India's then-largest-circulation magazine, the *Illustrated Weekly of India*, confessed freely that "we have made little or no impact on the villagers. And in return the village has very little impact on us. We view it as a quaint, backward otherworld, peopled by noble savages and dusky, full-bosomed (preferably bare-bosomed) lasses."

But the problem of relevance ran rather deeper. For a long time until the collapse of the Emergency broke their psychological shackles, Indian journalists had had every incentive to conform, and neither the resources nor the social sanction to acquire the authority that came from specialization. The vocation became a respectable kind of clerkship; the journalists' financial worries, their lack of research and travel facilities, the absence of a tradition of social inquiry, their fear of the consequences of governmental displeasure, and their own low social status in relation to those they sought to analyze combined to create a deskbound journalism that filled the news columns with undigested handouts and the editorial sections with strongly expressed but impotent comment. "The national habit of issuing statements at the slightest provocation," one editor had noted before independence, "has stifled journalism." In the first thirty years after independence the problem only got worse, and the scope of the statements only became narrower. "You get the impression," an English editor remarked, "that the entire nation has spent the previous day doing nothing else but exhorting each other, preparing votes of thanks to each other, or giving seminars for each other."

V. S. Naipaul wrote of how struck he was by the "limited vision" and "absence of inquiry" of Indian journalism; apart from the editorial pages, "there were mainly communiqués, handouts, reports of speeches and functions." Indian journalism, in his view, "matched the triviality [*sic*] of the politics; it . . . reported speeches and more speeches; it reduced India to its various legislative chambers."

Yet one of the first victims of the Emergency was the Indian press, whose role in helping create an atmosphere of freewheeling political anarchy was cited by the government as the reason for the introduction of severe censorship restrictions. The deputy minister for information and broadcasting declared in 1976 that "any distortion in the role of the mass media would result in grave imbalances that a developing society cannot afford. . . . What we, therefore, need in Indian journalism today is a spirit of inquiry rather than the luxury of opinions." What the minister, Dharam Bir Sinha, did not say was that opinions in consonance with the government's would not be considered a luxury. His prime minister, Mrs. Gandhi, was in no doubt about her relief at not having to wake up and read attacks on her actions in print, attacks that gave aid and comfort to her political enemies. When she locked up Jayaprakash Narayan and his fellow agitators and simultaneously silenced the press, she said, the nation gained doubly: "There was no agitation. The agitation was in the pages of the newspapers." Sinha argued, more sophistically, that freedom of the press had meaning only if it also worked to ensure justice to the masses. How could a government focus on the progress and well-being of its people, Indira's acolytes asked, if it was constantly being sniped at and undermined in the national media?

If the press was targeted as an instance of democracy's incompatibility with development, so, somewhat more surprisingly, were the basic rites of democracy itself, the process of elections. Since the proclamation of Emergency was soon followed by the postponement of the scheduled 1976 elections, Congressmen were quick to assert that voting alone did not constitute a democracy. Mrs. Gandhi, defending the postponement of elections, went so far as to say that "there had been more elections than necessary" in India, and that the violence and disruption that had accompanied them had severely threatened the very survival of the polity. "If the government was convinced elections would result in mass violence, hinder development activities and threaten the integrity of the nation," Mrs. Gandhi declared, "it could not stick to the ritual."

Under the provisions of the Forty-second Amendment to the Constitution, the powers of the independent judiciary were also curbed, with the specific intention of not affording judges the opportunity to sacrifice socioeconomic legislation at the altar of individual rights. The Emergency, which brought to the fore the question of whether Indian democracy has been obstructive of the ends of social justice, answered at least part of that question by significantly reducing the courts' capability for such obstruction.

Part of the problem, to critics of the judiciary, lay in its evolution as a bulwark of Indian rights against the colonial transgressions of the British, a legacy that made it the least politicized institution in Indian public life, but also, therefore, the least committed to the socialistic goals of the government in power. As a result it was accused of having tended, through at least the first three decades of independence, to place the fundamental rights it was created to defend above the social needs of equitable economic development. Since the Constitution lists the right to property in Article 19 as one of the fundamental rights of the Indian citizen, and since Article 226 allows him to petition the courts for writs staying any official action in derogation of his fundamental rights "and for any other purpose," the judiciary found itself the battleground for some of the stormiest encounters in Indian political history. Maharajahs turned to it in an effort to challenge the government's abolition of their privy purses; businessmen sought constitutionally to overthrow the bank nationalization ordinance; and landlords attempted to stem the course of agrarian reform by taking the issue out of the fields and into the courthouse. In all these matters, the judiciary, by faithfully interpreting the letter of the Constitution — if not its intent, as embodied in the non-justiciable directive principles of state policy — had upheld individual rights above those of the state. Not until the Constitution was amended on several occasions, to circumvent judicial reservations, did the courts acquiesce in

many pieces of legislation meant to promote social justice and economic
development.

The judiciary was thus blamed for in effect colluding with vested
interests to thwart development and social justice. Take, for instance,
the case of land reform. The issue was left to the states, where powerful landlord interests ensured that reforms either were not enacted or
were implemented in ways that preserved the landlords' power. The
failings of the local bureaucracies and the reluctance of state authorities to enforce even legislation they had themselves passed constituted
the first line of defense. Then came resort to the courts, the conventional practice being to obtain a judicial order staying implementation of land ceilings on one's property in order to use the time thus
made available to divide up the property among family and retainers,
or simply to bribe a menial court employee to block indefinitely the
case's movement up the court calendar. If all else failed, landlords influenced the local record keepers or *patwaris* to falsify the books. The
cautious operations of Indian democracy have also contributed to the
problem: initial reform legislation provided for the landlord to re-
take untenanted land for his "personal cultivation," which led to mass
evictions of tenant farmers, and to some sharecroppers "voluntarily"
surrendering their legal rights to landlords in the hope of salvaging
some relationship to the land, even as hired help. In fact, in West
Bengal, Bihar, and Uttar Pradesh the effect of the land reform legislation was initially to increase the numbers of landless laborers and
sharecroppers.

Scholars who studied the workings of land reform in India, from
Wolf Ladejinksy to Hung-chao Tai, had been virtually unanimous in
blaming the workings of democratic politics for its failures. According to Huntington and Nelson, "the evidence is overwhelming that
land reform — one of the most dramatic ways of enhancing both social equality and status level in rural society — is more likely to be
introduced effectively by noncompetitive and nondemocratic governments. . . . If [political] participation has expanded [as it has in India]
to the point where medium-sized landowners play an active role in

politics, land reform becomes difficult or impossible. Parliaments are the enemy of land reform." In the words of Ladejinsky, "The conclusion is inescapable: if the peasantry is to get what is promised, peaceful and democratically managed reforms are not going to fill the bill. Government coercion, whether practiced or clearly threatened, is virtually unavoidable."

．　　　．　　　．

So what did the suspension of democracy achieve in India? Within a year of the imposition of the Emergency, there was a great deal of testimony attesting to what government propagandists called the "gains of the emergency." As a graduate student in the United States, I culled the catalog of commentaries below almost at random:

> In India's new political order, discipline has become the watchword, the theme of slogans proclaimed from the sides of buses, and of speeches by politicians. In the disciplined new India, the universities, which used to be regularly paralyzed by rioting, are now tranquil; the black market in many commodities has diminished, and the pools of illegal, undeclared capital are drying up. (*The New York Times*, November 8, 1976.)

> There are no bus hijackings; the students are busy studying and sitting for their examinations instead of intimidating the invigilators. . . . The supply of food is not disrupted by strikes and bandhs. . . . Food prices are down. (*Far Eastern Economic Review*, August 13, 1976.)

> Officials attend office on time, trains run on schedule, bus queues are orderly, some cities (like Delhi) have been cleaned up, there are no strikes or lockouts, no closing down of schools or colleges. Prices of essential things, including food, have come down. (Khushwant Singh, *The Illustrated Weekly of India*, January 25–31, 1976.)

> Industrial production rose by a record 10.5 percent in the first four months of this year and the pace is being maintained. Man days lost from strikes, now banned, dropped by 74 percent in the second half of last year — from 17.1 million to 4.6 million. In the first four months of this year they had further declined to 2.34 million. Transport bottlenecks were eliminated; power supply has risen 13 percent, industrial outputs have in-

creased. . . . Even her left-wing critics acknowledge that much more land has been distributed and many more feudal ties on landless labor broken in the twelve months since the twenty-point program was announced than in all the years before. The Emergency has been used to short-circuit approaches to the courts by recalcitrant landlords intent on frustrating the program. (*Far Eastern Economic Review*, August 13, 1976.)

Developing a country under democracy, one wise old saw went, is like trying to play poker without bluffing. The Emergency attempted to demonstrate that the game is best played with a stacked deck; yet, to stretch the metaphor, the cards had been on the table a long time. For years Indians had worried that politics served merely the interests of the politicians, that democracy had become an end in itself, unrelated to the welfare of the masses, that responsible governmental action was constantly being impeded by politically responsive short-termism.

Even the successes of Indian political practice underscored these arguments. For, even as democracy politicized vast sections of Indian society to a remarkable extent, it led to political activities by persons often ill-prepared by education or orientation to exercise functions of public trust. And democracy also led to such activities being carried out for ends that were widely seen as destructive of the larger goals of the society and the state. Many worried that the primary function of Indian democracy had become to accommodate demands rather than to program and administer social progress. The result was a system of equilibrium that appeared more conducive to stability than to real change. As the strains on the polity increased, however, and demands began to be voiced in the streets and on factory floors rather than in Parliament or the press, even this stability was called into question. The "JP movement" brought this weakness to the fore by exploiting popular discontent in the form of mass protest agitations; responding to the movement politically paralyzed the administration and obstructed the fulfillment of its developmental goals. To sympathizers of the Emergency, not all cynics, the issue became quite plainly whether the democratic freedoms to dissent and organize opposition were more important than the government's need to mobilize the society toward greater socioeconomic justice. The Gandhian sage Acharya Vinoba Bhave, for instance, willingly legitimized the new order by declaring that obedience and order were the social imperatives.

So, during the Emergency, with normal democratic processes suspended, Sanjay Gandhi, dubbed by his critics the "Extra-Constitutional Center of Power," developed a reputation for efficiency based on his determination to cut through red tape and throw off the dead weight of tradition in order "to get the country moving." He defended the postponement of elections as a duty to posterity: "There are greater things by which the country is judged. The future generation is going to want a strong economy." That Sanjay expressed such views is not remarkable; what is remarkable, perhaps, is that he echoed theories given respectability in the past by Western scholars. Francine Frankel, an American, had written in 1969 that democracy was of dubious value in "an underdeveloped country where parochial values far outweigh national commitment, where economic conflict is superimposed on traditional regional, linguistic, and caste rivalries, where there is no firm consensus on acceptable rules of competition, and where economic surpluses are either static or growing much more slowly than are demands." The British scholar Angus Maddison had argued that even Nehru "could not have achieved all his social aims without breaking up the system of parliamentary democracy," and the sociologist Barrington Moore had theorized that "a strong element of coercion" was necessary before any effective change could come to India. Interestingly enough, most Western liberal analysts had consistently expressed their skepticism about the effectiveness of Indian democracy and linked it with the hope that the polity would not become so democratic as to challenge the Congress's ability to provide strong governance. Thus *The New York Times*, in dispatches between 1969 and 1971, frequently noted that Mrs. Gandhi's reduced power had forced her "to maneuver skillfully just to stay in office," a position that left her with little of the "flexibility" required to achieve socioeconomic progress; and before the 1971 elections the *Times* published this remarkable endorsement :

If Indira Gandhi and her moderately left-leaning New Congress Party can gain a working majority in Parliament, India will have one more chance to work out its staggering problems through the democratic processes of peaceful change. . . .

An indecisive election result, leaving Mrs. Gandhi in power but subject to the pressures of coalition partners, would mean more of the current indecisive drift toward anarchy. It could strengthen separatist tendencies. . . . [T]he democratic system can hardly survive unless this election produces a government capable of dealing more effectively with India's unsolved problems.

This argument could be carried a step further, and was, by Dom Moraes in the same paper:

I would say there is no adequate replacement for Mrs. Gandhi as prime minister of the largest free nation in the world. She is the only politician in India with a thoroughly modern mind. Democracy in the Western sense does not really work in India, and this is provable from the past: It is too large a land, with too many corrupt people in positions of power, and too many illiterate and uninformed people controlled by them. The ruthlessness, the autocracy, for which Mrs. Gandhi has been criticized seem to me, in the context of the country, essential to its prime minister. Without this ruthlessness, this autocratic touch, nothing would ever be done about anything in India.

The reason these issues are worth revisiting more than two decades after the Emergency is that there are still voices in the country suggesting that freedom is less important than bread; that strong, even dictatorial, rule is the only way to achieve results in India; and that had it not been for the excesses of the family-planning program, which led to compulsory sterilizations and incited a mass electoral revolt across northern India, the experiment in autocracy would even have been vindicated at the polls.

Mrs. Gandhi's critics based their opposition to her abrogation of Indian democracy on essentially three grounds: first, that the

Emergency was not really necessary and that it was proclaimed and then institutionalized for purely partisan purposes; second, that the abuses of authoritarianism far outweighed the failings of democracy; and, third, that the "gains of the Emergency" were either not as considerable as claimed or were ebbing away as the initial shock of its imposition wore off. Having given the advocates of autocracy a full hearing, let us review the counterarguments — and not just with hindsight: many of these points were made by Indians at the time.

The charge of petty partisan politicking stuck to the Emergency from the start. The constitutional amendments came in for by far the strongest criticism in Indian intellectual circles at the time, former external affairs minister and Bombay judge M. C. Chagla insisting that the Constitution already provided for "a system of ordered liberty and not license, not liberty without any restraint or without any control." (The Forty-second Amendment was repealed by the Janata government soon after Mrs. Gandhi's defeat.) Mrs. Gandhi's arguments that democracy was impeding social justice were dismissed on the grounds that her large parliamentary majority provided her the opportunity to effect any changes she wanted to, without proclaiming an Emergency for the purpose. The real target was opposition of any sort, not merely of the disruptive kind; the partisan statements of many Congressmen — notably Congress Party president D. K. Borooah's fatuous assertion that "the country can do without the Opposition; they are irrelevant to the history of India" and Sanjay Gandhi's declaration that "the future of the Congress is the future of India" — led to speculation that the amendment prohibiting "antinational activities" might be used to ban opposition political parties. (It was not, but the Emergency was clearly not a good time to contemplate a career as an opposition politician in India. The two opposition governments in office at the time were soon dismissed. Two decades later, in May 1996, fourteen of India's twenty-six states had governments run by parties other than the country's then ruling party, the Congress.)

The specific charges against the institutions of Indian democracy also did not stand up too well. The much-maligned judiciary, for instance, was just beginning to strike the balance between defending rights and promoting change when the government drastically intervened with its Emergency. The Supreme Court's decision in the 1974 Keshavananda Bharati case that the right to property was not part of the basic structure of the Constitution epitomized this change in attitude; and other "socioeconomic" legislation, from the Minimum Wages Act to the Contract Labor Abolition Act, had all been consistently upheld by the court. In industrial law, the rights of the employee had been supported over those of his employer; in other areas, the outlawing of discrimination and other social evils was supported by the courts, which also upheld quota-based affirmative-action policies. The entire trend of judicial behavior, one could argue, had tended toward affirming Parliament's right to bring about social and economic justice through progressive legislation. Curbing the judiciary's powers in the Emergency therefore proved both unnecessary and destructive. In the two decades since, the judiciary has taken its activism much further, converting itself into a far more effective agent of social change than Parliament or politicians.

Many of the other charges against the workings of Indian democracy were not vindicated either by their suspension during the Emergency or by subsequent democratic experience. Far from proving to be the unenlightened fortresses of the retrograde, the states have, as discussed elsewhere in this book, brought democracy closer to the people. Politics in India has expanded its reach to the poorest levels of society, so that democracy has brought dramatic transformations to Indian society, empowering the lower and "backward" classes as well as the former Untouchables (the Dalits). Equally important, the changes wrought through the democratic process have found greater acceptance, and are therefore assured of greater durability, than those imposed by fiat from New Delhi. Studies have shown, for instance, that the much-publicized abolition of bonded labor during the Emergency actually worsened the condition of bonded laborers. And, as Amartya Sen has pointed out, democracies are better at preventing famine than dictatorships.

Rulers are best condemned out of their own mouths. "The purpose of democracy," Mrs. Gandhi once declared, "is to involve more and more people in policy-making." Ironically, India became less and less democratic by Mrs. Gandhi's own criterion as the years wore on, till the authoritarian tendencies in her approach reduced policy-making to the decisions of an individual and a handful of her advisers.

The abuses of the Emergency far outweighed what little good it did. Minister Gokhale argued, logically enough, that "if the power is required by the authority for the good of the people, the possibility of abuse should not be used as an argument for denying such power to the authority concerned" — yet when the exclusive arbiter of "the good of the people" was precisely the authority seeking such power, abuse was always a distinct possibility. Most of the atrocities committed at the time had little to do with social justice: the mandatory resettlement of Delhi slum-dwellers in a cruel exercise in heartless cosmetology; forced sterilizations by officials anxious to meet targets for fear of losing their jobs; the lack of accountability of the bureaucracy and the police to the public or the courts; the harsh treatment of labor by businessmen certain that the government valued production more than it did wage demands (strikes were banned under the Emergency, but lockouts were not); the misuse of detention powers by vengeful and corrupt policemen; and the loss of judicial redress for arbitrary imprisonment. Even if these improved an economic indicator or two, Mrs. Gandhi, as Chagla put it, appeared to be ignoring the Gandhian dictum that the ends do not justify the means.

As to the third charge, that the Emergency did not achieve any real gains at all, the argument is more complex. The list of reported successes I quoted earlier (apart from the bizarre reference to bus hijackings, which few had seen as a major Indian problem) were real, and seen as such at the time. The Emergency capitalized on the belief that abandoning India's traditional democratic — and usually lax — practices and procedures might well provide the solution to the country's overwhelming problems. Take the bureaucracy, for instance: Anyone who has had the frustration of standing in four separate queues to cash a check, or seeing forms glumly filled out in quadruplicate and duly stamped by three different supervisors before some perfectly simple transaction can be effected, or known the seething rage of having to bribe a clerk to perform the function your taxes are already paying him to perform, will sympathize with the desire of many to see the bureaucracy firmly dealt with. Mrs. Gandhi's authoritarian experiment is gratefully remembered for the fact that in several ministries there was a sudden shortage of chairs when the customary 40 percent absenteeism rate suddenly fell to practically zero. But there was little evidence that the occupants of the chairs were any more productive after occupying them, nor was there any proof that a performance orientation is easier to obtain under autocratic conditions than democratic ones (if anything, tyranny makes bureaucrats less accountable). There is no denying that it will take an efficient, productive bureaucracy to effect social justice in the face of vested opposition from political quarters, but no proof exists that suspending democracy will in fact deliver one.

In any case, to her critics, Mrs. Gandhi's motives were fundamentally suspect; she was seen not as a dedicated socialist using emergency powers to effect changes she could not otherwise bring about, but as a schemer "slightly to the left of self-interest." An American analyst predicted soon after the Emergency was imposed that "if she does get the economy turned around, most Indians will say that authoritarian rule was worthwhile. But Mrs. Gandhi has never been much of an economic administrator, and she is far more interested in political tactics than economic reform." The New Delhi lawyer and civil libertarian V. M. Tarkunde argued that her objective "is not to remove Indian poverty, but to create a strong executive unhindered by the checks and balances which characterize every democratic constitution. That is why the fundamental rights of the people are being taken away, why the wings of the judiciary are being clipped, and why the deceptive doctrine of parliamentary sovereignty is being propagated." Whatever her motives, even a callow twenty-year-old graduate student like me was able to write in mid-1976 that "it is by no means certain that even the 'gains of the Emergency' will persist once the jolt of its imposition has worn off and a couple of bad monsoons occur."

The fact was that, despite the failings of democracy in India, Indian democracy did ensure that progress was made toward greater social justice. It was the vote that gave the lower strata of Indian society their power; the political clout of the "backwards" is directly correlated to their numerical strength at the polls. One striking example of democracy's direct impact on society was its effect on the iniquities of the caste system in Tamil Nadu, where Brahmins who had been dominant for millennia found themselves the victims of governmental "reverse discrimination" favoring the voting majority against whose numbers (and resultant political weight) the Brahmins could not hope to compete; as one local commentator put it, "the forces of democracy have turned the tables upon them." Though those who argued that democracy had impeded social justice had the elements of a case, there was enough evidence on the other side to prove the opposite.

In any case, it remained true that Indian authoritarianism could not long be authoritarian, that the nature of the country would have reasserted itself in the face of any long-term attempt at regimentation. We are too vast, diffuse, and varied a people to be ruled for long under the kind of restrictions Mrs. Gandhi sought to impose; "emergencies" can oblige us to snap to attention, but they wear off after a while. Any government would have had to accommodate other points of view sooner or later, incorporate alternative sources of power into the governing consensus; there are few countries less susceptible to sustained one-person rule. Yet that is precisely what was being attempted during the Emergency; as the American writer J. Anthony Lukas put it at the time, a trifle colorfully, "Even if only thirty million Indians played some active role in the old system, that is 29,999,998 more than today, when only two — a mother and her son — make any significant political decisions."

Despite the hyperbole, the point is well taken: this sort of overcentralization would have been impossible to sustain. One of the reasons Mrs. Gandhi called elections when she did in 1977 — apart from her misplaced conviction that she would win them — was that, without elections and the related trappings of democracy, she had no means, under "Emergency" rule, to renew her own standing, legitimize her rule and that of her party, identify the currents in society she needed to co-opt, receive feedback from the people, and convey a sense (as well as a mechanism) of political participation to the vast multitudes in whose name she claimed to speak. In any case, a one-party system, even one claiming to be oriented toward the promotion of economic development, risked discovering that it could meet popular demands (however feebly expressed) only by using economic resources — without the process of pluralist bargaining that democracy provides, which helps determine who gets how much and why. In a country as diverse and plural as India is, a wide range of demands are always going to arise that will have to be recognized, accommodated, and to some extent satisfied, if the polity (and the nation) is to survive. Emergency rule cannot provide the answer to such demands.

But this is not to suggest that, with the Emergency an increasingly distant memory, complacency about Indian democracy is warranted. First, some of the factors that made the Emergency possible are latent in the system; they were exacerbated and exploited by Indira Gandhi, but they have not disappeared with her. Second, other failings of democracy have either emerged or intensified since the Emergency, notably in the increasing corruption, violence, and criminalization of Indian politics. It is worth examining both of these concerns in the interests of advocating realism as well as principle — democracy without illusions.

Mrs. Gandhi throughout preferred to rule rather than reinstitutionalize, to control rather than reorient, to subvert rather than balance: she mastered tactics and ignored strategy, ruling the country as its democratically elected head but doing nothing to help strengthen its democracy. The Emergency merely marked the logical culmination of this approach. Mrs. Gandhi weakened or undermined the institutions she found obstructing her dominance — the judiciary, the presidency, the press, the cabinet, Parliament, the Congress Party — but she failed to replace them with alternative institutions of her own, preferring instead to exercise her authority through no recognized procedure (as with the largely arbitrary appointment of Congress chief ministers in the states) or autocratic and sometimes unconstitutional pressure (as with the doings of her son's "caucus" during the Emergency).

Part of the reason for the damage that Mrs. Gandhi was able to do to the Indian polity lay in India's political culture itself. Despite two orderly successions (after Nehru's death in 1964 and after Shastri's in 1966), India had failed to evolve sufficiently strong institutional structures or deeply entrenched political norms, so that when the system proved unable to cope with the mounting economic, political, and social crises of the late 1960s and early 1970s, the situation was ripe for the classic "man on horseback" who could impose order and purpose on the prevalent chaos. It may have been ironic that the man on horseback was a woman, but the metaphor is startlingly relevant. In a trivial decision early in her rule, Mrs. Gandhi revealed her attitudes to the wielding of power and to those who were subject to it. The decision related to the widespread criticism in India, especially from liberals and socialists, of the riding test administered to trainees in India's civil and foreign services. The critics considered the practice a relic of the colonial era; not so Mrs. Gandhi, who affirmed (in the account of an admirer, the diplomat K. P. S. Menon) that "riding had a psychological value. It instilled a feeling of self-confidence and fearlessness, qualities essential in men holding positions of responsibility. A man who could control a horse, said Mrs. Gandhi, would also know how to control a mob." Not surprisingly, Mrs. Gandhi was herself a good rider, and "self-confidence and fearlessness" were attributes she prized in herself.

Under Mrs. Gandhi, legitimacy came to adhere not to the system but to her. She characterized her critics as congenitally irresponsible, politically incapable, and electorally frustrated conspirators of dubious patriotism who were threatening India's democratic institutions by attacking her. Her final political nemesis, a family friend since her childhood, Jayaprakash Narayan, felt constrained to write to her from what he thought was his deathbed: "Dear Indiraji, please do not identify yourself with the nation. You are not immortal, India is." At that very time Mrs. Gandhi had acquiesced in the slogan "India is Indira and Indira is India."

This blurring of distinction between nation and individual was, to a great extent, reinforced by Mrs. Gandhi's own conviction that she was the embodiment of the popular will. It was a conviction she derived from her father's instinctive identification with the Indian masses. Nehru had always made much of his connection with, and responsiveness to, the public at large. "I found in India's countryfolk something . . . which attracted me," he wrote. "The people of India are very real to me in their great variety and, in spite of their vast numbers, I try to think of them as individuals rather than as vague groups." But his knowledge of them, inevitably for a busy prime minister, was largely intuitive: he believed he had his hand on the pulse of the Indian masses, that with each emotionally charged contact with an adoring crowd, he knew their feelings and hopes, understood what they wanted. Nehru tried to educate the public in his mass meetings with schoolmasterly explanations of his policies. But as one historian, R. K. Dasgupta, described it: "Nehru addressed the Indian masses as a democrat, but the Indian masses revered him as a demi-god. . . . In his last years he had no means of feeling the pulse of the people he wanted to serve. The masses were either mute or would throw at him their acclaim at crowded meetings."

A problem with leaders relying on their intuitive sense of the aspirations of the masses was highlighted by former diplomat Badr-ud-din Tyabji's requiem on India after Nehru: "Subjectivity still rules the roost, though the great Subject himself died in 1964. His successors now quibble over the contents of his system, though he had no system. He had only behaved like himself, and no one can do that any more for him."

One person was prepared to try. Indira Gandhi saw herself taking over the country in an apostolic succession from Nehru: "My father and I *went* to the people," she said to me once. "We talked with a large number. . . . We were in touch with the people [at large] . . . not just [with] limited sections." Mrs. Gandhi told another audience that "people from all over India — peasants and others — were always coming [to her childhood home]. I was meeting them. I was in touch with their problems. . . ." Mrs. Gandhi's direct contacts with the masses were, of course, limited to her morning *darshans* (essentially, brief "at-homes") and public meetings. At the latter she began poorly, an inarticulate and self-conscious speaker, but crowds came to see if not to hear her; yet initially they were often more curious than supportive, and the largest meeting she addressed during the 1967 election campaign was at Madurai, where her party failed to win a seat.

Despite her undoubted popularity at certain points of her career — particularly during the Bangladesh War of 1971 and for the year or two that followed — it is important to remember that Mrs. Gandhi never won a majority of the popular vote. It was India's first-past-the-post electoral system that, by rewarding pluralities against a fragmented opposition, gave her Congress Party its crushing majorities in Parliament.

Yet Mrs. Gandhi found it easy to impose herself. At least in theory, India was governed by the same principle of collective cabinet responsibility that characterized parliamentary government in Britain or elsewhere, but in practice she reduced the cabinet to a rubber stamp. Several factors contributed to this, among them the ministers' lack of interest and ability: many were incapable of formulating policy, preferring to act as monitors for decisions taken and plans initiated by their senior civil servants, and they functioned more as the presiding political heads of their ministries, handing out favors and exercising political clout, than as policy-makers in their respective fields. The bureaucracy, meanwhile, exploited both the ministers' incapacity and Mrs. Gandhi's policy of strengthening the officials' hands in order to curtail the power of the ministers. All this underscored the preeminence of the prime minister herself. Under her, the old notion of *primus inter pares* was replaced by a pseudo-presidential one in which the prevailing view was that it was the prime minister rather than the party that had obtained the electoral mandate, while the cabinet ministers were seen as merely those chosen by her to assist in the implementation of her policies. Accountability now rested not on the cabinet but on the prime minister, from whom all policy flowed. Most ministers were either politically dependent on her goodwill or unquestionably loyal to her; if not, they rapidly ceased to be ministers. The formal cabinet itself was downgraded by Mrs. Gandhi's reliance on a "kitchen cabinet" of close advisers from the earliest days. These were usually junior or middle-grade ministers who were her personal favorites: one analyst even distinguished between Mrs. Gandhi's "kitchen cabinet" and the "verandah cabinet," depending on the degree of their proximity to the prime minister.

One of her ablest foreign ministers, the late M. C. Chagla, told me of the manner in which the rest of the cabinet was treated: Mrs. Gandhi did not respect her colleagues, he said, and "took days to grant appointments" to them. She was frequently imperious in style: another observer noted that she would "ruffle her colleagues by her speech" and often "startle them by her studied silence." For their part, they betrayed an abysmal absence of integrity and self-respect in failing to respond to Mrs. Gandhi's centralization of authority and initiative. Mrs. Gandhi made it clear that independent ministerial action would not be tolerated, and they gave in without a fight. During the Emergency she neutralized relatively senior ministers by increasing the authority of their junior ministers or by granting independent charge of part of their portfolios to ministers of state. But even before the Emergency, the prime minister controlled the meetings of the cabinet, whose agenda was subject to her approval. She could change the agenda, postpone a meeting, or bypass the cabinet altogether, and when it actually met, she could and did steamroll a consensus. The actual meetings were largely a formality.

The extent to which her power had already superseded the cabinet's was illustrated dramatically in the very decision to proclaim the Emergency, which was taken by Mrs. Gandhi without consulting her ministers. The Emergency declaration had to be issued formally by the president of the Republic, but Mrs. Gandhi had devalued that office, first by throwing her weight to a rebel Congress candidate (V. V. Giri), thus precipitating the party split of 1969, and then, when Giri grew restive under her dominance, by replacing him in 1974 with an old loyalist, Fakhruddin Ali Ahmed. Ahmed, despite being advised against the constitutionality of signing an Emergency proclamation without the approval of the council of ministers, acquiesced in the declaration without demur. The cabinet was then summoned at 4:30 A.M. on June

26, 1975, after the wave of arrests under the Emergency had already begun, and confronted at a 6:00 A.M. meeting with a *fait accompli* to which they raised no protest.

If the cabinet was weak, the party system, both Congress and opposition, fared little better. One of the crucial indicators of the effective working of a democracy is the functioning of the opposition to the government. In the early days of independence, the Congress remained the party of consensus, its rivals parties of pressure, seeking to bring their criticism to bear on the dominant party, which had to respond in order to preserve its dominance. However, one-party dominance was not — as the Congress's setbacks in the 1967 elections demonstrated — integral to the political *system;* it was merely the chief feature of the political *situation.* Some observers prematurely discerned a change in that situation in the elections of 1967. One scholar of Indian politics, the Briton W. H. Morris-Jones, described what he saw as the emergence of a "market" polity,

> a system in which a large number of decisions are taken by a large number of participants who stand in positions of both dependence on and conflict with each other. The decisions are reached by a process of bargaining; no one is strong enough to impose his single will. . . . [T]he consistent trend of Indian politics over the past twenty years is clarified if we regard it as one of movement from a system in which the market element was rather small to one in which it is predominant and decisive.

That was credible from the perspective of 1967, but of course things did not stay long that way, and after 1971, to extend the metaphor, the "market" polity quickly gave way to one of state capitalism, with a virtual monopoly of goods and services in the hands of Prime Minister Indira Gandhi. The "market" is back in business after the elections of 1996, but there is no guarantee that what happened before cannot happen again.

The Congress Party, with its control of power and patronage, its nationalistic aura, its unique organization, its network of vote-banks, its hold on both business and labor, its virtual copyright on the names of Gandhi and Nehru, was uniquely able to thwart all political opposition for more than four decades. Until 1977, and again during 1980–89, the opposition never posed the most effective threat of a parliamentary opposition, the potential that it could form an alternative government. Devoid of the financial, organizational, and charismatic resources of the Congress and hopelessly fragmented, it functioned essentially as a collection of pressure groups within the ruling elite. Parliamentary eloquence and occasional public agitation offered limited opportunities; it was often more productive to attempt to influence certain outcomes through informal contacts with the Congress. Within each party, other Congress standards also prevailed — a centralist structure with little accountability of the top echelons to their rank and file, and a one-way flow of power from High Command to ordinary member.

During the years of Congress Party dominance, political opposition was a singularly unprofitable activity, since opposition parties had no patronage to dole out except occasionally at state level. Opposition politics was largely the domain of four types of people: those who resisted government simply, as Edmund Hillary might have put it, because it was there; the ideologues, who were dedicated to the proposition of a revolutionary change their own conduct did little to bring about (Calcutta overflowed with Communist leaders sporting Cambridge degrees and living in palatial ancestral homes); the "outs," those who had enjoyed the taste of power as Congressmen but who were, for a variety of reasons, no longer in favor with their party establishment; and the "down-and-outs," those whose direct interests were adversely affected by the policies of the national government. The last either turned to insurgency or were won over through policy concessions; the rest were either co-opted or ignored. (It was only in the 1990s — when literally any party could realistically contemplate the prospect of a share in power at the Center — that this paradigm ceased to be true.)

Of course, the opposition had a powerful forum — Parliament — and, formally, Parliament's powers were extensive. Above all, perhaps, it was the ultimate authority in regard to the budget, its financial control over the appropriations of each individual ministry affording it a means of influencing the government's actions. The Lok Sabha, the lower house of Parliament, met normally for three sessions a year, for a total of seven to eight months, so that the government was never really exempt from legislative scrutiny. The routine proceedings of Parliament included several devices for opposition pressure on the government. Each House began its day with a "Question Hour" five days a week, followed by a "Zero Hour" at which further issues could be discussed. Ministers and officials spent a good portion of their working days preparing briefs to respond to the questions arising in these forums. The preparation and paperwork this generated was reported to bring most other activity in the ministerial secretariats to a standstill. Nevertheless, the majority of "backbenchers" tended to be out of their depth: they knew how to get elected, but not how to legislate. (In 1971 the poet and journalist Dom Moraes penned an unforgettable picture of the Lok Sabha, where "in a far corner of the chamber, amidst the yells and the clatter of the bell, a few members from remote rural areas, heads pillowed peacefully on their arms, slept the sleep of the innocent and uninformed.") When the opposition posed a serious substantive challenge, the Congress Party's crushing majorities ensured that it was beaten back; as Atal Behari Vajpayee, one of the country's more able parliamentarians, put it, "we have the arguments; they have the votes."

Mrs. Gandhi also tended to look beyond Parliament to "the people" for support. A senior Gandhi aide pointed out to me once that parliamentary opinion on most subjects (with the notable exception of Kashmir) was not necessarily representative of the views of a large segment of the population, and that the government did not therefore feel obliged to respect it. The principle of the delegated authority of the elected representative to speak for his constituency did not seem to have made much headway in official circles. These various strands fused under Mrs. Gandhi in a denial of legitimacy to the opposition that rapidly became a hallmark of the political ethos and reached its apogee in the one-party rule of the Emergency. "Sometimes I feel that even our parliamentary system is moribund," Mrs. Gandhi told an early interviewer.

"Everything is debated and nothing gets done. Everything that can be exploited for political purposes is exploited. . . . Democracy implies an implicit acceptance of certain higher objectives; the government can be opposed but not national interests." The problem was, of course, that it was the government that defined the boundary between the two. While Nehru had been described as "simultaneously the official leader of the ruling party and the covert leader of the opposition" — a man who built up democratic institutions by according them a respect they could not of themselves command — Mrs. Gandhi treated the *right* to oppose as if it were her gift to the opposition. By early 1975 perceptive observers found the opposition living in mortal fear of her resorting to one-party dictatorship and postponing an election she might lose. The declaration of the Emergency confirmed this fear, the ultimate denial of legitimacy coming from Congress president D. K. Borooah's declaration that "those who are not committed to the policies of our beloved leader Indira Gandhi have no place in our body politic."

The fact that Mrs. Gandhi and Mr. Borooah are no longer with us does not mean that a future Indira cannot find herself a hundred other Borooahs. The problem is compounded by the illusion of consensus, a concept overvalued in Indian politics. The only consensus a democracy really needs is that it doesn't always need a consensus. In India, however, the political consensus was not that it was enough to debate, to resolve differences through democratic disagreement and a show of hands. As revealed with startling clarity in the way India's prime ministers have been chosen by successive victorious parties or coalitions, consensus in India transcended the democratic process. The need for unanimity in the political culture ran so deep that on the occasions of three out of the first four prime ministerial successions — Shastri's, Indira's, and Morarji Desai's as a Janata leader in 1977 — an unelected caucus of elders chose the "consensus" candidate. The "consensus" choice was then endorsed without exception by legislators often in no mood to be consensual, but unable or unwilling to challenge the procedural model. After being passed over in this way for Shastri in 1964, Desai bitterly denounced the "unhealthy" practice of using consensus "to claim unanimous support for the choice of a few people who are in positions of authority." But when he actually challenged Mrs. Gandhi for the prime ministry in 1966, he lost and learned his lesson: when he finally came to power in 1977, it was not after a vote among Janata Party legislators but as the hand-picked nominee of two elder statesmen, Jayaprakash Narayan and Acharya Kripalani. Of course, the manufacture of consensus around individuals is not always good long-term politics. Chandra Shekhar, outmaneuvered by V. P. Singh for the prime minister's job in 1989, nursed his bitterness long enough to bring down the Singh government and acquire the throne for himself for six months in 1991.

But consensus may disguise the absence of a choice based on criteria more substantive than caste or personality. Too often the quest for power has less to do with principle than with opportunism. Since there were no substantive issues except the question of whether the "outs" could get "in," the political landscape presented an illusory uniformity that theorists mistook for consensus. Either way, the system changed little; the status stayed quo.

This weakness for consensus in Indian politics might, at its worst, point to a susceptibility to autocracy. Indeed, the 1980 electorate's decision to bring back Mrs. Gandhi just three years after the excesses of her Emergency appeared to confirm the theory that India values a firm hand over a democratically squabbling multitude. In Indira Gandhi's India, "consensus" could be imposed in domestic matters and contrived in foreign policy. It did not necessarily represent shared political convictions or approaches to the world, but rather the preferences of a sociopolitical ethos that valued unanimity over dissension.

The decline of the Congress Party from the accession to power of Mrs. Gandhi to its electoral defeat of 1996 makes these concerns all the more relevant. As Congress president for a year in 1959, Mrs. Gandhi had used the party to push issues ahead of the Congress government; her role in mobilizing the party to bring down the elected Communist government in the state of Kerala was instructive. As prime minister, however, Indira Gandhi quickly began to see the other side of the picture. Initially the creature of the Syndicate, she allowed the party leaders to intervene in some decisions, such as the choice of her first cabinet (she was pressured by party notables, particularly Congress president Kamaraj, to include some senior Congressmen against her wishes). Friction quickly developed, however, between her and the party leaders.

Kamaraj had come to see a need for "new techniques of collective thinking" in the Congress, and called for greater coordination between the government and the party, the prime minister and the Congress president. During Shastri's prime ministry he had expressed his views on a number of major policy questions and made it clear that he expected to be listened to. In his presidential address to the Congress Party soon after Mrs. Gandhi's accession to the prime ministry, Kamaraj made clear his view of his own authority and the diminished importance of the prime minister. The party's responsibilities after Shastri's death, he announced, "have become too heavy for any one single person to shoulder." Mrs. Gandhi's "onerous responsibilities," he declared, would be shared by the party organization. "It is with great sense of humility that I approach these grave responsibilities and I seek your sympathy and guidance . . . to cope with the burdens that the nation as a whole has to bear."

Indira Gandhi, on the other hand, declared that as the representative of the nation she stood above Kamaraj, the representative of the party. She told an interviewer in September 1966 that "here is a question of whom the party wants and whom the people want. My position among the people is uncontested." Kamaraj, visibly angry, was reported to have been asking openly the next evening, "What did she mean?"

She soon made it clear what she meant. By 1969, using the issue of the election of India's ceremonial president, she split the Congress Party, holding on to power and driving Kamaraj into opposition — and irrelevance.

Ironically, Mrs. Gandhi split the party on (among other things) the issue of democratizing its functioning and guaranteeing the "inherent right" of Congressmen to debate every party and governmental policy: the "basic issue," she declared, "is whether the democratic process will prevail or not in the Congress." Nevertheless, it did not take her long after asserting her own control to stifle that very democratic process. She delayed internal elections, appointed her own men to every significant post, and treated the party president as a junior aide rather than as the leader of the organization that had brought the country to independence. This was partially because, as with the nation, Indira Gandhi identified herself with the party:

> [T]he Congress is very dear to me because some people joined at the age of fifteen, some people at the age of twenty and some at forty or fifty. But I was born in the Congress. There was no time when my home, since I was born, was not the center of all the major political movements, decisions and the meetings that took place and the whole of modern Indian history was being made there. . . . Nobody could be closer to the Congress or even more emotionally involved than I have been and I still am.

Her opponents, she claimed, "came in [to the Congress] when there was no question of sacrifice or suffering but merely of what could be got out of the party."

Though a travesty of the truth — Mrs. Gandhi, a daughter of privilege, never suffered the personal privations undergone by many of those she excoriated — this heritage, Mrs. Gandhi believed, qualified her to remake the party in her own image. The loss of the bulk of the Congress organizational wing in the 1969 split facilitated such a step, for she had largely to carry the party on her own shoulders. By 1969, at any rate, Mrs. Gandhi had come to the conclusion that the executive role of the party in government was more important than the organization wing — which, she now said, derived its own sustenance from the party's representatives in Parliament and government. The rapid subordination of the new Congress's organization to the prime minister followed.

Indira Gandhi showed that she could do without an organization when she led her party to victory in the 1971 polls largely on the strength of her personal charisma. Congress candidates campaigned mainly on her name and backing; the typical election poster showed her picture, not the candidate's, and mentioned him, if at all, in much smaller print than that accorded Mrs. Gandhi. Thanks in part to the opposition's slogan of *Indira Hatao* ("Remove Indira"), Mrs. Gandhi became the primary, indeed the only, issue in the elections. Congress election posters, instead of stressing positions, displayed slogans affirming that Mrs. Gandhi was "the only national leader whose image is enshrined in the hearts of the people." The 1971 elections were thus in every sense a personal triumph for Mrs. Gandhi, and firmly established her position at the top of both party and nation. With the historic military victory over Pakistan later that year in the Bangladesh War, Mrs. Gandhi was almost deified throughout India — the Muslim artist M. F. Husain, "India's Picasso," painted a triptych depicting her as the Hindu warrior goddess Durga — and criticism of her in the party was treated virtually as sacrilege.

Mrs. Gandhi then set about centralizing the party, which had in the past been a federal one characterized by strong state parties. She did this by reducing the power of the state organizations, eliminating the party bosses, placing her own nominees on key Congress decision-making bodies, nominating Congress chief ministers in the states instead of encouraging their free election by state legislators, personally appointing the Congress president, and deferring indefinitely intra-party organizational elections. Her control of the Congress presidency was an important instrument of her domination. After the party split, Mrs. Gandhi initially thought of assuming the position herself, but then decided to staff the presidency with frequently replaced loyalists. None of them was permitted to stay long enough in office to consolidate an independent base of support in the organization. Mrs. Gandhi bolstered her control at the top by ensuring that the Congress MPs below were dependent on her for political advancement, patronage, and party nominations (as well as material support) for elections.

Some sympathizers have suggested that Mrs. Gandhi's remolding of the party was aimed at making the Congress a more effective organization, a vehicle of performance rather than compromise. That interpretation may have been intellectually appealing to starry-eyed leftists at the time, but it is empirically difficult to sustain, for Indira Gandhi's personalization of power *increased* precisely as the party's ability to perform declined, through the economic and political crises of 1973–75. Her own record makes it all the more difficult to suggest that the changes she brought into the way the party was run could have been justified on the grounds of performance. The American political scientist Stanley Kochanek spoke of "de-institutionalization," saying, "The new Congress system is too personalized. It has failed to establish mechanisms for building support other than through the use of populist systems." This was as true of the party as it was of the cabinet. Indira Gandhi herself later admitted that the Congress under her "lacked a party apparatus," and after her defeat she conceded that she had neglected the task of party organization entirely. Yet, when she came back to power in 1980, she did nothing whatsoever to restore inner party democracy to the Congress.

The Emergency marked the culmination of a process of centralization that in its working had much less to do with performance than with the control of power. Even before the Emergency, the "new generation" of Congressmen in her leadership, far from being a well-knit "performance oriented" team, was an inchoate amalgam of her father's rejects (like K. D. Malaviya), traditional politicians (like Jagjivan Ram), family friends (like Uma Shanker Dikshit), regional bosses (like Bansi Lal), fiery idealists without ministerial experience (like Chandrasekhar), un-ideological office-seekers (like V. C. Shukla) and lapsed Communists in search of power (like Mohan Kumaramangalam). Together they proved unable to stop the political or the economic drift. The entire official edifice had the weight and stability of a frequently reshuffled house of cards. It came, therefore, as no great surprise when the Congress Parliamentary Board, meeting in June 1975 in the wake of the adverse court judgment against Mrs. Gandhi that might have unseated her, not only did not ask her to observe the proprieties and step down, but instead resolved unanimously that her "continued leadership as prime minister is indispensable for the nation." By then the realization had dawned that, as a letter-writer to *The Statesman* put it, "the Congress was so bankrupt" that it could not even nominate a temporary replacement for Indira Gandhi.

Another legacy of Mrs. Gandhi's style of governing was her use of advisers responsible only to her, of whose advice and services she availed herself as and when she chose — and who remained unaccountable to any democratic forum in the parliamentary system. Her personal staff came to include crude wielders of political clout, men who had risen from the clerical ranks by their adeptness at dispensing patronage and their penchant for effective political arm-twisting. The personal dominance of the prime minister was exercised through officials whose influence transcended their nominal powers. A single phone call from Mrs. Gandhi's "Additional Private Secretary," or even his personal assistant, was enough to goad ministers and secretaries into action. "There were no rules, no regulations, no precedents, no principles," wrote the eminent journalist Kuldip Nayar: " . . . all in the government waited at the end of the telephone line."

The stage was thus set for Sanjay Gandhi's unconstitutional control of policy long before the Emergency was actually proclaimed on June 26, 1975. At the same time, with the core of the party and its organization etiolated, Indira Gandhi had little choice but to turn to her son for support and sustenance during the Emergency. The Congress she had created was no longer capable of meeting an activist political challenge. Mrs. Gandhi, congenitally unable to trust others, feeling herself existentially "alone" and conscious that Sanjay was the only aide whose loyalty to her was unconditional, relied heavily on her younger son and most trusted confidant. It also helped that they lived under the same roof. Sanjay participated in daily meetings with the prime minister, toured the country alongside her and on her behalf, made speeches, and issued instructions to chief ministers, state party bosses, and even bureaucrats, over none of whom he enjoyed any formal authority. In the process he took the "de-institutionalization" of India to the limit.

His mother's cousin, B. K. Nehru, a distinguished civil servant and diplomat, may appear in hindsight to have overstated the case against Sanjay when he declared:

During the Emergency, Sanjay traduced all the fragile institutions of our democracy — the civil service, the judiciary, the press, the civilian control of the military. He gave preference to this civil servant or that judge, intimidated this journalist or transferred that soldier. He therefore demoralized the whole apparatus of government. In his short life, he destroyed all the fragile democratic institutions that had been nurtured in independent India. Thus, he made possible the dawn of a totally ruthless, disillusioned period, where each man is for himself, and for whatever he can get out of the society.

Even if exaggerated — Sanjay, for all his unfeeling malevolence, could not destroy Indian democracy singlehanded, and the institutions survived him, as India has survived other despots through its history — the indictment of a member of the family points devastatingly to the direction in which he was leading the country.

Sanjay Gandhi's "five-point program," the animating political philosophy of the Emergency, consisted of population control, slum clearance, tree-planting, literacy, and dowry abolition. Though it was a long way from the stirring aspirations of the Congress in its nationalist days, it was a useful enough agenda, if dreadfully limited in its vision — but it failed spectacularly on all fronts. The thuggish attempt to enforce sterilization and vasectomies, as well as to intimidate government servants (from officials to schoolteachers) into fulfilling arbitrary sterilization quotas or forfeiting professional preferment, set back the country's voluntary family planning efforts by a decade. The bulldozing of half a dozen slums in the national capital and the relocation of their inhabitants into areas where they were deprived both of infrastructure and of opportunities to earn a livelihood demonstrated the futility of slum clearance as an objective in itself: slums exist because their inhabitants have nowhere else to live, and because their residents conduct viable lives from them; improving slum conditions makes far more practical, economic, and indeed political sense than clearing them. Tree-planting is a laudable objective, but it was not pursued with any great energy; worse, little was done to control the ravages of deforestation undertaken by contractors with political connections to the ruling party. Literacy rates continued to stagnate, except in such states as Kerala, where the impetus for education predated Sanjay Gandhi and was pursued most vigorously by those who were implacably imposed to his aims. And as for dowry abolition, not only did the practice burgeon in the aftermath of the Emergency, but the 1970s and 1980s saw a record increase in the grisly phenomenon of "dowry deaths," with brides being burned in their kitchens by husbands and mothers-in-law for not having brought sufficient dowries into their marriage. Such crimes were committed, largely in the north, by precisely the kind of thrusting, materialistic, up-wardly mobile middle-class urban families who formed the backbone of Sanjay Gandhi's political support.

The fate of his "five-point program" merely confirmed that no na-tional figure in independent India has left a more futile political legacy than Sanjay Gandhi. When, a few years after his death, his widow, Maneka, along with a handful of former cronies sidelined by the post-Sanjay Congress, attempted to revive their political fortunes by starting an organization they named the Sanjay Vichar Manch (Forum for the Thoughts of Sanjay), they were greeted by a collective exhalation of disbelief, for how could anybody exalt the "thoughts" of a man who had no thoughts? A "Sanjay Action Forum" might have made some sense, for, in his impatience to "get things done," Sanjay was arguably a man of action. But not even his most committed admirers could have ac-cused him of being a thinking man; earlier, during the Emergency, he admitted in an interview that he read only comics. When, during the period of anguished mourning that Mrs. Indira Gandhi suffered after her younger son's death, the idea was floated to rename Delhi University after Sanjay, the howls of protest from the university's degree holders penetrated even the prime minister's maternal shield. The very thought of having our education devalued by attaching the name of an unedu-cable dropout to our degrees was bad enough. As one Delhi University classmate of mine exclaimed, "For God's sake, why rename a university after the man? Couldn't they find a garage?"

The passing of Sanjay and the elevation of Rajiv as Mrs. Gandhi's new right hand did, however, illustrate the extent to which the Con-gress Party had come to be dominated by one woman. Sadly, this occurred just when new groups of political actors were entering the national arena — representing the downtrodden, the marginalized, the fanatic — and when the challenge of accommodating and absorbing them required the vision of the Nehru generation. Instead, the political transformations occurring across India encountered not a flexible, imaginative, and great-hearted ruling class, but an atrophying system paying court to a petty autocrat. This moment of bathos gave us the depredations of Sanjay (farce as tragedy), the sycophantic syncopations of a depleted Congress leadership (tragedy as farce), and the unwise inciting of Sikh fundamentalism leading to the assault on the Golden Temple in "Operation Bluestar" (tragedy as tragedy).

"The Congress is no longer a party," wrote political scientist Ashutosh Varshney, "but an undifferentiated, unanchored medley of individuals sustained by patronage." Meanwhile, shorn of the opportunity to exercise real responsibility, Congress politicians used the party as a vehicle largely for self-gratification. By the time of Rajiv's ascent, the party overflowed with the sort of professional politicians we of the educated middle classes had come to despise, sanctimonious windbags clad hypocritically in khadi who spouted socialist rhetoric while amassing uncountable (and unaccountable) riches.

Rajiv Gandhi's searing portrait of his own party, in his presidential address to the Congress centenary celebrations in 1985, cannot be bettered as a portrait of its decline:

> Instead of a party that fired the imagination of the masses throughout the length and breadth of India, we have shrunk, losing touch with the toiling millions. It is not a question of victories and defeats in elections. For a democratic party, victories and defeats are part of its continuing political existence. But what does matter is whether or not we work among the masses, whether or not we are in tune with their struggles, their hopes and aspirations. We are a party of social transformation, but in our preoccupation with governance we are drifting away from the people. Thereby, we have weakened ourselves and fallen prey to the ills that the loss of invigorating mass contact brings.
>
> Millions of ordinary Congress workers throughout the country are full of enthusiasm for the Congress policies and programs. But they are handi-

capped, for on their backs ride the brokers of power and influence, who dispense patronage to convert a mass movement into a feudal oligarchy. They are self-perpetuating cliques who thrive by invoking the slogans of caste and religion and by enmeshing the living body of the Congress in their net of avarice.

For such persons, the masses do not count. Their lifestyle, their thinking — or lack of it — their self-aggrandizement, their corrupt ways, their linkages with the vested interests in society, and their sanctimonious posturing are wholly incompatible with work among the people. They are reducing the Congress organization to a shell from which the spirit of service and sacrifice has been emptied. . . .

We talk of the high priorities and lofty ideals needed to build a strong and prosperous India. But we obey no discipline, no rule, follow no principle of public morality, display no sense of social awareness, show no concern for the public weal. . . .

The speech made him deeply unpopular with the old guard of his own party, but (or because) it was true; and today, a decade later, it is truer yet. In his five years in office, Rajiv Gandhi reshuffled his cabinet no fewer than twenty-six times, but he came no closer to finding the right combinations of competence, integrity, and commitment he sought in a Congress Council of Ministers. He did not, of course, trace its decline to its manipulation and hollowing out by his mother, but he could not arrest it, and his successor, P. V. Narasimha Rao, did not even try. In the Congress's most recent stint in power — under the Rao government of 1991–1996 — intraparty elections were not held for four years, party appointments were at the pleasure of the prime minister (who went further than Mrs. Gandhi by simultaneously holding the post of president of the Congress Party, thereby preventing challengers to his authority from arising within its ranks), and Congress chief ministers in the states were appointed by New Delhi; worse, the top party leadership acquired a nationwide reputation for unresponsiveness and lack of accountability. (It is because many voters sense that the decay, corruption, and complacency of the Congress is less present in the BJP that that party has managed to appeal to some who do not share its "Hindutva" agenda.)

On the positive side, there is a remarkable stability to Indian politics, despite its apparent fragmentation. The French political philosopher Maurice Duverger classified political conflict within democracy in three ways: conflict over basic principles (as in Italy, where Communists and Christian Democrats contended); conflict over subsidiary principles (as in Britain, which offered a choice between social democracy and conservatism); and conflict without principles (as in the United States, where voters chose between two liberal-capitalist parties). Looking at the divergent platforms of the various parties, it might be thought that India falls into the first category. Yet, the platforms of the two Communist parties notwithstanding, the tenor and thrust of oppositional activity in general did not challenge the established consensus. This was ironically reaffirmed in 1977 when the former opposition, then the Janata coalition, restored the democratic consensus after its suspension by a Congress government, and again in 1996 when the basic policies of the defeated government were echoed in the Common Minimum Program agreed upon by the thirteen-party United Front coalition that replaced it. Even the two Communist parties did not challenge the national consensus on governance when they came to power in the states of Kerala, West Bengal, and Tripura; they ran capable liberal-democratic regimes in the Congress mold, working for evolutionary rather than revolutionary change. Beneath the chaos in the streets, opposition politics actually shored up the Indian democratic system. Every party claimed to represent the totality of the national interest in the quest for consensual national objectives. A conflict over subsidiary principles thus seems the fairest description of Indian politics, though it strikes many as a conflict without principles — in not quite the way Duverger intended.

·   ·   ·

Of the issues most famously raised by Prime Minister Rajiv Gandhi himself in his controversial speech to the centenary celebrations of the Indian National Congress Party in 1985, his excoriation of the political roots of Indian corruption resonated perhaps the most strongly with ordinary Indians. In remarks notable for their candor and freedom from cant, Rajiv declared:

> As the proverb says, there can be no protection if the fence starts eating the crop. This is what has happened. The fence has started eating the crop. We have government servants who do not serve but oppress the poor and the helpless, police who do not uphold the law but shield the guilty, tax collectors who do not collect taxes but connive with those who cheat the state, and whole legions whose only concern is their private welfare at the cost of society. They have no work ethic, no feeling for the public cause, no involvement in the future of the nation, no comprehension of national goals, no commitment to the values of modern India. They have only a grasping, mercenary outlook, devoid of competence, integrity, and commitment. . . . Corruption is not only tolerated but even regarded as the hallmark of leadership.

There are a number of reasons for the dramatic growth in political corruption in independent India. The obvious ones lie in the power that politicians have arrogated unto themselves in the "permit-license-quota Raj" ushered in by Nehruvian socialism. When so much of the country's basic economic activity is dependent on the issuance by government of permissions, waivers, licenses, and exemptions to regulations, the temptation for politicians and public officials to profit from their power to permit becomes irresistible.

The evolution of the relationship between business and politics has also played a part. The Indian nationalist movement in the days of the British Raj openly sought support and financing from Indian business houses; Mahatma Gandhi was assassinated at the home of business tycoon G. D. Birla, a major financier of the Congress Party. Even the socialist Nehru encouraged contributions by businessmen and companies to his party, and indeed to other parties: the Birla industrial house made it a point to contribute to all political parties, including the Communists (though the votaries of Marx received only a token contribution). Such contributions were made publicly, by check, and the figures were accessible to anyone interested, and officially tabled in Parliament by the minister of commerce. Prime Minister Indira Gandhi, however, whether out of cynicism or idealism — with her the two were often indistinguishable — declared such practices to be morally unacceptable in a socialist country, since they placed political parties in thrall to big money. She accordingly banned political contributions by companies. She could hardly have been unaware that her partymen promptly sought such contributions anyway, but no longer officially: the certified check was replaced by the briefcase under the table.

Businessmen had little choice but to play along with this arrant hypocrisy. For one thing, cultural attitudes were hostile to big business. Private gain was widely considered an ignoble motive, and capitalists seen as inherently selfish; the heated socialist rhetoric that dominated public political discourse put them further on the defensive. For them, it made sense to trade financial support in exchange for links with top government leaders. When Congress took a socialistic turn, businessmen preferred to stay in its good graces in quest of limited personal gains from the powers that be rather than to work to support a pro-business alternative like the opposition Swatantra Party (a pro–free enterprise grouping that flourished from 1959 to 1975, winning as many as forty-four seats in Parliament in 1967). This unctuous desire to curry favor with their sworn ideological enemies was hardly surprising. As Mrs. Gandhi noted cheerfully, "Our private enterprise is more private than enterprising."

The calculations were clearly short-term: the Congress was in power and therefore in a position to disburse licenses and other governmental favors in an increasingly controlled economy, whereas the party that pledged to eliminate all controls was too weak to offer the prospect of immediate returns. Swatantra general secretary Minoo Masani railed regularly against the "supine and cowardly attitude" of big businessmen, but they preferred to appease their critics rather than bankroll their supporters. Indeed, when the Congress leadership was contested between Mrs. Gandhi and the right-of-center Morarji Desai, businessmen financed the leftist prime minister in preference to the man whose views might have been more congenial to business. It was a relationship of breathtaking cynicism: businessmen supporting leaders who imposed state controls on business, knowing that their support would get the controls waived for them (but maintained on others). As the right-wing pro-RSS journal *Organizer* bitterly described big business's relations with Mrs. Gandhi: "And so they showered donations on her; and she showered licenses on them."

So, when the government passed a law banning company donations to political parties, the contributions were merely driven underground. "Black" or unaccounted money flowed to party coffers — and increasingly (because politicians are human, and particularly fallible examples of the species) into their private bank accounts as well. Politics became the route to amassing great wealth; humble socialists built impressive houses in their wives' names, acquired large farms, cars, and foreign bank accounts, and traveled abroad at the drop of a boarding pass. The government's role in making major international purchases — of weapons, oil, sugar, fertilizer, any major commodity that was being acquired in the name of the nation as a whole for public distribution — became a particularly lucrative source of corruption. The Indian taxpayer routinely paid a premium over the world market price for such goods, the difference disappearing into the pockets of assorted political middlemen, and a portion, presumably, going to the ruling party, to finance its increasingly expensive election campaigns. Since much of the "big" money was now collected centrally, Mrs. Gandhi and the party leaders were able to control the use of party funds better, to reward and punish others within the party.

The corruption endemic in the political system then pervaded Indian life, partially because the all-encompassing nature of the bureaucratic state obliged ordinary citizens to deal with government for so many of the essentials of their lives, from obtaining ration cards and gas connections to registering a deed of sale or buying a railway ticket. As the money-making of the politicians at the top came to be emulated by the functionaries below them, corruption became a way of life. Corruption, it is often argued, has existed in India at least since the days of the Mughal Empire, but today it has reached a level that leaves no citizen untouched. Even the wretched homeless in some cities have to pay for the right to sleep on the sidewalks.

This was not always the case. When I left India to go to the United States as a graduate student in 1975, I could honestly say that I had never needed to bribe an official for anything, from getting a seat on a train to getting a seat in a college. Today both of those activities, and a host of lesser and greater ones (installing a phone, building a house) afford opportunities for illegal gratification. And most ordinary Indians accept with a shrug that that is simply the way things have become. Indians' undeclared income has now reached such proportions that the "black" economy is estimated as being almost a third as large as the official one.

Acceptance of corruption is widespread, nowhere more so than in relation to politics, where the public seems to *expect* conduct that in any other profession would be grounds for dismissal. It is assumed that every politician must be "taking money"; the few who reputedly do not are regarded as saints. This has been true for some years, but now we seem to have reached a point where corruption, far from eliciting outrage, is not even considered an issue. Throughout 1991 I was told by journalists, businessmen, and officials — many with firsthand anecdotal evidence — that a recent short-lived government was the most corrupt, in terms of money made per day in office, than any in the history of free India. But not one of the many media or scholarly analyses of its seven months in office even bothered to touch on this shameful reputation; it was simply considered to be of marginal relevance to any assessment of its record. (This was particularly saddening, because among the ministers in the cabinet were men who had previously enjoyed exceptional reputations for integrity and commitment to principle; the fact that even such men felt that they should make the most of their opportunities in office to gratify themselves illegally was a source of profound disillusionment.)

When those who presume to lead the nation are not even held to such a basic standard of behavior, it is not just our public life that is degraded — it is all of us. Yet corruption does not even get punished by the electorate. Kalpnath Rai, a politician against whom the charges of malfeasance were plausible enough to oblige him to campaign from jail, won reelection to Parliament in 1996 from behind bars, a reward for his standing in the constituency that outweighed the accusations against him. And raising dishonesty as an issue is seen by most Indians, and the media itself, as terminally naive. "After all," one politically savvy journalist told me, "everyone is on the take, and everyone knows it — corruption is now a dog-bites-man story, not a man-bites-dog headline." What such widespread and pervasive cynicism does to the country's social fabric is another story — this time of the man-bites-man variety.

In Nehru's day the slightest hint of financial impropriety resulted in the enforced resignation of the responsible minister, the most famous cases involving the departure of Finance Minister T. T. Krishnamachari in 1958 and of Mines and Fuels Minister K. D. Malaviya two years earlier. As with so much else, the rot set in under Indira Gandhi. In 1971 a bank clerk named Nagarwala obtained 6 million rupees from a nationalized bank by the simple expedient of imitating Mrs. Gandhi's voice on the phone; though the man himself was arrested and jailed for the crime (he subsequently died in jail, an event that set the conspiracy theorists' tongues wagging), the implication was that it had been done before, that the prime minister had obtained money from the State Bank of India in the past just by asking for it.

But Mrs. Gandhi's opponents and successors were no better. Prime Minister Morarji Desai's son Kanti was widely considered an epitome of sleaze, though few specific charges were ever proven. In the 1980s, India suffered major defense-procurement-related scandals, involving the Bofors field artillery gun and the HDW submarine; many supporters of Rajiv Gandhi actually argued that the Bofors commission was actually a blow *against* corruption, because the ruling party was now making its electioneering money off one major deal rather than hundreds of little ones. The implication that these smaller deals would be corruption-free was, of course, completely bogus; if the big guns could make big money, petty politicians and bureaucrats argued, the smaller fry were entitled to their more modest shares, too.

The heart of the problem is that corruption is now embedded in the nation's economic, political, and bureaucratic system, since access to governmental decision-making has become a convenient source of moneymaking. Under our restrictive system of permits, licenses, and quotas designed to prevent the growth of monopoly capitalism, it was the offices of politicians and bureaucrats that became the new temples at which Indian entrepreneurs had to prostrate themselves to pray for favors and indulgences. The inevitable result has been not just the stagnation, inefficiency, bureaucratization, slow growth, and high unemployment we have already discussed — but also rampant corruption.

Hardly a month goes by without a new scandal emerging: in recent years oil, sugar, and fertilizer have all been bought at prices above the world market price, with the difference going to politically connected Indian middlemen and no doubt to their political patrons. When the most recent sugar scandal burst into the news in 1994 (corrupt Indians, by asking for contracts at prices above the going price, drove up the world price of sugar and cost the Indian exchequer millions of dollars), I was reminded of an episode at the end of August 1989. I was visiting London and driving with an acquaintance, the wife of a prominent NRI businessman, when she called her broker from the car phone. She instructed him to take a rather large position on sugar futures on the London commodities market. "We've been tipped off from a source in the Commerce Ministry in Delhi that the government will be importing large quantities of sugar before Diwali," she said, referring to the coming Hindu festival, at which vast quantities of sweetmeats are consumed. "It's easy money, really. All it takes is a phone call. Do you want to invest too?" I declined the offer. Sure enough, within days India entered the sugar market, the price went up, and a number of people like my acquaintance made small fortunes on the backs of the Indian consumer. (She is now a prominent politician herself, in a party that likes to consider itself incorruptible.)

On that occasion, no whiff of scandal reached the press, but journalists I consulted say that every government decision to make a large import order invariably enables someone to skim money off the top. (The industry minister of the new United Front government in 1996, Murasoli Maran, spoke publicly of the existence of a "kickback Raj" across the country, and in his home state of Tamil Nadu in particular, where "facilitation fees" of 10 to 15 percent were routinely charged by bureaucrats and politicians in return for government contracts.) There are, of course, other forms of corruption made possible by the statist economic system. In 1992 the Harshad Mehta scandal broke, involving the siphoning off of some 50 billion rupees (nearly one and a half billion dollars) from the financial system in a stock-market scam involving the collusion of banks, stockbrokers, senior executives of nationalized industry, and lurid stories of a suitcase full of large-denomination banknotes allegedly being handed over to the prime minister himself by the principal accused, Harshad Mehta. The case drags on in the Indian courts, but the losses are real and the damage to investor confidence in the financial system is palpable.

The economic reforms have done little to remove the capacity for administrative-financial malfeasance; instead, some critics have argued that they have permitted the sale of governmental assets and privileges to a limited number of beneficiaries within the system who know how to manipulate it to their personal advantage. This perception must be ended quickly if the reforms are not to be occluded by the pervasive miasma of corruption. One aspect of the impact of corruption on the economy to which not enough attention tends to be paid is the demoralization it promotes among the population at large, which has no means of earning or generating "black money" but is expected to pay it. Yet the acquisition of business prominence through exploiting the system, bribing the right functionaries, and ensuring that the considerable regulatory authority of the state is misused in one's favor is widely considered the Indian way to business success; at least one of the country's largest (and certainly most visible) publicly traded companies is said to have risen from very humble origins through precisely such methods.

Two corruption scandals in 1996 illustrated the point. In one, a British "pickle tycoon" of Indian origin, Lakhubhai Pathak, sued a controversial "godman," the highly influential Chandra Swamy, for having accepted a bribe of $100,000 to get him a government permit that never came; the piquancy of the case came from Chandra Swamy's VIP contacts, which included the Sultan of Brunei and the Saudi arms dealer Adnan Khashoggi, as well as former prime minister Narasimha Rao, and from Pathak's allegation that Rao himself had met with Pathak on the same occasion and assured him that his "work would be done." The second case was the "Jain *hawala* scandal," in which the Central Bureau of Investigation was prodded by the Supreme Court into filing charges against an impressive list of politicians whose names figured in the diaries of an illegal foreign-currency trader ("*hawala* operator" in local parlance) as having received payoffs from him. Judicial activism in both cases offers the only encouraging sign that India might at last be tackling its endemic corruption; but while there is satisfaction that at last some big fish are being asked to account for their assets, most Indians see these as just a slice of the tip of the iceberg, and the extent of corruption in their daily lives continues unabated.

These two were not the only corruption scandals to make the headlines in 1996. There was also the more classically political case of the alleged "JMM payoffs," in which Prime Minister Rao was alleged to have paid three crores of rupees (a million U.S. dollars) to wavering MPs of the Jharkhand Mukti Morcha, an autonomist tribal party, in order to induce them to cast their votes in favor of the Congress government during a 1993 no-confidence debate in Parliament. And in another case, Rao's son Prabhakar was charged with having received an unexplained sum of money from a Turkish company that had failed to deliver fertilizer for which it had, unusually, been paid up front by the government. Both cases are before the courts as these words are written, and the media began to suggest that even the arrest of the former prime minister was no longer inconceivable.

The Indian judiciary, which at its upper reaches still enjoys a reputation for incorruptibility that has been underscored rather than besmirched by the 1992 scandal that defenestrated one of their number (V. Ramaswamy, former chief justice of the Punjab High Court), is taking on corruption by obliging the investigative agencies to do their duty without succumbing to political pressures. Individual bureaucrats have also used their official positions to take stands of principle that have required both courage and sacrifice. The mixed fortunes of Bombay municipal official G. R. Khairnar, who used the full force of the law to demolish illegal constructions that had been built (in some cases by underworld figures) with the connivance of prominent city and state politicians, lost his government job but succeeded in mobilizing a popular crusade against corruption; he is now a public figure of some repute and a symbol of integrity (as well as, some people would say, mule-headedness, given his singleminded focus on implicating a specific political leader, former chief minister Sharad Pawar, rather than reforming the system as a whole). Other Indian administrators, notably H. S. Pirzada, who confronted the contractors illegally deforesting his district in Tamil Nadu in collusion with politicians and was transferred out of his job as a result, and K. J. Alphons, who challenged unauthorized constructions in Delhi and found himself suspended from the civil service, have demonstrated both the potential for those who try to buck the corruption built into the system, and the pitfalls of doing so.

The outstanding example of a civil servant almost single-handedly taking on an entrenched system and proving that nothing is unreformable is, of course, that of Chief Election Commissioner T. N. Seshan. With courage, arrogance, an unshakable faith in himself, and a breathtaking disregard for the conventions of Indian political life, Seshan took on the corruption that had grown in the national electoral system and in 1996 gave the country the fairest, least expensive general elections it had ever known. Organizing the world's largest exercise in electoral democracy — with 590 million eligible voters, more than five hundred registered political parties, nearly fifteen thousand candidates in 535 constituencies, and more than 800,000 polling stations requiring 44 million pounds of ballots — Seshan used the largely dormant powers of his office to the full, imposing a Model Code of Conduct that had been agreed upon nearly three decades earlier and disregarded ever since, assigning 1.6 million policemen and 1,650 observers to ensure that its provisions were strictly adhered to, demanding daily accounts of expenditure (which were compared to the estimates of his own observers), and threatening convincingly to disqualify any candidate or party caught violating his stringent rules. (This struck terror into the hearts of the mendacious: a journalist from the Delhi *Observer* hilariously recounted how her paper's name sent candidates and campaign workers scurrying for cover — since they had understood her to be an *election* observer!)

Announcing that he would destroy the "three M's — money power, muscle power, and minister power," that had distorted past Indian elections, Seshan strictly imposed the legal spending limit of four and a half lakh rupees ($13,150) permitted each candidate, a figure so laughably out of touch with contemporary political reality that no one stayed within its limits if they could afford not to. (Though actual expenditure varies from constituency to constituency, *India Today* estimated in early 1996 that each major contestant for the South Bombay seat in the Lok Sabha planned to spend five crore rupees, more than a hundred times the permitted amount.) Any irregularities resulted immediately in polls being countermanded in the affected area and repolling ordered in more than a thousand places, effectively negating the habitual intimidation and "booth capturing" (the takeover of polling stations by thugs who proceed to stuff the ballot boxes with votes for their candidate) that had prevailed in certain lawless areas of northern India, particularly Bihar and Uttar Pradesh. The ubiquitous posters and graffiti displayed in public spaces and even on the walls of unwilling private citizens were ordered removed; election meetings had to end by 10:30 P.M.; the use of loudspeakers was restricted, and the propensity to appeal to voters on "communal" grounds, or to exhort them by incitations to hatred, was forbidden on pain of punishment; and votes were counted under the unblinking gaze of a video camera recording every ballot passing through the hands of the returning officers. The result was an election that was widely considered dull, colorless, uneventful, and boring — but was unquestionably the freest and fairest India had ever known.

"Anyone who had one-tenth of this job would quail at the challenges," Seshan was reported as saying of his efforts to rein in India's irrepressible politicians. "When people ask me if I'm Jesus, I say, 'Sorry,

I'm only Moses."' The commandments he brought down to Indian electoral politics were, however, out of the ordinary. One of his decisions was to outlaw the use of small animals among the electoral symbols adopted by each party to aid illiterate voters. Past elections had witnessed candidates strangling birds symbolizing their opponents, so Seshan decided to allow only larger creatures as symbols on the sound principle that "you can't easily wring the neck of an elephant or tiger."

Seshan stands out because of the scale of his achievement and the nationwide impact of his efforts. But even his successes have only made a dent in the problem of the system fostered under Congress Party dominance, a system of patronage and jobbery, kickbacks and payoffs, bribery and malfeasance. Elections are a tool, but the entire system needs an overhaul: there is little point in having a smooth-running tractor if the field it is meant to plow is overflowing with refuse. That is not too great an overstatement of public attitudes to Indian politics today.

Indeed, for proof that independent India still has a long way to go to evolve the kind of democratic civil society dreamed of by Nehru, one has to look no further than the criminalization of political life in India, the dimensions of which have been graphically described by a former top civil servant, ex–cabinet secretary B. G. Deshmukh, in searing terms:

> Anti-social elements, including blackmarketeers, have always tried to cultivate politicians to safeguard their interests and also to protect them from the due process of law. Before Independence, their efforts did not make any headway. . . . The pre-Independence political leadership consisted of gentlemen who had unblemished character. Almost all of them gave up [a] comfortable living and even lucrative professional positions to enter politics only to serve the people of the country. It was unthinkable for any anti-social element to approach them for favors, direct or indirect. . . . Since independence, . . . politicians started finding that anti-social elements were . . . quite useful for getting funds for fighting elections. These elements also [discovered] the attraction and convenience of holding political positions which not only gave them social status but also a certain immunity. . . . When the politicians started realizing that their party apparatus was not fully capable of mobilizing voters or that their opponents [did better] by

adopting irregular methods, a general feeling [arose]. . . . that there was nothing wrong in taking the help of anti-social elements. This phenomenon led to various irregular electoral practices. With the help of the brutal force or muscle power at the disposal of these anti-social elements, unscrupulous politicians [altered electoral rolls or interfered with the vote]. . . . Booth capturing and bogus voting naturally followed. This gave rise to organized groups and in some cases even organized gangs which were available for a price to a politician. In some areas, groups of certain castes and communities formed such gangs . . . to enforce their will on the electorate. . . . When this situation became all-pervasive, anti-social elements thought that instead of merely fighting somebody's battle, they could themselves enter the fray. They had the inherent advantage of money power and muscle power. Since most of the political parties were interested only in winning elections, they did not mind giving tickets [party nominations] to such candidates howsoever undesirable they may be. This was the beginning of the end.

Deshmukh's indictment points to the most dangerous phenomenon of independent India's political life, the criminalization of politics. One might even speak of it as the politicization of criminals, for (as he suggests) many a law-breaker has found it useful to become a law-maker. The CPM member of Parliament Harkishan Singh Surjeet told me that of the 535 members of the lower house (Lok Sabha) of India's Parliament in 1996, as many as a hundred may have had criminal records. India's police, never quite paragons of law enforcement and frequently subject to political interference, found more reasons for demoralization in the discovery that the very criminals they were pursuing or seeking to prosecute could become their political masters the next day.

A few weeks into the term of the United Front government, the press revealed that its minister of state for home affairs, Mohammed Taslimuddin, had no fewer than eighteen criminal cases pending against him in the courts, not for overenthusiastic electioneering or politically linked offenses but for the entirely unparliamentary activities of kidnapping, rape, molestation, and attempted murder. Taslimuddin, who had not actually been convicted in any of these cases yet (but against whom the evidence had been found to be plausible by a committee appointed by the legislative assembly of his home state, Bihar), finally resigned, but not before alleging religious bigotry on the part of his accusers (he is a Muslim, and the government felt obliged to defuse the charge by appointing another Muslim MP to the job). To the newspaper-reading middle class, the fact that someone with this sort of background could even be considered for such august office was dismaying enough, without the post in question being in the ministry entrusted with supervising India's internal law-and-order machinery (including the police, internal security, and intelligence; though the government pointed out that those departments of the ministry were supervised directly by the cabinet minister, not the minister of state, the fact was that when Taslimuddin held office, no cabinet minister for home affairs had yet been appointed). Worse still was the realization that it is precisely the criminal connections and conduct of some politicians that gives them the clout to become viable candidates for high office in the first place; Taslimuddin had, after all, been nominated for a ministerial berth by the powerful chief minister of Bihar, Laloo Prasad Yadav.

If there are, as Mr. Surjeet believes, ninety-nine other Taslimuddins in the present Parliament, it is more than a disturbing statistic. Sociologists have long analyzed the class composition of India's legislatures and traced the important change from a post-independence Parliament dominated by highly educated professionals to one more truly representative of the rural heartland of India. The typical member of Parliament today, the joke runs, is a lower-caste farmer with a law degree he's never used. But the electability, particularly from the northern states, of figures referred to openly in the press as "Mafia dons," "dacoit [bandit] leaders" and "antisocial elements" is a poor reflection on the way the electoral process has served Indian democracy. The resultant alienation of the educated middle class means that fewer and fewer of them trouble to go to the polls on election day. Whereas psephological studies in the United States have demonstrated that the poor do not vote in significant numbers in national elections, the opposite is true in India; it is the poor who are willing to take the time to queue up in large numbers in the hot sun, believing their votes will make a difference, whereas the relatively more privileged members of society, knowing their views and numbers will do little to influence the outcome, have been increasingly staying away from the polls. Voter studies of the 1996 elections demonstrated that the lowest stratum of Indian society, the "very poor," vote in numbers well above the national average, while graduates turn out in numbers well below.

The abstention of the highly educated from the polls is only a symptom of a more debilitating loss of faith in the political process itself. Only 25 percent of Indians questioned in a Gallup poll in April 1996 expressed confidence in Parliament, whereas 77 percent said they trusted the judiciary. Defections and horse-trading are common, political principle rare. The spectacle of legislators in one state assembly after another being "paraded" before a speaker or a governor to prove a contested majority, or — worse still — being "held hostage" in hotels by their leaders so they cannot be suborned by rivals until their claims to majority are accepted, has done little to inspire confidence in the integrity of India's parliamentarians. Their occasional descent into brawls on the floor of the assemblies, which have recorded numerous instances of fisticuffs, jostling, and the flinging of footwear, is hardly likely to inspire reverence either. (It is hardly surprising that respect for the country's political parties has not grown. In 1968, 41 percent of the Indian people believed it made no difference which party was in power in the country, and when asked to identify themselves with a political party, 67 percent indicated no affinity to any in particular. In a 1996 poll, the figures had not changed significantly: 69 percent declared that they did not feel close to any political party, and 63 percent answered "no" when asked if they felt India's elected representatives cared for the people.)

But far more dangerous to Indian democracy than the deficiencies of its guardians is the scale of violence in the country. Violence is an inescapable reality for the newspaper reader; one cannot turn the pages of the press without being sickened by the daily occurrence of riots, clashes, rapes in custody, incidents of the powerful taking the law into their own hands (typified by the frequency with which the press reports episodes of poor women being stripped naked and paraded through the streets of villages to humiliate them or members of their family into doing as they are told). The democratic Indian state seems to be able to do little to end such occurrences, though individual police officers, administrators, and judges have shown great courage and commitment in the pursuit of justice. The Marathi newspaper *Navakal* once compared the Indian state to the drunken husband who contributes nothing to the household himself but beats his wife to obtain the money she has worked hard to earn — a telling image in a country where such domestic events are commonplace. There is no doubt that the combination of violence and corruption, flourishing with impunity under the protection of the democratic state, discredits democracy itself: too many cynics see democracy in India as a process that has given free rein to criminals and corrupt cops, opportunists and fixers, murderous musclemen and grasping middlemen, kickback-making politicos and bribe-taking bureaucrats, Mafia dons and private armies, caste groups and religious extremists. Of course this is a caricature of a far more complex reality, but it is a plausible enough portrait of what the middle class sees to lead thoughtful Indians to worry about the viability of democracy itself.

And yet our own inherent incompetence offers grounds for hope. Democracy is not always the most efficient form of government, but it is vastly preferable to those systems in which the police are the most efficient organ of the state. The occasional corruption, ineptitude, and complacency of the Indian police is properly the subject of anguished criticism by Indians, but in these qualities may also lie the best hope for the survival of Indian democracy.

.   .   .

What makes political conflict endemic in any state? Economic need is an obvious part of the answer; politics is the pursuit of economics by other means. Individuals and groups in quest of means to satisfy their economic desires seek political power in order to advance their interests; this is a basic fact of any polity. In order to pursue power, they organize themselves, in most democratic systems, into political parties, each party united by a common set of political principles that articulate their convictions about how society should be organized (usually to the greatest benefit of their supporters). In a strong multiparty system, the party is identified clearly with core beliefs and traditions that its supporters share, and it deals with differences of emphasis or personality within that framework of beliefs through self-regulating mechanisms that resolve disputes without threatening the basic party structures. In India, neither has been the case; except for a handful of "ideological" parties (the Communists, the Swatantra for a brief period, and the Jana Sangh and its successor the BJP), there is a profusion of parties that all believe in more or less the same thing (socialism, secularism, nonalignment, affirmative action, state control of the "commanding heights" of the economy). Nor are there effective internal elections or comparable processes for resolving intraparty differences; whenever a dispute gets serious enough, the party splits or the disgruntled individual leaves the party, with the result that most of India's major politicians have at one time or another served under more than one party affiliation (and in many cases four or five). Whereas in most other democracies, a politician changing party is a major development calling for dramatic headlines, in India parties have become mere labels, to be peeled off and replaced as convenient.

The weakness of the party system has meant that all too often politicians organize themselves around other identities than party (or create parties to reflect a particularist identity). It is ironic that one of the early strengths of independent India — the survival of the nationalist movement as a political party, the Congress Party serving as an all-embracing, all-inclusive agglomeration of all the major political tendencies in the country — turned out, in hindsight, to have undermined the evolution of a genuine multiparty system. There is no doubt that the political dominance of the Congress, its maintenance of support through a complex process of networking and exchange, its agglomerative ecumenism, all made the party a major integrative institution in independent India. But had the nationalist movement given birth to, say, three parties — one right-of-center, one social democrat, one Communist — a culture of principle might have evolved in India's political contention. Instead the survival of the eclectic Congress for decades as India's dominant party stifled this process, and opposition to it (with a few honorable exceptions, such as Rajaji's pro-free-enterprise Swatantra Party between 1959 and 1974) emerged largely in the form of the assertion of identities to which the Congress was deemed not to have given full expression.

These identities tend, in the Indian context, to involve caste or religion; the Bahujan Samaj ("Majority People's") Party is a party of and for the Dalits or "Untouchables," the Akali Dal a party of and for Sikhs, and so on (though there are, of course, Untouchables and Sikhs in other parties as well). The result is that instead of parties distinguished by political principle, Indian politics too often offers the spectacle of a choice between different group identities. Where divisions occur within such identities — as in the two Dravidian parties in Tamil Nadu spawned from the same anti-Congress movement in the state — the choice becomes one between personalities, not principles. Differences that in other democracies might produce intraparty rivalries lead, in India, to new parties altogether.

This is not merely a lament for the loss of principle in our country's political debate; it is also a dirge, because clashes between groups organized around sectarian identities tend to have more destructive consequences than clashes between socialists and free-marketers. No Indian election has been wholly free of violence, though the 1996 elections organized by T. N. Seshan came close; still, it is a sad commentary on our society that we are able to congratulate ourselves on an election in which "only" seven people were killed.

An added complication in India is the extraordinary role, for a democracy, that the state has come to play in the economic life of the country, so that competition for political power in the state has become competition for the power to control, to regulate, and to benefit through the process of appropriating, dividing, and distributing the economic resources of the state. For a while the Indian government was able to use this power to stem internal conflict by subsidizing crucial interest groups, co-opting leaders of traditionally "backward" or underprivileged communities, ensuring that no region or religion felt underrepresented in the highest offices of the state, and balancing competing interests by ensuring that no one group was seen to be gaining or losing more than the others in the way in which the state arranged its affairs. But these methods could only go so far; Untouchables mollified with reserved seats in Parliament and the state assemblies began to ask themselves why they could not transform their votes into political power for themselves; "backwards" saw their cabinet posts as tokenism and hungered for the top office in each state; some religious or other minorities rejected the state itself, feeling that nothing less than separation could guarantee them the power that their numbers could never give them in India as a whole. (It is an attitude chillingly reminiscent of the notorious remark made by a Yugoslav politician as that country was breaking up in 1991: "Why should I be a minority in your state when you can be a minority in mine?")

The most vital challenge for Indian democracy remains the need to contain and accommodate these inevitable clashes of interests, eliminating the need (and even the temptation) for marginal groups to resort to violence to pursue them. The strength of Indian democracy has always lain in its willingness to permit the expression of all varieties of political opinion; those who cannot be heard by their words will want to be heard through their bombs. But this alone is not enough; the institutions of the Indian democratic state must also be able to deliver what all democratic states are expected by their citizens to deliver, namely national security and economic prosperity. If corruption, maladministration, and political failure result in a citizenry that feels insecure and deprived, the resultant disillusionment with the system can lead to violence and destruction that could destroy democracy itself.

There is some unlikely anecdotal evidence for this fear. In India the biggest hit film of 1996 was *Indian,* a Tamil film that went on to national success in a dubbed Hindi version, *Hindustani,* and was then entered for a foreign-language Oscar. The eponymous hero of the film is a serial killer who stalks through the movie murdering one archetype after another of the Indian establishment — a policeman, a politician, a revenue official, a senior administrator, and so on. Each killing was greeted in the movie halls of the nation with prolonged applause; friends reported witnessing standing ovations. This was not film criticism of the "I saw a movie being shot, and the actors deserved to be" variety: the audience's own fantasies about the punishment of the powerful were being sublimated on screen. The level of popular cynicism this reflects about the workings of Indian democracy in the eyes of the "common man" suggests that many wrongs still need to be set right.

The significant changes in the social composition of India's ruling class, both in politics and in the bureaucracy, since independence is proof of democracy at work; but the poor quality of the country's political leadership in general offers less cause for celebration. Our rulers increasingly reflect the qualities required to acquire power rather than the skills to wield it for the common good. The democratic process has attracted figures who can win elections but who have barely a nodding acquaintance with ethics or principles, and are untroubled by the need for either. Too many politicians are willing to use any means to obtain power. Even the time-honored device of the dodgy campaign promise has sunk to record lows. One leading politician, now a cabinet minister, became chief minister of India's most populous state after promising that, if elected, his first act in office would be to abolish an ordinance that prevented college students from cheating on their exams (the ordinance forbade outsiders to smuggle crib sheets into the exam halls, regulated the examinees' freedom to leave the exam hall and return to it, and so on). He won the youth vote and (as a champion of the "backwards" and the Muslims) the elections in a landslide, and he was as good as his word; within seconds of taking the oath of office, he withdrew the anti-cheating ordinance.

Sadly, this politician's willingness to elevate political expediency above societal responsibility is all too typical of his fellow politicians today. The profession of politics has attracted many who are unprincipled, inept, corrupt, or even criminal. As Rajiv Gandhi recognized, their quest for power is unaccompanied by any larger vision of the common good, any sense of responsibility to the society as a whole. But they do get elected, repeatedly; for one of the failures of Indian democracy has certainly lain in its inability to educate the mass of voters to expect, and demand, better of their elected representatives.

One relevant development appears to be the passing of the towering "great figure" from the Indian political stage. The last two were both Gandhis, Indira and Rajiv, and for most of their time in power the organized opposition possessed no leader of national standing (defined as an individual seen by more than 10 percent of the electorate in public opinion polls as a worthy alternative candidate for prime minister). Today three of four parties can put forward a credible prime minister, partly because the success of Narasimha Rao and the mere ascent of Deve Gowda have broadened popular acceptance of what constitutes credibility in that role. Equally, though, there is no national political figure who enjoys the admiration and support of the majority of the electorate; we have no Snow White, only the Seven Dwarfs.

The basis of democracy is, of course, the rule of the *demos*, the people — the rule, in other words, of all rather than few. Democracies uphold the right of the general body of citizens to decide matters of concern to society as a whole, including the question of who rules them in their name. A democracy changes governments by free and fair elections, guarantees rights and privileges to individuals and minorities, and seeks to promote the participation of ordinary individuals in decision-making. All this, and more, may be found in Indian democracy; but much more needs to occur to entrench both the institutions and the habits of democracy among both the leaders and the led. Winston Churchill was right in describing democracy as "the worst form of government except [for] all those other forms that have been tried." India's challenge is not to perfect it, but simply to make it better than it now is.

9

India at Forty-nine

Notes Toward an Impression
of Indian Society and Culture Today

*T*he night I arrived in Delhi on a visit in January 1996, the elevator at the Maurya Sheraton took us up to the twelfth floor in
a breathtaking six or seven seconds. "Remarkable," I commented
admiringly to the friendly hotel employee in a maroon sari and busi-
nesslike pageboy haircut, who had draped a three-kilogram marigold
garland around my neck as I stepped across the threshold. "We couldn't
have ascended faster in the U.S. of A."

She took my praise in stride, as well she should have. Jet-lagged after an eighteen-hour journey from New York, I had failed to notice that
this was not some superfast new elevator technology that the Maurya
had brought into Delhi, but rather some highly creative labeling. When
I finally woke and looked out my window, I realized that what the
elevator buttons had called the twelfth floor was in fact the second.
The gleaming Maurya elevator had merely taken me for a ride — and
a shorter ride than I'd imagined.

I couldn't keep the accusatory tone out of my voice the next time I
ran into the maroon sari. "Twelfth floor, huh?" I said pointedly. "I didn't

think liberalization meant being liberal with the facts."

She was surprised that I had taken offense. "Our foreign visitors much prefer to think of themselves as being on the eleventh and twelfth floors than the first or second," she replied with wide-eyed innocence. "And they don't look out the windows that much."

Welcome, I thought, to the new India. An India I was discovering for the first time: an India of five-star hotels, welcoming garlands, and smooth-talking hotel staff, where nothing is quite what it seems (not even the elevator buttons), where windows are not meant to be opened and appearances are the only reality.

. . .

Time for a pause, right there. I'm beginning to do exactly what I've always criticized the Naipauls for doing: drawing grand, sweeping conclusions from the flimsiest of anecdotal evidence. After all, one cannot be unaware that in trying to paint even an impressionistic portrait of contemporary Indian society and culture, one is recalling a concept so undefinable that T. S. Eliot was cautious enough to call his book on the subject *Notes Toward the Definition of Culture* and George Steiner, two and a half decades later, could do no better than subtitle *In Bluebeard's Castle* as *Notes Towards the Redefinition of Culture*. I have neither the desire nor the ability to attempt to define or redefine this slippery term; one cannot entirely forget the pro-Nazi poet Hanns Johst's declaration, "When I hear the word 'culture,' I reach for my gun." Nonetheless it is a word I cannot escape in outlining my concerns and impressions in this chapter. By "Indian society and culture" I mean the social heritage and contemporary life of Indians, the mental and creative artifacts produced by the Indian people in the course of their ongoing lives and within their particular life conditions. In the Indian context, even so narrow a usage embraces something rather vast and varied, from the five-star hotels with which I began this chapter to the homeless sleeping huddled on railway platforms, from the classical schools of Indian dance to the village equivalents of the whirling dervishes, from the ancient Sanskrit epics to the B-movies of Bollywood, from stories retold around rural fires to those recycled on the television screen, from the patterns daubed on the walls of mud huts to the postmodern canvases now sold regularly at high-priced auctions by Sotheby's — none of which I intend to discuss in this book. Since Indian society and culture are so broad and undefinable, I shall only try to touch on a small portion of what is visible to a middle-class Indian. In doing so I seek to be illustrative rather than comprehensive; and in any case what follows is not just impressionistic and subjective, but even leaves out many of my own obsessions — Indian cricket, for instance, and Indian cinema — as belonging elsewhere.

At the beginning of *The Labyrinth of Solitude*, for more than four decades a seminal work on Mexican society and culture, Octavio Paz muses: "At one time I thought that my preoccupation with the significance of my country's individuality . . . was pointless and even dangerous. Instead of asking ourselves questions, it would be better, I felt, to create, to work with the realities of our situation. We could not alter those realities by contemplation, only by plunging ourselves into them. We could distinguish ourselves from other peoples by our creations rather than by the dubious originality of our character, which was the result, perhaps, of constantly changing circumstances. I believed that a work of art or a concrete action would do more to define the Mexican — not only to express him but also, in the process, to re-create him — than the most penetrating description." Paz went on to overcome his hesitation and write a compelling portrait of his countrymen, but his point here is both a call to action and a suggestion that a country essentially defines itself. The impressions that follow accept both premises entirely.

.   .   .

I had averaged a visit home each year since leaving India for postgraduate studies in the United States more than twenty years ago, but I had always stayed with family and friends, of whom thankfully I still have several across the country. This time, however, I was in India not on holiday but for work, to address a United Nations peacekeeping seminar and to accompany the UN's future secretary general Kofi Annan on a series of official meetings. As a result I was seeing another India, the India we present to foreigners. It was a curiously disorienting experience.

Don't get me wrong; I'm not complaining. It's difficult to complain about a standard of hoteliering I have rarely come across in four continents in the course of a peripatetic professional life: overwhelmingly attentive staff who were far more numerous than their counterparts in the developed world and far more capable than their counterparts in the developing world; startlingly efficient housekeeping; and food of a deliciousness and variety that Western cuisines would be hard put to imagine. One could gladly exchange a week in paradise for a week in the Maurya Sheraton, and not notice the difference.

Provided one doesn't look too closely at the bill.

What should an Indian make of a room rent that costs more, in one night, than any of the hotel's diligent staff make in a month? Of a telephone system that charges seven rupees a pulse for *local* calls, when a one-rupee stamp will carry a thick letter to the other end of the country? Of an efficient laundry that will wash and return your socks the same day, for ten times the price you paid to buy them? Of a hospitable lounge where bowing waiters will ply your guests' children with three-inch half-glasses of Fanta at ninety rupees each, *plus* tax, a sum on which the waiters themselves could eat and drink for a week?

I had come to India and found America, or at least as good an imitation of America as India can manage, with a price tag that even Americans, except those on expense accounts, would gag at. And what is more, though the charges seemed to have been calculated in dollars and then converted to rupees, I found this India patronized by as many Indians as Americans. So, if anyone was out of touch, it was me.

It certainly wasn't the beggar woman, a mewling infant at her breast, who approached my rented Contessa at an intersection. I offered her my largest coin, and she practically thrust it back at me: *Babuji, do rupye se kya hoga?* ("What can I do with two rupees?") If two rupees aren't enough for a beggar in today's New Delhi, one wonders why the government bothers to mint any of the smaller coins. As hotel doormen expect ten-rupee tips for letting you into your car and railway porters start their tariffs at three figures, I imagine the rupee going the way of the lira or yen, becoming the indivisible base monetary unit as the paisa ceases to have any value at all.

. . .

The sums one routinely hears about in the capital certainly tend to confirm my prediction. Lakhs (one hundred thousand, the sum I grew up thinking of as the psychological if not the numerical equivalent to the American million) are discussed as if they were small change; the new Indian entrepreneurs are *crorepatis*. (A crore is a hundred lakhs, or ten million rupees: it was not so long ago that the very idea of a *crorepati* in our stifled and taxed economy was as fanciful as a unicorn in the Purana Qila zoo.) Outside the international five-star circuit, of course, the talk was all of the *hawala* scandal, of sprawling multi-crore farmhouses and the diaries kept in them, and of the dramatic change the latest scandal was going to bring about in the nation's political fortunes. Much of the excitement seemed, however, to be confined to journalists, who as a tribe tend to hear earthquakes when others merely slam doors. "This is terrific!" one media man said to me about the *hawala* affair shortly after interviewing me on the more prosaic questions of United Nations peacekeeping. "It's the biggest story since independence!"

Ordinary Indians were more blasé; I did not meet a single person who *didn't* think all politicians were corrupt anyway. Their attitude to the *hawala* scandal was a combination of "What's new?" and "So what?" For the newspapers to wax indignant about the names in Mr. Jain's list of pols on the take is rather like finding a "P" page of the telephone directory and concluding that only Patels have phones. The few politicians on whom the press and the Central Bureau of Investigation were focusing represented those who received money from one rather small-scale operator during one particular year. It is a safe assumption that there are other politicians who have taken money from other operators in different years, quite probably in amounts that would dwarf those dispensed by the meticulous Mr. Jain; but they have been lucky enough to have been suborned by people less diligently devoted to the art of double-entry bookkeeping.

The truth is that whereas Americans demand of their politicians standards that don't exist in their society at large (ask Gary Hart), most Indians accept conduct from politicians that we wouldn't tolerate in our neighbors. As a people we tend — and I know all generalizations are risky — to be open, hospitable, generous, truthful, faithful, and scrupulously honest, and we expect our friends and relations to be the same. Two classes of people are, however, exempt from those norms: politicians and movie stars. Such larger-than-life figures enjoy a societal carte blanche to lie, cheat, dissemble, and commit large-scale larceny, adultery, and tax fraud; only murder is a little more difficult, though even there a major politician and a leading film star have been released from jail after allegations of offenses that might have earned lesser men fates worse than death. So what the media mavens discovered is that their journalistic enthusiasm isn't entirely mirrored on the street; Indians *expect* their politicians to be dishonest and duplicitous, and are not surprised to have their assumptions confirmed.

.   .   .

Much of the clamor about India's economic reforms has focused on the somewhat chimerical "Indian middle class," a construct that may be sociological but is not entirely logical. The popular myth is that this middle class is some 300 million strong — larger than the entire domestic market of the United States — and, together with a very rich upper class, has both the purchasing power and the inclinations of the American middle class. Today's economic mythology sees this new Indian middle class as ripe for international consumer goods; India's television channels and glossy magazines overflow with ads for foreign brand-name products ranging from Daewoo Cielo cars to Ray-Ban sunglasses. That is why Kellogg's rushed in with their corn flakes; Nike got India's then cricket captain to endorse their sports shoes (sparking off an unintended controversy since his name, Mohammed, is also that of the Prophet and could not adorn an item so lowly as footwear);

Mercedes-Benzes are already rolling off the automotive production lines; and Johnnie Walker Black Label Scotch became an Indian brand, not just one purveyed by smugglers. (It was once said that more bottles of Johnnie Walker Black Label were sold in India than were distilled in Scotland; now the joke will literally come true.)

But Kellogg's has been dismayed by the weak response of the market; Nike is far from turning a profit; Mercedes knows it will sell very few Benzes; and Johnnie isn't walking with quite the same strut as before. The reason is simple: the Indian middle class is not quite what it's cracked up to be in the West.

Most members of the Indian middle class are quite content with their *idlis* or *puri-bhaji* for breakfast, and have no desire to eat expensive bits of shredded cardboard instead, merely because their American counterparts do. Most find Indian-made Bata shoes expensive enough; Nike's prices are simply out of reach. The potential Mercedes ownership in any country is pretty limited, but in India less than a tenth of one percent of the population can even dream of earning enough money to own one. And Johnnie Walker came in just as Indian Scotch drinkers were discovering the virtues of the better Indian whiskies at one-fourth the cost.

A survey conducted between 1986 and 1994 by the National Council of Applied Economic Research (NCAER) in New Delhi has largely debunked the myth of the Indian middle class. After questioning 182,600 urban homes and 99,150 rural households, the survey found that India's consumers could be divided into five classes, not three: the very rich (6 million people, or 1 million households), the "consuming class" (some 150 million, or half the conventional estimate), the "climbers" (a lower middle class of 275 million), the "aspirants" (another 275 million who, in America or Europe, would be classified as "poor"), and finally the destitute (210 million). But the worst news for foreign consumer-goods marketers was that it is only among the million households of the very rich that there exists a sustainable interest in the products of Kellogg, Nike, Mercedes-Benz, or Johnnie Walker. Of course the others buy goods — but these are more basic, and cheaper, than multinational corporations produce. If you're selling tea or cooking oil, you have a vast Indian market, spanning all five classes; leather sandals or rubber thongs reach half the population; but sport shoes that cost a chauffeur's monthly take-home pay? Forget all but the smallest group at the top.

Not that Indians aren't spending more and acquiring more. Since the 1980s, there has been a Reaganesque boom of buying. On a visit to rural south India (Tamil Nadu and Kerala) in mid-1996, I was struck by how many houses were of "pukka" construction rather than mud or thatch, and even more by how many of the most ordinary village homes had some sort of vehicle parked outside — in most cases a bicycle, but there were also scooters, other two-wheelers, and in some cases cars. An astonishing number of roofs sprouted television antennas, and a few houses even sported a satellite dish. This empirical, if unscientific, evidence is confirmed by the NCAER study. Forty million Indians own television sets, even if many of those are black-and-white sets bought secondhand and reconditioned for 1,500 rupees (forty-four dollars). All but the most destitute own wristwatches, bicycles, and portable radios. Some 40 million households (approximately 240 million people) bought electric irons and kitchen equipment. Cumulatively, the NCAER survey concluded, India has a "consuming population" of 168 million to 504 million people. But what they consume, and how much they can afford to pay for it — linked to an indifference to global brand names that is the legacy both of four thousand years of traditional civilization and forty years of self-reliant protectionism — does not suggest that dollar signs will light up soon in the eyes of too many foreign manufacturers of brand-name consumer goods.

· · ·

Some have seen in Indian society a constant struggle between two distinct attitudes to life: those exemplified by the elevated, sophisticated spiritualism of the renunciatory Vedanta philosophy and their opposites, the materialist, hedonistic, amoral (and atheistic) *charvakas*. To those analysts, Indian society reflects this dualism in the constant struggle between opposed tendencies — the stark white simplicity of the *dhoti* or *mundu* (the ankle-length waist cloth worn by most Indian men) versus the richly colored silk sari of the women, easily the most alluring garment devised by humankind; the culinary asceticism of the vegetarian Gandhi or the nut-eating (and urine-drinking) Morarji Desai versus the complexity and richness of the most varied, subtle, and challenging cuisine on earth; the fatalism of the poor and oppressed versus the cupidity and greed of the corrupt and powerful; the nonviolence of Gandhi versus the militarism of a potential nuclear power with the fourth-largest army in the world. And then there is the most basic duality of all, that between "India" and "Bharat." India, the country I have been writing about, has shot satellites into space, boasts in Bombay a business capital with the highest commercial rents in the world (higher than Manhattan or Tokyo), has had the most rapid televisual growth of any country on earth, and is the country whose first-ever cellular telephone call was made (in English) between the Communist chief minister of West Bengal and a millionaire Telecommunications minister in Delhi. "Bharat," the indigenous India that speaks Hindi, lives in village huts, plows the fields, has no phones to use, observes caste rules, and rejects (or resents) all the trappings of secular modernism.

Be that as it may — and surely such a dualism can be found in any country? — one area in which Bharat is winning over India appears to be in the naming game. The self-appointed guardians of the *Bharatvasis* are convinced that the names India has given its cities and landmarks reflect the colonization of a national sensibility, a process they are determined to reverse whenever they have the chance. So the Shiv Sena–led government in Maharashtra has renamed the state capital Mumbai, proscribing the use of the word Bombay for any official purposes. This strikes me as the equivalent of a company jettisoning a well-known brand name in favor of an inelegant patronymic — as if McDonald's had renamed itself Kroc's in honor of its inventor. "Bombay" has entered global discourse; it conjures up associations of cosmopolitan bustle; it is attached to products like Bombay gin, Bombay duck, and the overpriced colonial furniture sold by "the Bombay company." In short, it enjoys name recognition that many cities around the world would spend millions in publicity to acquire. "Mumbai" was already the city's name in Marathi; but what has been gained by insisting on its adoption in English, aside from a nativist reassertion that benefits only sign painters and letterhead printers? The Shiv Sena went one step further and renamed the city's main railway station, Victoria Terminus, an Indo-Gothic-Saracenic excrescence universally known as "VT" and completely devoid, in everyone's imagination, of any association with the late Queen-Empress. "VT" is henceforth to be known as "Chhatrapati Shivaji Maharaj Terminus." Try telling that to a Bombay taxi driver.

Not to be outdone, the DMK government in Madras, which had, in an earlier spell in office, renamed the state of Madras "Tamil Nadu" ("homeland of the Tamils"), decided that the city of Madras would be similarly renamed. The chief minister had been informed that "Madras" was actually a Portuguese coinage, derived either from a trader named Madeiros or a prince called Madrie (just as Bombay came from the Portuguese "Bom Bahia" or "good bay.") "Madras is not a Tamil name," announced the chief chauvinist to justify his decision to rename the city "Chennai." Once again, name recognition — Madras kerchiefs, Madras jackets, Bleeding Madras, the Madras monitoring system — went by the board as "Chennai" was adopted without serious debate. More unfortunately, however, the chief minister had overlooked the weight of evidence that "Madras" was indeed a Tamil name (derived, alternative theories go, from the name of a local fisherman, Madarasan; or from the local Muslim religious schools, *madarasas*; or from *madhu-ras*, the word for honey). Worse, he had also overlooked the embarrassing fact that "Chennai" was not, as he had asserted, of Tamil origin. It came from the name of Chennappa Naicker, the raja of Chandragiri, who granted the British the right to trade on the Coromandel coast — and who was a Telugu speaker from what is today Andhra Pradesh.

So bad history is worse lexicology, but in India-that-is-Bharat, it is good politics. This is not a new development, for names had been changed since soon after the British left. Such Anglicized affectations as "Cawnpore" and "Poona" had become "Kanpur" and "Puné" respectively to reflect the way the names were actually pronounced, and Mysore state had become Karnataka to resurrect the proud tradition of what the British had called the "Carnatic" region. But after fifty years of independence, isn't it time to start drawing the line somewhere? Was it really necessary for Keralites, who had gotten used to calling their capital Trivandrum in English and Thiruvandooram in Malayalam, to jettison both abbreviated forms for the glory of "Thiruvananthapuram"? Or to insist that Trichur, which is in fact a close approximation of the popular local pronunciation, be re-spelled "Trissur," which must have been dreamed up by Kerala's sole surviving illiterate?

What's in a name? Shakespeare asked, and of course the trains will be just as crowded at Chhatrapati Shivaji Maharaj Terminus as they were at VT. But are we so insecure in our independence that we still need to prove to ourselves we are free? Is there no comfort, after all, in being able to take places for granted, without the continuing sense that they are still susceptible to being renamed? In parts of India it is customary for a bride, upon marriage, to take on a new name — not just a surname, but a first name — chosen by her husband's family. It is as if the rulers of Bombay and Madras wanted to show that they were now the lords and masters of these cities, and to demonstrate the change by conferring a new name upon them. For what these aggressive nativists are doing is demonstrating that they are now in charge, that the old days are over. They are asserting their power, the power to decide what a thing will be, the power to name — for if one does not have the ability to create, one can at least claim the right to define.

.   .   .

One point at which the two Indias converge is in the process of celebration. Festivals and *mela*s define our need for escape, and India has more of them than any other country; we also take more time off, with a choice of forty-four official holidays for a variety of religious and secular occasions, ranging from Republic Day to Id-e-Milad, the birthday of the Prophet Mohammed. The birthdays of Guru Gobind Singh, Guru Ravidas, Maharishi Valmiki, and Mahatma Gandhi are also legitimate excuses to have a day off, as are the ascensions of Buddha, Christ, and Mahavira of the Jains, as well as the Hindu festivals of Mahashivaratri and Ganesh Chathurthi, in honor of the gods Shiva and Ganesh respectively. Throw in the Parsi New Year and the Shia Muharram, and you can see how secularism has deferred to religion, to the benefit of the indolent of all faiths. But of course the secular harvest festivals of Dussehra, Onam, and Vaisakhi, the festival of lights (Deepavali), the spring festival (Holi), and the day of brotherhood (Raksha Bandhan, when women tie colorful *rakhees* to the wrists of their brothers, who are thus pledged to protect them) are celebrated too. Add to all these the 104 weekend days, annual leave, casual leave, compassionate leave, and sick leave, and it is perfectly possible for a government employee to work a third of the days on the calendar and legitimately collect a full year's salary.

Of all the various ways of measuring the relative underdevelopment of nations, from GNP tables to the Human Development Index, the one that I would like to see conducted is the Holiday Index. My theory is that the poorer the country, the more holidays it gives itself, and the more festivals it conducts. But is it that we are poor because we have so many holidays, or that we have so many holidays because we are poor? Festivals and *mela*s, mass gatherings of the many united around a common event, are the holiday events of the poor; the rich have no shortage of opportunities to enjoy themselves by themselves, whereas the poor have few outlets and pleasures other than communal ones. So poor countries need more holidays and public festivals than rich ones do, to give people the chance to amuse themselves. For an Indian villager a day at the local *mela* is his opera ticket, tennis tournament, and beach vacation rolled into one — and in celebrating it he experiences some of the happiness that Thomas

Jefferson told us it was the duty of government to allow him to pursue.

.   .   .

One sign of the way in which the new economics of post-reform life in India has changed things can be found in an institution that is surprisingly directly affected despite having nothing to do with liberalization — the Indian army. The army has resolutely refused to let down its standards, but in the new India it's hurting. In a land where there are usually a hundred viable candidates for every job, the army is suffering from a shortage of officers. A colonel in the Paratroop Brigade told me that instead of the twenty-two officers he should have had to run his battalion, he had only ten. One of his majors, a bright and self-confident flier, freely confessed his intention to take his skills into the burgeoning private sector. There was a time when service to the nation was rewarding in every sense, including the material; but as our economy has opened and grown, our soldiers, diplomats, and administrators are finding themselves the poor cousins of the businessmen, bankers, and television talk-show hosts of the new India.

.   .   .

The army has taken a tragic toll in casualties in counterinsurgency operations over the past decade (starting with its "peacekeeping" efforts in Sri Lanka, which went so sadly awry), and this may have diminished its appeal. Or perhaps not — for we, as a nation, have become appallingly blasé about violent death. Indians are a people with great reverence for human life; we celebrate birth and infant survival in a host of rituals, acknowledge obligations to even distant relatives, and mourn visibly and publicly when death takes a loved one away from us. Yet we live today with a daily human toll that should be shattering: for years we woke to headlines telling us that thirty a day were killed in Punjab, five or ten in Assam and Kashmir; today Punjab is calmer, Kashmir still tense. At least a hundred others elsewhere in the country lose their lives every month in riots, caste conflict, or election violence. Despite the relative calm of the 1996 elections, in which "only" seven people died, we do not seem to be able to exercise our democratic rights without spilling blood. And natural (or, if often manmade, at least nonpolitical) disasters compound the misery. To take the period of just over a year preceding the writing of these words (from August 1995 onward), the litany of disasters becomes a dirge. If I were to ignore the dozens of deaths in buses driving off roads, collapsing buildings and bridges, and laborers poisoned by adulterated food or illicit drink, I would still be left with a horrific list: five hundred railway passengers were killed in an accident at Firozabad near Agra in August 1995; some seven hundred (mainly primary-school children) were incinerated in a fire in an enclosed space at the local school in the northern town of Mandi Dabwali in December 1995; another hundred were crushed in stampedes at Hindu pilgrimage sites in north India in July 1995; nearly seventy died after eating at a canteen in the textile town of Bhiwandi, near Bombay, in August 1996; and more than two hundred died of cold and exposure after avalanches disrupted the annual Hindu pilgrimage to the holy cave of Amarnath in Kashmir the same month (ironically the first time in some years that the state's Muslim insurrectionists, who had attempted to disrupt previous pilgrimages, had allowed them safe conduct). In one horrendous week in November 1996, 351 aircraft passengers were killed in the world's worst midair collision, just off Delhi, and some 2,500 (plus countless others rendered homeless) by a cyclone that ravaged Andhra Pradesh state.

But India goes on. When they speak of political violence, sophisticated journalists and senior officials claim, at least in private, that the country is big enough and resilient enough to cope indefinitely with a couple of "Ulsters." As for the other tragedies, even parliamentarians content themselves with expressions of outrage, the award of cash compensation to the families of the victims, and the launching of yet another inquiry whose report will be filed routinely like the hundreds that have preceded it on the official shelves. Foreigners see our acceptance of these quotidian deaths — many of which now rate only a few column inches on the inside pages of most newspapers — as confirmation of Indian "fatalism." As an Indian I ask myself what this daily hemorrhage is doing to the quality of the national blood. Why do the deaths of Indians not result in more changes of policy, of procedure, or of personnel? Why must we accept that some loss of life is "inevitable," rather than oblige those who order our lives to be accountable and reward them when they do take successful precautions? I fear that our willingness to live with random and frequent death is damaging our collective psyche in ways whose lasting harm we may come to see too late.

.　.　.

In death, as in life, we are not individuals. The family is the quintessential Indian social unit. We are neither individualists in the Western mode (India is not hospitable terrain for "atomic man," since India is not a society in which atomized individuals can accomplish much) nor are we capable of the self-sacrificing ecumenism that idealistic communism demands. Instead, we operate within the cocoon of a family unit, not necessarily nuclear, which generates our most vital support (practical, material, psychological) and the most important of our social duties and obligations. The family may involve parents, children, and their spouses; decreasingly common, but still prevalent, is the extended "joint" family spanning several generations and several branches of the family tree — uncles, cousins, and in-laws all living together or nearby and relating to each other as in a nuclear family.

Sometimes the notion of "family" extends more broadly to a clan or a caste group, or even to friends and neighbors in a village. I cannot remember a time, growing up in India, when there wasn't a young man from either of my parents' villages in Kerala — sometimes not even a close relation — living in our flat while my father arranged for him to have some professional training and got him a job. That was in the nature of things in our society; it was expected that my father, as one who had done well, would help others to get their start in life. India is not a welfare state — the government provides little to its unfortunates — but it is a welfare society in which people constantly help each other out, provided they feel a connection that justifies their help.

Unfortunately, our sense of community largely stops there. Very few Indians have a broader sense of community than that circumscribed by ties of blood, caste affiliation, or village. We take care of those we consider near and dear, and remain largely indifferent to the rest. There are Indian charities, both religious and secular, but their work barely scratches the surface of the problems of the people as a whole.

At a more trivial level, it is common to find sumptuous luxury apartments in buildings that are filthy, rotting, and stained, whose common areas, walls, and staircases have not been cleaned or painted in generations. Each apartment owner is proud of his own immediate habitat, but is unwilling to incur responsibility or expense for the areas shared with others, even in the same building. My mother once asked her "sweeper-woman" in Delhi to sweep the stairs of her building as well. The woman, who would have been paid extra for the chore, was astonished at the request. "But why should you, madam?" she asked. "The stairs don't belong to you."

This attitude is also visible in the lack of a civic culture in both rural and urban India, which leaves public spaces dirty and garbage-strewn, streets potholed and neglected, civic amenities vandalized or not functioning. The Indian wades through dirt and filth, past open sewers and fly-specked waste, to an immaculate home where he proudly bathes twice a day. An acute consciousness of personal hygiene coexists with an astonishing disregard for public sanitation.

Not surprisingly, India is home to many of the world's most polluted cities. The air in Calcutta or Delhi is all but unbreathable in winter, when exhaust fumes, unchecked industrial emissions, and smoke from countless charcoal braziers in the street rise to be trapped by descending mist and fog. A French diplomat friend, undergoing a routine medical check after serving three years in Calcutta, was asked how many packs of cigarettes he smoked a day. When he protested that he had never smoked in his life, his doctor told him to try another excuse; three years of breathing Calcutta's air had given him lungs resembling a habitual smoker's. A visiting Australian environmental official told a Calcuttan friend that if Brisbane reached a tenth of the

Bengali city's pollution levels, every factory in town would be closed down.

As a result of such unchecked pollution, respiratory diseases are rife in urban India. Factories belch noxious black clouds; effluents pour untreated into rivers; sewage systems reek and overflow. Nature conspires with dilatory sanitation workers: Surat, a thriving Gujarat city of traders, mill workers, and diamond cutters, suddenly hit the world headlines after fifty-two cases of plague were diagnosed there in 1994. And of course, deforestation and overcultivation take their own environmental toll on rural India. Though the Chipko Andolan (which urged rural women to hug trees to prevent their being cut down by rapacious contractors) has had an impact in the forested hills of north India, environmental consciousness remains limited elsewhere across the country, despite some examples of positive action, such as the cleaning up of Surat by its municipal commissioner and the environmental rulings of the Supreme Court's "Green Judge," Justice Kuldip Singh. Governments pass regulations, then regularly ignore them. Meanwhile, more and more cars reach India's congested roads, more poisons and toxins flow into our water and air, and more small factories open up that do not meet pollution-control standards. But they will never be closed down, because unemployment is a greater political danger than lung cancer.

A 1996 World Bank study estimated that air pollution killed more than forty thousand people annually in the six Indian cities it had surveyed, including 7,500 in New Delhi alone. The capital has more than 200,000 vehicles and many thousand factories, which add some two thousand tons of pollutants each day to the air above the city. When the Australian cricket team played there in November 1996, the manager said the air was so unfit to breathe that his players' performance was affected. With respiratory illnesses, cardiovascular diseases, and lung ailments all caused by pollution, the total health costs for the country resulting from illnesses caused by pollution were estimated at 340 billion rupees ($9.7 billion), some 4.5 percent of India's gross domestic product. Ecologist Anil Agarwal looks at these figures starkly: they mean "that the entire economic growth for the year is being wiped out and development has taken place solely at the expense of the environment."

This dismal picture, coupled with lax pollution-control measures and corrupt enforcement of environmental regulations, reflects the sad state of the Indian ecology in the last years of the twentieth century. This does not, however, prevent politicians from using environmental issues to delay major developmental projects, as witness the hue and cry over environmental objections to the Cogentrix power project for electricity-starved southern Karnataka. The fact that, without the Cogentrix project, Indians would have to use far more polluting methods to obtain a fraction of the energy required, does not seem to trouble the "green" politicians unduly. If the choice is between being polluted and poor and being polluted and prosperous, I have no doubt that most Indians would be happy to choke and splutter all the way to the bank. It would be best, of course, if we could achieve prosperity without pollution, but that goal seems, for now, an elusive chimera.

. . .

India has the second-largest population on earth, after China, and by all accounts is set to overtake its giant neighbor by 2020. Its population continues to grow at a rate of 2.1 percent, and fertility is just about as high as it's ever been — while some improvements in basic health care have caused mortality rates to drop appreciably since independence. In the last twenty years the Indian population has grown by a number greater than the entire population of the United States.

The consequences of population pressure are well known: a mounting challenge to keep feeding a populace expanding beyond the capacity of the food producers to cope with it, and a growing gap between the availability of water, health care, and education on the one hand and the number of people seeking those essentials on the other. Less well known, but equally disastrous, are the ecological consequences: deforestation, the degradation of agricultural land, and a decline in the ability of the land to support the people. The beggars in the streets, the homeless sleeping on sidewalks and railway station platforms, are evidence of a population well beyond what the country can provide for. India's chronic problems of landless labor, and its continuing tendency to rely on inefficient, labor-intensive practices in industry and agriculture, are also reflections of overpopulation. Worst of all, India adds an Australia to its population every year, but it does not have the resources to create what that population would need — another 127,000 new schools, 373,000 more schoolteachers, 2.5 million new houses, 4 million more jobs, 190 million meters of cloth, and 12.5 million quintals of food grain each year.

Instead, India currently spends over a billion dollars annually on its domestic population-control programs, only a scant $55 million of which comes from foreign sources. India adopted a national population policy in 1952, when it was one of the first countries in the world to do so. But there were powerful reasons for the population explosion. As the sociologist Mahmood Mamdani pointed out, people aren't poor because they have too many children; they have too many children because they are poor. Children are an asset in a poor family; they are potential sources of labor, and when they grow up they constitute the only social security insurance policy an Indian has. Nor does a poor family have to spend money to educate its children; they can be put to work instead of being sent to school. And since the family is never sure whether and how many of the children will survive to productive adolescence in a land bedeviled by famines, disease, epidemics, and violence, it is wise to have as many children as possible to compensate for those who won't make it. Such attitudes were compounded in traditional culture by the respect given to the father of many sons, by the low status of women, and by high female illiteracy. People had children because they didn't know any better.

So poverty breeds overpopulation and overpopulation breeds poverty (indeed, one can simply say, poverty breeds). How can one deal with it? India has tried pretty much every population-control device, some with less success than others (the failure of intrauterine contraceptive devices in the 1960s, for example, resulted from women suffering bleeding and IUCD rejection but finding no medical officers to attend to them). After the disastrous experiment with compulsory sterilization during the Emergency, the backlash against which brought down the Indira Gandhi government and set back the country's family-planning efforts by a decade, the government is dealing with population problems across a broad front. India's basic population policy is still to reduce fertility — not by surgically curbing the production of children (though vasectomy and tubectomy "camps" still flourish, especially in the rural areas) but by improving health, education, and literacy so as to reduce the incentives for people to produce more children. Still, sterilization remains by far the most prevalent method of family planning. And the average age of Indians choosing to be sterilized is in the thirties, when they have already produced more children than was good for them or the country.

India officially aims at achieving "replacement-level fertility" (in other words, each couple producing only two children, leading to zero population growth) by the year 2000. It is a tall order. The government has been assiduous in promoting family planning, with massive advertising campaigns on radio and television and on public billboards (or for that matter, on the sides of houses and barns in the countryside). The family-planning symbol of an inverted red triangle, and the stock image of a happy nuclear family of father, mother, boy, and girl ("we are two, we have two" goes the slogan), are widely familiar across the country (with subtle variances in the facial characteristics of the family to correspond to regional patterns). But though consciousness has been raised, action does not necessarily follow. Three times as many women are aware of contraception as use it. Abortions are legal, widely available, and generally safe, but many women do not have the knowledge (or the courage) to avail themselves of the option.

Tying family-planning services into rural health clinics as part of integrated health care is one effective method of overcoming resistance to it. Even something as simple as rural electrification has an impact on population growth — give people other things to do in the dark, and they might not make quite so many babies. But the most successful programs are those in states with high female literacy rates, as in Kerala, or where women play important roles in society — again as in Kerala. An educated woman demands and receives better care for herself and her sick children, ensures better standards of personal and domestic hygiene, has more say in running her household, and is more resistant to cultural pressures to produce large numbers of children. The best contraceptive is education.

. . .

India has made only uneven progress in educating its population. Whereas most districts in Kerala, following the introduction of free and compulsory education by an elected Communist government in 1957, have attained 100 percent literacy, the national literacy level still hovers around the halfway mark; the current figure is 52 percent. The traditional explanation for the failure to attain mass education is two-pronged: the lack of resources to cope with the dramatic growth in population (we would need to build a new school every day for the next ten years just to educate the children already born) and the tendency of families to take their children out of school early to serve as breadwinners or at least as help at home or on the farm. Thus, though universal primary education is available in theory, fewer than half of India's children between the ages of six and fourteen attend school at all.

Despite the plausibility of the usual explanation, some critics have suggested that the real reasons are more sinister: that there is, if not an actual conspiracy, a set of attitudes among the country's decision-makers that militate against extending the benefits of education to the ignorant masses. Too much learning, these critics point out knowingly, would undermine the social order, put ideas of clerical jobs into the heads of peasants, and disrupt the hierarchical Indian society that the elite really wants to preserve. "Illiteracy," says American journalist Barbara Crossette, an adherent of this view, "insures that the masses will remain powerless." I find this theory excessively cynical, but it is possible that my instincts are shaped by my experience of Kerala, and that such an explanation might be valid in less enlightened parts of India. But national policy is undoubtedly in favor of education, or at least of promoting literacy. As a child at school, I remember being exhorted to impart the alphabet to our servants under the Gandhian "each one teach one" program; and many of us were brought up on Swami Vivekananda's writings about the importance of education for the poor as the key to their upliftment. But it is true that, forty-nine years after independence, progress has still been inexcusably slow, and that Indian politicians are all too quick, as Mrs. Gandhi was, to take refuge in sharp rejoinders about not drawing the wrong conclusions from the illiteracy figures. Education, Mrs. Gandhi would often say, was not always relevant to the real lives of village Indians, but India's illiterates were still smart, and illiteracy was not a reflection of their intelligence or shrewdness (which they demonstrated, of course, by voting for her).

Fair enough, but Kerala's literate villagers are smart too. The saddest aspect of India's literacy statistics is the disproportionate percentage of women who remain illiterate. More attention to improving the lot of Indian women in general, empowering them to make decisions about such matters as reproduction and family expenditure, and improving their access to health care, would undoubtedly have benefited Indian society as a whole, notably by reducing the country's population. But not just that: freeing India's ordinary women from millennia of subjugation would have liberated for the country the productive talents of half the population, which for millennia have been left to languish exploited, abused, and taken for granted, but all too rarely fulfilled.

(Kerala is, as usual, an exception. It is one of the few states in India where women outnumber men. The 1991 census counted 1,040 women for every 1,000 Kerala men; the all-India figure, a reflection of the neglect of girl children, was 929 women per 1,000 men. Of 13,400 abortions conducted at a Delhi clinic in 1992–93, 13,398 were of female fetuses. In Kerala, female life expectancy exceeds that of males.)

Remarkably enough in the circumstances, India's middle-class women have excelled in professions other societies traditionally reserved for men. There have been Indian women doctors, engineers, lawyers, editors, chief executives, airline pilots, and, most famously, a woman prime minister, well before such positions opened up to their female counterparts in the Western world. When I was at school in the late 1960s, as feminist consciousness was beginning to rise in the West, an international survey of sexism (though they didn't call it that) was conducted in high schools around the world. Respondents were told a story that ended in a riddle: A man is driving with his father and has a serious accident. The father is critically injured and rushed to the hospital; the man, who is uninjured, is waiting anxiously outside the operating theater when a white-coated surgeon strides out, embraces him, and weeps, "My son, my son." The question was, how could this be? The man's father was injured and being operated upon. How could the surgeon then say, "My son, my son"? The answer, of course, is that the surgeon was his mother. Indian students, in a country whose first woman doctor graduated in the 1890s, had little problem with the riddle: over 90 percent of them got it right. Respondents in the West were stymied: whereas in Sweden some 30 percent answered correctly, in the U.K. only 12 percent of students got it right, and in the United States the figure dropped to around 5 percent. The students (including girls) weren't stupid; they simply couldn't conceive of a woman surgeon, whereas educated Indians had grown up seeing women doctors their whole lives. The irony is that these same Indian men have come to maturity in a society that still allows the majority of its women to waste their lives in housewifery or social subjugation.

· · ·

Galloping modernization has done little, however, to dampen enthusiasm for that traditional Indian institution, the arranged marriage. Parenthood in India still implies a responsibility for getting your offspring wedded respectably, particularly if the progeny in question is female. Growing urbanization and the displacement of families by the processes of economic development have, however, made it less easy to rely on traditional village or clan networks to find a suitable spouse. Thus was born the matrimonial advertisement, that uniquely Indian updating of a millennial social practice, re-created in the atomized world of the popular newspaper, and translated across the barriers not only of culture but of language. Whereas the jaded West has its own "lonely hearts" personals in which "DWM" (divorced white male) seeks beautiful well-proportioned female for music, companionship, and unmentionables, India's matrimonial ads are placed by anxious parents whose intentions are entirely honorable. As an index to current preoccupations, though, they offer a window not just into Indian middle-class society, but also into the innovative contributions modern India has made to the evolution of the English language.

"Correspondence invited from educated, charming, U.S.A./Canada settled girls for Punjabi Arora industrial production engineer" reflects the inevitable aspiration for NRI-hood among India's upwardly mobile professionals, though the degree of precision about the advertiser's subcaste (Arora) suggests that "U.S.A./Canada" values have not yet sunk very deep. "Caste no bar" says the well-worn phrase advertised by the enlightened; but equally typical is "South Indian Brahmin father seeks *compatible match* for computer professional son," which could as well read "non–South Indian Brahmins need not apply."

Other codes are equally conventional. Males of any age remain, like Peter Pan, always "boys," even when they are gingerly described as "mature" or "fifty-three," but women over twenty-five descend from girls to "spinsters" and rarely presume to demand much from their prospective mates. The women are always "fair-complexioned" and "beautiful." If the color of their skin tends more to Naomi Campbell's than Claudia Schiffer's, they are described creatively as "wheatish," a particularly Punjabi coinage that combines the notion of brownness with the robustly positive associations of the north's premier agricultural crop. If she is also "homely," this does not mean, Occidental dictionaries notwithstanding, that she is plain or bad-looking, merely that she is good at housework and is not a restless soul constantly seeking to be out of the house. (Most men looking for a bride through the matrimonial columns of a newspaper are likely to be looking for a "homely" girl.) Desirable females who have graduated from (or at least attended) missionary schools are advertised as "convent-educated," though in these days of inflationary advertising tariffs, that can be abbreviated to "convented." Similarly, a college graduate is "degreed," and if she is "convented, degreed," you can overlook the fact that she is also "wheatish-complexioned" and/or not "homely." The ad might also assure you that she is "from status family," which carries with it both pedigree and connections. Dowries, nominally illegal, are never sought or offered openly in the ads, but a prospective bridegroom declaring "girl only consideration" is not just stating the obvious, but assuring the intended bride's family that no other considerations, especially pecuniary ones, will intervene.

Like anything composed and set in type by human hand, matrimonial ads are also prone to producing howlers, and I have spotted a few in my random perusals over the years. "Wanted a simple-minded bride," is an oft-repeated classic, but what is one to make of the family looking for a "housebroken groom" or the one that seeks "a broad-based boy"? The father who offers his "innocent divorcée daughter" is not suggesting that she is a wide-eyed simpleton, or even just that she was not the guilty party in the divorce; instead, he is signaling clearly that her marriage was never consummated, for "innocence" is a euphemism for virginity whenever the candidate is of an age or situation to be suspected of having lost hers (just as the request for an "understanding" mate seeks a man who will forgive such a loss). I doubt, though, that the liberal family declaring, at the end of its ad, "caste, creed, no bras" was really looking for a feminist who had burned her underclothes. Indian newspapers are as prone to printer's devils as matrimonial advertisers are to clichés.

.   .   .

The lowly place of women in India goes back to the Manusmriti, the codes laid down by the venerable lawgiver Manu some three thousand years ago. But not all of India's ancient legacies are iniquitous.

While some of the more extravagant claims by Indian chauvinists about the achievements of the ancient Hindus — such as that India invented flying vehicles and hydroplanes around 2000 B.C., or anticipated the Darwinian theory of evolution — have been understandably ridiculed, there is evidence to suggest that extraordinary insights into atomic theory and into the physiological (and alchemical) properties of mercury existed in ancient India and were lost in later times. There is no doubt at all about the accomplishments of the astronomer Aryabhatta, who proved that the earth is round and revolves around the sun, a thousand years before Galileo was censured for arguing the same; about Bhaskaracharya's understanding of gravitation a millennium before Isaac Newton; about the invention, credited largely to Gritasamada, of the zero and the entire system of decimal numbers (which was learned by the Arabs and thence reached the West, giving the world "Arabic numerals.") The Arabs themselves referred to mathematics as *Hindsat*, "the Indian science." Nor do scholars contest India's claim to have produced the first surgeon, Susruta, whose methods (and tools) of surgery, including plastic surgery and prostheses for amputees, pioneered the field; to have given the world quadratic equations and trigonometry; to have set out the principles of grammar and phonetics; to have raised questions of philosophy and psychology in the Upanishads a thousand years before they had occurred to anyone in the West; and to have developed an imaginative literature, from the animal fables of the Panchatantra to the sophisticated dramas of Kalidasa, that inspired — according to the Chinese scholar Lin Yutang — Aesop, Boccaccio, Emerson, Goethe, Herder, Hesse, Schopenhauer, and the *Arabian Nights*.

Where has this inventive tradition disappeared in today's India? The leading citizens of the land of Susruta travel abroad for major operations. There is no recent scientific discovery of consequence ascribed to a resident of India; Indians have won Nobel Prizes in the sciences only after emigrating and acquiring American passports. The last Indian mathematical genius, the ineffable Ramanujan, died in the 1920s. Our "cutting edge" achievements are in fields pioneered by others, from missile technology to software development. Are we, the heirs to that extraordinary tradition, doomed to be a nation of secondhand imitators, building upon the ideas of others? I do not believe so, but perhaps that is because I do not want to believe it. Looking around today's India, though, there is little doubt that the explosion of creative energy one does see is confined to the realms of theater, music, clothing design, and literature. Indian minds are undoubtedly grappling with major scientific challenges, but they are doing so in Chicago or California, not Calcutta.

.   .   .

The print media received a tremendous fillip from the post-Emergency hunger for news and comment, and it has not looked back since. Both newspapers and magazines have improved immeasurably since the days when Naipaul and Shils judged them, and though the news columns still devote too much space to speeches and announcements, the feature pages — particularly of the news magazines — offer a range and quality of information and comment unparalleled in the developing world. The problem remains, though, that what is otherwise called the "mass media" is actually the "class media" in its reach and assumptions. But in a country where only a minority reads anything at all, this is not too surprising. The written word may not be "relevant" to half the population, but it is vital to the life and thought of the other half.

Nonetheless, I couldn't help noticing, on my last visit to India, that practically everyone I knew in the print media has now gone into television (in some cases in addition to their work for the press). The new India seems to have more TV production companies than fast-food restaurants, though I am inclined to predict that the ratio will reverse itself in the coming years. But I couldn't turn on the TV or return a phone call from a journalist friend without seeing yet another familiar face on the box, earnestly discussing the Fate of the Nation in sound bites rather than column-inches.

What does this all mean? Either that we don't read and write as much as we used to, or that the audiovisual media pays better than print, or that sounding off before a camera takes less time and effort than writing an article, or all of the above. India, or at least the lettered half of it, used to pride itself on its literacy; now it seems we are joining the boob-tube culture of the Western world.

. . .

Today's India offers its residents more choices than ever — on where to work, but also on what to buy, what to drive, and what to listen to.

I was struck, after a gap of just eighteen months since my previous visit, by the visibly increased "globalization" of Indian life — the profusion of billboards advertising Western brand names, the multiplicity of vehicles on the roads that were *not* Ambassadors and Fiats, the advent of a new pop music that owes more to trends in London and New York than to anything out of Bollywood. (Surfing audio channels on Air India, I had to listen attentively to realize that the lyrics I was hearing were in fact in Hindi, or at least primarily so — so American was their sound, their accent, their very intonation.)

I grew up in an India that was obsessed with *swadeshi*. National self-respect seemed to require that we made everything we needed here, however badly — from outmoded cars to outstanding colas. Today we seem to have lost our paranoia about foreign goods, and our even greater paranoia about foreign investors. One of the lessons of history is that you can learn the wrong lessons from history; ever since the East India Company came to trade and stayed on to rule, our rulers have seen the shadow of the imperialist behind every foreigner with a briefcase. Now at last we seem to have outgrown such fears, except for the Luddites and troglodytes who smashed Kentucky Fried Chicken's premises in Bangalore and the politicians who are still trying to close KFC down in Delhi.

I am a vegetarian myself, but I can't for the life of me see what threat is posed by a handful of fast-food outlets aimed at feeding fat Indian chickens to fatter affluent Indians and foreign tourists. If anything, Indian chicken farmers are likely to gain by selling their poultry at dollar-inspired rates to KFC. Those who claim that either their livelihood or their sense of identity is threatened by the presence of a foreign food shop have neither a worthwhile livelihood nor a worthwhile identity to protect. There are thousands of Indian snackeries, with our traditional fast food at a fraction of the price of McDonald's or KFC; the sheer scale of the challenge makes it extremely unlikely that these "multinational" franchises will drive them out of business. Those who fear and resist them are no better than the buggy-whip manufacturers who protested the invention of the automobile because it would deprive them of their work. Time, and the automobile, passed them by. A similar fate awaits the ill-behaved politicized peasantry of Bangalore.

. . .

One more proof of the double-edgedness of change came during my January 1996 visit to India, when the *Asian Age* ran a front-page headline screaming "Sushmita to (Un)dress Up for Cup." The story went on to announce that the former Miss Universe, Sushmita Sen, would be the "major attraction" at the cricket World Cup opening ceremony at the Eden Gardens a month later. Indians are inordinately proud of Ms. Sen, and of her friend Aishwarya Rai, Miss World the same year; the pair gave India the distinction of being the only country to have ever had both the reigning Miss World and Miss Universe at the same time. The paper quoted an Italian, of all people, the chairman of something called Half Moon Image Consultants, as declaring that Sushmita would project "the true beauty of Indian womanhood" while "taking off her clothes." (How the planned "undressing" would sit with the ceremony's chief guest, Chief Minister Jyoti Basu, the man who had banned Samantha Fox from Calcutta for fear that she might take off her clothes, was not mentioned.) "I am going to make her look an Indian like never before," the Half Moon Signore added.

So, I thought, it has come to this. The world's most knowledgeable cricket audience needs a firm of "image consultants" (from a land where the only crickets they've heard of are insects or cigarette lighters) to manufacture a seventy-five-minute "laser show" before it can launch a cricketing event. The erstwhile capital of Indian culture needs an Italian to make one of its citizens "look Indian." And the organizers' notion of advance public relations is to drop teasers about the readiness of a symbol of contemporary Indian womanhood to undress. I thought such things only happened *with* the full moon, not *under* a Half Moon.

If this is globalization, I found myself musing, give me *swadeshi* any day.

In fact, the World Cup opening ceremony did prove an unmitigated disaster. The Half Moon plan to make Sushmita "undress" (the Italian had intended, it transpired, to dress her in the flags of all the participating nations, which she would peel off one by one and hand to the respective captains, ending up draped in the Indian tricolor) was abandoned among the general public outcry. However, the lasers went awry, the costumes did not turn up in time (leaving delegations to be escorted by T-shirt-clad damsels whose jeans did not justify their ends), and the Italians made no allowances for the wind that blows in from the Hooghly at that time of year, resulting in a situation for which only one Italian word could apply — fiasco.

. . .

The term might not have been too inappropriate for the next popular event of global cultural significance (that is, with "world" in the title) to take place in India — the 1996 Miss World contest. After all, with two previous Miss World winners and a couple of close runners-up having come from India, and the national pageants for an assortment of Miss Indias having enjoyed increasing (and uniformly positive) publicity, it seemed quite a coup for movie superstar Amitabh Bachchan when his company won the right to stage the global contest in Bangalore.

He reckoned without his compatriots' maddening capacity for opportunistic mischief-making. The contest was immediately condemned by a coalition of radical feminists, Hindu fundamentalists, and Marxist youth as exploitative of women and offensive to Indian culture; as journalists flocked to report their every utterance, some twenty organizations leaped on the bandwagon. (No one, it seems, asked them why their puritan passions had not been stirred earlier, since beauty contests involving Indian women had taken place across the country for decades.) The convenor of the feminist group Mahila Jagran Samiti (Movement to Awaken Women) threatened to immolate herself in protest and to organize a wave of similar suicides by her colleagues. One male member of the Democratic Youth Federation of India, a twenty-four-year-old tailor, actually set himself alight at a bus stand and succumbed to his burns.

With the militant Farmers' Association — the same folks who trashed a Pizza Hut outlet earlier — threatening to torch the cricket stadium in which the contest was to be held, more than fifteen thousand policemen and security guards had to be assigned to protect the venue and the contestants. Bachchan was provided two personal bodyguards, a dozen policemen to screen visitors, a bulletproof automobile, and a police escort car; and the eighty-nine beauties found their hotel, the idyllic-sounding Windsor Manor Sheraton, ringed by security personnel drawn from such agencies as the Border Security Force and the Rapid Action Force. Meanwhile, much to the disappointment of those who had bought tickets in Bangalore, the swimsuit section of the pageant was shifted to the Indian Ocean island country of the Seychelles, in order not to further inflame (if the expression may be excused) the sensitivities of the protesters. Soon enough, somebody thought of indulging the national passion for litigation, and the courts entered the fray, ruling with typical stuffiness that the contest could go ahead provided there was "no indecent exposure of the bodies of participants amounting to obscenity and nudity." The feminists promptly announced they would sneak into the event and set fire to themselves anyway. It is an old rule of the protest business: Threaten the worst; it keeps the media interested.

The contest proceeded without incident, except for the arrests of a few hundred demonstrators, but the fierce and voluble hostility of the protesters tarnished India's international reputation immeasurably. The world press wrote of Indian xenophobia, which until recently one might have thought a contradiction in terms. Barbara Crossette, in *The*

New York Times, observed that, in the words of one of the organizers, a "Stone Age mentality" had surfaced. She saw a parallel with situations in which "would-be business investors look on with chagrin as mobs attack foreign-backed projects the country needs badly." India's image as a tolerant land of live-and-let-live, a congenial environment for every idea and practice, will not easily recover from the coverage of the Miss World contest.

This may well have been the protesters' intent, because their noisy cantankerousness was at least in part aimed at the increasing liberalization of Indian life, of which the Miss World contest was merely a visible (and literal) embodiment. Indian leftists are not all reconciled to the entry of India into the world economy, and a beauty contest provides evocative images of neo-imperial penetration that were a recurrent subtext of the feminists' agenda. (Their incendiary, if matchless, convenor, a law student named K. N. Shashikala, regularly denounced the "commercialization of women by multinational corporations.") There is little doubt that the visible evidence of foreign intrusion, from Kentucky Fried Chicken to international brand-name stores, can be manipulated by politicians in ways that homegrown evils cannot; it is easier to mobilize people against symbols they cannot touch, to which they feel no affinity, and that can be portrayed as a sign of external dominance of the country.

But the other objection raised by the protesters was equally troubling, and that was to the alleged contamination of "Indian culture" by an international beauty pageant. The entire point about Indian culture is that it embraces both the *burqa*-clad Muslim woman and the Bombay model (and former Miss Universe runner-up) who posed nude for a shoe advertisement; that it honors the lush erotic statuary of the temples of Khajuraho, where amatory couples cavort in explicit positions in stone, while frowning on kissing in public; and, what is more, that it accommodates both middle-class prudery and an economic reality that obliges many poor rural women to go about bare-breasted because they cannot afford the cloth to cover themselves. Which version of "Indian culture" does a glittering parade of well-dressed (and occasionally underdressed) foreign women offend?

The question is troubling because, in late November 1996, the self-proclaimed defenders of Indian culture took on one of the greatest figures of contemporary Indian culture, the painter Maqbool Fida Husain. Husain, arguably India's leading artist of the second half of the twentieth century, is not above painterly opportunism — he shamelessly cultivated Indira Gandhi, and a shoddy mural he has scribbled onto the walls of the Indian Permanent Mission in New York is an embarrassment to his art — but his critics were not taking him on either political or aesthetic grounds. Instead a mob, objecting to a Husain painting of the Hindu goddess Saraswati in the nude, destroyed several of his works at an exhibition in Ahmedabad, outraged in particular that a Muslim artist should have taken such liberties with their faith. The eighty-year-old artist's life, and the safety of his paintings in public collections, were directly and explicitly threatened.

Husain had, in fact, drawn liberally from Hindu iconography in his work, and goddesses and *apasara*s were among his favorite figures: he had depicted Prime Minister Indira Gandhi as Durga after the 1971 war, and, less controversially, painted a series featuring the film actress Madhuri Dixit as Menaka in 1995. But rather than feeling flattered that a Muslim should have so readily sought inspiration in the Hindu tradition, the fundamentalists challenged his right to do so. "No Muslim has the right to portray our deities any way he wishes," declared the founder of the Bajrang Dal, which represents the more lumpen of the Hindutva brigades, going on to demand that Husain's "objectionable paintings" should be immersed in the sacred river Ganga so that they might be simultaneously cleansed and destroyed.

I am tempted to say, with passion and feeling, that this is not Hindu behavior; indeed, the very fact that the Saraswati drawing most objected to was first revealed to the public twenty years ago, without incident, suggests that most Hindus, left to themselves, would not think twice about it. But what is Hindu behavior these days is not defined by the tolerance preached by Vivekananda. A politicized Hinduism has arisen, which reacts to real or imagined slights the way some Muslims reacted to Rushdie (indeed, all that is missing is the Hindu equivalent of an Ayatollah with a *fatwa*, but, thank God, Hinduism doesn't have one). The Hindutva leaders are guilty of the worst kind of me-tooism; they have seen governments pandering to the offended sensitivities of minority communities, and they want to show that they can be offended too. In the process they are doing their own faith a disservice. They are dragging Hinduism — as they manifest it — into the mire of an intolerance that is foreign to its very nature.

Perhaps the only answer is to fight philistinism with culture. The Hindutva leaders should all be sent on an educational tour of Khajuraho. After that, they might consider even the transported Miss World swimsuit contest rather tame.

. . .

The two world events are behind us now. Bangalore, increasingly as cosmopolitan a city as Bombay, will be learning a number of lessons from its experience with the feminist fringe. Calcutta will take a long time to recover from the crowd misbehavior that marred the semifinals of the tournament it so grandly inaugurated under the Half Moon. But the gaudy and ultimately disastrous extravaganza at the Eden Gardens failed to conceal what had become increasingly apparent to me in my regular visits to the place I have, for nearly three decades, considered my hometown: Calcutta has become a backwater.

I write these words in disappointment. When, as a twelve-year-old in late 1968, I first learned of my father's transfer from Bombay to Calcutta, where his newspaper was headquartered, I embraced the news with great excitement. Calcutta still had the lingering aura of the former First City of the British Empire, a place of importance if no longer of grandeur. It was the bustling commercial metropolis of the jute, tea, coal, and iron and steel industries; more important, it was the city of Eden Gardens, of College Street, of Firpo's and Trinca's (and — recalling the whispers of wicked uncles — the Golden Slipper, the acme of all Indian nightclubs). It was the city of the peerless

Nobel Prize–winning litterateur and visionary Rabindranath Tagore, of India's greatest filmmaker, Satyajit Ray, and (in a way that defined the grace of a bygone age) of the patron queen of high culture, Lady Ranu Mukherjee; for juveniles of less exalted cultural inclinations, it had India's first disco (the Park Hotel's suggestively named "In and Out") and, in *JS,* India's only "with it" youth magazine. Former Calcuttans still spoke of the brilliance of the Bengali stage, the erudition of the waiters at the Coffee House, the magic of Park Street at Christmas. Calcutta seemed immeasurably more exciting than money-obsessed, glitzy, second-rate Bombay.

The excitement faded quickly enough — overshadowed by power cuts, poverty, potholes, pavement-dwellers, political violence, paralyzed industry. But for all its problems, Calcutta still retained, amid the dirt and the degradation, the despair and the disrepair, many of the qualities that had made it important. Sometimes, paradoxically, its worst problems served to enhance its importance — as when the Bangladesh crisis brought refugees, a government in exile, and the world media to the city. Today, ironically, the problems seem fewer: reforms in the Bengal countryside mean that destitute villagers no longer flock to Calcutta for survival, power cuts are rare, and nineteen years of Left Front rule have given the city a measure of political stability unimaginable two decades ago. But Calcutta matters much less to the rest of India than it did when its troubles were greater.

Calcutta's commercial importance is negligible. A great deal of industry has fled; little new has risen in its place. Some major firms ostensibly headquartered here have in fact moved the bulk of their operations elsewhere, leaving a shell to bear the designation "registered office." Jute has collapsed as a product of consequence with the development of new synthetic materials; tea is in the doldrums, and while world prices are stagnant, Indian tea is being supplanted in international markets. One of the reasons that "load-shedding" does not regularly plunge the city into darkness is that nothing succeeds like failure: the exodus of major industry has reduced demand for power consumption. Businessmen and professionals alike talk openly of moving. Calcutta has little to offer the rest of the world.

Culturally, for all its achievements, Calcutta has been reduced to a provincial capital. The city continues to be the custodian of the best of the Bengali tradition, but it no longer produces work that the rest of India looks up to for inspiration. The major innovations in theater, in art, in music, in writing, even in cinema, are taking place elsewhere in India. Calcutta's intellectual life, including in the pages of its newspapers, does not dominate — let alone anticipate — the national debate. Some of the best Calcutta journalists have left the city; even Bengali editors with everything going for them here prefer to thrive in Bombay and Delhi, and non-Bengalis who made their reputations in Calcutta have chosen to preserve them elsewhere. Calcutta is left with its *bhadralok*, its Bengali bourgeoisie, who stay not because, but in spite, of what the city offers them.

Of course all this is not purely Calcutta's fault; it cannot help the increasing centralization of *everything* in the capital, and the corresponding desire of many ambitious and talented people to move to where the action is. But the city fathers are responsible for Calcutta's failure to provide the civic amenities one can take for granted in any other major Indian city — and for the widespread sense that Calcutta, complacently resting on its past laurels, no longer cares whether it matters to the rest of India or not. When a great city collectively loses the desire for greatness, its lights dim in more ways than one. It used to be said that when Calcutta catches a cold, the rest of India sneezes. Today, if Calcutta has a cold, the rest of India looks away — and hopes that the virus isn't catching.

•   •   •

By contrast, Delhi can now afford to indulge in debates about being too successful. For some years, most of us Indians were ostentatiously proud of our capital city. Its broad avenues, late-colonial architecture, and general air of well-ordered self-importance went well with popular notions of what the nation's premier city and seat of government should be like.

When the aging colonial capital designed by Sir Edward Lutyens was given a multi-crore-rupee facelift before the 1982 Asian Games, the new highways, overpasses, and tourist hotels made our Rajdhani presentable as well as patrician. New Delhi, its inhabitants tended to assure impressed visitors, wasn't like the rest of India. And they meant it as a compliment.

But today a new stereotype is gaining ground in urban India. The glossy feature pages Indian newspapers have recently sprouted on weekends describe a city of which the thinking Indian writers of these articles are anything but proud. To them, Delhi typifies an India that has lost its soul, the epitome of a new concrete culture of "black money" and five-star hotels divorced from tradition, the arts, or the refinements of the higher life.

All that was worth cherishing in old Delhi, they moan, has now given way to the overpass and the fast-food counter, both serving hustling transients who feel no sense of belonging to the city and don't even know the history behind the addresses on their visiting cards. This is not just the sneering of a few highbrow columnists. It is, in fact, a view widely held among educated Delhiites, especially those who have lived in the capital for more than two decades.

The irony is that the analysis is not new. It was first voiced in the Magadhan-Mauryan period, from the sixth to the third century B.C., when a similar process of social change and urbanization, following major political transformation, also provoked anxious and self-critical debate. The Indian intellectuals of two thousand years ago were similarly torn between nostalgia for an idealized past and self-confident optimism about the triumphs of urban cosmopolitanism.

Even more ironically, the cosmopolitans are doing rather worse this time around. The major difference is probably the intervening phase of British rule. The British-educated Indians who were, in Macaulay's words, "interpreters" between them and the masses did not want to train men of action, doers, businessmen, or industrialists who might compete with their mercantile classes. As a result, the minds of

Indians were shaped by words, not goals; we are adept at literature and history, but contemptuous of mere striving. No wonder we cannot appreciate a city that places effort and success above ideas and memories.

The intelligentsia decry New Delhi as a parvenu city. It was created by those who had lost everything in the partition of the subcontinent — men and women of the Punjab, Sikhs and Hindus uprooted from the land that had been the home of their ancestors for countless generations, rejects of history who had to carve out their own futures. They worked and struggled and sweated to make it. They were unencumbered by the baggage of the past, for the past had betrayed them. They succeeded — and as a result of their efforts, they created the first truly postcolonial Indian city.

So people who had trudged across the frontier as refugees today drive shining Marutis across overpasses; people who had lost their houses now sup in five-star hotels. But instead of applauding them, educated Indians tend to curl their refined lips in scorn. The crass materialism of the archetypal Delhiite is sniffed at, his lack of culture ridiculed, his ignorance of history deplored. Literate India laments the transformation of a Delhi that was once a byword for elegant poetry, Mughal manners, and courtly civilization.

Delhi may indeed have had its attractions, but it was also a moribund place steeped in decay and disease, ossified in communal and caste divisions, exploitative and unjust. Today's New Delhi — not the musty bureaucratic edifices of government, but the throbbing, thriving agglomeration of textile factories and cycle-repair shops, industrial fairgrounds and film studios, nightclubs and restaurants — is a city that reflects the vigor and vitality of those who have made it. It provides and reflects a stimulus, unfamiliar to the Indian intelligentsia, of enterprise and risk-taking; its people are open and outward-looking. They may have forgotten their history, but they remember their politics. They may not know *why*, but they know *how*.

New Delhi has enshrined performance and effectiveness as more important measures of human worth than family name or pedigree.

If, in the process, it has also placed a premium on vulgar ostentation rather than discreet opulence, so be it. The new rich could not have run the old clubs, so they built the new hotels. The "five-star culture," for all its vulgarity, is more authentically Indian than the "club culture" it has supplanted, a musty relic of proto-colonial dress codes and insipid English menus.

It is true, of course, that New Delhi lacks a coherent cultural focus. Its very structure of disaggregated "colonies" ensures that the capital is really twenty townships in search of a city. But if Calcutta symbolizes urban Indian civilization, thank God New Delhi is not civilized. The capital epitomizes development as Calcutta epitomizes culture; it is not a city indifferent to the basic needs of its citizens. Nor is it lacking in creative endeavor. Today, fueled by the money and the people that have poured into the city, there are more plays, exhibitions, and concerts on any single day in New Delhi than anywhere else in India. It was not so two decades ago.

New Delhi is also a cosmopolitan society in the international sense. We have always been an overly self-obsessed people, and the autarchic and protectionist years since independence have increased our self-absorption to an alarming degree. Four decades of restrictive economic policies have drastically reduced, in other cities, the frequency of routine contact and interchange between Indians and foreigners. New Delhi is the one place in India where this is still possible and Indians of every class can benefit from relating to the outside world, and seeing themselves in its eyes.

Throughout Indian history there has been a link between urbanization and prosperous development, because cities were centers of contact with the outside world. This urban openness and economic energy lay behind the importance of the ports on India's western coast. With the advent of jet travel, geography is no longer determinant; the "coast" may move inland. New Delhi is India's contemporary equivalent of those port cities of a bygone age — bustling, heterodox, anti-ritual, prosperous. For all its inadequacies, it is a symbol of a country on the move, the urban flagship of a better tomorrow. It will lead India into the twenty-first century, even at the price of forgetting all that happened in the other twenty.

. . .

It was Calcutta, however, and not Delhi, that featured most recently in a Hollywood film. If Calcuttans had had their way, however, the film of *City of Joy*, based on Dominique Lapierre's 1986 best-seller about poverty and piety in this Bengali city, might never have been made.

Director Roland Joffe was quoted as saying he had an easier time making *The Killing Fields* on the Cambodian border and *The Mission* in the jungles of Colombia than filming *City of Joy* in Calcutta. His crew were subjected to a variety of forms of vocal protest, ranging from editorials and lawsuits to demonstrations and (in one episode) bombs being thrown on the set. A Bengali reporter covering the picketing died after allegedly being beaten up by two of Joffe's assistants. The courts kept the crew's cameras idle for part of the spring, before allowing restricted public filming on holidays.

Calcutta is no stranger to cultural controversy: its citizens once rioted and burned trams to protest a Paris writer's expulsion from the Cinémathèque Française. On the face of it, *City of Joy*'s troubles seemed to confirm India's reputation for thin-skinned hypocrisy. The protesters were angry about the film's focus on the city's despair and degradation; the filmmakers point out, not unreasonably, that these do exist. Calcuttans dreaded yet another depiction of poverty, prostitution, and urban squalor unleavened by any acknowledgment that their city has for more than two centuries been India's cultural capital, a metropolis of art galleries, avant-garde theaters, and overflowing bookshops, whose coffeehouse waiters speak knowledgeably of Godard and Truffaut. The filmmakers retorted that that may well be true, but that's not what their film is about: it's about poverty and suffering and death — all of which can be found in good measure in Calcutta's slums — and about the resilience of the human spirit in the face of tragedy. They see their work as a tribute to Calcutta, a city of misery that is nonetheless a city of joy. Those who want them to turn their cameras on the other Calcutta, Joffe says, are only trying to camouflage the painful reality.

Perhaps — but whose reality? Lapierre's book was ostentatiously burned by some among those he wrote about, the residents of the slum of Pilkhana. Even those who do not condone the violence and extremism of some of the protesters sympathized with their objections. The way they tell it, the book was bad enough; with the film, Calcutta will become the favorite pinup of the pornographers of poverty. Westerners are going to munch popcorn in air-conditioned theaters as they stare at flickering images of dying Indian babies. This seemed to them a new kind of voyeurism, which has no interest in the totality of the Calcuttan reality, only in that part of it which titillates the Western conscience. And don't forget the risk of racism: in the book and in the film, they argued, the Indians would be shown as poor wretches who need cinegenic whites to give them succor. Calcutta doesn't matter for itself; in the book, it is merely the backdrop for the beatification of a Polish priest and the self-realization of an American doctor (played in the film by *Dirty Dancing*'s Patrick Swayze).

The more thoughtful of the Calcutta protesters argued that they would have no problem with a different film on the same subject. They are proud of Indian directors, like Satyajit Ray, Ritwik Ghatak, and Mrinal Sen, who have made vivid and convincing films on Bengali poverty. Neither Lapierre nor Joffe, those protesters pointed out, feel the same empathy. Worse, by focusing on Western protagonists, they implicitly deny the dedication and sacrifice of thousands of Calcuttans — rich, poor, and middle-class — who have devoted their time and their resources to helping their fellow citizens. Even Mother Teresa couldn't have achieved a fraction of what she has done without her overwhelmingly Indian legions of volunteers and nuns, none of whom happen to look like Patrick Swayze. Indians are struggling, with dignity and selflessness, to overcome their own problems. The book and the film, they suggested, do them a disservice.

It was a persuasive case, passionately argued by Calcuttan intellectuals, among them my wife. And yet I found myself deeply ambivalent about it. As an Indian, I don't particularly relish what Lapierre did in his book; I am reminded of Mahatma Gandhi, sixty years earlier, calling the American traveler Katharine Mayo's *Mother India* a "drain-inspector's report." As a writer, though, I was troubled by my Calcuttan friends' implicit condoning of censorship; they seemed to be saying to Lapierre and Joffe, "This is *our* poverty, *you* can't depict it." I could not accept that, any more than I can accept the suggestion that Peter Brook had no right to make his version of *our* epic, the Mahabharata.

I cannot accept the notion that the suffering of the Third World's underclass is not a fit subject for First World filmmakers. On the contrary, I believe it is vital to get the media of the haves interested in the problems of the have-nots. I was aware that, in aiming at a Western audience, Joffe would frame his story from the perspective of the outsiders, just as Candice Bergen got more footage in the film *Gandhi* than a dozen Indian figures with a greater claim to a share in the Mahatma's life. The Indian poor, I was convinced, would be the objects of Mr. Joffe's lens, rather than its subjects; *City of Joy* would be less their story than Patrick Swayze's. Like the Calcutta protesters, I resented that, but unlike them, it is a price I was willing to pay.

I argued that I would be willing to risk a bad, even exploitative, film in defense of the principle that Joffe has as much right to make a film about India as I have to set my next novel in America. And — just as Candice Bergen's presence helped get Gandhi's message to a vast new audience — I knew that Joffe's film could do far more to make the West's rich aware of the East's poor than the more authentic films of Third World directors, which won't garner any Academy Awards or reach a fraction of the audience that I expected *City of Joy* to. For those two good reasons, I appealed to the Calcutta protesters: You have made your point; let us now give the filmmakers a chance to prove that they have one worth making.

When I saw the finished film (in a largely empty New York theater), I discovered my assumptions had been completely wrong. I wasn't just mistaken: the outcome was the opposite of what I had so knowingly imagined. Far from moving mass audiences and sweeping the

Oscars, *City of Joy* didn't do well at the American box office; its message of compassion failed to reach a new audience, and the film nearly sank Patrick Swayze's career. But the movie did, to my surprise, humanize its Indian characters: the rickshaw-puller played by Om Puri is as much the hero of the movie as Patrick Swayze's American doctor or Pauline Collins's Irish nurse. I don't know if the Calcutta protesters influenced this treatment, but the film certainly showed up their protests as misguided. Perhaps the city would have had a larger box office if they had found a way to put Candice Bergen in it after all.

. . .

Whenever Indian food is mentioned, the non-Indian says with a knowing nod, "Ah yes, curry." Unfortunately, though, there is no such dish. "Curry" simply means any dish with a gravy, and there are several hundred of those in each of the many styles of cooking that make up Indian cuisine.

Food is, of course, no exception to the golden rule of diversity that applies to all things Indian. The variations between different styles of Indian cooking are far greater, to Indian palates, than the differences between, say, French and Italian cuisine would seem to a European. In India those distinctions emerge from a variety of factors: geography (regional traditions), climate (the availability or absence of certain foods, oils, and spices), and religion (communal preferences and taboos). And *within* each of those is the rampant individualism of all Indian life, that basic principle of improvising within broad basic rules that applies to everything from Indian classical music to Indian political conventions. Each individual cook varies the ingredients and methods of each dish, so that no two Indian dishes of the same name actually taste identical. This is a far cry from the idea of sprinkling a spoon of "curry powder" into a pan to make a dish "Indian." "Curry powder" does not exist in India: instead there are some forty different major spices and several dozen other seasonings from which an Indian cook chooses each time, varying the quantity, proportion, order, and method in which each is used. The idea of a standard mixed powder for all purposes would be greeted with horror in an Indian kitchen.

The list of cultural, regional, and religious variations is extremely long. Some are a result of history: the north, with its recurrent experience of invasion from Persia and Central Asia and several centuries of Muslim rule, was inevitably influenced by Persian, Afghan, and Central Asian cuisine. The resultant style of Indian food, "Mughlai," is what is usually found in Indian restaurants around the world. (Indeed, some regional Indian cuisines can be found in no restaurant at all; until one opened in 1996, you would have been hard pressed to find a Bengali restaurant in Calcutta, the capital of Indian Bengal, perhaps because it was assumed that anyone who had acquired a taste for Bengali cuisine could always go to someone's home to indulge it.) But if Mughlai food is what most people think of as "Indian," it has, to an Indian palate, almost nothing in common with the rice-*sambar*-and-coconut cuisine of the relatively uninvaded south.

These culinary variations simply demonstrate again how the pluralism of India is reflected in its cuisine. The country's diversity affects:

· *What people like to eat.* For instance, most Hindus (the exceptions being westernized ones) do not eat beef or pork; Muslims generally (again, unless they are very westernized) eat beef but not pork. Bengalis are renowned fish-eaters; people from Andhra like their food extremely "hot." Most Brahmins are vegetarian, but Brahmins from Kashmir and Bengal are not; indeed, they insist on meat or fish even on such auspicious occasions as weddings, where other Indians would be inclined to serve vegetarian fare to underscore the purity of the event. The distaste for beef makes it the cheapest meat in India and helps explain the absence for decades of a McDonald's or a Burger King in such a vast country. (McDonald's finally opened its first outlet in Delhi in 1995, with vegetarian burgers the star attraction on the menu.) The sublime *idli*, a steamed dumpling of ground and fermented rice and *urad* lentils, and its crepelike sibling the *dosa*, are staples of the south, but virtually unknown in the north (though one evidence of "national integration" is their increasing availability at least in the bigger cities).

• *What people are able to eat.* Mushrooms are a delicacy in the extreme north, but cannot be found elsewhere in the country. People in rice-growing areas often can conceive of no other grain, so that in past famines starving people have rejected wheat. Fish is popular near coastal areas and rivers, but the relatively poor quality of preservation and transportation makes it scarce, and sometimes unsafe, elsewhere.

• *What food is cooked with.* Kashmiris use saffron, which is an expensive delicacy in other parts of the country; but whereas Kashmiri Hindus use asafetida and reject garlic, Kashmiri Muslims do exactly the opposite. Coconut in various forms — shredded, grated, pulped, blended, sprinkled — abounds in Kerala cooking, but is totally absent in Mughlai. Red and green chilies are used around the country, but their proportions decrease with latitude, so that the seemingly illogical equation between hot climates and "hot" food is underscored in India.

• *How food is cooked.* In cuisines where many dishes are fried, the "cooking medium," as it is called in India, becomes very important. Mustard oil gives Bengali dishes their unmistakable taste, but other Indians dislike its sharp odor. Coconut oil is preferred in Kerala, but vegetable oils, including sesame seed (*til*) oil, are more popular in the north. Oil is, of course, the cooking medium of the budget-conscious: only *ghee* (clarified butter) will do for those who can afford it, and can afford to disregard their cholesterol count.

• *How food is eaten.* Most Indians eat Indian food with their hands, forks and knives being an affectation and an inconvenience. But whereas northerners confine themselves to the very tips of the fingers, southerners use the whole hand to mix and pick up food. Where Muslims might think nothing of dipping their hands into a communal dish, Hindus are careful not to let the hand they are eating with touch anyone else's plate, let alone a bowl others have to help themselves from.

• *What food is eaten on.* In the south, food is served on a large banana leaf, which is first washed by the eater. In the north and west, the *thali*, a round metal tray laden with small bowls for individual portions of each item, is customary. The westernized urban Indian uses a porcelain plate, to the disapproval of the orthodox, who note that animal bones go into its making.

This catalog of contrasts does not even begin to take into account the endless variations in each individual home. Some of these reflect personal preferences, others long-held family traditions, a particular way of cooking a dish handed down from generation to generation. Many of the dissimilarities result from the way in which the cook uses the spices and seasonings for which Indian cooking is famous. "Spicy" does not mean "hot": what burns the tongue in Indian cooking is the *chili,* red or green, which is too often used by indifferent cooks to disguise the mediocrity of their cooking. In a country of strong smells and brilliant colors, Indians like their dishes to look and taste different from each other, not uniformly "hot." Chilies only came to India with the Portuguese, who had discovered the natives growing them in America, so it is somewhat ironic that westerners should identify them with India. The major Indian spices — cumin and coriander (leaves, seeds, ground powders), turmeric, the pleasantly scented "three C's" (cardamom, cinnamon, and cloves), or fennel and mustard seeds — are all both mild and fragrant. They are each used in different ways, separately or together, to enhance the variety of flavor of Indian dishes. As Madhur Jaffrey explains:

> Sometimes we leave the spices whole and fry them, sometimes we roast the spices and at other times we grind them and mix them with water or vinegar to make a paste. Each of these techniques draws out a completely different flavor from the same spice.

Since each item or ingredient can be treated this way, the possibilities are literally endless: a simple potato can be cooked with one spice or an almost infinite combination; each spice can be used in a different way each time; or a different method (boiling, baking, roasting, frying, mashing, sautéing, enveloping in different flours, etc.) can be applied within each technique. Early in this book I wrote whimsically of three hundred ways of cooking the potato: given the variations I have just described, that must be considered a very conservative estimate. In our food, as in our civilization as a whole, India affirms yet again that it is a singular land of the plural.

.   .   .

These sketchy impressions are partial in both senses of the word: they express my view of a number of random issues that caught my eye, and they are noteworthy for what they omit of Indian society and culture — not just caste and religion (which are treated elsewhere in this book), but the buying and burning of women, crime, sex, sport, and especially music, dance, theater, and Indian cinema (which are not). There is no particular reason for my selection. But society and culture are abstractions, whereas India is something real and tangible to every Indian. When I think of India, I think of steaming breakfast *idlis* and pungent coconut chutney, of lissome women in saris the colors of paradise, of the throngs of working men pouring from a brown-and-ocher train; I hear the roar of the white-specked blue ocean lapping up at sandy beaches, the clear, calm stillness of the snow peaks, the cacophony of city traffic; I imagine the sun shining off the marble and stone of our greatest monuments, the rain falling vigorous and life-renewing upon the drying plains, the breeze stirring the green stalks of the paddy fields in my village. I remember how, each time I come home, I stand in the sun and feel myself whole again in my own skin.

10

A Future Without Shock

I remember beginning the New Year of 1993 with a depressing visit to India. It is not an adjective I ever expected to use about my visits home; nothing had in the past diluted the exhilaration that was my usual response to being back there. If anything, that exhilaration had increased on recent visits; India had seemed at last to be turning the corner, to be breaking out of the rut of economic stagnation that had condemned it to what cynical economists had dubbed "the Hindu rate of growth." There was real talk of the nation at last unshackling the statist controls that had fettered the creative energies of her hardworking, thrifty, notoriously entrepreneurial citizenry. Headlines spoke of India as "a giant on the move" and "a tiger uncaged." Business journals wrote approvingly of her new economic policies; in late November 1992 *The New York Times* published a flattering profile of Narasimha Rao, the septuagenarian prime minister who was presiding over this thrilling if overdue transformation. And then it all seemed to fall apart.

On the sixth of December 1992, howling mobs of Hindu extremists tore down a disused mosque in India's northern heartland. In the frenzy that followed that wanton act of destruction, the streets of sixty-five cities and towns erupted; two thousand were killed in rioting, several tens of thousands injured, billions of dollars worth of property destroyed. Barely had calm and order been restored when the city of

Bombay, *urbs prima in Indis,* the country's thriving commercial capital, blazed again in an orgy of organized violence against its Muslim minority. When that too was put down — but only after hundreds more lives were lost, thousands more livelihoods shattered — the next act in the tragedy followed. A series of thirteen bombs exploded across the city in a well-planned and orchestrated terrorist assault on Bombay's nerve centers, including its newly computerized Stock Exchange. When another huge explosion rocked Calcutta days later, and the United States urged its citizens to cancel planned trips to New Delhi, the questions began to be asked: "Is it all over for India? Can India ever recover from this?"

Of course the answers were no and yes, but outsiders cannot be blamed for asking existential questions about a country that so recently had been seen as poised for takeoff. The factors that point to India's potential — its size, its human resources (particularly a skilled, educable, and inexpensive workforce), its burgeoning middle-class market, its thriving democracy — also point to its pitfalls. Was the country simply too vast, too riven by differences, too torn apart by ancient and incomprehensible hatreds, to be taken in the direction that Malaysia, Indonesia, and now even China were going?

India can recover from the physical assaults against it. It is a land of great resilience that has learned, over arduous millennia, to cope with tragedy. Within twenty-four hours of the Stock Exchange bombing, Bombay's traders were back on the floor, their burned-out computers forgotten, doing what they used to before technology changed their styles. Bombs alone cannot destroy India, because Indians will pick their way through the rubble and carry on as they have done throughout history.

But what *can* destroy India is a change in the spirit of its people, away from the pluralism and coexistence that has been our greatest strength. Equally, there are vital areas of life, political and economic, in which India cannot afford *not* to change. As the country nears the fiftieth anniversary of its independence, it is undergoing a period of ferment in which profound challenges have arisen to the secular assumptions of Indian politics, to the caste structures underpinning society, and to the socialist consensus driving economic policy. Any one of those three changes would be significant enough to send political scientists scurrying to their keyboards; all three occurring simultaneously point to a dramatic transformation. Where is India heading?

.   .   .

India has some serious problems. Three vital border states, Kashmir, Assam, and Punjab, have suffered secessionist ferment in the 1990s, and though Punjab seems to have turned the corner, violence has become endemic in the country, with bomb blasts (and their accompanying tragic toll) a frequent occurrence even in the capital. Until T. N. Seshan astonished the country and the world with his conduct of the 1996 elections, it seemed that amid assaults, intimidation, and "booth-capturing" (ballot-stuffing by thuggery), we were unable to exercise our democratic rights without spilling blood. And as if we did not have enough violence of our own, terrorism is also imported: Rajiv Gandhi's killing in an otherwise tranquil Tamil Nadu state occurred at the hands of Sri Lankan "Tamil Tigers" who had crossed the Palk Strait, bringing their murderous campaign for a separate homeland onto Indian soil.

Corruption, violence, sectarianism, the criminalization of politics, and widespread social tension all mounted during a period when a degree of economic liberalization opened up a new entrepreneurial ferment. A new consumer culture was born amid a population of whom 65 percent live below a tragically low poverty line and 25 percent earn less than twenty-five dollars a month. As the visible consumption of color TV sets, VCRs, and automobiles increased, there was more for the have-nots to aspire to, and more for the hungry and frustrated to resent. The competitive ferment has erupted through all the fissures in Indian society — farmers and peasants raging against the cities, Hindus bitterly protesting the "pampering" of the Muslims, Assamese revolting against being reduced (by Bangladeshi immigrants, Calcutta capitalists, and Delhi bureaucrats alike) to second-class citizens in their own state. A combination of India's own economic choices and external factors has left the country with a colossal economic challenge, with chronic fiscal deficits, an increasingly disastrous balance of payments, a deficient infrastructure, and mounting unemployment and inflation.

The social ferment engendered by economic change is also a key factor in the communal violence following the Hindutva resurgence of the 1990s. The youths who smashed the Babri Masjid wore the shirts and trousers of lower-middle-class urban youth, men whose opportunities have not matched their expectations, and who are taking out their resentment on the visible Other. Various sections of Hindu society are seeing their status and privileges threatened by bewildering processes of change: affirmative-action programs for Dalits and "backward classes," trade liberalization, economic reforms that have brought foreign employers into the country, remittances from Gulf labor that have made nouveaux riches out of their Muslim neighbors. A worldview resting on timeless assumptions has been jolted by the realization that you can't take anything for granted anymore.

The list of Indian woes seems endless. And we haven't even mentioned the widespread illiteracy (still 48 percent of the population), the calamitous consequences of accelerating deforestation, the stifling levels of water and air pollution, the decline of the once-reputed administrative system (too many members of India's prestigious civil services are reported or rumored to be indulging in petty, and not-so-petty, corruption), the cripplingly congested and outdated education system. Worst of all, the sheer effort of combating insurgency has besmirched India's once-proud record as a rare Third World democracy. There are increasing reports, primarily by Indian civil liberties organizations, of human rights violations in counterterrorist operations; and the army, still deservedly admired by most Indians, is beginning to show the strains of being called out again and again to do a job it was never meant to do. The state has become a battleground of sharply defined identities where sectarian interests have replaced national loyalties as the banner around which rival forces rally — and this has, inevitably, raised concern about the future of India.

·   ·   ·

Nearly half the Indian population lives below a poverty line that has, to put it mildly, been drawn just this side of the funeral pyre: to be poor in India is to be unable to manage the basic elements of human subsistence. No per capita income figures, no indices of calorie consumption, can capture the wretchedness that is the lot of the Indian poor, whether destitute amid the dust of rural India or begging on the sidewalks of its teeming cities. To be poor is to be born of a malnourished mother in conditions where your survival is uncertain; to survive with inadequate food, clothing, and shelter, without the stimulation of learning or play; to grow unequipped intellectually or physically to be a productive member of a striving society. That such conditions still afflict 350 million Indians is worse than a tragedy — it is a shame.

The challenge of Indian democracy is to meet the basic material needs of all Indians while accommodating their diverse aspirations within the national dream. Economic policies are central to political prospects; the failures of the Nehruvian economic path have contributed directly to some of the political strains that have beset Indian democracy. An economy that welcomed foreign investment sooner, and thus offered a wider range of employment possibilities to India's youth, might well have kept them off the streets and weakened the temptations of agitational and insurrectionist movements. State-directed industry simply did not have the absorptive capacity to soak up rural surplus labor; nor could an overregulated economy, in which even Indian capitalists were prevented from freely reinvesting their own profits, generate enough jobs to employ the graduates of the country's colleges. The result was a shiftless, angry mass of alienated young people, prey to the incitements of demagogues of various hues, from the fundamentalist (Bhindranwale in Punjab) to the ideological (the Naxalites in Bengal). One of the less-appreciated consequences of Indian socialism was the dangers it created for Indian democracy.

The dominance of the state in the national economy had other negative repercussions. The sector of the economy that grew most in independent India was neither the agricultural nor the industrial, but the bureaucratic. In other words, regulation became a more important economic activity than production. As the state became all-pervasive, it was also the only available focus for discontent. If jobs were not available, it was the state's fault; if there was not enough food on the table, the government had failed. In turn, the state was the only available means for redressing its own failures, and when it took steps that alienated its citizens, they had nowhere else to turn but to (or against) the state. Would despairing young men have taken to immolating themselves in the streets in protest against the V. P. Singh government's decision to guarantee reservations of government jobs to "backward castes," if the government was only a minor option among many for a graduate job-seeker?

The economic reforms ushered in since 1991 — and whose continuation under an avowedly left-of-center United Front (UF) government in 1996 suggests that they are indeed irreversible — have been steps in the right direction. But the progress made so far, with the hesitancy characteristic of a government looking over its electoral shoulder, has been limited largely to the removal of restrictions on investment, a partial deregulation of industry, and the easing of some controls on trade and foreign exchange. Much more needs to be done to attract investment in labor-intensive enterprises, to channel foreign and private-sector money into infrastructure development (our roads are an abomination, our national highways little better than country paths), to liberate existing small-scale industries from crippling bureaucratic restrictions and promote the establishment of additional ones, to reduce the discretionary powers of officialdom over economic activity, and to eliminate the influence of the criminal underworld. The speculators and racketeers on the make who have inevitably cashed in on the early stages of liberalization are an unnecessary evil and must be curbed. The stock exchange scam manipulated by Harshad Mehta, the millions of rupees flowing into and out of illegal accounts, as borne out in the Jain *hawala* scandal, are symptoms of a way of doing things that liberalization ought to have rendered irrelevant. Deregulation of the economy must, paradoxically, be accompanied by more effective regulation of the way in which the deregulated economy works.

Above all, more Indians must develop a stake in the reforms. Economic change must reach the ordinary Indian; it must, as it has done in Malaysia and Indonesia, result in a visible improvement in the standard of living of the overwhelming majority of the people, including the poorest of the poor. This means that liberalization must produce not only shinier foreign cars for the affluent, but jobs for the unemployed, food for the hungry, and spending money in the hands of the needy. Otherwise the political support for economic reforms will melt away. The market will hold no magic for those who cannot afford to enter the marketplace. Conversely, if liberalization comes to mean the liberating of the creative energies of the Indian people, involving them in the grand adventure that development can become, it will have the effect not merely of producing growth and prosperity but of giving Indians of all classes and backgrounds a psychological stake in the new India — an India that they see as serving their interests.

This could be the key that opens the door to more generalized prosperity for Indians as a whole. The Indian businessman and writer Gurcharan Das argues that "even if we do nothing else but merely ensure that we don't close the economy — don't reverse the reforms we have made — and improve the quality and quantity of education, the momentum of the global economy will carry us on its shoulders." Self-reliance as an end in itself is increasingly irrelevant for economies in today's interdependent world; but individual self-reliance in a free and fair economic environment could yet transform the lives of India's people.

But who is the "us" this momentum will carry forward? As Das implies, it must apply to Indians as a whole, not just a favored and opportunistic elite. Sundeep Waslekar has suggested, in his *South Asian Drama*, that the subcontinental elites were historically largely intermediaries rather than producers, men who earned their living in colonial times through rents and commissions acquired through managing and trading the wealth of others, rather than by generating profits and wages or creating their own wealth. As a result, Waslekar argues, these intermediaries preferred, when they came to rule in postcolonial times, to acquire coercive instruments of state control, giving them power over the repressive mechanisms of the state and thereby over the sources of wealth generated within it. The political systems of the subcontinent reflect this economic pattern in that "democracy has been used as a set of procedures to acquire control of the institutions of governance by the same set of people who could in any case acquire such monopolist control in other systems merely because of their position in society by birth." Though the argument is a little overstated — the dramatic changes in the social composition of the Indian Parliament since independence, for instance, do not suggest the perpetuation of a ruling class that could have acquired such power in any other system but the democratic — Waslekar is right to point to the connection between an economic policy of controls and a political ethos of control. The corruption that has become so widespread in India reflects this reality; it is spawned by a politico-economic culture that rewards access over action, and permits over-production and influence over investment. Waslekar puts it trenchantly:

> If people can generate wealth on their own, they will be happy to do so. But if they have to depend on those who manage wealth for licenses, quotas and subsidies, they will consider the management of wealth more attractive than its creation. Under such circumstances, competition for management is bound to take place to the detriment of wealth creation.

There is clearly, therefore, a vital need to reduce the role of the state in the economy as a precursor to improving the political content of Indian democracy. The task is hardly comparable to that which the countries of the former Soviet Union have undertaken; after all, Bombay's stock market was established in 1875, and Indians have long experience in capitalist modes of doing business. Capitalists less dependent on favors from the state are, one might suggest, also likely to forge a more creative partnership with labor, whose value in the productive equation will rise as the importance of bureaucratic management declines. It is interesting that the economic consensus has shifted visibly. The Common Minimum Program (CMP) agreed upon in mid-1996 by the thirteen-party left-of-center coalition known as the United Front, which includes two Communist parties, suggests that a new bottom line has been drawn in economic policy, incorporating the reforms adopted since 1991. The fact that these parties have all agreed to the reform-oriented CMP suggests that the country is no longer likely to return to the unproductive self-sufficiency of the past, even under parties whose rhetorical commitment to the poor echoes the justifications for the old approaches.

Meghnad Desai, the expatriate Indian economist (and British lord), has written that the economic reforms have indeed helped only the rich. "But," he adds, "it is more accurate to say that the reform has cleared a space in which business can grow and the middle classes will benefit, and that the reforms have not gone sufficiently deep in removing older vested interests — of the subsidized farmers, the loss-making public enterprises, and the interest-subsidized industries — in order to create room for redistribution to the poor." That must be the ultimate yardstick for judging the effectiveness of India's economic liberalization.

To make this work, India will need to maintain a system of governance that incorporates both the responsiveness of democracy and the imperative of stability — one that brings along all those who benefit directly from the reforms (businessmen, traders, private-sector employers, professionals, service providers) and those who will benefit indirectly in the longer term (the salaried middle classes, the general consumer, the prospectless unemployed, and eventually the poor, who have no better alternatives under the old system) into a "grand coalition" against the vested interests. Because economic progress requires time, and a degree of immunity from short-term political calculations, it is difficult to see such a process occurring amid the expediency and opportunism that characterize India's electoral politics. With one state or another going to the polls practically every few months, Indian politics offers a shifting kaleidoscope of short-term alliances, unprincipled compromises, and the sight of governments forming or falling on the basis of caste and personal considerations. This is hardly propitious ground for the kind of sustained political commitment that economic reform requires. "Right now," declared Lord Desai, writing just before the 1996 elections, "the political system is too fragile, elections occur too often, and cause far too many reversals of policy. This is a very big obstacle to fundamental and irreversible economic reform." It may therefore be time to look at a possible reform of the system, and we will do so shortly.

But it is important to stress that any systemic reform must not favor stability at the expense of democracy. It is true that democracy works in some ways against the larger, long-term national interest in economic policy. It privileges short-term considerations, like the populism that infected the Andhra polls of November 1994; the attitude is to seek licenses or benefits now, not to sacrifice for long-term development. It makes hard choices difficult, because of the political consequences of such necessary decisions as public-sector layoffs or the elimination of subsidies. Equally, however, it involves all shades of opinion in the problem by obliging them to exercise power in the states or the Center and to confront the same choices in the process. No wonder all the three governments that have held national office in 1996 remained committed to the same basic consensus around economic liberalization. And democracy sometimes serves as a force for responsible governance by placing restraints on how far politicians can go in their profligacy; if they are so spendthrift as to provoke high inflation, voters will turn them out. As Manmohan Singh, the architect of reform under Prime Minister Rao, put it:

> In the short term, democracy may be an impediment to growth, but it is not a disadvantage in the long run. Political pluralism is the wave of the future. . . . Political societies that are rigid and monolithic are like command economies. They can produce very rapid growth in the short term, but in the long run it's not sustainable.

This is a message that is being heard in influential Western circles. Karen Elliott House, international president of Dow Jones, wrote in *The Wall Street Journal* in early 1995 of the importance to future investors of India's democracy and traditions of the rule of law:

> While democratic systems like India's or the U.S.'s frequently seem less decisive and act more slowly than authoritarian ones, when policies are vetted and voted they have a durability that authoritarianism's arbitrary moves can't match. . . . What India has to recommend it [over China] is a future based on longer trends, deeper traditions and more profound tensile strengths.

Before reexamining the system, it is also essential to accept that any political system in India must take into account the diversity of the country. The vexed question of identity is one from which there is no escape in today's developing societies, and India is no exception. The plethora of sectarian agitations, religious clashes, and movements for secession or autonomy reflect periodic breakdowns in the ability of the state to convince sections of its people that their economic and political aspirations are being (or even can be) met within the state structure. Sometimes conflict arises from the competition for resources, at other times from contention for power (though power is not merely an end in itself, but a means to control the distribution of resources); but it is always predicated on the assertion of identity, a particularist identity distinct from that of the rest of the nation. Problems arise when the identity that is sought to be asserted is rigid and nonnegotiable, rather than one that is divisible (into alternative political loyalties) or fungible (through accommodation into the regional or national mainstream). The demand for a distinct territory — whether for an autonomous region, as with the Gurkhas of northern Bengal; for a separate state within the Indian Union, as with the Jharkhandis; or for complete secession and independence, as with Kashmir and some of the northeastern insurgencies — is symptomatic of this desire for self-realization, rather than an ultimate objective in itself. Each group is saying, "Give us our own space, in which we can feel we belong, we call the shots, we determine our own fate." For India to survive as an effective democracy, it has to be able to acknowledge and accommodate the various identities of its multifaceted population. Yet to give in to each demand is to generate new victims and new minorities.

There is no easy answer, but democracy is the only technique that can work to find one. In a pluralist state it is essential that each citizen feels secure in his or her identities (and, as I have explained, there will always be more than one identity for each citizen). Indians have to come to understand that while they may be proud of being Muslims or Marwaris or Mallahs, they will be secure *as* Muslims or Marwaris or Mallahs only because they are also Indians — in other words, that it is their Indian identity that gives them the framework within which to satisfy their material needs, to compete and coexist with other members of the broader society, to work and trade in a larger marketplace, to contend for political office and feel physically secure behind defensible borders. The institutions of political and economic democracy are the only ones that can provide each Indian with the sense that his interests can be pursued fairly and openly alongside those of others. Strengthening those institutions is the vital task of the next fifty years.

Recent trends may in fact give heart to those who believe that economic liberalization and political democracy will inevitably make sectarianism and bigotry impossible. Market forces militate against fundamentalisms; the rupee, though not quite yet as almighty as the dollar, does not recognize the faith of the man making or spending it. Many a Hindu businessman depends for his profits on a Muslim worker or tailor or weaver, who in turn depends on the Hindu for his employment; they thus develop a vested interest in keeping each other safe. A riot against the Muslim artisans of the Hindu sacred city of Benares (Varanasi) would deprive Hindus of the traditional masks and paraphernalia required for their annual Ramlila; without those industrious and experienced Muslim hands, Benares Hindus could not celebrate their own religious epic, the Ramayana. A compelling study led by Harvard's Ashutosh Varshney of six pairs of Indian cities — each city comparable demographically to the other in the pair, but one prone to communal riots and the other not — has recently established that the prior existence of social networks of civic engagement across communal lines is the key to preventing violence. Where Hindus and Muslims work together, interact together, and need each other, they tend not to attack or harm each other. This insight suggests that a governmental policy of actively encouraging the establishment of intercommunal associations (clubs, unions, committees, trade arrangements) could help promote communal peace even in the most riot-torn environments. Civic action is the key, more so than political conciliation.

But politics also provides a dynamic toward cooperation. "The majority of our people understand that the country has to be run on the basis of consensus, not confrontation," said Atal Behari Vajpayee, even before his BJP government's inability to find support from the "secular" parties spelled the end of his brief stint as prime minister. The BJP's experience of obtaining but failing to hold on to power has taught it that it cannot hope to rule India without broadening its base beyond the votaries of Hindutva. The only way the BJP can hope to lead a government in India is by including other parties, or on the basis of a program attracting secular voters and appealing to India's minorities. Yet such an expansion of the BJP's sources of support will simultaneously dilute the threat its extremist wing poses to the pluralist governing consensus.

At the same time, there is no cause for complacency about Indian democracy, which some critics have suggested merely reduces the population to "election fodder." There is no doubt that electoral democracy is one of India's greatest political achievements, and that the sight of the rural poor turning out in vast numbers to vote is an extraordinary affirmation of human political freedom. But democracy is a process, not an event; elections alone do not a democracy make. The great socialist leader Jayaprakash Narayan once compared Indian elections to sheep choosing a shepherd, and it sometimes seems as if our political system merely perpetuates the abuse of the people, for the people, by the people. All too often the electorate seems to have a choice only amongst recurrent agents of misrule. What is vital in India, as elsewhere, is not just to hold free and fair elections, but to create and sustain institutions that entrench democratic habits in both the rulers and the ruled.

It is arguably of equal importance that political democracy needs economic content, and even more that it gives a sense of involvement and belonging, as well as empowerment, to all Indians. The processes of electoral democracy have mobilized the country's "backward" castes to great effect, but our political, economic, social, and administrative structures do not always help ensure the efficient delivery of results. Change is therefore necessary, though in India it is rarely unavoidable.

In a country as diverse as India, the interests of various groups of Indians will tend to diverge, and political contention is inevitable. The major challenge for Indian democracy is therefore to absorb and resolve the clashes that may arise between contending interests, while ensuring the freedom, safety, security, and prosperity of all Indians. A paradox is that the state reaches deep into the lives of most Indians, but the effectiveness of its structures is still weak and its capacity to mobilize the people for common endeavors is limited. Equally, too many citizens feel powerless, unable to influence the direction of the system. If the failings that undoubtedly exist in Indian democracy — particularly those relating to corruption and to the criminalization of politics — are not dealt with rapidly, there is a great danger that the public at large could lose faith in democracy itself. At one point in September 1996, the presidents of all three of the country's leading political parties — P. V. Narasimha Rao of the Congress, L. K. Advani of the Bharatiya Janata Party, and Laloo Prasad Yadav of the Janata Dal — were all simultaneously under indictment for alleged criminal wrongdoing. Every country, no doubt, gets the quality of political leadership that it deserves, but (even without implying the guilt of any of these indictees) it is difficult to imagine the sins that have made Indians deserve the level of venality, bigotry, dishonesty, incompetence, and just plain criminality they have had to put up with from some of their political representatives in recent years. The forms of our democratic institutions may have had their origins in the West, but their content and the culture that underpins them are firmly rooted in Indian society. We cannot escape our responsibility for what we have made of our democracy.

Africa has responded to the dangers of political divisiveness by resorting to the non-Indian solutions of the one-party state and, more recently, the no-party state. The one-party state worked more or less successfully in Tanzania, where, under Julius Nyerere's enlightened and statesmanlike (if economically unsuccessful) leadership, it became a force for uniting a disparate congeries of tribes and clans into a viable nation-state. The no-party state is being tried in Uganda, where President Yoweri Museveni has argued that political parties are dangerously divisive because they function differently in Africa than in Western democracies. In the West, he suggests, parties draw from all sections of society, since they are organized around issues of principle or to defend class interests; in Africa parties are organized on a tribal, ethnic, or regional basis, therefore do not draw from all sections of society, and as a result threaten societal cohesion. Museveni's answer was to ban all political parties in Uganda, permitting opposition by individuals rather than groupings. But while aspects of his analysis are relevant to India — for there are communal and regional parties that represent impermeable and therefore divisive identities — India also has parties that are organized ideologically on Western lines and transcend such divisions, so the Museveni analogy does not apply. And in any case it is inconceivable that any Indian government could deny its citizens the fundamental right to organize politically on whatever basis appeals to them, including those of caste, religion, or region. The country already has more than five hundred registered political parties, and while some critics suggest these merely exaggerate the fault lines in Indian society, one might see their profusion as evidence of the contrary, for not even plural India has five hundred credible sources of serious political division.

At the same time the increasing devolution of authority to the locally elected village *panchayats*, local councils, set in motion by Rajiv Gandhi in 1989 and gathering momentum ever since, has brought democratic empowerment to the grassroots. There can be no better education in democratic rights than the chance to exercise them yourself, and with two and a half million villagers elected to positions on the *panchayats*, governance has come to mean more to ordinary men and women than ever before, making democracy a genuinely mass phenomenon.

Yet there is no denying the disillusionment that does exist in India with aspects of Indian democracy. All too often, democratic politics appears to be practiced in India as an end in itself, unconnected to the welfare of Indians. As a result, one disturbingly encounters, in conversations across middle-class India, a frequent wistful longing for benign authoritarianism. It is startling to me, for instance, how the Emergency is remembered in many middle-class homes as a time of order and relative honesty in government, when officials came to work and didn't ask for bribes, when the streets were free of agitations and demonstrations, and when blackmarketeers and hoarders were locked up along with troublesome politicians. Political contention breeds inefficiencies, and the subcontinental penchant for taking our differences to the streets in the form of strikes and agitations undoubtedly costs the country a great deal in lost production. Slogans do not fill stomachs, and, when shouted too loudly and too often (along with those inventive Indian forms of proletarian coercion, the *gherao, dharna,* and *hartal*), could well scare off foreign investors. Democratic politics also distorts the complexity of governance, predicating political judgment to the short-term logic of the next election, making difficult visionary decisions (especially those that involve short-term individual pain for long-term societal gain) impossible. This is why authoritarianism holds some attraction for those who genuinely claim only to have the national good at heart. Democracy, they say, doesn't deliver the goods, it merely impedes their delivery.

Tyranny usually serves the interests of those who are themselves untouched by it, so autocrats and dictators everywhere have always enjoyed some popular support. In India, I had thought the decisive repudiation of the Emergency in the elections of 1977 had ended the allure of authoritarianism for all time, but I was wrong. In December 1993 a major polling organization questioned respondents in India's leading cities about whether they thought the problems of the country could best be tackled through democracy or dictatorship. A startling 58 percent chose dictatorship; in Bombay and Madras, cities whose populations are considered better educated and more cultured than Delhi's, over 70 percent preferred dictatorship to democracy. Democracy, in their minds, was associated with inefficiency, corruption, and argument, the inevitable side effects of political conflict.

So it was not entirely surprising to read in the newspapers in January 1996 that a venerable nationalist hero, the former Orissa chief minister Biju Patnaik, had proposed, amid the wave of scandals engulfing the government, that the army should take over the country. As it happened, the week that comment appeared, my official work obliged me to spend a lot of my time in India in the company of army officers. They were unanimous in their embarrassed rejection of the suggestion made by the grand old man of Orissa politics. It was not surprising that they disclaimed any interest in taking on the running of the country; like all true professionals, they only wish to do what they are trained to do well. But equally important, getting involved in governance would only ruin one of the few institutions in the country that has not yet been besmirched by the prevailing mores.

The army is still a splendid advertisement for India. The qualities it prizes and the ones it instills in its men from their earliest days as cadets in the Indian Military Academy (IMA) are those that are increasingly rare in our country: high standards of performance, honesty, hard work, self-sacrifice, incorruptibility, respect for tradition, discipline, team spirit. The army has no place for bigotry in its ranks: prejudice or discrimination on account of caste or religion are completely unknown. I spoke to young cadets at the IMA, and marveled at the values and aspirations they were proudly taking into adulthood. ("The honor and security of your country come first, the honor and safety of your men come second, your own personal safety comes last," says the IMA motto, and it was clear that everyone there, from the commandant to the youngest cadet, takes this credo very seriously.)

But the best of India can only be preserved by insulating the army from the pressures of the worst of India — from the unceasing contention of region and religion, from the national habit of cutting corners, from the selfishness and indiscipline of the prevailing ethos, and from the politician's practice of profiting from the power to permit. Mr. Patnaik appears to forget that the very qualities he wants the army to bring to government are the ones the army would lose if it stayed in government.

As I watched the massed bands of the armed forces "beating the retreat" outside Rashtrapati Bhavan, with the skirl of bagpipes incongruously rising over the turbaned riders of the camel corps silhouetted against the Delhi twilight, I was filled with admiration. No one knows how to put on a splendid show better than our armed forces, a point underscored a few days earlier at the Republic Day parade. The precision marching of our soldiers, the colorful variety of the states' floats, the pluralism of India on display in the uniforms, headgear, visible ethnicities, and even the heights of the different military units, the moving sight of the widowed mother receiving the medal so heroically earned by her officer son, all suffused me with pride and gratitude. Pride and gratitude, too, for the fact that the beribboned uniforms were on the marchers, not on the reviewing stand. The Indian Army knows its place — and takes it with honor.

Mr. Patnaik was soon reported to have retracted his statement, or at least claimed to have been misquoted, but inevitably his disclaimer failed to get the same attention as the original remark. That it struck a chord among the antipolitical middle class was, however, troubling. A Gallup poll in April 1996 found that 84 percent of Indians expressed confidence in the army, while only 25 percent trusted Parliament. The level of disillusionment with democratic institutions, by comparison with an institution widely seen as meritocratric and incorruptible, was revealing. But it does not suggest that people would prefer the army to rule them — rather, that they wished their political institutions would acquire some of the characteristics they admired in the army.

India is unusual in that democracy there is not an elite preoccupation, but one that matters most strongly to ordinary people; as sociologist Ashis Nandy puts it, "The poor seem more committed to it than the ultra-rich." Nandy argues that "democracy in India is neither an imported consumable nor the creation of an enlightened, determined minority. It is a style of governance that has neatly fitted the lifestyle of a majority of Indians." The poor turn out to vote in greater strength than elsewhere, because they know their numbers make a difference and they are able to bring about change through their ballots. (It is striking how the electoral strength of the poor has served India's Communist parties so well, not to foment revolution against Indian's "bourgeois democracy" but to bring about evolutionary change in Kerala and West Bengal.) Former prime minister V. P. Singh, who has spoken of angry Indians using the vote to express their anger, declared in 1996 that "there is no cynicism about elections among the poor and lower castes. For them, every election means a little more power."

Foreign journalists covering Indian elections are often struck by the faith in the process shown by the poorest of India's citizens. As John Burns wrote in *The New York Times* in April 1996 from the village of Luckham in Kerala's tea-growing hill country:

> What permeated the mood was something as old as independent India itself — the sheer pleasure of taking part in a basic democratic rite, the business of appointing and dismissing governments, that has survived all of the disappointments that Indians have endured in the past half-century.
>
> On election days, the burdens of poverty and corruption and of a creaky economic system are put aside, and India celebrates. Many voters dress especially for the occasion. . . . None quite voiced the thought, but those who came in a steady stream to vote seemed to be saying that India may have fallen far behind its neighbors in the struggle for prosperity, but as long as it can choose its governments, it can hope for better in the future.

"It is my duty to vote," Burns quotes a sixty-year-old tea picker as saying, "like everybody else. More than that, I don't really know."

It is a beginning, but voters like him are already beginning to know more than that, and to assert their rights in the process. Manmohan Singh was right: in the long run, only a participative, pluralist democracy will prove sustainable.

.   .   .

The quotidian functioning of Indian democracy has also undergone dramatic changes. We have seen how Mrs. Gandhi inherited a strong and relatively autonomous prime ministry, and, while initially fettered by strong party leaders, asserted her dominance in a significant transformation of the nature and conventions of Indian prime ministerial authority. The personal nature of her power was underscored in the vast influence of her close advisers, who frequently bypassed existing decision-making channels and were not above breaking a rule they couldn't bend. While formal institutionalization existed in the shape of party organization, cabinet, and committees, Mrs. Gandhi in practice ignored these institutions or, at best, used them to ratify decisions over which they had little control. The expression of public opinions did not always imply the existence of public opinion — or at least of effective opinion — in a land impeded by illiteracy, poor resources, and every imaginable socioeconomic constraint. Political communication was often a one-way process, frequently tutelary and with little expectation of an upward filtration of ideas or demands from the populace. Intellectuals who exercised themselves on policy questions were ignored, co-opted, or corrected, but rarely heeded; interest groups, where vocal, were manipulated. The opposition parties shared, to a great extent, the assumptions of the government. Where they transcended this worldview, it was frequently in impractical or demagogic terms, unrelated to realistic evaluations of interests and costs. Where they further went beyond these limitations and articulated coherent objections to policy or suggestions for change, they were routinely overridden by the government's numerical majority. Worse, the Gandhi administration increasingly came to question the legitimacy of opposition inputs, treating opposition criticism as only destructive. The nature of governmental authority under Mrs. Gandhi "deinstitutionalized" the policy-making structure and militated against the possibility of bureaucrats compensating for the prime minister's limitations. Then, in the decade after Indira Gandhi's death, India moved strikingly in the opposite direction, toward a system of fragmented power, coalition rule, and political federalism. Today the concern is less about authoritarian centralization and more about the risks of pluralist decentralization.

Some degree of regionalism and regional feeling is inevitable in a country the size of India. Though the China war in 1962 united Indians as nothing else had done since the freedom struggle, there were voices raised in Kerala wondering why the sons of that state, more than two thousand miles away to the south, should spill their blood for a patch of snow-covered Himalayan land; and I heard a similar speech in my mother's village during the equally popular 1971 war over Bangladesh. But these were minority views, and it is to the credit of Indian democracy that they were allowed to be expressed. Southern separatism had always seemed the greatest danger for a country ruled from New Delhi (which is why Mahatma Gandhi had quixotically called for the capital to be shifted to the hot and dusty town of Nagpur, which had the sole merit of being located in the geographical center of the country). In the state of Madras (later to be renamed Tamil Nadu), a combination of anti-Brahminism, Tamil pride, and resentment at the north's attempts to impose Hindi on the country as a national language fueled the rise of the Dravida Munnetra Kazhagam (DMK). The DMK spoke of seceding to form a separate "Dravidastan," defeated the Congress Party in state elections in 1967, formed a government, and was quietly co-opted into the Indian democratic system. The conversion of the DMK from a separatist movement into a regional political party (now split into several offshoot parties), allied with "national" parties at the Center and a partner rather than a threat to the unity and integrity of the country, is one of the great unsung achievements of Indian democracy.

At the same time, India's federalism was distorted most thoroughly when the "national" parties, particularly the Congress, were in power. Few things are more revelatory of the sham of India's federalism, and more humiliating to the pride of Indians in the far-flung states, than the way in which Delhi interferes in the appointment — one cannot rightly say election — of the chief ministers of the states. Though the chief minister is supposedly elected by the majority party in the state legislature, this only happens in practice if that party is a "regional" party (i.e., one whose roots are local and whose top leadership is the state leadership itself). Otherwise the "national" party in Delhi imposes its choice of chief minister on the state legislatures, while rival contenders for office fly (or, as Indian newspapers prefer to put it, "airdash") frantically to Delhi to press their claims on leaders far removed from the state and its immediate concerns.

Indian federalism was, in practice, far more strongly centralized than the Constitution suggested, particularly in the era of Prime Minister Indira Gandhi, whose arbitrary appointments and dismissals of chief ministers in the states reduced federalism to a farce. ("I came in because of Madam," admitted one bewildered chief minister of Andhra Pradesh upon his unceremonious exit, "and I am going because of her. I do not even know how I came here.") Article 356 of the Indian Constitution permits the central government to dismiss a state government and impose federal or "President's Rule," a provision intended to be used in the event of a breakdown of normal government but one frequently misused by Indian prime ministers after Nehru to get rid of inconvenient opponents (the article, used just eight times in the first fourteen years of India's independence, was applied on nearly seventy occasions between 1965 and 1987). The ceremonial governor, a replica in the states of the president at the Center, has been used far more as an agent of the central government to control (and recommend the dismissal of) a state government than as the disinterested constitutional figurehead the office is supposed to represent.

The overall issue of Center-state relations was studied extensively (more than 4,900 pages) and intensively (with 247 separate recommendations) by a commission headed by R. S. Sarkaria, a distinguished Sikh Supreme Court justice, who labored nearly five years to study the subject. Predictably, the Sarkaria Commission's report (denounced by some critics as "halfhearted" for its failure to advocate a constitutional overhaul) was shelved by the Indira Gandhi government as soon as it was submitted, though the indications are that its recommendations — ranging from the sparing use of Article 356, to increasing the powers of the states and appointing nonpolitical governors — have struck empathetic chords in the United Front.

The UF government marks a radical departure from the old way of doing things because, for the first time, the government in Delhi is really a coalition of state governments. Many of its constituents — such as the Telugu Desam of Andhra Pradesh, the AGP of Assam, the DMK of Tamil Nadu, and the Tamil Maanila Congress — are state parties with neither a base nor aspirations outside their states, who see the interests of their states as the first purpose of their politics. None of them can realistically aim for power at the Center except through a coalition. This is also true of the "national" parties in the UF: the Communists have only ever held power in three of India's twenty-six states, Kerala, Tripura, and West Bengal, and even the prime minister's party, the Janata Dal, which likes to think of itself as a national party, is a credible force in only three states, Bihar, Karnataka, and Orissa. Most central ministers are nominees of far more powerful state chief ministers, and use their federal positions to advance the interests of states in general, and of their states in particular.

Under pressure particularly from Andhra Pradesh chief minister N. Chandrababu Naidu, who has emerged from relative obscurity as a savvy champion of states' rights and a coalition-builder par excellence, the United Front government has agreed to devolve much more power, and the concomitant financial resources, to the states. The Nehru-era institution of a Planning Commission, drawing the states into a national framework plan and leaving them little room to develop their own priorities, has turned out to be a potent tool of centralization; it has also, on occasion, served as a political tool, cutting down planned outlays for opposition-ruled states. Crucially, the practice of the federal government transferring development resources directly to local bodies in the districts, a classic instance of the centralization practiced in the name of federalism, is to end; Naidu argued that the money should go to the state governments, which would be better able to set priorities and allocate funds than a distant national bureaucracy. (It would also improve accountability for development performance, which would now rest with the states rather than the faraway national government.) The Common Minimum Program adopted by the UF provides for all centrally sponsored development schemes to be finally transferred to the states. But the catch lies in resource generation: as the central government cuts taxes to stimulate growth, it has less and less money to spend on the states. In recent years, states have proved enterprising in raising their own investment funds abroad, particularly from their own expatriate populations. Few have been more successful than traditionally entrepreneurial Gujarat, few as indefatigable as Communist-ruled West Bengal.

Not all observers see these developments as entirely positive. Columnist Rajeev Srinivasan is trenchant:

> After centuries of oppression, today we finally have a nation, one that is even beginning to awaken. One that can marshal its resources, . . . stand up to canny foreign capitalists and demand concessions as the ticket to enter the billion-person market they salivate over. At this crucial juncture, to let the states follow their own selfish (and competing) agendas would be disastrous. . . . It would be unpardonable to give in to some romantic notion about federalism and allow our nation to fall apart.

The *Financial Times* editorialized, as India's election results emerged in May 1996: "Perhaps the greatest threat posed by such a [coalition] government is to India's fragile fiscal stability. Since each regional party has a strong incentive to insist on the largest amount of spending and the least amount of taxation in its own area, a coalition of regional parties could bankrupt India." But it went on to suggest that "the entrenchment of a more decentralized federal structure" would oblige the states to "take more responsibility for their fates and the central government would be restricted to providing the framework within which they operate, in addition to defence, foreign policy and a sound currency."

There are more and more signs of "a more decentralized federal structure." Prime Minister Deve Gowda startled the country in his Independence Day address on August 15, 1996, by announcing that his government had decided to grant separate statehood — under the name "Uttarakhand," though the variant "Uttaranchal" is now being mooted — to the hill districts of the northern state of Uttar Pradesh. There had, fortunately, been no violent agitation making such a demand, so the government could not be accused of having caved in to pressure; rather, the prime minister seemed to be acknowledging that the giant size of a state like Uttar Pradesh (which, if it were independent, would be the tenth most populous country in the world) made effective government increasingly difficult. Inevitably, the establishment of Uttarakhand will give rise to similar demands from Jharkhandis, Bodos, Gurkhas, Ladakhis, and others, who see statehood as an answer to the alleged neglect of state governments whom they consider unresponsive to their groups. A further reorganization of states to create smaller units less distant from the reach of the state capitals may not be immediately on the cards. (Indeed, some might well argue that the last thing India needs is half a dozen additional sets of governments, bureaucracies, and political offices.) But a first step has been taken toward recognizing that the key units of government must come closer to the people government is meant to serve.

There is much to be said for "de-centering Delhi." It is a refreshing change for India to see the national capital in the hands of those whose roots are in the distant soil and not in the federal ministries. The process has also made some unlikely converts. A case in point is UF finance minister Chidambaram, a Congress politician with a long record of ministerial office at the Center. His conversion to regionalism occurred just before the 1996 elections, when the national party ignored his advice and entered into an alliance with a deeply unpopular regional leader, leading him and others to set up a Tamil Congress party that resoundingly defeated the candidates of the parent body. Chidambaram today speaks of an irreversible change in the nature of federal politics in India — one that will remain valid even if, as is widely rumored, his party decides to merge back into the national Congress. "National parties, if they are to survive, have to convert themselves into federal parties," he declared. "We cannot have centralized, centrally run national parties. They are simply becoming increasingly unacceptable at the local level."

But regional decentralization can create as many problems as it solves. States begin thinking of themselves virtually as independent political entities, even when they are ruled by parties serving side by side in the same coalition government in New Delhi. The UF government was not very old when a major row erupted over the construction of the Alamatti Dam on the Krishna river between Karnataka (the state of Prime Minister Deve Gowda) and Andhra Pradesh (the state of Mr. Chandrababu Naidu). Karnataka's work on the dam was, it was feared, likely to reduce the water flow into Andhra; a request by Andhra to suspend the construction was, however, rejected. The problem was seen as much as a political one among constituents of the ruling United Front as a problem of national governance; indeed, the prime minister's first instinct was to refer it to a UF Steering Committee panel of four UF chief ministers rather than to an organ of the central government. The controversy drags on as of this writing, but its outcome is less important than the fact that it is a problem arising within India that is dealt with as a quarrel between two entities defending the interests of Kannadigas and Andhraites, rather than as an issue for a national government to settle in the interests of *Indians*.

The fears of excessive regionalization in India echo recent arguments in Africa, where most countries are essentially artificial political constructs superimposed on an array of tribes, clans, and linguistic groups whose diversity is comparable to India's. The African experience with national government in the face of such potential disunity is instructive. For years the answer was seen to lie in centralized, one-party government; with the economic and political failures that followed, African countries have moved away from that formula, and in many countries this has enhanced regional and tribal consciousness. As the formerly all-intrusive state has, under pressure from the World Bank and the IMF, granted economic autonomy to far-flung regions and individual economic actors, rural and minority populations have developed a greater consciousness of their own identity. In Africa this has been abetted by the decline of the detribalized professional class that was in the vanguard of anticolonialism, and that has, in many places, ceded its place to ethnic elites whose power comes from authority over their own regions or tribes. In some African states the writ of the central government does not run much beyond the capital; observers report increasing instances of unregulated trade, local unsanctioned taxes, regulations imposed by regional authorities, all at variance with official "national" policies. The journalist Richard Dowden describes a continent in which "the bureaucrats are being replaced by the barons, the state by the region." This has not happened in India, largely because of the continuing power of the national civil services, the "steel frame" of the British (and now Indian) Raj. In parallel, barriers to interstate commerce and the movement of labor are falling, but the process is occurring within orderly structures that have so far held up better than their African counterparts.

Nonetheless, the fragmentation of the electorate manifested in the 1996 elections is seen by many as another serious threat to Indian democracy. Even the BJP draws most of its support, and all of its parliamentary seats, from just eight states and union territories out of a total of thirty-two in the country — twenty of which returned no BJP legislator at all. The election of regional parties running on state-specific issues and electoral calculations raises the risk of India becoming ungovernable at the center. The pan-Indian elites with a "national" view of Indian affairs have been supplanted by those for whom the only realities are provincial ones. One veteran politician and rival of Deve Gowda's, Ramakrishna Hegde, has warned of the dangers of "municipal politics at the national level." As Britain's *Financial Times* thoughtfully editorialized in the wake of the election results, "The question is how to make democratic politics produce effective government at the all-India level. It is beginning to look as though politics as usual are no longer able to provide the answer."

．　　　．　　　．

Where, then, can one find grounds for any optimism at all about India as it enters the brave new world of the twenty-first century?

It may seem unforgivably complacent, at a time when the Soviet Union has unraveled and Yugoslavia has torn itself apart, and when the ideal of the multiethnic state has rarely seemed more discredited, to say that India has survived crises before and will do so again. But it is true: whereas no one convincingly predicted the breakup of the USSR, *every* observer of India in the 1950s and 1960s predicted its collapse, dissolution, descent into dictatorship, or revolutionary transformation, and all were proved wrong. There is a remarkable resilience about the Indian state, one that is sustained by an intangible sense of nationhood and shared destiny. India is a country held together, in Nehru's evocative image, by strong but invisible threads that bind Indians to a common destiny. Indians are comfortable with multiple identities and multiple loyalties, all coming together in allegiance to a larger idea of India, an India that safeguards the common space available to each identity, an India that remains safe for diversity. It is this quality, taken for granted by most Indians, that foreign analysts tend to miss; and it is this quality that will prevent the disintegration so widely predicted for my country.

Of course, one can look beyond the bad news to ample evidence of good. There are the remarkable levels of food production and distribution that enabled the country to withstand a drought in 1987 that would have cast the specter of famine across any other developing country. (Yes, India has conquered starvation, though not yet hunger.) There is the profusion of skilled workers, talented professionals, inventive technicians, and able managers at all levels of Indian industry. There is the entrepreneurial spirit that, when unshackled at last, has begun to prove a remarkable engine of growth. There is the very stability of the economy — for decades a vehicle of slow but steady growth — that suggests a capacity to absorb and transcend the problems that now beset it. There is even the immense size of the country, which has converted serious insurgencies into "local" problems, leaving most of the rest of India unaffected and ensuring that the center holds even when things fall apart on the periphery. Above all, there is the flawed miracle of Indian democracy, which has given the country a functioning political system, based on a written Constitution and incorporating an extensive register of civil liberties, that has successfully allowed the expression of — and has so far managed to contain in relatively harmonious concordance — the competing claims of the various forces in Indian society. Since independence, Indians have sought to define their interests within differing coalitions and alignments, making political bargains within a common framework of democratic rules. Things work in what John Kenneth Galbraith called, not unaffectionately, a "functioning anarchy." Despite all its stresses and strains, the system has brought about several peaceful changes of government through the ballot box. And it is within this system of political pluralism that one finds hope for the vital changes necessary to surmount India's current crisis.

After all, conflict is inevitable in any diverse society, where groups (defined in a variety of ways) contend for opportunity and influence. The real question is whether there are successful, workable mechanisms for dealing with, and resolving, such conflict. Indian democracy has, despite all the stresses and strains we have described, proved to possess such mechanisms. But all institutions must change and adapt if they are to survive in a turbulent world, and India's democratic institutions are no exception to this rule.

So what should be done to improve the prospects for India's future? For a land of maddening paradoxes, the answer may lie in a seeming contradiction: greater decentralization on the one hand, and a switch to a presidential system on the other. To explain this, a small digression into constitutionalism is necessary.

One of the more interesting statistics to emerge from the psephologists after the 1991 general elections is that Rajiv Gandhi's assassination may have swung as many as 40 seats to his party. Had the former prime minister been allowed to conclude his campaign unscathed, the Congress Party would have had no more than 180 seats in the Lok Sabha, with the extra 40 going to three other parties. In that scenario, even the minority government that Narasimha Rao put together might have been impossible to form. By voting three political groupings of roughly equal strength into Parliament, the Indian electorate would have produced a recipe for governmental instability. And instability is precisely what India, with its critical economic and social problems, could not afford; without his stable government, Rao could never have embarked on the economic reforms that have begun to bring solvency, if not yet prosperity, to India.

A human tragedy, therefore, brought the nation a breathing space. Then, five years later, what might have happened in 1991 did occur: no majority party emerged, and an uneasy coalition of thirteen parties, backed "from the outside" by the Congress, came to power. The United Front government survives because no political party wants another election; but its fragility is underscored by the dissensions within the coalition, which expelled two leading national figures within weeks of assuming office, and by the fact that the Congress is in opposition in many states while supporting the government at the Center, and could be prompted at any time to withdraw that support. While the government lasts, the time has come for Indians to ask ourselves whether the country can again afford to keep taking the risk that our elections might produce inconclusive results and unstable governments.

Pluralist democracy is our greatest strength, but its current manner of operation is the source of our major weaknesses. India's many challenges require political arrangements that permit decisive action, whereas its parliamentary system increasingly promotes drift, factionalism, and indecision. That system has not only outlived its utility; it has in fact become clear that it is unsuited to Indian conditions and is primarily responsible for many of our principal political ills.

To suggest this is political sacrilege in New Delhi. Like the American revolutionaries of two centuries ago, Indian nationalists had fought for "the rights of Englishmen," which they thought the replication of the Houses of Parliament would both epitomize and guarantee. Clement Attlee was intrigued, as a member of a British constitutional commission, to note that Indians considered the Westminster system "the only real one for democracies"; when he suggested the U.S. presidential system as a model to Indian leaders, "they rejected it with great emphasis. I had the feeling that they thought I was offering them margarine instead of butter." Even our Communists have embraced the system with great delight, reveling in their adherence to British parliamentary convention (down to the desk-thumping form of applause) and complimenting themselves on their authenticity. One veteran Marxist legislator, Hiren Mukherjee, used to assert proudly that former British prime minister Anthony Eden had felt more at home during Question Hour in the Indian Parliament than in the Australian. Indian faith in the parliamentary system was reaffirmed in the open jubilation of the country's political class when the postwar regimes of Pakistan and Bangladesh both opted to discard the presidential form of government in favor of the parliamentary; in the open regret when the latter nation reverted to it (and when Sri Lanka adopted a presidential system in 1977); and in the public outrage expressed in most of the editorial columns that Mrs. Gandhi should, during the Emergency, have contemplated abandoning the parliamentary system for a modified form of Gaullism.

Yet the parliamentary system assumes a number of conditions for its successful operation that simply do not exist in India. It requires the existence of clearly defined political parties, each with a coherent set of policies and preferences that distinguish it from the next, whereas in India a party is merely a label of convenience that a politician adopts and discards as frequently as a Bombay film star changes costume. The Congress party is a fuzzy agglomeration of every political tendency, from Marxist to corporatist. The principal opposition parties, whether "national" or regional, are just as vague about their beliefs: every party's "ideology" is one variant or another of centrist populism, and their separate existence is a result of electoral arithmetic, not political conviction. With two exceptions — the Communists, who are not serious contenders for national office except as part of a larger coalition, and the pro-Hindu BJP, whose actual electoral manifesto has little to do with the reasons for its appeal — India's parties all profess their faith in the same set of rhetorical clichés, notably socialism, secularism, a mixed economy, and nonalignment, terms they are all equally loath to define. (Even the BJP, till a few years ago, proclaimed its belief in "Gandhian socialism." Gandhi, of course, was not a socialist, but that may have been the BJP's point.)

So India's parties are not ideologically coherent, take few distinct positions, and do not base themselves on political principles. As organizational entities, therefore, they are dispensable, and are indeed cheerfully dispensed with at the convenience of politicians. The sight of a leading figure from a major party leaving it to join another or start his own — which would send shock waves through the political system in other parliamentary democracies — is commonplace, even banal, in our country. (One prominent politician, the suave Ajit Singh, has switched parties seven times in the ten years since 1986.) In the absence of a real party system, the voter chooses not between parties but between individuals, usually on the basis of their caste, their public image, or other personal qualities. But since the individual is elected in order to be part of a majority that will form the government, party affiliations matter. So voters are told that if they want a Mrs. Gandhi as prime minister, or a local film star as their chief minister, they must vote for someone else in order to accomplish that result indirectly. It is an absurdity only the British could have devised: to vote for a legislature not to legislate, but in order to form the executive.

The fact that the principal reason for entering Parliament (or a state assembly) is to attain governmental office poses two problems. First, it limits executive posts to those who are electable rather than to those who are able. Second, it puts a premium, in India's political culture, on defections and horse-trading. The Anti-Defection Law of 1984 was necessary because in many states (and, after 1979, at the Center) parliamentary floor-crossing had become a popular pastime, with lakhs of rupees, and many ministerial posts, changing hands. Now musical chairs is an organized sport, with "party splits" instead of defections, and for much the same motives.

Worse, in the states, the parliamentary system permitted the perversion of the popular will by its potential for manipulation from the Center. Chief ministers have notoriously been imposed by New Delhi upon state governments formed by the ruling party, without reference to the electorate or indeed to the state legislators themselves. One result has been endemic bickering and "dissidence," with legislators rushing off to the capital to intrigue against a chief minister who can be brought down just as easily by central fiat. Another has been — at least in three states — a resort to extraconstitutional methods to force change.

Genuine autonomy would have eliminated the basis for secessionism; as the United States knows all too well, strong local governments are the bedrock of national democracy. The disrepute into which the political process has fallen in India, and the widespread cynicism about its pretensions to federalism, can be traced directly to the workings of the parliamentary system.

So can much of India's political corruption. In the states it emerges from the need to keep legislators happy in order to remain in power, and in the Center from the need to finance not just a national election campaign but 542 local ones, all costing several times the legal limit. As a result the honest politician is as rare as unadulterated milk, and just as difficult for the system to digest.

How is all this relevant to the challenges identified in this book? The parliamentary system in India has created a unique breed of legislator, largely unqualified to legislate, who has sought election in order to wield (or influence) executive power. It has produced governments more skilled at politics than at policy or performance. It has distorted the voting preferences of an electorate that knows which individuals it wants, but not necessarily which policies. It has permitted parties that are shifting alliances of individuals rather than vehicles of coherent sets of ideas. It has subverted federalism by reducing the autonomy of state leaders (though this has changed with the 1996 elections). It has promoted nationwide corruption, and it now threatens national instability. We must transform it.

The case for a presidential system of either the French or the American style has never been clearer. A directly elected chief executive in New Delhi would have stability of tenure free from legislative whim, would be able to appoint a cabinet of talents, and, above all, would be able to devote his or her energies to governance, and not just to government. The Indian voter will be able to vote directly for the individual he wants to be ruled by, and the president will truly be able to claim to speak for a majority of Indians rather than for a majority of MPs. To offset the temptation for a national president to become all powerful, and to give real substance to the decentralization essential for a country of India's size, an executive chief minister or governor should also be directly elected in each of the states. Those who reject a presidential system on the grounds that it might lead to dictatorship may be assured that their fears are misplaced; Mrs. Gandhi's brief stint of Emergency rule proved that the parliamentary system confers no immunity from tyranny, and the powers of the president would, in any case, be balanced by those of the directly elected chief executives in the states.

· · ·

Change must come to India. In one sphere it has already come: the opening up of the economy inaugurated by former prime minister Narasimha Rao has released long-pent-up creative energies that — with sufficient foreign investment and credit — can still transform India into, if not another Asian tiger, at least the missing lynx. The frustrations of unemployment are the cause and the fuel for many of India's political extremists; a growing, unshackled economy would provide them more productive outlets for their aspirations. The advantages of a common Indian market are also a powerful antidote to secessionism — once each state has the political autonomy and the economic freedom to take advantage of its benefits.

Political change is also inevitable. When, in the wake of the 1996 elections, I wrote in *The New York Times* that the increasing decentralization they portended might not be a bad thing for India, a Yugoslav diplomat at the United Nations came up to me, his brow furrowed in concern. "I have served in India," he said, "and I liked your article. Except for one thing. Don't encourage all this talk of decentralization. It is dangerous. Believe me, I know what I am talking about. Don't make the mistakes we made." I thanked him for his concern, but remain convinced that there is too much holding India together for that change to take the form of a Soviet- or Yugoslav-style balkanization. Yet the evident failings of the current way of running things point clearly in the direction I have outlined above — toward a system for making pluralism work better. The alternatives are either chaos or an order imposed by force (which eventually leads to chaos).

Indian solutions are already being found in India and by Indians. The proliferation of human rights groups, women's groups, groups organizing the rural peasantry for purposes ranging from the ecological to the gynecological, all testify to the way in which democracy has acquired greater content at the grassroots. Our future depends on our ability to educate our children, develop the potential of Indian women, provide opportunities to the historically underprivileged, diminish unproductive conflict between communities, and prevent the abuse of the human rights of our fellow citizens. All this is happening, and it is happening from within. Outsiders can help, but the good they do could easily be outweighed by the baggage they carry: a country still recovering from two hundred years of colonial rule does not take kindly to criticism by foreigners. The best kind of change is that which comes from within, and Indians are changing, meeting Indian aspirations, raising Indian standards in all these fields.

There are grounds for hope, but not for certitude. At least it can be said that India's destiny lies in the hands of Indians. They might seize it with the vision of a new India of revivified pluralism, an India that accommodates vast diversities and is yet greater than the sum of its contradictions. Or — for India is also capable of this — its fate might be decided by the petty calculations of those who only know how to manipulate the system for short-term gain. *Satyameva Jayate,* says our national motto: "Truth Always Triumphs." But no one knows which truth it will be.

When I published *The Great Indian Novel* in 1989, I surprised many friends by my concluding emphasis on dharma, an ancient concept that I have occasionally translated in the present volume as "faith."

But "faith" conveys only a small portion of its meaning. Dharma is perhaps unique in being an untranslatable Sanskrit term that is, nonetheless, cheerfully defined as a normal, unitalicized entry in an English dictionary. The definition offered in *Chambers Twentieth-Century Dictionary* is "the righteousness that underlies the law; the law." While this is a definite improvement on the one-word translation offered in many an Indian Sanskrit primer ("religion"), it still does not convey the full range of meaning implicit in the term. "English has no equivalent for dharma," writes P. Lal in the glossary to his "transcreation" of the Mahabharata, in which he defines dharma as "code of good conduct, pattern of noble living, religious rules and observance."

My friend Ansar Hussain Khan, author of the polemical *Rediscovery of India*, suggests that dharma is most simply defined as "that by which we live." Yes — but "that" embraces a great deal. An idea of the immensity and complexity of the concept of dharma may be conveyed by the fact that, in his superb analytical study of Indian culture and society, *The Speaking Tree*, Richard Lannoy defines dharma in at least nine different ways depending on the context in which he uses the term — from "Moral Law" to "righteousness." Lannoy also quotes Betty Heimann's 1937 work *Indian and Western Philosophy: A Study in Contrasts*: "Dharma is total cosmic responsibility, including God's, a universal justice far more inclusive, wider and profounder than any western equivalent, such as 'duty.'"

I mention dharma again because it may be the key to bridging the present gap between the religious and the secular in India. The social scientist T. N. Madan has argued that the increasing secularization of modern Indian life is paradoxically responsible for the rise of fundamentalism, since "it is the marginalization of faith, which is what secularism is, that permits the perversion of religion. There are no fundamentalists or revivalists in traditional society." The implication is that secularism has deprived Indians of their moral underpinnings — the meaning that faith gives to life — and fundamentalism has risen as an almost inevitable Hegelian antithesis to the secular project. The only way out of this dilemma is for Hindus to return to dharma — to the tolerant, holistic, just, pluralist Hinduism articulated so effectively by Swami Vivekananda.

I do not believe, in any case, that there is a clear-cut distinction between the religious and the secular in Hinduism. Some scholars of Hinduism argue that India has not traditionally accepted the notion of a separation between dharma and *moksha* (salvation), on the one hand, and the secular values of *artha* (wealth) and *kama* (pleasure) on the other. The Hindu's secular pursuit of material happiness is not meant to be divorced from his obedience to the ethical and religious tenets of his faith, which makes the distinction between "religious" and "secular" an artificial one; there is no such compartmentalization in Hinduism. The secularism avowed by successive Indian governments, argues Professor R. S. Misra of Benares Hindu University, is based on *dharma-nirpekshata* ("keeping apart from dharma"), whereas an authentically Indian ethic would ensure that secular objectives are *infused* with dharma.

I find this view persuasive but incomplete. Yes, dharma is essential in the pursuit of material well-being, public order, and good governance; but this should not mean turning public policy over to *sant*s and *sadhu*s, or excluding any section of Indian society from its rightful place in the Indian sun. If we can bring dharma into our national life, it must be to uphold, rather than at the expense of, Indianness. Secularists are reproached not so much for their modernism as for their lack of a sense of their place in the grand Indian continuum, their lack of dharma. In my view, to live in dharma is to live in harmony with one's purposes on earth, not necessarily in a traditional way. Dharma today must accompany doubt and diversity; it must accept that there is more than one Truth, more than one Right, more than one dharma.

Contradictory? Hinduism has always acknowledged the existence of opposites (and reconciled them): pain and pleasure, success and failure, creation and destruction, life and death, are all manifestations of the duality inherent in human existence. These pairings are not contradictory but complementary; they are aspects of the same overarching reality. So also with the secular and the sacred: a Hindu's life must involve both. Indian thought has always assumed that new beliefs are inserted into old ones, rather than set up in opposition to them, which is why philosophical, ideological, and even religious challenges to Hinduism have simply been absorbed into the faith over millennia. New ideas emerging from new experiences refresh and alter the traditional ideas based on old experiences, but do not replace them. One does not have to believe in a cyclical view of history to accept the Upanishadic idea of the constant rebirth of the timeless. India is arguably the oldest continuing civilization in the world, one that, in essence, has throughout remained connected to, and conscious of, its own antiquity (whereas Greeks, Egyptians, and Persians had to rediscover or reinvent a past from which history had ruptured them). Secularism can only be effective when reconciled with, and assimilated into, this continuing civilization.

In an essay in the London *Athenaeum* in 1915, Ananda Coomaraswamy responded defiantly to the challenges posed by modernity to India's essential identity by enunciating a universal proposition:

> Each race contributes something essential to the world's civilization in the course of its own self-expression and self-realization. The character built up in solving its own problems, in the experience of its own misfortunes, is itself a gift which each offers to the world. The essential contribution of India, then, is simply her Indianness; her great humiliation would be to substitute or to have substituted for this own character (*svabhava*) a cosmopolitan veneer, for then indeed she must come before the world empty-handed.

Or, as Yeats would have it, hollow-hearted. If the "cosmopolitan veneer" of secularism were indeed a *substitute* for all that is worth cherishing in Indianness, our hands would be empty indeed. But if it infused our Indianness as our Indianness infuses our worldliness, that would be a triumph. This is what our secular parties need to learn if they are to combat effectively the threat of the Hindu resurgence.

I, too, am proud of my Hinduism; I do not want to cede its verities to fanatics. To discriminate against another, to attack another, to kill another, to destroy another's place of worship, on the basis of his faith is not part of my dharma, as it was not part of Vivekananda's. It is time to go back to these fundamentals of Hinduism. It is time to take Hinduism back from the fundamentalists.

•   •   •

"Anyone who wants to understand the modern world," wrote William Rees-Mogg in the London *Times* on March 11, 1996, "must make a personal passage to India, which has the deepest and most resilient culture of the four likely economic superpowers of the next century, more stable and politically advanced than China, not yet denatured by the modernism of the United States and Europe." Rees-Mogg sees the continuity of India's traditions as its greatest strength while predicting for it the status of an economic superpower in the twenty-first century. Neither thought would have occurred to most Indians.

Such predictions may be unduly optimistic. Rees-Mogg's calculation was based on the premise of 7 percent growth in India until 2025, against 2.5 percent growth in the "mature economies," giving India, the United States, and the European Union the same GDP in thirty years. (China, by the same projection, would be much bigger than any of the three.) But his analysis rested implicitly on a confident answer to the central dilemmas posed in my introduction to this book: Indian democracy, he concluded, has "solved the constitutional problem" and so will be able to manage the inevitable processes of political change and economic growth. I believe that, provided Indians keep the faith, he may well be right.

The questions with which I began this book are not merely academic debates; as I recalled in the introduction, they are now being enacted on the national and world stage, and the choices we make will determine the kind of India the youth of today will inherit in the twenty-first century. John Kenneth Galbraith once spoke of India being in a state of "suspenseful indecision." As independent India nears its fiftieth birthday, the time has come to end the suspense and decide.

I believe that, yes, Indians will stand for democracy, openness, tolerance, freedom.

Yes, democracy can be unbearably inefficient, but efficiency without democracy can be simply unbearable.

Yes, regionalist decentralization could be dangerous, but devolution of power — accepting that answers to every question in Dharwar are not necessarily found in Delhi — can strengthen democracy rather than dilute it. In many ways the United Front coalition represents a reaffirmation of the aggregative style of the Indian nationalist movement, which had been denatured by the centralism of Indira Gandhi.

Yes, we are not by nature a secular people — religion plays too large a part in our daily lives for that — but Indian secularism should mean letting every religion flourish, rather than privileging one above the rest, while ensuring that the tradition of dharma infuses both public policy and private conduct. After all, there are too many diversities in our land for any one version of reality to be imposed on all of us. Hinduism is a civilization, not a dogma. Worse, the version propagated by the proponents of Hindutva resembles nothing so much as the arguments for the creation of Pakistan, of which Indian nationalism is the living repudiation. Hindu resurgence is the mirror image of the Muslim communalism of 1947; its rhetoric echoes the bigotry that India was constructed to reject. Its triumph would mark the end of India, and that, I am convinced, Indians will not let happen.

And finally, yes, we can drink Coca-Cola without becoming Coca-colonized. I do not believe that Indians will become any less Indian if, in Mahatma Gandhi's metaphor, we open the doors and windows of our country and let foreign winds blow through our house. Our popular culture has proved resilient enough to compete successfully with MTV and McDonald's; there is probably a greater prospect of our music and movies corrupting foreign youth, especially in other Asian and African countries and among subcontinental expatriate communities in the developed world, than of the reverse. Besides, the strength of "Indianness" has always lain in its ability to absorb foreign influences and to transform them by a peculiarly Indian alchemy into something that belongs naturally on the soil of India. The language in which this book is being published in India is just one example of this.

The independence generation, newly freed of the incubus of colonialism, was deeply mistrustful of the outside world. After all, the British had come to trade, and stayed on to rule: foreign investors were therefore seen as the thin end of a neo-imperialist wedge. The result was stagnation and underemployment, as we turned away investments that would have created jobs and strengthened infrastructure, while we tried to divide an ever-shrinking economic pie. (I have often wondered how much of our political troubles can be laid at the door of our economic choices. Youth and students without economic prospects in a rigidly controlled economy were ready material for agitations and militant movements: had we opened up the economy earlier, they might have been recruited by MNCs rather than by terrorist gangs.) Today even Communist China has learned to transcend history, to put the past in its place and open the doors to the future. India's youth have no colonial hang-ups to hobble them; they can look with confidence, not fear, at what the outside world has to offer them.

I began this book by recalling my own cynicism as an adolescent in the India of 1975. Which way will India's youth turn? In resolving these great debates of our time, their challenge is not only to develop, and take pride in, the "sense of belonging" whose absence I bemoaned as a nineteen-year-old. It is also to sustain an India open to the contention of ideas and interests within it, unafraid of the prowess or the products of the outside world, wedded to the pluralism that is India's greatest strength, and determined to liberate and fulfill the creative energies of its people. Such an India can make the twenty-first century her own. Back in 1975, I ended my article with the words, "Perhaps our citizens of tomorrow will be of a different breed." Perhaps they already are.

Glossary

The glossary below defines not only Indian terms and words used in the book, but words whose usage in Indian English carries connotations not always evident to non-Indian readers.

agitations Street demonstrations, usually around a particular cause, and often as part of a broader movement involving mass rallies and protest marches.

Amethi District in Uttar Pradesh, political constituency of Sanjay and Rajiv Gandhi.

backwards Members of the intermediate castes, or "Other Backward Classes," a term invented by a British colonial census official and retained by the government of India ever since. The "backwards" themselves show no discomfort with the term, since in India's quota-laden system (see *reservations,* below) "backwardness" is a guarantee of political privilege. The "backwards," it should be stressed, are not at the bottom of the caste system (see *Dalits,* below).

Bangladesh crisis of 1971 The crisis resulting from the military crackdown by the Pakistani Army in East Bengal, then a province of Pakistan, following the victory by a Bengali nationalist party in elections that were intended to end military rule in Pakistan. The army crackdown, followed by a declaration of independence by Bengali leaders, resulted in the largest refugee crisis of the modern era, when more than 10 million refugees streamed across the border into India. The crisis ended in war in December 1971, when the Indian Army took East Pakistan in fourteen days, giving birth to the new independent republic of Bangladesh.

Bhagavad Gita   "The Song of the Lord," an episode interpolated into the ancient epic the Mahabharata, in which Lord Krishna expounds some of the most important philosophical doctrines of Hinduism to the warrior Arjun, who is assailed by doubt on the battlefield. The Gita, as it is simply known, is a transcendent explication of faith and an appeal to disinterested action in the name of duty; it is considered amongst Hinduism's most sacred works.

Bollywood   The popular film industry of Bombay.

bonded labor   A system of indentured servitude, in which a worker is "bonded" to work for a creditor until a debt is paid off, which usually means in perpetuity.

Brahmins   Members of the highest caste in Hindu society, traditionally priests and scholars; still a dominant elite.

charvakas   Followers of an ancient school of skeptical philosophy that propounded materialist doctrines.

communal(ism)   Sectarian(ism). The word has a negative connotation in India that is absent in England or America; "communal" does not suggest "community" in the sense of cooperative harmony, but in Indian usage explicitly means identifying exclusively with one's own religious community, to the detriment of others. In India, a "communalist" is a bigot; "communal violence" refers to sectarian rioting.

Congress, Congressman   Shorthand for the Indian National Congress and its members. American readers should not confuse the Congress with the Parliament. The Congress, founded in 1885, is India's oldest political party; it led the nationalist movement for independence and won the first five of India's General Elections. The Congress's nationalist old guard was sidelined after a split engineered in the party in 1969 by Prime Minister Indira Gandhi, whose crushing victory in the 1971 elections reduced the rump to irrelevance. After its defeat at the hands of the Janata Party in 1977, the Congress split again, with the faction led by Mrs. Gandhi baptizing itself the Congress-Indira, or Congress-I. Mrs. Gandhi's return to power in the 1980 elections made hers the dominant party to claim the Congress label, and though several splinter groups have broken off over the years (and for the most part re-merged into the parent party), the Congress Party of the last decades of the twentieth century is identified completely with the Nehru-Gandhi family.

crore Equal to 10 million. Indians count in *lakhs* (100,000s) and *crores*, rather than millions and billions.

Dalits "The Oppressed," an appellation preferred since the 1970s by the new generation of those at the bottom of India's caste system, who have been known variously as "Untouchables," "Harijans" (Mahatma Gandhi's term for them, which translates as "People of God," and which many Dalits find patronizing), or "Scheduled Castes" (a bureaucratic term derived from their listing in a Schedule attached to the Indian Constitution).

Delhi, New Delhi India's capital, built on the site of seven previous capitals stretching back over the millennia. *Delhi* refers generally to the teeming old town, and *New Delhi* to the well-planned city laid out by Sir Edwin Lutyens in the 1920s and 1930s, but the two merge seamlessly into each other, and Indians usually speak of "Delhi" to refer to the common conurbation as well as to the seat of the national government.

dharna Agitation (see above).

Emergency A period of autocratic rule in India from June 26, 1975, to February 22, 1977, during which freedoms Indians had long taken for granted, including freedom of the press and of assembly, were suspended, opposition politicians were jailed, and dissent was suppressed (for details, see Index). The Emergency ended with Prime Minister Indira Gandhi's comprehensive defeat in the elections of February 1977.

Ezhava A "backward caste" in Kerala, socially disadvantaged but economically and politically powerful.

hartal A general work stoppage, often bringing an entire town or area of a city to a standstill.

Hindi, Hindu, Hinduism, Hindutva *Hinduism* refers to the religion of 82 percent of Indians, whose adherents are called *Hindus*. *Hindi* is the language of northern India, and is officially the country's "national language" (and it has nothing to do with Hinduism; not all Hindi speakers are Hindu, and not all Hindus are Hindi-speaking). *Hindutva* ("Hinduness") is the name given to the movement for Hindu resurgence, led by a number of groups loosely and inaccurately described as "Hindu fundamentalists."

Hindu Code Bill   The legislation, passed in 1956, that amalgamated, revised, and supplanted a wide variety of "traditional" practices in Hindu family law (see *Personal Law*, below). Among other things, the Hindu Code Bill outlawed polygamy (which had been legal for Hindus in some parts of the country), permitted women to inherit property, and defined the legal status of the Hindu Undivided Joint Family.

Jainism   A reformist faith nearly contemporaneous with Buddhism, founded by Mahavira (540 – 468 B.C.), with several million adherents scattered all over India, particularly in the north and west. Unlike Buddhism, Jainism did not seek or win followers abroad. Its principal tenets include nonviolence, penance, self-control, moderation, and charity. Though Mahatma Gandhi was not a Jain, his beliefs echoed Jainism in many ways.

Jharkhand   A region of northern India straddling eighteen southern districts in the state of Bihar, inhabited principally by "tribals" — Indian aborigines — who have long demanded a separate Jharkhand state of their own within the Indian Union. The support of members of Parliament elected from the Jharkhand region on the ticket of an autonomist party, the Jharkhand Mukti Morcha (JMM), proved crucial to the survival of Prime Minister Narasimha Rao's minority Congress government (1991–96).

liberalization   The opening up of India's protected, overregulated economy to greater competition, global investment, and foreign trade.

Mahabharata   One of two great epic poems of Hindu civilization, the other being the Ramayana. The Mahabharata is the world's longest epic poem — some five times the length of the Bible — and contains the famous declaration, "What is here is nowhere else; what is not here, is nowhere." Few other works in world literature could make such an extravagant claim, but in doing so, the two-thousand-year-old Indian epic poem is not defending a closed structure: rather, the Mahabharata has had so many accretions over the years in constant retellings that there is practically no subject it does not cover. The dramatic central narrative, if the tale of the dynastic rivalry between the Pandava and Kaurava clans may be called that, has been so thoroughly the object of adaptation, interpolation, and reinterpretation that the Mahabharata as we now have it overflows with myths and legends of all sorts, didactic tales exalting the Brahmins, fables and stories that teach moral and existential lessons, bardic poetry extolling historical dynasties, and meandering digressions on everything from law to lechery and from politics to philosophy. Whenever a particular social or political message was sought to be imparted to Indians at large — at least over the thousand years the epic took to arrive at its settled shape in around A.D. 500 — it was simply inserted into a retelling of the Mahabharata. Which is why I used the epic as the framework for my own satirical retelling of twentieth-century Indian history, *The Great Indian Novel.*

melas Fairs.

Nairs A caste native to Kerala, occupying an intermediate social position below the Brahmins (who are known as *Namboodiris* in Kerala) and above the "backwards." Nairs traditionally were warriors, landlords, farmers, and professionals.

Onam A Kerala harvest festival.

Partition The division of British India in 1947 into the sovereign independent states of India and Pakistan. Partition was the demand of the Muslim League party, which wanted a separate homeland for India's Muslims, and was resisted by Mahatma Gandhi and the Congress Party, which had fought for a secular, pluralist, undivided India. Partition was accompanied by rioting, massacres, and refugee flows, with some 13 million people displaced as non-Muslims crossed into India and Muslims migrated to Pakistan. (The two halves of the new country of Pakistan were separated by some 1,500 miles of Indian territory: twenty-four years after Partition, the eastern wing seceded to become the republic of Bangladesh.)

Personal Law The Indian term for "family law," i.e., law governing marriage, divorce, inheritance, and worship; in India, minority communities are permitted by legislation to follow their own "Personal Law," administered by their own priests and religious leaders.

Ram Janmabhoomi "Birthplace of Ram," the name given by Hindus to the site of the Babri Masjid mosque in Ayodhya, which many believe to have been built on the grounds of an earlier temple commemorating the birth of the Hindu god-king Ram. The "Ram Janmabhoomi agitation" was a movement led by the votaries of Hindutva to replace the mosque with a temple to Ram on the site; it culminated in the destruction of the disused mosque by a mob in December 1992.

Ramayana   One of two great epic poems of Hindu civilization, the other being the Mahabharata, which it probably precedes in composition. The epic tells of the adventures of the god-king Ram (or Rama) of Ayodhya, his love for his wife Sita, his banishment to the forest following the machinations of a jealous stepmother, the kidnapping of his wife by the Lankan demon-king Ravana, and his great war, aided by a monkey army, to destroy Ravana and recover Sita. Ram is worshiped as an incarnation of God by Hindus; Mahatma Gandhi's dying words were "Hé Ram" — Hail Ram. The story of the Ramayana remains a vital part of the folk traditions of a number of no-longer-Hindu Asian countries, including Cambodia, Indonesia, and Thailand.

Raj   Literally "kingdom" or "reign," as in "British Raj," but also used to mean "state system," as in "India's permit-license-quota Raj."

reservations   Quotas, i.e., reserved seats (in colleges, in the bureaucracy, in Parliament, etc.) for specific disadvantaged groups, such as the Scheduled Castes and Tribes (see below) and "Other Backward Classes."

Scheduled Castes and Tribes   A bureaucratic name for India's outcastes, so called because the specific castes suffering from the stigma of untouchability and aboriginal tribes are listed in "Schedules" attached to the Indian Constitution.

secularism   In Indian usage, not irreligiousness, but rather the doctrine that no religious community shall be favored by the state, and that religion will play no part in public policy or personal advancement. In practice, secularism in India has often meant multireligiousness.

Sikhism   A syncretic faith, founded in the Punjab in the fifteenth century by Guru Nanak (1469–1538), which attempted to combine elements of Hinduism and Islam, notably the universalism of the former and the monotheism and egalitarianism of the latter. As a result of Muslim persecution the Sikhs converted themselves into a martial faith under Guru Gobind Singh (1675–1708); all Sikh men use the name "Singh," or "lion," and though Sikhs represent only 2 percent of the Indian population, they make up 25 percent of the Indian armed forces. Sikhs wear five outward symbols, the "five K's": *kesh*, or long hair; *kangha*, or comb; *kara*, or steel bangle; *kachha*, or short drawers; and *kirpan*, or sword.

Male Sikhs are generally recognized by their uncut facial hair and tightly wound turbans. An overwhelming majority of Sikhs are ethnic Punjabis, though as enterprising migrants they may also be found scattered throughout the country. Partition hit the Sikh community particularly hard, since millions had to abandon ancestral homes, livelihoods, and shrines in what became the new Muslim state of Pakistan.

Untouchability   The stigma placed on the lowest of India's castes and those outside the caste structure, who literally could not be touched by a high-born Hindu for fear that contact would be polluting. Untouchability was outlawed by free India's Constitution — whose principal draftsman was an Untouchable, Dr. B. R. Ambedkar. It is still practiced in many parts of rural India, though caste discrimination is a punishable offense and prosecutions occasionally occur.

Upanishads   Literally "esoteric doctrines," a series of some 150 treatises in prose and verse going back to the sixth century B.C., which contain some of the most sophisticated and profound philosophical inquiries of the ancient world — on such topics as the nature of the godhead, the origins of the universe, the knowability of the soul, and the connections between mind and matter.

Vedas   Literally, "divine knowledge," the Vedas are the basic (but not the only) holy books of Hinduism, consisting principally of Sanskrit hymns written between 1500 and 1000 B.C. There are four principal Vedas: the Rig Veda, the Yajur Veda, the Sama Veda, and the comparatively recent Atharva Veda.

Vedanta   Literally, "the end [or object] of the Vedas." The orthodox school of Hindu philosophy.

Acknowledgments

Many of the ideas in this book have engaged me for some time, and over the years I have expressed views in print on several of the subjects touched upon in the preceding pages. Parts of the text of the present book, in somewhat different form, have therefore appeared in the following publications: *The New York Times, The Washington Post, The Statesman, The Telegraph, The Times of India, Indian Express, Business India, Mid-Day,* the *Straits Times,* the *Far Eastern Economic Review, CEO/International Strategies, Bostonia,* and *Civilization,* whose cooperation is gratefully acknowledged.

A special word of appreciation to Kofi Annan, Secretary-General of the United Nations, for encouraging me in my literary moonlighting. Nothing in this book, of course, engages the United Nations in any way or represents anything but my purely personal views — as the notice on the copyright page makes clear.

I would like also to thank David Davidar for talking me into writing this book and for guiding me generously to its completion; Jeannette Seaver, Dick Seaver, and David Martyn for their enthusiasm, editorial skill, and forbearance; my literary agents Mary Evans and Deborah Rogers for their many efforts; and David Curzon, for a passage from Ananda Coomaraswamy. I am especially grateful to "c.p." for reading the manuscript with diligence and insight, and for believing in the book;

to Rosemary Colaco and Vikas Sharma, for their help; and to my family, for bearing with my neglect of them as I wrote.

Thanks, too, to the many others who contributed, in big and little ways, to making this work possible. Above all, there is India itself — "The sole country under the sun," Mark Twain wrote a century ago, "that is endowed with imperishable interest . . . , the one land *all* men desire to see, and having seen once, by even a glimpse, would not give that glimpse for the shows of all the rest of the globe combined." I am, of course, solely responsible for what I have made in these pages of the glimpses afforded to me of my beloved and impossible homeland.

Index

Gandhi, Rajiv (*continued*)
41–42, 46–47, 171, 324, 350;
critique of Congress Party, 44,
252–53, 254–55
Gandhi, Sanjay, 24, 33, 36–37, 43,
48, 228, 230, 249–51, 252
Gandhi, Sonia, 23–26, 46–47, 49, 137
"Gandhian socialism," 352
Ganesh (Ganapathi), 59–66, 286
Ganga River, 11, 12, 115, 133–34
Garten, Jeffrey, 177
gender discrimination, 81, 144
General Agreement on Tariffs and
Trade (GATT), Uruguay round,
181–82
General Electric, 172
General Motors, 172
Germany, 11, 19, 123, 157
Ghana, NRIs in, 144–45
Ghatak, Ritwik, 315
gheraos, 211, 337
Giri, V. V., 239
globalization, 4, 172, 196–98, 302–4
Goa, 12, 105
Gobind Singh, Guru, 286
Gokhale, H. R., 205, 232
gold crisis (1991), 159–60, 171
Golden Temple, Amritsar, assault on
(1984), 37–38, 252
Gore, Al, 184
Gowda, H. D. Deve, 108, 124–25,
274, 345–46, 347, 348
Granth Sahib, 52
Great Britain, 254; NRIs in, 144–45,
146, 149, 150, 151, 153, 155–57,
168, 169, 260. *See also* England
and entries at British
Great Indian Novel, The, 6, 60, 356
Green Revolution, 177
Gritasamada, 300
Group of 77, 196
Gujarat, 30, 113, 345

Gulf War, 159
Gurkhas, 332, 346
Guyana, NRIs in, 144–45, 146

Haj pilgrimage, 120
Half Moon Image Consultants, 303,
304, 308
handloom industry, 188
Hanuman, 134
Harijans ("Children of God"), 20,
95, 111. *See also* Untouchables
hartal, 337
Haryana, 45, 217
hawala scandal, 279, 327
Hegde, Ramakrishna, 348
Heilbroner, Robert, 203
Heimann, Betty, 357
Herzl, Theodor, 128
Hillary, Edmund, 241
Himalayan agitations, 138
Himalayas, 11, 70
Hindi, 74, 78, 93, 113, 124, 342;
speakers, 11, 48, 112, 283
Hindu, term, 54–55, 103
Hindu chauvinism, 4, 56–57, 59, 110,
138, 361; fanatical or extremist, 58,
77, 134, 139–41, 359. *See also* Hindu
fundamentalism; Hindutva movement
Hindu civilization and culture, 130,
132–35, 137, 205, 361
Hindu Code Bill, 120, 121
Hindu fundamentalism, 54, 56, 304,
307, 333, 357, 359; and the "Global
Conference" (Washington, D.C.,
1993), 139–41. *See also* Hindu
chauvinism
Hinduism, 9, 12, 54–56, 70, 77, 112;
and caste system, 104, 105, 107,
122; as a civilization or culture (*see*
Hindu civilization and culture);
festivals, 66, 131, 286; gods, 60–66,
133; nature of, 54–55, 59, 66,